A DOCUMENTARY HISTORY OF JEWISH IMMIGRANTS IN BRITAIN, 1840–1920

Best Wishes

David Englander

For
Rosemary

A DOCUMENTARY HISTORY OF JEWISH IMMIGRANTS IN BRITAIN, 1840–1920

Edited and compiled by
DAVID ENGLANDER

LEICESTER UNIVERSITY PRESS
LEICESTER, LONDON & NEW YORK

Distributed exclusively in the USA and Canada by St. Martin's Press, Inc.

Leicester University Press
(a division of Pinter Publishers Ltd)
25 Floral Street, London, WC2E 9DS

First published in Great Britain 1994

© Introduction and editorial apparatus David Englander 1994

Distributed exclusively in the USA and Canada by St. Martin's Press, Inc., Room 400, 175 Fifth Avenue, New York, NY 10010, USA

David Englander is hereby identified as the author of this work as provided under Section 77 of the Copyright, Designs and Patents Act 1988.

British Library Cataloguing in Publication Data

A CIP catalogue record for this book is available from the British Library

ISBN 0 7185 1517 X (hb)
    0 7185 1520 X (pb)

Library of Congress Cataloging-in-Publication Data

A Documentary history of Jewish Immigrants in Britain, 1840–1920 / edited and
  compiled by David Englander.
    p.   cm.
  Includes bibliographical references and index.
  ISBN 0-7185-1517-X. – ISBN 0-7185-1520-X (pbk.)
  1. Jews – Great Britain – History – 19th century – Sources. 2. Jews –
Great Britain – History – 20th century – Sources. 3. Great Britain –
Ethnic relations – Sources. I. Englander, David, 1949– .
DS135.E5D63 1994
941'.004924–dc20
                                                  93-26495
                                                           CIP

Typeset by Mayhew Typesetting, Rhayader, Powys
Printed and bound in Great Britain by Biddles Ltd of Guildford and King's Lynn

Contents

List of figures

List of tables

Preface

Politicians and generals need luck; historians need friends – kind generous sorts willing to listen to their ideas, read their drafts, encourage and advise them. So many, I know, have been unsparing with their time and knowledge that it would be impossible to acknowledge them all without impairing my publisher's sanity! I must, however, express my thanks and appreciation to Professor William J. Fishman of the University of London, Professor Aubrey Newman of the University of Leicester and to Mr David Kessler of the *Jewish Chronicle*. Sally and Peter Brander have allowed me to draw upon their memories and unrivalled knowledge of what was once Jewish East London, and I am grateful to Dr Angela Raspin, senior archivist, at the British Library of Political and Economic Science for her help and unfailing courtesy; to Mr Charles Tucker, archivist to the London Beth Din for assistance with certain rare documents; to Rickie Burman and her staff at the London Museum of Jewish Life; to the local history librarian, Tower Hamlets Public Library; to the Greater London Record Office; to Age Exchange Theatre Company, and to the super-skilled staff of the Jennie Lee Library at the Open University. Transcripts of Crown-copyright records in the Public Record Office appear by permission of the Controller of H.M. Stationery Office. Grateful acknowledgement is made to Wm Collins Sons & Co Ltd for permission to quote from *Still Dancing* (1987) by Lew Grade; to Gerald Duckworth & Co. and Pantheon Books, New York, for permission to quote from *East End Jewish Radicals 1875–1914* (1975) by William J. Fishman; to Valentine Mitchell for permission to quote from *The Balfour Declaration* (1961) by Leonard Stein; and to Peter Halban for permission to quote from *Jewish History Essays in Honour of Chimen Abramsky* (1988) edited by Ada Rapoport-Albert and Steven J. Zipperstein. Every attempt has been made to obtain permission to reproduce all material in this book. Copyright holders of material which has not been acknowledged should contact the publisher. Thanks are due to Mrs Wendy Clarke, my secretary, who has again triumphed over my appalling handwriting to create a legible manuscript and to Alec McAulay and Vanessa Harwood of Leicester University Press who have turned it into a handsome book. Daniel Englander and Matthew Englander have been marvellous as usual. My greatest debt of all, though, is to Rosemary

O'Day, for her love, support and wonderful intelligence. To her this book is dedicated.

David Englander
Department of History
The Open University
January 1993

Introduction

When in 1886 Charles Booth started his investigation into the condition of the people in London, the effects of Jewish immigration from Eastern Europe had begun to register both in Whitechapel and in Westminster. Pogroms in Russia and the expulsion of the Poles from Prussia led to a rapid increase in the number of Jews in Britain and concern about the absorptive capacities of East London where the bulk of them settled. The first of several parliamentary enquiries had already considered the issues raised by 'foreign immigration' while the effect of the newcomers upon wages, sanitary conditions and living standards supplied the subject of everyday exchanges in pubs and clubs and of anxious comments in polite periodicals.[1] Jews were news. In the course of the next twenty years or so the Jewish immigrant was the subject of four major departmental reports, four select committees and two royal commissions.[2] Seldom have so few been scrutinised by so many!

There was also a lively tradition of private inquiry. Its forms varied with the purpose for which the information was required. Joseph Jacobs (1854–1916), the father of Anglo-Jewish statistics, a talented and unjustly neglected figure, was preoccupied with the measurable characteristics of the minority population and primarily concerned to present a reasoned quantitative description of its many parts.[3] George Halpern, by contrast, in his brief but suggestive monograph on Jewish workers in London, was more concerned with the review of the mass of data that had already been accumulated rather than the generation of fresh evidence.[4] Investigative journalism of a meliorist kind, such as that undertaken by *The Lancet* into the housing and working conditions of the immigrant community, was also less innovative, merely reporting an unconventional subject in a conventional manner.[5] Others gathered information for routine administrative purposes or in pursuit of a particular project. Valuable information on immigrant occupations, acquired by the Poor Jews' Temporary Shelter or the Jewish Board of Guardians, represent examples of the former; the wealth of detail on the self-governing, self-supporting institutions of the immigrant quarter, amassed by the United Synagogue in connection with the East End Scheme, illustrates the latter.[6]

Rather different in kind were the great social surveys of the period, the

Booth Inquiry into the life and labour of the people in London and the Toynbee Hall Inquiry into the Jew in London.[7] It would have been unthinkable for Booth and his associates to omit the Jewish community from their survey. The extraordinary emergence of East London Jewry and its influence upon the earnings and occupations of the metropolitan poor directly addressed the central concerns of late Victorian social science and rendered its inclusion in Booth's investigation automatic. The Jewish presence was monitored and explored through a number of carefully conducted studies which, for precision and penetration, were without precedent. The coverage was wide as well as deep. An extended study of the Jewish community, which embraced customs, beliefs and institutions, was specially commissioned. Immigration and the immigrant trades were also made the subject of detailed studies. Booth, like Mayhew before him, obtained much of his information from representative figures and the direct testimony of eye-witnesses. Mayhew's methods, alas, cannot be checked; Booth's can. The notebooks in which the interviews and impressions of Booth and his associates were recorded are extant. Not only do they allow us to inspect his methods, they also supply a vast amount of additional information that was not included in the published survey.[8] Would that it were true of the Toynbee Hall Inquiry into the Jew in London.

'Questions of poverty, of crowding, of industrial displacement, of insanitary life – insofar as they are connected with Jews, are invariably connected in the public mind with the foreign Jew', wrote one of Booth's assistants.[9] Official inquiries reflected these priorities. The scope of *Life and Labour of the People in London* was likewise limited by the problematic supplied by 'pauper immigration'. The position of the Jews as a minority immigrant group was neglected, as were their politics and, above all, their religion. Judaism, was seen as a system for the acquisition and diffusion of transferable skills. Sacred learning adapted to secular purposes transformed the immigrants into a race of brain workers with whom no one could compete. The Toynbee Hall Inquiry, by contrast, was far more sensitive to Judaism as a spiritual force within the immigrant community, more aware of the fraught relations between native and immigrant Jews and acutely conscious of the tensions between the minority and majority populations in the area of settlement.

The origins of the inquiry were as much local as general. Jewish immigration transformed the possibilities of settlement work in East London in much the same way as it had transformed parish work. Toynbee Hall, which at times seemed to have lost its place in the locality, required information on the future development of the Jewish community as much for internal use as for the guidance of the public. Of particular concern was the probable extent of assimilation. 'Will the Jew . . . yield to the meek forces of toleration what he has never yielded to persecution?' asked Canon Barnett. Or would he simply acculturate, '. . . remain a Jew while he becomes a better Jew, and in this way add a new element to the British national life?' Barnett, who was aware of local sentiment and the growth of political anti-Semitism in Europe, thought that a similar outcome should not be excluded from any investigation into the probable futurity of immigrant Jews in Britain.[10]

The Toynbee Hall Inquiry, published in 1900, took the form of two individually-authored essays. The trustees were fortunate in the selection of writers. Charles Russell, an Oxford graduate and administrator in the Indian Education Department, spent the year between graduation and employment in and about Whitechapel interviewing Jews in their homes, clubs and meeting places. His report, which at times is unsympathetic and unfriendly, is informative, shrewd and cogent. A criticism and commentary was supplied by Harry S. Lewis (1861–1947), a Cambridge Wrangler and Toynbee Hall resident who was also a Jewish minister and local councillor with a profound knowledge of the Jewish East End. Lewis, who shared many of the attitudes of Anglo-Jewry towards his co-religionists, and made no attempt to disguise them, had a much better understanding of the immigrant community and was '. . . thus able to enter fully into its feelings and aspirations and . . . set these clearly before the Gentile reader'.[11]

Unpublished material pertaining to the immigrant experience is varied in quality and quantity. Some of the best comes from official holdings. Particularly noteworthy are the Home Office, Metropolitan Police and Registrar General Papers kept at the Public Record Office. Taken together they reveal the interaction of the state and the Jewish minority over a wide range of issues. Police observation, for example, played an important role in the formation of opinion and policy with respect to immigration and public order issues connected with Russian Jewish opposition to military service during the First World War. The authorities, fearing political subversion, closely monitored the attitudes and activities of the Jewish radical movement. The Yiddish socialist press was read by Special Branch with all the assiduity of the modern doctoral student. Copies of handbills, posters, pamphlets and other ephemera, gathered by careful coppers, have also been preserved in the Home Office files.[12] The Registrar-General Papers, by contrast, are valuable for the light they shed on the acculturation of the immigrant particularly with respect to marriage and divorce. The general correspondence files of the Metropolitan Police supply a series of snapshots, taken from various angles, of the immigrant quarter and its problems.[13]

Behind these varied inquiries and probings lay deeper issues concerning the possible integration of the Jewish immigrant into British society. Questions of status were fundamental. Could Jews be patriots? What was their place in a Christian country? Were they a racially exclusive and unassimilable minority? Could they be trusted? Could you work with them or live with them? Contemporary responses were varied. Out and out pessimists, like Goldwin Smith or Arnold White, who saw Jews as a harmful influence, favoured legislation to exclude alien immigration. Not all anti-alienists, though, were anti-semites. Charles Booth and his circle, critical and prejudiced though they were, were not fearful of modernity and did not share the catastrophic vision of those who were. Once the period of adjustment was completed, there was every expectation that the newcomers would take their place as useful members of society. Policemen, local administrators, teachers, social workers and clergymen, who were in daily contact with the immigrant community, were also often more hopeful. So were the lay and ecclesiastical leaders of Anglo-Jewry who, as much for self-protection as anything else, developed a whole range of programmes and projects for the socialisation of their co-religionists from the East.[14]

The immigrants themselves had different views. Their experience in Britain needs to be seen in relation to the disintegration of the autonomous corporate structure of traditional Jewry and the movement towards individual participation in state and society which constitutes the principal theme of Jewish history between 1700 and 1900.[15] The transformation of Jewish life should not be regarded as a uniform or unvarying process of modernization. The persistence of Orthodoxy and weakness of Reform Judaism, or the character of English Zionism compared with German Zionism, underscore the importance of the environment in explaining particular outcomes.[16]

Immigrants from Eastern Europe, it is now clear, provided a substantial contribution to the Jewish population in Britain from the 1840s onwards. The volume of immigration rose dramatically with the intensification of persecution after the assassination of Tsar Alexander II in 1881. In the next twenty years an estimated 125,000 East European Jews settled permanently in Britain. Who were they? Where precisely did they come from and why? What previous industrial experience did they possess? What was the place of religion in their lives? What were their ideas and images of Britain and how were their hopes and fears modified by settlement in these islands? The answers are not always straightforward, but there are no shortages of source materials from which they might be constructed. Memoirs, diaries, correspondence, school reports, press reports, police reports, public and private inquiries, synagogue and charity records, handbills and pamphlets, state papers, publications of representative institutions, oral testimonies, photographs – have all been included in the selection presented here. None of these sources is at present easily available to students or general readers. I have tried to represent a wide range of original documentary and visual texts that will not only add immediacy and depth to our understanding of the experience of one particular immigrant minority, but will also be found relevant to the situation of other religious and ethnic minorities who struggle for an identity in a multi-faith society.

The book is divided into nine sections. Section I, 'The Jewish Immigrant' illustrates the causes of emigration and the complex nature of the migration process. Section II, 'Anglo-Jewry: Status and Institutions', tries to define the character and shape of the receiving community and reveal the ways in which immigration from Eastern Europe posed problems for a native orthodox establishment that sought to mediate relations between the minority and the state. Section III, 'The Jewish Quarter', takes us into the heart of the settlement localities. We look at family life, popular culture and the effects of host-minority relations upon spatial patterning. Section IV, 'Getting a Living' provides a vivid illustration of life at the margins as seen through the immigrant trades. With Section V, 'Protest and Politics', we again see the immigrant as agent trying to master the inhospitable environment. The salient features are identified and the radical response given. Section VI, 'Religion', looks at the heritage the immigrants brought with them and the new conditions of life in Britain. Section VII, 'Education and Improvement', illustrates the key role of formal schooling in the acculturation process and the secondary importance of leisure provision in ironing out the Ghetto bend from immigrant children. Section VIII, 'The Jewish Question', samples the evidence for the growth of anti-Jewish feeling, illustrating its local character and the comparative unimportance of ideological anti-Semitism until after the First World War. Section IX, 'Jews at War', 1914–18', looks at the political problems posed by Jewish military participation and the social and religious consequences of Jewish war service.

Each section has a short introduction and each individual document has a headnote which supplies essential contextual information together with details of the source and location. Words enclosed in square brackets consist of matter that is not in the original text but has been inserted by the editor to make grammatical sense or elucidate the text. All editorial deletions are shown by ellipses (three points; or, for a long deletion, ellipses on a new line, followed by a line space). Suggestions for further reading are included in a separate section. Unfamiliar terms and names are given in the glossary below and there is a chronology to enable readers to locate key developments in time and place. Extracts from published sources are taken from the appropriate English editions published in London unless otherwise stated.

This collection of original material is designed primarily for students of social history and those interested in Jewish Studies. It is intended for use with standard texts such as V.D. Lipman, *A History of the Jews in Britain Since 1858* (Leicester, 1991), G. Alderman, *Modern British Jewry*, (Oxford, 1992) or popular studies such as W.J. Fishman, *The Streets of East London* (1979). It is not a substitute for these and other original works. Our aim is to indicate the range and richness of the material that is available, to convey some idea of the texture of life as it was lived, to enable readers to engage in historical debate and further study, and to encourage them to do so.

Notes

1 See evidence of Rev. R.G. Billing, *Royal Commission on the Housing of the Working Classes*, Parliamentary Papers XXX (1884–5) qq. 4989–5305; W.J. Fishman, *East End Jewish Radicals 1870–1914* (1975) p.69.

2 Departmental reports from the Board of Trade were on the sweating system in Leeds and in the East End of London (1887–88) and on the volume and effects of immigration from Eastern Europe with a special report on women's work (1894). Parliamentary reports include select committees on emigration and immigration (1888–89), the sweating system (1888–89), Sunday closing (1905) and Sunday trading (1906) as well as the Royal Commissions on labour (1892–94) and alien immigration (1903).

3 Joseph Jacobs *Studies in Jewish Statistics* (1891); *Statistics of Jewish Population in London 1873–1893* (1894). See, too 'Dr Joseph Jacobs: Memorial Meeting', *Transactions of the Jewish Historical Society of England*, VIII (1915–17), pp. 129–52.

4 George Halpern, *Die jüdischen Arbeiter in London* (Berlin, 1903).

5 See 'Report of Special Sanitary Committee on the Polish Colony of Jew Tailors' *The Lancet*, 3 May 1884; 'Report of Special Sanitary Commission on Sweating

among Tailors at Liverpool and Manchester', *The Lancet*, 14–21 April 1888; 'Report of Special Sanitary Commission on the Sweating System in Leeds', *The Lancet* 9–16 June 1889.

6 See Council of the United Synagogue, *Report of the East London Enquiry Commission* (1885). On the East End Scheme see V.D. Lipman, *Social History of the Jews in England 1850–1950* (1954), pp. 127–31.

7 Charles Booth, *Life and Labour of the People in London* 17 vols. (1889–1903), C. Russell and H.S. Lewis, *The Jew in London, A Study in Racial Character and Present-day Conditions* (1900).

8 See Rosemary O'Day and David Englander, *Mr Charles Booth's Inquiry: Life and Labour of the People in London Reconsidered* (1993).

9 British Library of Political and Economic Science, Booth Collection A39 fo. 7.

10 Russell and Lewis, *Jew in London*, p. xxvii.

11 Ibid., pp. x–xi.

12 See Sharman Kadish, *Bolsheviks and British Jews: The Anglo-Jewish Community, Britain and the Russian Revolution* (1992).

13 See David Englander 'Stille Chuppah (Quiet Marriage) Among Jewish Immigrants in Britain', *The Jewish Journal of Sociology*, XXXIV, (1992), pp. 85–109.

14 See E.C. Black, *The Social Politics of Anglo-Jewry 1880–1920* (Oxford, 1988).

15 For a general survey, see David Englander (ed.), *The Jewish Enigma An Enduring People* (1992).

16 See S. Sharot, *Judaism, A Sociology* (Newton Abbott, 1976).

I
THE JEWISH IMMIGRANT

On the eve of the mass migration from Eastern Europe British Jewry comprised an estimated 60,000 persons. From less than two score families at the time of the Resettlement the community had grown continuously and at times dramatically. The Anglo-Jewish population registered a twenty-five fold increase during the course of the eighteenth century and expanded steadily thereafter. The 25,000 souls enumerated in 1800 had become 35,000 by 1850 and the numbers went on rising. The expansion of the population was not due to natural increase alone. Continuous immigration – from Germany, Holland, and above all from Poland – supplied a significant annual increment to the ever-growing proportion of native-born Jews (**doc. 1**).

The volume of immigration from Eastern Europe rose sharply following the pogroms of 1881–82 and the promulgation of restrictive legislation by a reactionary Tsarist regime. The attitude of the Russian government towards the Jews was capricious and coercive, alternating between liberal and repressive versions of Russification, until, after the assassination of Alexander II, it froze into a relentless hostility. Jewish insecurity was sustained by continued popular violence, propaganda and discrimination. Jews were driven from the countryside and cooped up in the towns of the Pale of Settlement; they were excluded from the public service, denied education and delivered into the hands of a corrupt bureaucracy and a bloodthirsty mob (**doc. 2**).

Population growth, enforced residence in the Pale of Settlement and discrimination in employment meant that most Jews belonged to the lowest stratum of the unemployed proletariat or of artisans and small masters (**doc 3**). Migrants from Eastern Europe were fleeing as much from the poverty and desperation of a congested labour market as from fears of personal violence. Few left legally. The Tsarist authorities, though keen to see them go, nevertheless withheld the passports that would have let them go properly. In most cases it did not matter. Few Russian Jews wanted to return, especially young men who had absconded to avoid compulsory army service. Those who for one reason and another did wish to go back were liable to be arrested for failure to fulfil their military duties (**doc. 4**). The difficulties created were to become particularly acute during the First World War when, to appease internal critics, the British government decided to deport non-naturalized Russian Jews who were unwilling to serve in the British Army. But by that time, the Russian Jewish population in Britain included a large number of refugees who were active participants in Russian revolutionary politics. Their presence underscores the continuing involvement with the country and the people they had left behind, as, indeed, does the migration process itself.

Between 1880 and 1914 no less than two million Jews left Eastern Europe for the United States, Canada, the Argentine, South Africa and France. About 100,000 settled in Britain. Who were they? When did they arrive? Where did they settle? How did they relate to other resident national minorities? The evidence for vital registration is reasonably complete. Would that we could say the same for the data on age-structure, marital status, occupation, migration and birthplace. The distribution of the newcomers is fairly clear, the volume and chronology of immigration less so (**docs. 5(a)–5(d)**). The imperfections in the data, however, do not obscure the larger picture. The demographic dimension remains important both in terms of family and community and also in relation to the wider environment, for there seems little doubt that the speed and scale of emigration was a potent influence upon the degree of prejudice that was engendered in the receiving population.

They came weekly by steamer from Libau, Hamburg, Rotterdam and Bremen and landed at Hull, Grimsby and London. Those without friends or relatives to receive them were robbed blind by Yiddish-speaking touts and tricksters working in cahoots with low lodging house keepers or, worse still, with white slavers (**doc. 6**). Their expectations were mixed. Some were deeply pessimistic. How, they wondered, could assimilation be resisted in such an environment? Was it not better to suffer and be still rather than traipse to England only to see one's children become *goyim*? The spiritual condition of Anglo-Jewry certainly gave cause for concern. Others, by contrast, rejected such a strategy on the grounds that the prospects for spiritual growth were greater among the living than among the dead. Personal experience of pogroms was not required; the well-grounded suspicion that one was an agenda item in an officially sanctioned programme of destruction was sufficient incentive to be up and off. Such knowledge might have been acquired from the local newspapers; more often than not it came from bolder spirits, earlier migrants, mainly family and friends, who wrote to encourage those left behind. Herschell Eisenstadt, a cabinet maker from Odessa, who came with his brothers to London and then persuaded his sister's family, the Winogradskys, to settle in Brick Lane, is a perfect illustration of the chain migration process (**docs. 7(a)–7(d)**).

The men went first. Wives and children arrived after lodgings and employment had been secured. It was a trying time for all. In some cases, emigration proved preparatory to desertion. As with the Protestant refugees of the sixteenth century, removal to England enabled emigrants to escape from domestic difficulties. Mrs Berman's concern that her husband Moshe, should make a go of it in England and send for herself and the children or return quickly to Saulen, supplies a poignant comment on the disruptive effects of emigration and the anxieties it created (**doc. 8**).

Those who decided to make their home in Britain were encouraged, particularly by their native co-religionists, to become naturalized British citizens. Associations were formed in London and the provinces for this purpose. The £5.00 naturalization fee and the literacy test that accompanied it were not only evidence of the acculturation of the newcomer; the applicant's petition and the processing thereof also supply useful, and under-used, documentation on the character and condition of the would-be Briton (**doc. 9**).

1. Wandering Jews, 1864

Source: W. Gilbert, 'The London Jews', *Good Words*, V (1864), pp. 867–68

Apart from its demographic importance Jewish immigration before the mass exodus of the 1880s exerted a significant influence upon the character of the Jewish minority. Dissimilarities in the level of acculturation and assimilation as between native and immigrant were striking. Jews were never an undifferentiated mass.

A mitigating circumstance however may be mentioned in the demoralisation of the low London Jews, and that is the continued influx of foreigners. In Holland, Germany, and Poland, the synagogues are in the habit of taking advantage of the wide-spread reputation for charity of the more respectable members of the Hebrew community in London, and shipping off all those whose chronic cases of poverty or irreclaimable vagrant habits threaten to be a burden on themselves; and the result is, that as the richer London Jews reform their demoralised or ignorant brethren, this continued influx of the worthless throws them back again, and frequently to such an extent, that only those who conscientiously and religiously carry on a good work can make head against it. Annoyed as they justly are at the results of this immigration of poverty and ignorance, their hospitable latch-string is never drawn in against their foreign co-religionists, and they commence the work *de novo*, and in time succeed in reclaiming those who to the casual observer would appear almost incapable of reformation. Few can form an idea of the poverty and degradation of many of the foreign Jews that are sent into England; still fewer could form an idea of their numbers. The foreign synagogues frequently contract with the captains of steamers for their passage at two shillings a head, and thus rid themselves of the incubus, while the poor creatures they thus inhospitably send away arrive in this country in a state of utter destitution. Nobly do the richer London Jews meet this most unjust infliction, and immediately set to work to succour and reclaim the unfortunates. In the first place, after providing for their urgent wants, they refuse all further succour, unless those having children send them to some school, justly calculating that their first duty is to train up the child in the way it should go. This at first sight would appear no difficult object to accomplish; but the contrary is the case; the lower class of foreign Jews seem perfectly indifferent to the question of education; they frequently appear to think a regulation of the kind almost an act of tyranny, and seek to evade it by all means in their power, and nothing but strict determination on the part of the charitable English Jews could make them obey so reasonable a law. At the same time it should be remarked that the aversion to education appears to vary considerably with the different foreign nationalities, the Dutch being more amenable to reason on the point than the Germans, and the Germans on their side less obstinate than the Poles. Anything short of savages can hardly be more demoralised than many of the Polish Jews on their first arrival in this country. Dirt, stupidity, and obstinacy, with scant sentiments of integrity, seem to be the principal features in their characters.

2.   The May Laws enforced, 1890

Source: The Annual Register (1890), pp. 338–40

Jewish immigration came in waves associated with the deterioration of the environment in Eastern Europe. The first wave was triggered by the crisis of 1881–82 in the Russian territories; the expulsion of the Poles from Prussia in 1886 brought fresh arrivals; and a further influx followed the mass expulsions from Moscow and Kiev in 1890–91. The shocks and crises at the opening of the new century brought boatloads from Roumania followed by others fleeing from the Kishinev pogrom of 1903, the Russo-Japanese War of 1904 and the post-revolutionary persecutions of 1905–6. One such incident is described below.

. . . The religious and political persecution which is still practised in Russia with all the fervour and cruelty of the zealots of the Middle Ages was this year brought into a strong light by the treatment of the Jews. . . .

. . .

In July last, . . ., the following measures based on the "May Laws", though not officially promulgated as a new imperial ukase, came into effect:–

1. Jews throughout Russia (and including Russian Poland) were henceforth to reside in towns only, and not in the country. No Jew was

any longer to be permitted to own land or even to farm land. All Jewish landowners, farmers, and agricultural labourers were to be expelled from their village homes, which meant that, unless they had saved the means of subsistence, they would be reduced to beggary. To intensify the severity of this edict and widen its scope, the Government officials included many hundreds of small towns in the category of country villages, and expelled the Jews from those towns. Tens of thousands of souls were thus liable to be rendered homeless.

2. Jews had hitherto been allowed by law to reside in only sixteen of the counties (*gubernie*) of Russia. But the law had not been enforced against Jewish merchants in many important commercial centres outside those provinces – such as Riga, Libau, Rostoff, etc; for, by a Ministerial circular of 1880, Jews long established in such towns were permitted to remain there unmolested. The law was now to be strictly enforced.

3. Jewish artisans who in like manner had, under the law of 1865, been permitted to settle temporarily in places outside the sixteen counties, were now to be expelled from those places.

4. Jews were no longer to be allowed to be in any way connected with mines or mining industry, nor even to hold shares in any mine.

5. The Jews were henceforth to be practically debarred from partaking of any educational advantages, whether in schools, gymnasia, or universities. Hitherto they had been allowed admission subject to the limitation that their number should not exceed 5 per cent of the total number of students.

6. The legal profession, in which heretofore a large number of Jews in Russia had achieved great success, was in future to be closed to Jewish students. A law had already been put in force requiring the special sanction of the Minister of the Interior before a Jew, qualified by examination, may practise. Since the promulgation of the law not a single sanction has been given, and it is understood that none will be given.

7. Jews were henceforth prohibited from following the professions of engineer or army doctor, or from filling any Government post, however subordinate.

In the days of the Emperor Nicholas it was a subject of reproach to the Russian Jews that they were all traders and not producers. That reproach has since been wiped away, and now an enormous proportion have become skilled artisans, agriculturists, and professional men, all adding largely to the wealth of the empire. But under the new repressive laws all this communal progress was to be reversed, the artisan, the farmer, and the professional men were all to be ruined, and those who survived the persecution were to become traders in the overcrowded towns. It was estimated that the total number of persons who would be expelled from their homes under the new law would not be far from one million. The consequent migration and the congestion of the starving fugitives in those cities where Jews were still to be allowed to dwell would be so dangerous, and possibly so pestilential, in its results, that it seemed as if only one object could be contemplated by the instigators of these persecutions – namely, the total extermination of the five million Jews of Russia. . . .

3.   Jewish industrial life in Russia, 1905

Source: A. Weiner, 'Jewish Industrial Life in Russia', Economic Journal, XV (1905), pp. 581–84

Immigration into Britain at the turn of the century was predominantly Jewish. British official statistics included the birth place and nationality of the newcomers but little else. The following document summarises the demographic, occupational and educational characteristics of the people from the Pale.

The present article, based on indisputable facts collected by a Russian of great authority, aims at dispelling some of the ignorance prevailing in English minds on the industrial life of the Jews in the Russian Empire.

The Pale Since the days of Catherine II the Jews have been huddled together in the "Pale of Settlement," defined by the "Laws Concerning the Jewish Population" of 1804 to consist of White Russia, Lithuania, Novarossia, Courland, Caucasia, and the Astrakhan province. Even this limited territory has been gradually narrowed and reduced, and the cordon drawn tighter round the hapless Children of Israel, so that the Pale now comprises only the towns and *myestechkos* (the unit of urban administration) of the fifteen Western and the ten Polish provinces. An exception is made in the case of graduates of Universities and of merchants of the First Guild, whose right of domicile and movement throughout the Empire is unrestricted. The privilege can only be accorded, even to those otherwise entitled to it, on payment of a special tax of 1,000 roubles (£100) per annum. It will cause no surprise, therefore, that of the 5,200,000 Jews enumerated at the last census (1897) only 4.1 per cent lived outside the Pale. By driving the Jews out of the village and rural districts a narrower ghetto – a sort of *imperium in imperio* – has been created. In many of the larger towns the Jews form over 60 per cent of the population.

Agriculture On one or two occasions the Russian Government has attempted to deal with the monster it has itself called into being. In the beginning of the last century it endeavoured to induce Jews to become agriculturists. Israelites desirous of returning to the calling of their fathers were permitted to buy and lease land and settle upon it. As usual the zealous officials exceeded the intentions of the Government, and went to the length of expelling Jews from the towns and forcing them to become agriculturists. This benevolent attitude of the autocracy did not, however, endure for more than half a century, and an era of restriction set in. In 1864 Jews resident in the provinces under the jurisdiction of the Governor-Generals of Wilna and Kieff were prohibited from buying or leasing land, while in the following year Jewish agriculturists were permitted to abandon their occupations and migrate into other trades. The crowning achievement of the series of the restrictive ordinances were the "Laws of May, 1882," which drove the Jews out of the villages of the Pale itself. But even this sudden change of policy did not succeed in driving all the Jewish agriculturists from the land. About 76,000 of them, divided into 296 colonies, are still scattered over 23 of the 25 provinces of the Pale, cultivating an area of 113,030 "desayatins" (about 323,000 acres), or an average of 4.3 acres (nearly) per head, a quantity obviously ludicrously inadequate to the successful pursuit of agriculture. Moreover, as the law prohibits the acquisition of land, the competition for leaseholds raises rents to an unprofitable level. Hence the colonists are extremely poor and ill-provided with stock or implements.

Trades and Crafts Debarred from agriculture, excluded from the professions and the Military and the Civil Services, driven from the industrial areas, the Jews have had perforce to turn to trade and commerce. According to the census already quoted, over 13.6 per cent of the whole Jewish population within the Pale were described as artisans, a proportion which is more than double that prevailing in the whole population of the provinces of Germany adjacent to the Pale, where the conditions of life are otherwise similar. Even this number is on the increase. Thus between 1887 and 1897 the percentage of artisans in the province of Kowno rose from 8.4 per cent to 12.4 per cent, in Mohilev 9.6 per cent to 15 per cent, and Volhynia 9.7 per cent to 15 per cent. In some towns these abnormal rates are vastly exceeded, *e.g.*, in Radom 33 per cent, in Slonim 35 per cent, and in Vinnitsa 42 per cent of the Jewish population are artisans. Yet these three towns are but typical of a large number of others within the Pale. The trades into which Jews flock in the largest numbers are tailoring, shoe-making, joinery, baking, meat-purveying and slaughtering, turning, smith's and general mechanic's work, all of which require considerable physical strength and little capital; they account for more than 60 per cent of the total Jewish artisans. This dangerous concentration within such a narrow industrial compass leads to merciless competition; wages are forced down to the lowest margin of subsistence, the conditions of life being thus rendered intolerably hard and precarious. Even in Poland, where the Jewish artisans are better off than elsewhere, tailors in 33 per cent of the towns earn less than 250 roubles (£25) per annum, in 47 per cent from 250 to 300 roubles (£25 to £30), and in 20 per cent above 300 roubles (£30) per annum. The average wages of shoe-makers do not exceed 150 roubles (£15), of laundry women 100 roubles (£10), and of female lace-makers 45 roubles (£4.10s) per annum. Although the purchasing power of the rouble is sometimes as much as 50 per cent above its nominal value in English currency, it is still clear that with the earnings just mentioned starvation must be the constant companion of the bulk of the Jewish workers. The foregoing figures are corroborated by the statistics of the Jewish Charity Organisations dispensing relief at Passover. Nearly 19 per cent of the whole Jewish population have to be assisted to celebrate the "Festival of Freedom," the anniversary of the Exodus from Egypt.

Schools and Universities In 1887 the Government promulgated a law limiting the number of Jews in the Secondary Schools ("Gymnasien und Realschulen") and Universities. Within the Pale they were not to exceed 10 per cent of the total number of students in the provinces of Moscow and St. Petersburg, 3 per cent of the Christian students, and in all other provinces 5 per cent of the total. An immediate decrease in the number of Jewish students followed this Governmental measure, more especially in the educational districts of Wilna and Kieff. In the years 1899 and 1900, 383 candidates sought admission to the four Universities of Kieff, Kharkoff, Odessa, and Dorpat, but only 110 were successful in obtaining a place. In some of the Universities Jews are only admitted when an insufficient number of Christian students seek to enter these higher educational institutions. These restrictions form an effectual barrier against any Jews who aim at earning a livelihood by the practice of an honourable profession. It is not to be wondered at that the various branches of trade and commerce are so overcrowded. Nor is there any hope of mitigation while the present bureaucratic policy holds its own, and while the more enlightened views of the thinking public are disregarded. The resolutions of the Congress of Professors and Tutors of High Schools in April last, and of similar assemblies of Journalists, of Shop Assistants, Town Councils, notably the Town Council of Wilna, the centre of Lithuanian Jewry, recommending that the Jews be placed upon a footing of equality with other nationalities of the Empire, form the best reply to the plea of the Government that public opinion would not tolerate the removal of Jewish disabilities. Such a policy seems certainly justified by the experience of Western nations, and is the only one that the Russian Government has not yet applied to remedy the unhappy lot of the Jew, for which its own legislation and administration in the past have been so largely responsible.

4.   Russian Military Service Regulations, 1912

Source: PRO HO 45/10819/318095/110, Committee of Delegates of the Russian Socialist Groups in London, *What Awaits Those Who Will Be Deported To Russia?* (1916)

The avoidance of military service, with its brutality, discrimination and physical maltreatment, underlay a good deal of Jewish migration. East End Jewish radicalism was in no small measure sustained by memories of army service and the fearful expectations of reservists who might be forced to return.

According to Article 145 of the law promulgated on the 23rd June, 1912, amending the Military Service Regulations, and Article 514(2) of the Penal Code, vol. xv., part 1:–

All Russian subjects abroad who have not, at the proper time, presented themselves for military service, are liable, upon their return to Russia, whether they have appeared voluntarily or not, after the 15th February of the year following that in which they were called, and provided they are below the age of 34, to imprisonment for a period of from eight months to one year and four months; and all those who have attained the age of 34, to the forfeiture of all special rights and privileges, either personally acquired or belonging to their status, and to imprisonment in a correctional prison for a period of from one year and a half to two years and a half.

5. The human aggregate

a) Jews in the UK, 1891–1921

Source: The Jewish Year Book

No precise figures exist for the size of the Jewish population. The estimates in the following table give a rough idea of the numbers involved.

Number of Jews in the United Kingdom, 1891–1921

Year	Number	Actual increase or decrease	% increase or decrease
1891	101,189	–	–
1901	160,000	+ 58,811	+ 58.1
1905	227,166	+ 67,166	+ 41.9
1911	237,760	+ 10,594	+ 4.6
1916	257,000	+ 19,240	+ 8.1
1921	300,000	+ 43,000	+ 16.7

b) Jewish population, 1871–1911

Source: Census of England and Wales, 1871–1911

Although the census made no specific enumeration of Jews, scholars reasonably assume that Jews constituted the vast majority of immigrants from Russia and Russian Poland. The increasing percentage of women underscores the importance of family migration in the formation of the immigrant community.

		Russians	Russian Poles	Rumanians	All aliens
1871	M	1,724	4,385	–	63,025
	F	789	2,671	–	37,613
		2,513	7,056		100,638
1881	M	2,639	6,097	64	74,097
	F	1,150	4,582	27	43,934
		3,789	10,679	91	118,031
1891	M	13,732	11,817	437	115,886
	F	9,894	9,631	297	82,227
		23,626	21,448	734	198,113
1901	M	34,013	11,562	1,850	151,329
	F	27,776	9,493	1,446	96,429
		61,789	21,055	3,296	247,758
1911	M	33,312	17,289	1,992	167,762
	F	29,550	15,390	1,730	117,068
		62,862	32,679	3,722	284,830

c)   Age and marital status of immigrants in England, 1911

Source: Census of England and Wales, 1911, *Birthplaces (and Ages and Occupations of Foreigners)*, vol. IX, Parliamentary Papers, [Cd. 7017], LXVIII (1913), pp. 176–77

Data on the ages of immigrants and their marital status confirm the significance of family migration and provides a basis for comparison with other immigrant groups. The second table displays the distinctive marriage patterns of Jewish men and women and highlights peculiarities in respect of rates of marriage, numbers of children and widows; the first indicates the source of the exceptionally high Jewish birth rate.

Age and marital status of immigrants in England, 1911

	Russians and Russian Poles		Foreign born (Excluding Russians and Russian Poles)	
		%		%
Total population	95,541		189,289	
Females	44,940	47.0	72,128	38.1
Males	50,601	53.0	117,161	61.9
Sub groups		% of all women		% of all women
Females 15–44	30,875	68.7	48,004	66.0
Children in population	9,344	9.7	10,764	5.6
Unmarried females	13,077	29.1	37,722	52.3
Unmarried females over age 15	9,482	21.1	34,909	48.4
Widows	3,909	8.7	7,789	10.8
		% of all men		% of all men
Unmarried males	18,216	36.0	60,920	52.0
Unmarried males over age 20	10,018	19.8	52,109	44.4

Condition as to marriage and age of immigrant
males and females in England and Wales, 1911

Russians and Russian Poles

Age	Unmarried			Married			Widowed		
	M	F	%	M	F	%	M	F	%
All	18,247	13,113	33.0	31,257	27,895	62.0	1,097	6,932	5.0
under 10	2,050	2,015	100.0						
10–15	2,699	2,580	100.0						
15–20	3,450	3,527	99.9	11	67	1.0			
20–25	4,898	3,520	70.0	1,184	2,488	30.0	4	16	0.0
25–35	3,917	1,144	19.0	11,816	10,108	80.0	51	258	1.0
35–45	788	181	5.0	10,108	8,193	91.0	167	665	4.0
45–55	283	72	3.0	5,463	4,187	86.0	248	934	11.0
55–65	105	37	3.0	2,396	1,635	72.0	279	1,141	25.0
65–75	34	20	2.0	878	439	57.0	226	700	41.0
75–85	20	14	6.0	174	64	43.0	102	184	51.0
85+	20	3	23.0	15	5	21.0	20	34	56.0

Non-Russians and Russian Poles

Age	Unmarried			Married			Widowed		
	M	F	%	M	F	%	M	F	%
All	61,305	37,734	52.0	51,997	26,579	42.0	3,859	7,815	6.0
under 10	2,681	2,559	100.0						
10–15	2,733	2,791	100.0						
15–20	11,293	6,842	98.0	25	159	2.0	2	1	0.0
20–25	17,387	7,960	88.0	1,360	2,072	12.0	13	29	0.0
25–35	16,470	8,679	51.0	14,510	9,134	48.0	158	440	1.0
35–45	5,332	4,100	27.0	16,181	7,607	69.0	406	990	4.0
45–55	2,477	2,502	22.0	10,962	4,631	68.0	753	1,716	11.0
55–65	1,197	1,340	19.0	5,890	2,109	60.0	934	1,933	21.0
65–75	573	722	18.0	2,462	739	44.0	1,002	1,795	38.0
75–85	164	214	16.0	563	136	29.0	515	795	55.0
85+		25	9.0	44	8	19.0	76	116	72.0

d)   Jewish marriages, 1857–1906

Source: S. Rosenbaum, 'A Contribution to the Study of Vital and Other Statistics of the Jews in the UK', *Journal of the Royal Statistical Society LXVIII*, (1905), p. 549; *Jewish Chronicle*, 31 January 1908

The following tables show that immigrant Jews married earlier and more often than the general population.

Marriage rates among Jews in London per 1,000
aged 15 and over in 1903

	Jews	London
Men	28.4	27.1
Women	31.7	22.8
Both Sexes	30.1	25.0

Proportion of Jewish marriages per 1,000
total population in London 1857–1906

Date	Jewish marriages per 1,000
1857	9.1
1873	10.0
1884	12.0
1893	21.1
1901	32.2
1906	39.5

6. Point of arrival, 1887

Source: PRO Mepo 2/260, Herman Landau to Major General Sir Charles Warren, Commissioner of the Metropolitan Police, 24 July 1887

Herman Landau (1844–1924) was a successful banker and communal leader. An immigrant himself, he was the moving spirit in the foundation of the Poor Jews' Temporary Shelter in London and remained close to the East End and its concerns. The letter printed below underscores the need for police action to prevent the newly-arrived from being dispossessed before they had left the quayside.

In compliance with your kind suggestion I have the honour to state in writing the sad plight in which many immigrants (especially those landing in the Thames) find themselves in. Those arriving by the London General Steam Navigation Company's vessels are in the majority of cases disembarked at St. Katherine's Wharf where a limited number of very decent English porters assist the Immigrants from the ship with their luggage at a very reasonable charge, but since none of these can speak German, they are unable to direct the Immigrants to the addresses which they usually bring with them to their friends, neither can they make them understand that their safest and in the end cheapest mode of reaching their destination would be by taking a cab, but no sooner are the Immigrants landed than their own countrymen address them in their own language in apparently the kindest possible manner, asking them if they have any addresses to go to and offering to take them and their luggage thither for a reasonable amount and in many cases pretending to act the Good Samaritan, offering to conduct them to their destination gratuitously. This is done not only for ulterior motives but to avoid holding any arguments at the Wharf, by which they might lose the privilege of being allowed there. They then conduct them to so-called lodging houses, one man conducting while the other takes the luggage either by hand or on a barrow. The carrier of the luggage who is one of the fraternity, then demands some exorbitant sum for his services and that in a manner well calculated to intimidate a poor stranger for not unfrequently any remonstrance on the part of the passenger is met by blows. The master and mistress of the lodging house then urge the passenger to settle with the porter immediately; pretend to make some compromise honourable to the poor victim, who in the end is mulcted in about five shillings in addition to the sum already paid by the ships side. The luggage is retained in the house and when the passenger asks why he is not taken to the address he had given, the landlord tells him the address is not in London at all but in the country and that it would cost from one to five pounds to take him there and they urge these strangers to take refreshments and rest awhile in their house. A

Figure 1   Just landed, 1901   Those without relatives or friends to meet them became a target for dispossession by the 'sharks' and charlatans who infested the quayside (G.R. Sims (ed.), *Living London*, 3 vols (London: Cassell, 1901), I, p. 49).

large number fall into this trap and are even induced to deposit for "safety" with the landlord any valuables or money they may have which they never recover again. The landlord and his confederator having obtained as much money as they possibly could to purchase the ticket for this pretended long journey into the country (in the last case that has come to my knowledge the sum of fifty shillings was thus obtained) the victim is taken to Liverpool St. Station and sent to Tottenham or some of the Metropolitan Railway Stations. The Immigrants arriving by foreign steamers, principally German, suffer if possible even more. These are put into small boats in mid-river under the supposed superintendence of a river policeman who tries in vain, not knowing their language to assist them and in the end has to content himself with counting the number of parcels each passenger brings. The waterman's charge per passenger is supposed to be fixed at three pence, but this in the case of Immigrants is disregarded and much higher charges are made. On landing they are immediately met by these loafers of whom there are about sixty or seventy all in league together and located in the manner before described.

If I may venture to suggest all this could be remedied by having a policeman or someone in authority present at every disembarkation, able to speak German for the large majority of Immigrants landing on the Thames, though not natives of Germany can understand that language. I would further suggest that a certain number of respectable men knowing German be permitted by the authorities to act as porters, having distinctive numbers on some prominent part of their dress with a fixed tariff of charges: that either the ships officers or the policeman on duty at the disembarkation should be required to enter the address of the Immigrants together with the number of the porter who is to conduct him thither. Of course one porter could conduct more than one, for the addresses they usually bring are in the East End of London and all within a comparatively small radius.

I point this fact out to show that a decent man could earn from one to two pounds a week with ease provided that all unauthorised persons be prohibited from carrying on their nefarious trade as at present. I may also mention that a very great number arriving here are simply en route to America or some of the Colonies. To the latter these lodging house keepers represent themselves as agents to various Shipping Companies and by these means either rob them of the whole of the passage money or hand them a ticket which does not carry them to their destination. On this subject Captain Wilson, at the Emigration department of the Board of Trade will be able to throw considerable light; all this must and does result in leaving a very large number of destitute foreigners on these shores.

7. Why Britain?

a) A Leeds tailor explains, 1898

Source: J.A. Dyche, 'The Jewish Workman', Contemporary Review, LXIII (1898), p. 50

John Alexander Dyche (1867–1939) was born in Kovno, Lithuania and went to the United States in 1900 after fourteen years as a trade union organiser in England. From 1904 he was the Secretary General of the International Ladies' Garment Workers' Union in New York. Here he explains the circumstances that prompted him to quit Russia and take his chances as a penniless 'greener' in Leeds.

. . . Not only was religious persecution the direct cause of the emigration of large numbers of Russian Jews, but indirectly it is responsible for the emigration of the great majority of them. To take myself for an example, I did not leave my native country because I was expelled either for political or religious reasons; but nearly every day brought me news of fresh expulsions, of new *ukases* against the people of my race, and I was asking myself, Where is this going to stop? Whose turn will be next? And I decided to leave the country where I could get neither justice nor mercy. I certainly have not come to live in English fogs for the mere pleasure of it. My case is typical of that of most Jewish immigrants. . . .

b)   The view from H (Whitechapel) Division, 1888

Source: PRO Mepo 2/260, Report on Immigration of Foreigners, 28 July 1888

Police observation supplies a useful insight into the condition of the newcomers with an account of the political and social pressures that prompted their migration.

With reference to the above subject I beg to state that in my opinion immigration has been on the increase for some time past and apparently more so during the last two or three years, but there are no police records to which a return could be based shewing the increase.

The Immigrants are no doubt attracted to the United Kingdom by the prospect of obtaining a better livelihood and enjoying more freedom than they would in other countries.

They are quiet, inoffensive, and industrious, making the most of what they earn and generally abstemious as regards intoxicating liquors it being seldom they are seen the worse for drink in the streets. They have but little regard for cleanliness either in their dwellings or their persons. Upon their arrival here those without money appear to live either upon the charity of persons of their own nationality or by assistance from the various charitable institutions which have been established to meet such cases until they obtain employment or are assisted to emigrate.

They congregate in the poorest parts of Whitechapel and Spitalfields which consist principally of narrow streets and courts and which are very much overcrowded as in many instances more than one family occupy the same room. Their social condition is low.

There are several clubs at which Dramatic and Musical entertainments are provided. Dancing also takes place at times; there are also many coffee and catering houses to which they resort and play cards and dominoes and no doubt frequently gamble.

The effect of the overcrowding by the immigrants has been to drive our own population from the districts now inhabited by the former. Morally I do not think it has made any difference, commercially tradesmen

complain that trade has fallen off owing to the foreigners not spending so
much money, also that they have been the means of reducing the price of
labour in those trades at which they work. I cannot learn that there is any
system under which these poor people are brought to this country but
they are more probably induced to come by the accounts given them by
their friends who are here but owing to the circumstances in which, in
many cases they arrive, they easily become the victims of designing
persons who use them as the means of bringing down wages, they being
willing to turn their hands to anything.

c) Lew Grade remembers, 1912

Source: Lew Grade, Still Dancing (Wm Collins Sons & Co Ltd 1987), pp. 18–20

Lew Grade (Louis Winogradsky), the Russian-born television producer and
impressario, recalls the circumstances that brought him with his parents and
younger brother Boris (Bernard Delfont) from Odessa to Brick Lane in 1912.

. . . At the age of five and a half I was completely unaware of the political
situation in Russia and wasn't even aware of the pogroms or the anti-
Jewish attacks happening around the country. . . . If my parents suffered
any mental anguish at what was going on – and I'm sure they must have
– they never let it show. All I knew was that suddenly my father was
packing his bags in order to go on a long journey across the sea. Just
how long he'd be away, nobody knew. The country he was going to was
called England and the year was 1912.

Three years earlier my mother's three brothers had decided there was
no future for the Jews in the Ukraine, and had emigrated to London.
They were all cabinet-makers, . . . the third and oldest, whose name was
Herschell, was the least successful, but, as it turned out, the most
supportive. He was adamant that we should leave Russia before it was
too late, and it was his letters that persuaded my father to come to
England and begin a new life there.

My father was away for three months before he finally sent for us. I
later found out that he had insisted that my mother learnt to speak
Yiddish while he was away, because without any English we'd be lost in
the East End of London. At home, you see, we only spoke Russian.

I have no memory of our upheaval at all. But on the few occasions I
have heard my mother talk about the journey . . . to London, she spoke
about the hazards involved and how unpleasant it had all been. It
certainly couldn't have been easy for a young women, aged twenty four,
to have to undergo such a traumatic move with two young children aged
nearly six and three and a half to care for. But my mother, I have to say,
was always an extraordinarily determined woman. Her family came above

everything else in life, and there were no hardships or deprivations she wouldn't suffer for their well-being. . . .

. . .

We were met at the docks by my father, who, in three months, had somehow managed to spend most of the capital he'd brought out with him. He was always keen on gambling, . . . At any rate, our first lodgings were in Brick Lane, in the East End. We were just one of the many Jewish immigrant families living in that area, and my initial impressions of the place were not good. . . . Brick Lane was bleak and rather dark, and so were the two rooms we lived in. . . . For the first time in our lives we were really poor, and, on top of this, I could barely make myself understood because all I could speak was Russian. Years later, my mother, who – she'll pardon me if I say so – liked to exaggerate a bit, used to claim that she had to borrow money from relatives and friends to pay the rent, and that she and my father often used to go without food themselves to see that her "kinder" had sufficient. She claimed that there were times when all we had in the house was an apple or a couple of slices of bread, and that she'd lost so much weight she weighed only six stone. All this may be true, of course. But my own memory is that, while there was no money for luxuries, we never went hungry. I know we were helped by our "poor" relative, Herschell. My mother's other two brothers, who were in a far better position to help because they both had their own business, weren't nearly as generous. They lived in Dalston, which at the time was a very posh area. I remember on the rare occasions that we were invited to visit them, it was a real event. A big deal.

d) *Observations of a Polish Jew, 1888*

Source: Minutes of Evidence taken before the Select Committee on Emigration and Immigration (Foreigners), Parliamentary Papers, XI (1888), qq. 2265–267

Herman Landau, who came to England from Poland in 1864 and subsequently played a significant role in the socialisation of his fellow co-religionists, explains why English freedoms were not regarded as an unqualified benefit by the people from the Pale.

2265. Has that persecution ceased now? — Yes, certainly; the acute part of it has ceased. With your permission, I should like to state that there seems to be an idea abroad which, owing to my having been in England so many years, I can easily understand, that emigration has a certain amount of charm to a great number of English people, but it is not so with Poles and Russians. I may tell you, from my own experience, that when a young man in Poland or Russia leaves for abroad it is considered quite a disgrace to his family; I can assure you that that is positive fact.

2266. You do not think that they have a great distaste for it, do you? — No; they consider it disgraceful, because they have the idea that the religious observances cannot possibly be kept up anywhere except in the country where they were born; and various other social reasons. So that really there is a great reluctance on the part of the people there, the Jews especially, to leave their country, and if they do so, it is merely by compulsion.

2267. Is it police compulsion? — It is police compulsion in a way. They are told, you must not be this and you must not be that; you must not live in this part of the empire, and you must not live in that part; you must not cultivate land. You would scarcely credit it when I tell you that a man is not allowed to drive with his own vehicle and horses into a place like Kieff, a very large city. He is prohibited, simply because he is a Jew; and he is not allowed to drive his own equipage into the city.

8.   Won't you come home dear Moshe? 1888

Source: Minutes of Evidence taken before the Select Committee on Emigration and Immigration (Foreigners), Parliamentary Papers, XI (1888), q. 1376

Moshe Berman was one of the millions of Russian Jews who, despairing of any permanent improvement in their condition, left the shtetl in search of better things. The resultant disruption of family life is well illustrated in the poignant correspondence from the wife he left behind.

To my dear and faithful Moshe Berman. I inform you that we are all, God be blessed, well. May God grant that we should hear the same of yourself. . . . your son Kirve held your letter in his hand and was very glad, continually asking, "when will father come". My dear Moses, you write that you are very bad off and earn very little; have I not told you before in Saulen, that you should not separate from us and leave me and the children alone; but you continually answered that wherever you will be you will be better off than in Saulen. And now you write that you repent having gone there at all. But believe me, dear husband, I and the children are worse off here than you are there. . . . Now, my dear Moses, do write me what is to take place now. God knows when we will see each other! You are bad off there and I am bad off here, and cannot earn anything. Please let me know if there are any means for you to come back to Saulen. . . . And who knows better than I do the state of your health. . . . I send my kind greetings to Mr and Mrs

Isaac for their benevolence to my husband Moses, and I pray of you to endeavour to find some means for him to enable him to find some bread for himself and his family, for besides God and yourselves I have nobody to apply to. . . .

9. Becoming an Englishman: petition of Jacob Amdur of Kovno, 1903

Source: PRO HO 144/718/110316, Petition and police report respecting application for a certificate of British Naturalization by Jacob Amdur, 5 August 1903

Naturalization and denization records supply additional data on the migration process. Individual applications include the length of time of residence in Britain, marital status, age, occupation and country of origin, number of children, information on parents, names of guarantors and a police assessment of the applicant's moral worth.

To the Right Honorable
His Majesty's Secretary of State,
for the Home Department

Naturalisation
_____

The humble
Memorial of

Jacob Amdur

1   Memorial
_____

of 102 Commercial Road
in the Parish of Stepney
an Alien

Sheweth
1. That your Memorialist is a subject of Russian Empire having been born at Breslau (sic) in the Province of Kovnow on the 20th day of December, 1870 and being the Son of Elliot Bear Amdur and Rachel Amdur both subjects of Russia
2. That your Memorialist resides at 102 Commercial Road Stepney E. in the County of London and is of the age of 32 years and is a Butcher
3. That your Memorialist is a married man and has 3 children residing with him viz:–
    Annie aged 3 Years
    Dinah aged 2 Years and
    Esther aged 7 months
4. That your Memorialist's settled place of business is at 102 Commercial Road Stepney E.

5. That your Memorialist has for five years within the period of the eight years last past resided within the United Kingdom, viz.–
   at 91 Commercial Road Stepney E. from September 1896 to June 1902 and at 102 Commercial Road E. from June 1902 to the present time
6. That your Memorialist intends to reside permanently within the United Kingdom of Great Britain and Ireland
7. That your Memorialist seeks to obtain the rights and capacities of a natural born British Subject from a desire to be able to discharge all duties pertaining to a Natural born British Subject and to enjoy all privileges of such

Your Memorialist therefore humbly prays that a Certificate of Naturalisation may be granted to him in pursuance of the Statute 33 Victoria Chapter 14 intituled "An Act to amend the Law relating to the legal condition of Aliens and British Subjects"

Witness
C.J. Bridhain
Solicitor
83 Finsbury Pavenor EC   [Signed] Jacob Amdur

METROPOLITAN POLICE (Criminal Investigation Department)

REPORT of the results of inquiries concerning the Application for a Certificate of British Naturalization by *Jacob Amdur*

5th August 1903

Name and Profession of Applicant	If declarations of Residence have been inquired into, and found correct	If the Sureties are respectable and responsible Persons	Reasons for which Naturalization is sought	REMARKS
Jacob Amdur a Butcher	The declarations of residence have been enquired into and found correct	The sureties are respectable and responsible persons, householders and natural born British subjects	The applicant is a respectable man and according to enquiry at the addresses given has lived in this Country for the last eight years; intends to remain permanently and wishes to enjoy the privileges of a British subject	The sureties speak well of applicant as a respectable man and I see no reason to doubt their statements

John Walsh Insp.

W. Melville   Superintendent

II
ANGLO JEWRY:
STATUS AND INSTITUTIONS

The enforcement of religious conformity within a liberal capitalist setting represented something new in the historical experience of the Jewish people. Until the Resettlement of the Jews in England in the mid-seventeenth century and their subsequent dispersal throughout the English-speaking world, lay and spiritual leaders had relied upon the repressive apparatus of the state-supported self-governing communities, the *kehillot*, for the maintenance of social and religious discipline. The more tolerant environment that prevailed in Britain and her colonies made the search for an alternative basis of Jewish communal discipline obligatory. Religious pluralism and the withholding of state assistance meant that social and spiritual control would have to be re-set within a voluntary and associational framework (**doc. 1**). Renegotiation and relocation were not, however, uniform processes. One need only compare the subordinate status of Reform Judaism in Britain with its salience in the United States to appreciate the variant outcomes.

The growth of effective community-wide organisation was a product of the Victorian era. Four institutions were of primary importance – the Chief Rabbinate, the United Synagogue, the Board of Deputies and the Jewish Board of Guardians. Together they gave Anglo-Jewry its distinctive centralised hierarchical character. During Queen Victoria's reign the hitherto autonomous rabbinate was replaced by an ecclesiastical establishment under the supervision of a Chief Rabbi in whose hands great powers were concentrated. The form of worship and religious observances, and all matters of religious administration of synagogues within his jurisdiction, were under his supervision and control. No person could preach or officiate in the service of the synagogue without his approval; candidates for the ministry likewise required his certification as to their religious and moral fitness (**doc. 2(a)**).

The emergence of the Office of the Chief Rabbi did not, however, exhaust the process of institutional innovation. The formation of a Jewish Board of Guardians in 1858 addressed the social condition of the community in much the same way as the Office of the Chief Rabbi addressed its spiritual condition (**doc. 2(d)**). The centralisation and control of charitable assistance formed part of a coherent programme designed to equip the Jewish poor with marketable skills preparatory to their incorporation in an enlarged and prosperous middle class. Co-operation in the field of relief work also provided the basis for the integration of the autonomous metropolitan Ashkenazi congregations within a unitary structure. Established in 1870, under the authority of an Act of Parliament, the United Synagogue sought to do for the Jewish minority what the Church of England did for the Protestant majority. Uniformity within the United Synagogue was in no small measure secured by the provisions whereby the Chief Rabbi assumed sole responsibility for the form of worship and all matters connected with the religious administration of that body and its subsidiary charities (**doc. 2(b)**).

The process of centralization, completed with the creation of the United Synagogue, was essentially the work of the acculturated elite who controlled communal resources. The same aristocracy of finance also dominated the Board of Deputies, which though formed in the eighteenth century, only came into its own in the struggles for emancipation of the 1830s. This elite comprised a cousinhood of well established merchant princes, bankers and professional persons – some Liberal, some Conservative – but all possessed of a common commitment to the social advancement of Jewry and protection of its recently acquired civil and political rights. To their wishes the mass of Jews were expected to conform. They not only constituted the lay leadership of the community, but also gave support and direction to the Office of the Chief Rabbi. The Chief Rabbinate was, indeed, as much the ecclesiastical mouthpiece of the patriciate as the President of the Board of Deputies was its secular spokesman (**doc. 2(c)**).

Under the guidance of these prudent pragmatists, the Jewish community created an institutional framework for the regulation of majority-minority relations and the socialisation of their co-religionists from the Pale. The process of adjustment, which made for integration without loss of identity, was accomplished without fundamental changes in the nature of the State. The space required for Jewish worship and observances – the keeping of the Sabbath, ritual slaughter of meat, religious marriages etc. – was small and easily accommodated within the pre-existing pattern of Church-State relations. Jewish exceptionalism posed no threat to the Anglican Establishment; nor was the privileged position of Christianity within the State disturbed (**docs. 3(a)–3(f)**).

The civil authority, though not directly involved in the management of the community, was not unsupportive. The Board of Deputies was recognised as the essential intermediary between the state and the Jewish minority; the primacy of the Chief Rabbi owed much to state support. It was the role of the Chief Rabbi in relation to marriage and divorce, and above all his privileged position in the registration process, on which his authority rested (**docs. 4(a)–4(c)**). The Jewish ecclesiastical authorities received preferential treatment from ministers of the crown and officials who valued their advice and approved of the responsible manner with which it was tendered. Questions concerning the status of marriage or the validity of a divorce, particularly among Jews of foreign extraction, were by arrangement referred to the Chief Rabbi and the Beth Din. Both the Chief Rabbi and the Board of Deputies were, in fact, willing to invite State intervention into the management of the community in order to enforce their authority over recalcitrant immigrant congregations and their rabbis as was revealed by the controversy over Jewish irregular marriages (**docs. 5(a)–5(c)**). But it was the confusion of State security with religious conformity during the First World War which revealed the nature and limits of the special relationship that had been created (**docs. 6(a)–6(c)**).

1.   Faith and freedom, 1847

Source: Minutes taken before Evidence of the Select Committee on Sunday Trading (Metropolis), Parliamentary Papers, IX (1847), qq. 1131–146, 1214–216

Henry F. Isaac lived at No. 203 Whitechapel Road, and, with his brother, was the proprietor and freeholder of the general mart in Houndsditch called Phill's Buildings. His observations on the prevalence of Sunday trading among the Jews also supplies a useful commentary on the voluntarist character of Jewish communal organization and the problems of religious authority arising therefrom.

1131.   *Chairman.* May I ask you whether persons of the Jewish persuasion who should open their shops on the Saturday, would be affected by any order of the church? — They are not at all restricted.

1132.   You would not be put out of your church? — Certainly not. For instance, if a person is regardless of his Sabbath, we say he is regardless of his faith, and it may be spoken of in society; but as to affecting him either in his synagogue or in his business, not at all; we are entirely free agents as to that.

1133.   Mr. *Brotherton.* There is no penalty? — None whatever; no restriction in the synagogue.

1134.   Mr. Alderman *Copeland.* It is a purely voluntary act on your part, to observe the Sabbath? — Yes . . .

1135.   State at what time on the Friday night you close, and when your Sabbath begins? — At sunset winter and summer, from sunset to star rise. On Saturday we have no market . . . On . . . the Jewish holidays . . . the . . . Jews . . . will not attend to any business. We open our mart, provided that the holidays fall on week-days, for the benefit of the Christian community, and those that have stalls; I have been sent for by the elders of the synagogue, and admonished by the rabbi, that I am opening the mart, which is giving an opening for Jews, if they felt disposed to trade. . . .

BOARD FOR THE AFFAIRS OF SHECHETA.

NOTICE TO THE JEWISH PUBLIC.

NOTICE IS HEREBY GIVEN, that

selling meat on a Stall in Wentworth Street, DOES NOT HOLD the LICENSE of the Board and that all Meat, &c., sold by him is according to Jewish Law Trifa (מרפה) and prohibited to be eaten by Jews.

London.   1901. Sivan 5661   By Order,
M. VAN THAL,
Investigating Officer

באָרד אָפ שחיטה

נאטים צום אידישען פּובליק.

עם ווירד היערמיט בעסאנמ געמאכם דאם

וואם פערקויפם פלייש אויף א סמאל אין ווענמווארמ
סם. האם נים קיין לייסענם פון דיא באָרד אף שחיטה
אונד לוימ דעם אידישען דין איז אלעם פלייש א.ז.וו.
וואם ער פערקויפם מרפה און איד׳ז מארן עסנים עסען

לונדן מון תרס״א: מ. וואן מהאל. אנוועסמניסנ: אפסער

ש״יד ינ׳אן רזוקעריא מאנ אה. ראבבינעאדשם. אז קאסטער׳סך מם׳ם.

Figure 2 A 'kosher' warning, 1901 Notices posted warning shoppers from patronising unsupervised butchers underscored the significance of an informed public opinion in the enforcement of Jewish religious law (G.R. Sims (ed.), *Living London*, 3 vols (London: Cassell, 1901, II, p. 32).

1137. Mr. *B. Wall.* How many holidays are there in the year? . . .

I should say twelve at least.

1139. Mr. Alderman *Copeland.* Some of those you keep very rigidly? —
Very rigidly indeed; in fact the whole of them; they have no power in
compelling us to close our marts on those particular days, therefore that
shows directly that we are quite free agents as to faith.

. . .

1214. Do they get meat from those who are licensed by the rabbi? —
They must be licensed by the rabbi before they can sell. The inspectors
are paid by the congregation and the killers too.

1215. With regard to those retail butchers, how do they manage on the
Sabbath-day; do they keep their own shops open? — No. If you were to
pay 20*l.* for an ounce, you could not get it, nor yet is a baker open; no
business whatever. It matters not what it is, they do not open. In fact, the
bakers and the butchers are under the surveillance of the rabbi and the
elders. For instance, if a butcher did anything wrong, the rabbi would not
allow the congregation, at least he would admonish them, and say, "You
are not allowed to eat or deal with that man; I do not consider that he
is," what is called, "clean according to the faith."

1216. In fact, a man is reached by a civil power, whether his conscience
acts upon him or not, and he is incapable of selling? — Yes.

2.   Institutions

a)   *Laws and Regulations for all the Synagogues in the British Empire, 1847*

Source: C. Roth, "The Chief Rabbinate of England", in I. Epstein, E. Levine and C.
Roth eds., *Essays in Honour of the Very Rev. Dr J.H. Hertz* (1942), pp. 382–83

The centralised and authoritarian character of the Chief Rabbinate was largely
the work of Nathan Marcus Adler (Chief Rabbi, 1845–1880) and his son
Hermann (Chief Rabbi, 1880–1911). Both were strict disciplinarians requiring
total submission from those who acknowledged their spiritual authority. Together
they dominated the life of Anglo-Jewry in one of its most formative periods. The
Laws and Regulations for all the Synagogues in the British Empire, issued by
N.M. Adler in 1847, signified the new order in the making. The first section
included the following:

The duty of superintending the Synagogue, as far as religious observances
are concerned, devolves on the Chief Rabbi . . .

The erection of a new Synagogue must have the sanction of the Chief Rabbi, and the formation of a new Congregation must have the sanction of the Chief Rabbi, besides that of the Board of Deputies.

b) The United Synagogue, 1870

Source: An Act for Confirming a Scheme of the Charity Commissioners for the Jewish United Synagogues, 14 July 1870 (35 & 36 Vict. c.116)

The United Synagogue has rightly been likened to the Anglican Establishment (Jewish Branch). Its conception as a Jewish analogue of the National Church was thwarted by Parliament which declined to create a Jewish version of the Church of England at the same time as it was disestablishing the Church of Ireland. The scheme for the creation of the United Synagogue included the following provisions:

The laws and regulations at the time of the establishment of this scheme or at any time previously thereto in force relating to the synagogues following, (that is to say,) the Great Synagogue, St. James's Place, Aldgate, in the city of London; the Portland Street Branch Synagogue, Great Portland Street, in the county of Middlesex; the Hambro' Synagogue, Church Row, Fenchurch Street, in the city of London; the New Synagogue, Great St. Helen's, Bishopsgate, in the city of London; and the Bayswater Synagogue, Chichester Place, Harrow Road, in the county of Middlesex; and to the subsidiary charities of the said respective synagogues; and the constitutions of the said respective synagogues; and the treaty or treaties at the time of the establishment of this scheme, or at any time previously thereto, in force between the said respective synagogues or any of them, are hereby annulled.

The synagogues herein-before named shall unite and form one institution, to be called "The United Synagogue," ק״ק כנסת ישראל, and shall be the present constituent synagogues of the said institution, each of the said synagogues, whether the same has been independent, or a branch of any other or others of them, being one of such constituent synagogues; and the subsidiary charities of the synagogues herein-before named shall be subsidiary charities of the United Synagogue. . . .

The objects of the institution to be called "The United Synagogue" shall be the maintaining, erecting, founding, and carrying on, in London and its neighbourhood, places of worship for persons of the Jewish religion who conform to the Polish or German ritual, the providing means of burial of persons of the Jewish religion, the relief of poor persons of the Jewish religion, the contributing with other Jewish bodies to the maintenance of a Chief Rabbi and of other ecclesiastical persons, and to other communal duties devolving on metropolitan congregations, and other charitable purposes in connexion with the Jewish religion.

The form of worship in each of the constituent synagogues shall be in accordance with the Polish or German ritual.

c) *Observations on the Board of Deputies of British Jews, 1851*

Source: Henry Mayhew, *London Labour and the London Poor*, 4 vols (1861), II, p.130

Henry Mayhew (1812–87) was a remarkable social investigator who, apart from personal observation, relied upon interviews with representative figures, high and low, to produce an engaging portrait of the Jewish community. The following, first published in 1851, reveals the work of the Board of Deputies and its standing with the civil authorities.

. . . I have before spoken of a Board of Deputies, in connection with the Jews, and now proceed to describe its constitution. It is not a parliament among the Jews, I am told, nor a governing power, but what may be called a directing or regulating body. It is authorized by the body of Jews, and recognised by Her Majesty's Government, as an established corporation, with powers to treat and determine on matters of civil and political policy affecting the condition of the Hebrews in this country, and interferes in no way with religious matters. It is neither a metropolitan nor a local nor a detached board, but, as far as the Jews in England may be so described, a national board. This board is elected triennially. The electors are the "seat-holders" in the Jewish synagogues; that is to say, they belong to the class of Jews who promote the support of the synagogues by renting seats, and so paying towards the cost of those establishments.

There are in England, Ireland, and Scotland, about 1000 of these seat-holders exercising the franchise, or rather entitled to exercise it, but many of them are indifferent to the privilege, as is often testified by the apathy shown on the days of election. Perhaps three-fourths of the privileged number may vote. The services of the representatives are gratuitous, and no qualification is required, but the elected are usually the leading metropolitan Jews. The proportion of the electors voting is in the ratio of the deputies elected. London returns 12 deputies; Liverpool, 2; Manchester, 2; Birmingham, 2; Edinburgh, Dublin (the only places in either Scotland or Ireland returning deputies), Dover, Portsmouth, Southampton, Plymouth, Canterbury, Norwich, Swansea, Newcastle-on-Tyne, and two other places (according to the number of seat-holders), each one deputy, thus making up the number to 30. On election days the attendance, as I have said, is often small, but fluctuating according to any cause of excitement, which, however, is but seldom.

With religious or sacerdotal questions the Board of Deputies does not, or is not required to meddle; it leaves all such matters to the bodies or tribunals I have mentioned. Indeed the deputies concern themselves only with what may be called the *public* interests of the Jews, both as a part of the community and as a distinct people. The Jewish institutions, however, are not an exception to the absence of unanimity among the professors of the same creeds, for the members of the Reform Synagogue in Margaret-street, Cavendish-square, are not recognised as entitled to vote, and do not vote, accordingly, in the election of the Jewish deputies. . . .

d)   The Jewish Board of Guardians, 1859

Source: Board of Guardians for the Relief of the Jewish Poor, *First Half-yearly Report, 1 July–31 December 1859* (1859)

The formation of the Jewish Board of Guardians in 1858 provided a basis for the integration of the autonomous Ashkenazi congregations within a unitary structure and constituted something of a landmark in the centralisation of Anglo-Jewry. The Board sought to reduce duplication, eliminate extravagance and restore order to the provision of charitable assistance — in short, to apply the principles of 1834 to the Jewish poor.

. . . This report being the first of the kind issued by the Board, it begs, in the first instance, to call the attention of the community to the circumstances that led to its foundation, the wants it was intended to meet, and the principles upon which it was based. For these purposes it is necessary to take a retrospect of the growth and progress of the community, since its re-establishment in this country, and to enumerate the various means which, from time to time have been adopted, to deal with the mass of pauperism which always existed in our midst.

It is certainly to be deplored that in this country a large amount of pauperism has always existed and still exists among us. But this stage of things cannot wholly be laid as a reproach to our community, either as regards the poor themselves, or as the result of a defective system of relief. It is to a great extent the result of the position the Jews have been compelled to occupy in most countries of their adoption. The honest attainment of independence involves a two-fold condition – industry, and a field for its exercise. The Jew is certainly endowed with no less energy or aptitude than his neighbour, for acquiring the necessary skill to enable him with God's Blessing, to supply himself with the means of subsistence; but he has been in olden times even in this country, and in later times in other countries, the victim of pernicious laws, which oppressed and restrained him. Restrictive laws have not been few in number, nor have the countries that enacted them been limited, whereby the Jew was for centuries, and in some places is still, shut out from following all industrial and honourable pursuits.

These restrictions led to their natural results; the few possessed of indomitable perseverance and commanding genius, managed to win their way to wealth and fame, despite every obstacle, but the many, sunk in wretchedness and ignominy, and steeped to the lips in poverty, sought the refuge of those more favoured countries, where the exceptional laws were less rigorous, and where consequently the fortunes of our community were brighter. Hence, the influx at an early date after our second settlement, of the "Jewish Poor" into England; an influx which was considerably stimulated by an increasing toleration, and still more by the absence of military conscription, and which continues to the present day.

. . .

. . . in 1859, the community with forty thousand souls, had, despite its increased intelligence, its enlarged means, and continued material progress, made but slight modification or improvement in the machinery for the dispensing of synagogal relief, which machinery was barely sufficient with a population of 8,000 in 1753. True it is that since 1800, the establishment of communal philanthropic institutions, free schools in the east and west, asylums for the old and the young, the widow and the orphan, charities for the needy and the blind, have remedied many of the grosser evils pointed out by Mr. Colquhoun, and freely admitted by Mr. Joshua Van Oven. Cheerfully and gladly must it be owned that the benefactions of private individuals and families have since that period permeated the community with a never-failing stream. Gratefully must it be acknowledged that "the women of Israel", of all conditions, from the highest downwards, have for some years past, brought, and still bring to bear, all the softening influences of refined minds and gentle hearts to ameliorate the condition of the poor, by visiting them in their homes, training their children in the school, and by example and precept pointing out to them there the path in which they should go. Still, the great bulk of the poor, with a large proportion of adults, and a majority of strangers, were not amenable to these influences; and even where these efforts could be brought to bear, much of the good was neutralised by the want of a concentrated organisation, wherein they might culminate, and imposition might be detected and checked.

Charities were multiplied and supported with no unsparing hand; but each charity moved, and still moves, in a circle of its own, and the poor still remained individually unknown, though their increasing numbers attracted attention and caused anxiety. A new charity frequently only opened a door of easy access to the sturdy, impudent beggar, who forced entrance to trade but too often on the nobler sympathies of our nature; and the truly unfortunate poor, – the shame-faced, the suffering, and the heart-broken, were debarred, self-debarred from these numerous charities established for their welfare, and, from being unknown and unsought, they were left to pine and to perish.

This state of things, admitted again and again on all hands, became greatly aggravated on the removal of the more wealthy to the west end of the metropolis. Formerly, when rich and poor lived in close proximity, the association of locality afforded some kind of intercourse, imperfect though it was. The rich and the poor were not as now estranged and apart. The worthless and the beggar were at least partially known as such to the donor; and in the instance of the worthy and respectable – when suffering became too keen, when perhaps the little ones cried for bread, when the aged were stricken down by the sharp tooth of famine, or paled before disease, and the exposure was made, the wealthy then knew personally their respectable neighbours, and believed them as such; but with the westward emigration both these conditions changed, and to the advantage of the beggar. The beggar, by profession unknown intimately to the donor, and known only by his importunity, had now more facilities for plying his not unsuccessful trade; while the needy but industrious man, unknown, for he had never asked before, was but too often confounded with the beggar, and became the victim of another's wrong-doing.

Formerly, with the poor man close at hand, the wealthier neighbour could not overlook his wants. It was easy to besiege the rich man's door, and to obtain by reiterated solicitation relief for that distress, now frequently unknown; for were it properly known, we may feel assured that change of residence has not altered the donor's heart, and that relief would soon be forth coming.

To put an end to this confounding of "evil with good," and to open a new channel, into which the several streamlets of charity might ultimately converge and unite, was long the anxious wish of every intelligent mind in the community. Various suggestions had from time to time been proposed, such as the amalgamation of our charities, and the "whole question" was frequently agitated; . . . It was at last felt that "perfection" cannot be arrived at by one gigantic bound, but must be the result of continued efforts at improvement; and with this conviction it was deemed the safer and wiser course to usher in a better state of thing with a reorganisation of the Synagogal system of relief. . . .

. . .

. . . *the Board of Guardians for the relief of the Jewish Poor* at length commenced operations on 1st July, 5619. The Board has since that period steadily pursued its onerous labours; meetings of the relief committees have been held twice in every week as provided for by the laws of the Board. The first meeting of the relief committee was held on 7th July, and there have been in all fifty-one meetings of the relief committees.

Two thousand and thirty-three applications from eight hundred and thirty-two individuals appear in the register of the Board as relieved by the relieving committees. In addition to this, the clerk who has power to give relief in kind to urgent cases, has received nearly six hundred applications and ministered to the wants of the applicants. Tabular statements of the Board's operations have been published every month, and an analysis of these tables, showing the number of cases relieved and the nature of the relief given, appears in the appendix to this report.

The relief administered, (in furtherance of the great aim of the Board, viz. to relieve the necessitous and discourage pauperism), has consisted, in a great measure of gifts of provisions, and of the necessaries of life, and also during the winter months of coals, clothing, and blankets. In addition to this, and encouraged by the liberality of D. Benjamin, Esq., who forwarded the munificent sum of one hundred pounds towards creating a fund specially for this purpose, the Board has advanced loans to one hundred and fifty-nine individuals to assist them in obtaining a livelihood.

The Board also, in the month of September (when the particulars and conditions of most of the poor were already recorded on its register) established a *mendicity department*, and invited its subscribers to apply to it for information as to the merits of any applications they might individually receive for relief. The Board cannot but greatly regret the limited use which has been made of this department . . .

The Board can but repeat the intimation it originally made; its register contains the full particulars of everyone of the 832 individuals that had been relieved to the end of the year, viz., their occupations, means of subsistence, number in family, native place, the period of their residence here, the school at which their children attend, and above all, as far as could be ascertained, the amount of public or other relief they have received. A reference to all these particulars before relief is given, must materially assist the distribution of true and discriminate charity, and the Board begs to reiterate that its register is at the disposal of every one for reference, and that its clerk will be happy to forward written information to any subscriber who will kindly apply for the same.

. . .

But with all these drawbacks, the Board cannot but flatter itself that much good has been accomplished, and that some of the objects for which it was established have been attained. It is certainly proved on the evidence of persons unconnected with the Board, that there is less of clamorous mendicancy at the doors of individuals, and that which still remains may by a more extended use of the Board's mendicity department be entirely suppressed. *The poor also are never relieved without enquiry;* instead of a hearsay account based on casual information through the beadle of the Synagogue, the home of each applicant is visited by the investigating officer, and searching enquiries instituted into his condition. The pauperising system of money gifts is also superseded except to an especial class of cases; instead of money, provisions and firing, which are certainly less open to abuse than money gifts, are freely given. During the winter months also distributions of blankets and flannel, hitherto almost confined to benefactions by benevolent individuals, have been made to deserving cases. Care is taken to urge and enforce on applicants the necessity of sending their children to our excellent schools, and with what results the returns of the schools as to the number of children attending will soon show. Lastly and above all, the machinery for relief has been in constant working order and always at hand; no person of the Jewish community need now suffer absolute hunger; the clerk is at hand, and is empowered and prepared to afford the necessaries of life, till the case can be enquired into and dealt with by the committee, which instead of distributing *once a month* as was the practice formerly, meets *twice in every week*. With the greatest satisfaction, and without fear of contradiction the Board can state that the result of this is shown in the fact which impartial evidence establishes, that there is less absolute distress among the Jewish poor now, than in any former winter.

. . .

Lastly, and above all, the Board would indeed consider its report imperfect, did it not take this occasion to allude to an almost patent fact that in a great measure mars its best efforts, and which keeps the poor "poor indeed," viz. – the homes of the poor. As a rule, the homes of the poor, such as the vast majority are at present, may be said to create poverty. While the homes are squalid, ill-ventilated, and therefore disease-breeding, the energies of the poor are cramped, their moral natures are frozen, and their chances of raising themselves above their present condition in life very limited indeed. The home, which should be the school of the affections, is here little better than a hovel – stript, both for the parent and the child, of its sweet charm and holy influence. These homes are in every way unfavourable to moral culture, to energetic exertion, or to religious training. The father, spiritless, strays away from home, to forget, if possible, the wretchedness of his miserable abode; and the child, thus neglected, seeks in evil company, in low pursuits, or in the exciting pleasures within its reach, false though such are owned to be, an equivalent for the solid happiness and blessings of home, and its sacred associations. While the home is such as described, the school may open its door to thousands, the Synagogue may instil the beautiful lessons of Scripture, institutions upon institutions may multiply, and Boards of Guardians may sit nightly to detect imposition and to relieve poverty; but the poor will remain devoid of those energies that command success of the virtues that shine, and of the habits that bless. The Board trusts, therefore, that it may consider it within its legitimate functions to suggest, at no distant day, a scheme for bettering the homes and dwellings of the poor.

3. Status of the Jews

a) Jewish exceptionalism: statement of Chief Rabbi, 1906

Source: Minutes of Evidence taken before the Joint Select Committee on Sunday Trading, Parliamentary Papers, [275] XIII (1906), q. 802

Special provision for Jewish observances — be it the keeping of the Sabbath, religious marriages, education etc. — represented a claim for distinctive treatment within a unitary legal system. The negotiation of these claims within the existing framework of the civil law constituted the principal work of communal leaders. Here Chief Rabbi Hermann Adler sets to.

Duke of *Northumberland* – continued
802. I suppose you recognise that it is not a very usual thing in legislation to exempt a particular religious community from the operation of the law. It is done in the case of Factory Acts; but is it done in any other case for the Jew? — Certainly, there is special legislation as regards the Marriage Acts. The Jews are specially mentioned. These provisions are no doubt well known to you. There are certain sections in the various Acts in the reign of William IV., and during the reign of her late Majesty there were several provisions referring to Jews, giving them certain exemptions. It is not obligatory upon them that the marriages should take place within a registered building. Marriages may be solemnized within their houses. It is distinctly stated that these provisions only refer to cases where both persons profess the Jewish religion. Therefore, there is ample precedent. Likewise, there is a clause stating that where the day of voting for Members of Parliament is on a Saturday the Registering Officer may mark the Balloting Paper on behalf of the Jew, who, from conscientious scruples, declines to do so on that day. Therefore, there is undoubtedly precedent for exceptional and considerate legislation on behalf of the Jews.

b) Marriage Act, 1836

Source: An Act for Marriages in England, 17 August 1836 (6 & 7 Will. 4, c. 85)

Apart from the maintenance of Jewish identity, provision for the registration of Jewish religious marriages served to raise the standing Board of Deputies whose President became the designated authority for certifying the Marriage Secretaries of Synagogues to whom Marriage Registers would be furnished.

II And be it enacted, That the Society of Friends commonly called *Quakers*, and also Persons professing the Jewish Religion, may continue to contract and solemnize Marriage according to the Usages of the said Society and of the said Persons respectively; and every such Marriage is hereby declared and confirmed good in Law, provided that the parties to such Marriage be both of the said Society, or both Persons professing the Jewish Religion respectively, provided also, that Notice to the

Marriages of Quakers and Jews.

Registrar shall have been given, and the Registrar's Certificate shall have issued in manner herein-after provided.

. . .

IV And be it enacted, That in every Case of Marriage intended to be solemnised in *England* after the said First Day of *March* according to the Rites of the Church of *England*, (unless by Licence or by Special Licence, or after Publication of Banns,) and in every Case of Marriage intended to be solemnized in *England* after the said First Day of *March* according to the Usages of the Quakers or Jews, or according to any Form authorized by this Act, One of the Parties shall give Notice under his or her Hand, in the Form of Schedule (A.) to this Act annexed, or to the like Effect, to the Superintendent Registrar of the District within which the Parties shall have dwelt for not less than Seven Days then next preceding, or if the Parties dwell in the Districts of different Superintendent Registrars shall give the like Notice to the Superintendent Registrar of each District, and shall state therein the Name and Surname and the Profession or Condition of each of the Parties intending Marriage, the Dwelling Place of each of them, and the Time, not being less than Seven Days, during which each has dwelt therein, and the Church or other Building in which the Marriage is to be solemnized; provided that if either Party shall have dwelt in the Place stated in the Notice during more than One Calendar Month, it may be stated therein that he or she hath dwelt there One Month and upwards.

Notice of every intended Marriage to be given to the Superintendent Registrar of the District.

. . .

XVI And be it enacted, That the Superintendent's Certificate, or, in case the Parties shall have given Notice to the Superintendent of different Districts, the Certificates of each Superintendent, shall be delivered to the officiating Minister, if the Marriage shall be solemnized according to the Rites of the Church of *England*; and the said Certificate or Licence shall be delivered to the Registering Officer of the People called *Quakers* for the Place where the Marriage is solemnized, if the same shall be solemnized according to the Usages of the said People; or to the Officer of a Synagogue by whom the Marriage is registered, if the same shall be solemnized according to the Usages of Persons professing

Superintendent Registrar's Certificate or Licence to be delivered to the Person by or before whom the Marriage is solemnized.

the Jewish Religion; and in all other Cases shall be delivered to the Registrar present at the Marriage, as herein-after provided.

. . .

XXXIX And be it enacted, That every Person who after the said First Day of *March* shall knowingly and wilfully solemnize any Marriage in *England*, except by Special Licence, in any other Place than a Church or Chapel in which Marriages may be solemnized according to the Rites of the Church of *England*, or than the registered Building or Office specified in the Notice and Certificate as aforesaid, shall be guilty of Felony (except in the Case of a Marriage between Two of the Society of Friends commonly called *Quakers*, according to the Usages of the said Society, or between Two Persons professing the Jewish Religion, according to the Usages of the Jews); and every Person who in any such registered Building or Office shall knowingly and wilfully solemnize any Marriage in the Absence of a Registrar of the District in which such registered Building or Office is situated shall be guilty of Felony; and every Person who shall knowingly and wilfully solemnize any Marriage in *England*, after the said First Day of *March* (except by Licence) within Twenty-one Days after the Entry of the Notice to the Superintendent Registrar as aforesaid, or if the Marriage is by Licence within Seven Days after such Entry, or after Three Calendar Months after such Entry, shall be guilty of Felony.

Persons unduly solemnizing Marriage guilty of Felony.

c) Workshop and Factory (Jews) Act, 1871

Source: An Act for exempting persons professing the Jewish religion from penalties in respect of young persons and females professing the said religion working on Sundays, 25 May 1871 (34 Vict. c.19)

Legislation to enable Jews to register for Sabbath exemptions from the laws regulating factories and workshops, negotiated with the Home Office by the Board of Deputies, illustrates the search for space within a Christian polity.

Whereas it is expedient to amend the law for the purpose of exempting persons professing the Jewish religion from penalties in respect of young persons and females professing the said religion working on Sunday:

Be it enacted by the Queen's most Excellent Majesty, by and with the advice and consent of the Lords Spiritual and Temporal, and Commons, in this present Parliament assembled, and by the authority of the same, as follows:

Exemption from penalties as to Jews.

1. No penalty shall be incurred by any person in respect of any work done on Sunday either in a workshop or in the tobacco manufacture by any young person or woman professing the Jewish religion; provided that,

(1) The workshop or manufactory is in the occu-pation of a person professing the Jewish religion, is on Saturday closed until sunset, and is not open for traffic on Sunday:

(2) That such workshop or manufactory is open on Sundays to the officers duly authorised by the Factory and Workshop Act, 1867:

(3) The total number of hours of labour of such young person or woman in any one week or day or period of twenty-four hours at such workshop or manufactory does not exceed the total number of hours of labour in any one week or day or period of twenty-four hours allowed by the Workshop Regulation Act, 1867.

Definition of work-shop.

2. "Workshop" shall mean workshop as defined by the Workshop Regulation Act, 1867.

d) Ballot Act, 1872

Source: An Act to amend the Law relating to Procedure at Parliamentary and Municipal Elections, 18 July 1872 (31 & 36 Vict. c. 33)

Special facilities to prevent discrimination against Jews in the electoral process were included in Part I of the First Schedule of the Ballot Act as shown below.

. . . 26. The presiding officer, on the application of any voter who is incapacitated by blindness or other physical cause from voting in manner prescribed by this Act, or (if the poll be taken on Saturday) of any voter who declares that he is of the Jewish persuasion, and objects on religious grounds to vote in manner prescribed by this Act, shall, in the presence of the agents of the candidates, cause the vote of such voter to be marked on a ballot paper in manner directed by such voter, and the ballot paper to be placed in the ballot box, and the name and number on the register of voters of every voter whose vote is marked in pursuance of this rule, and the reason why it is so marked, shall be entered on a list, in this Act called "the list of votes marked by the presiding officer." . . .

e) Shechitah imperilled, 1891

Source: Jewish World, 20 November 1891

The delicate balance between the minority religion and the state might be disturbed when large sectors of opinion were at variance with Jewish religious practises. The ritual slaughter of animals for food provides one such example. The Chief Rabbi hesitated to enforce the strictest standards lest it provoke an increasingly vociferous animal rights lobby.

The Chief Rabbi then gave the following explanation. Some eight or ten months ago, he said, a Society called Chevra Machzike Hadath, submitted to the Beth Din certain alleged grievances relating to the sale of Kosher meat, especially with regard to certain fat that was said to be sold to the poor as Kosher and was not so. The Beth Din thoroughly investigated those complaints, and assured the Chevra that no one who required Kosher meat and fat had any difficulty in obtaining it. True, there were in the Community certain individuals who were unfortunately not so particular, but those who wished to have meat that was in all respects Kosher according to Jewish law could obtain it. . . Why it was imperative to crush such a movement was because every rule of humanity that could be observed was observed in the slaughter houses under the Board's control. But in the case of these people, who came over here uncultivated and uncivilised, there was every reason to apprehend that such precautions would not be observed. The consequence would be that the Society for the Prevention of Cruelty to Animals would step in and, confounding the Chevra with the whole Community, would condemn Shechita as an act of cruelty.

f) The Sunday question and the Jews, 1906

Source: Minutes of Evidence taken before the Joint Select Committee on Sunday Trading, Parliamentary Papers, [275] XIII (1906), q. 2884

Opposition from the Jewish community held up the reform of the Sunday trading laws. Here President of the Board of Deputies David Lindo Alexander (1842–1922) justifies Jewish claims for exceptional treatment.

. . . Let me say at the outset that the Jewish community recognise as fully as their Christian fellow-citizens the extreme importance of the principle of one day's rest in seven, and I therefore wish it to be clearly understood that I hold no brief and claim no special treatment for those Jews who trade on the Jewish Sabbath as well as on the Sunday. On the contrary, I would gladly welcome legislation which would prevent them from working on more than six days a week. My attendance here to-day is solely on behalf of the observant section of Jewish shopkeepers and costermongers, a very large number of whom would be most seriously and, as I submit, most unjustly affected (if not completely ruined) by a general enforcement of Sunday closing. It is a matter of common knowledge that the poorer classes find it difficult enough already to earn sufficient in the six days of the week to support themselves and their families, and therefore to impose on the poorer members of the Jewish population compulsory abstention from business on Sunday – which would leave them with only five days of the week in which to earn their living, unless they violate the observance of their own Sabbath – would not only amount to unjust and unequal treatment, but would inevitably lead to a very large increase in the poverty and misery already prevailing in the poorer districts of London and the provinces. The result would be that many of the poorest Jews would be compelled to work on their Sabbath in order to keep body and soul together, and I say that a general enforcement of Sunday closing which, while compelling the Christian to observe his Sabbath, would have the effect of driving a considerable and industrious section of Jewish traders to break theirs, would be a violation of the principle of religious equality. To quote the words used by Lord Tweedmouth in his recent speech in the House of Lords, "the case of the Jews must be carefully considered and provided for in a generous manner," . . .

It may be instructive to consider one by one the main arguments advanced against any special exemption in favour of Jews, and to examine the grounds on which they are based. In the first place, it is said that Jewish members of the population must submit to the national customs in return for the liberty and advantages which they obtain in this country, but this argument treats all Jews as foreigners. There are no doubt, many Jews who are aliens, but the greater proportion of the Jewish traders are by birth or by naturalisation British subjects, and, as such, quite as much entitled to work on six days of the week as their Christian fellow citizens, so that as regards such Jews at all events the argument completely fails. Moreover, the argument entirely disregards the economic side of the question. It cannot, I submit, be to the best interests of this country to deprive thousands of small traders, whether they are British subjects or aliens, of the means of obtaining their livelihood, and this would unquestionably be the result of a general Sunday Closing Act, containing no exemption in favour of Jews. The next point taken is that the Jews in claiming an exemption in their favour are asking for an indulgence which their ancient legislators denied to the foreigner in a Jewish state. But as to this I am informed by the chief Rabbi that Jewish law does not impose on the foreigner any obligation to observe the Jewish Sabbath, and as the Chief Rabbi has in his evidence before this Committee explained the Jewish law on this subject, I need not further dwell on this point. The next argument, viz., that an exception allowing Jews who close on Saturdays to open on Sundays would lead to many Jews employing Christian labour on a Sunday can be disposed of in a few words. Such employment would not be possible under an exempting clause worded in the way proposed by me, for it expressly provides that a Jewish trader is not to be entitled to the benefit of the exemption unless he employs Jewish hands only on the Sunday. I thought it only fair and reasonable to impose such a condition on Jews, seeing that the object of legislation is to secure, as far as possible, a six days' week for work and one day for rest. It has, however, been suggested to me that Christian employees might possibly object to a condition prohibiting Jewish traders from employing Christian assistance on the Sunday, but I submit that it is not open to those who oppose any exemption in favour of Jews to complain that it will lead to the employment of Christian labour on Sundays, and in the same breath to object to a condition providing against such employment. The next two points may very conveniently be considered together. It is alleged (1) that some Jews employ Christians to transact their business during the Jewish Sabbath, and then open on Sunday; and (2) that, in some districts, Jews do not close at all on Saturday, but keep open on seven days a week, and it is said that it is the competition of such Jews that is felt so keenly. As regards the first of these allegations, I maintain that it is not borne out by the evidence before this Committee.

. . .

and as regards the second allegation, although some Jews no doubt may be found to open on seven days a week the number of Jews who do so is comparatively small. As a general rule the Jewish trader observes his Sabbath by complete abstention from business from sunset on Friday to nightfall on Saturday. But even if the allegations in question could be established (which I maintain they cannot be) the competition complained of would be entirely got rid of by adopting such a clause as I have indicated: for under it no Jew who trades on Saturday either personally or through an agent would be allowed to trade on the Sunday. A further argument put forward, and apparently much relied on is that Jewish traders are at liberty to open on Saturday night after the termination of their Sabbath. In reply to this argument I must point out that in the summer months when the Sabbath terminates very late, the opportunities which Jewish traders have for doing business on a Saturday night are limited to a very short space of time. For instance, during many weeks both before and after Midsummer Day, the Jewish Sabbath does not end until after 9 o'clock in the evening, and although in the winter they have a longer Saturday night for doing business, still they get a shorter day on the Friday, for they have to close business on Friday in the winter as early as 3.30 p.m. I wish to press home the fact that the observance of the Jewish Sabbath involves complete abstention from business from sunset on Friday to nightfall on Saturday, which covers a period of time varying from 25¼ hours in winter to 27¼ hours in summer, so that put it as one may the Jewish trader who keeps his Sabbath has throughout the year less than six days a week left him for carrying on his business, and it is therefore idle to say that he will get an unfair advantage if he is allowed to open on Sundays. On the contrary, the Jew is already severely handicapped in his trade, for in addition to observing his Sabbath he has to abstain from business on thirteen other days in the year – namely, the Jewish Festivals. . . . The argument that a Jew opening on Sunday forces a Christian to open on that day in self-defence has no substance in it. The main trade done by Jews on Sunday is with their fellow Jews, who would in all cases prefer to give their custom to a Jewish trader. With their fellow Jews they can talk Yiddish and discuss communal affairs, and have many points in common which they have not with Christians. Moreover, the Jewish trader knows the tastes of his fellow Jews and is therefore better able to cater for their custom. This argument for compulsory closing on Sunday is therefore merely an excuse for crushing Jewish competition in trade. I have now dealt with every argument used against an exemption in favour of Jews, and it only remains for me to say that I have carefully considered other alternatives to the amendments proposed by my Board, but find that none of these, such as local option or a plebiscite of the inhabitants, or exemption in particular districts, will meet the exigencies of the case. I therefore claim on behalf of the Jewish community that any Bill introduced on the subject should contain all the three amendments framed by my Board, and in particular a clause exempting Jews from the operation of any general restriction against Sunday trading, provided they observe their Sabbath by complete abstention from business from sunset on Friday to sunset on Saturday and only employ Jewish assistance for their Sunday trading. . . .

2887. You are aware that Sunday trading is illegal at present? — I quite admit that; but we must not lose sight of the fact that the Act of Charles II. is almost a dead letter at the present day. It embraces many more subjects than Sunday trading; it provides for everybody going to church, and so on. Therefore we live in a very different time to that in which the statute of Charles II was passed. . . .

So far as Jews are concerned the present state of the law works satisfactorily, and the Jewish community do not ask for any alteration. But if there is to be new legislation, we claim the protection provided for by my three amendments.

4. Religious conformity, the State and the Jews

a) The Beth Din, 1851

Source: Henry Mayhew, *London Labour and the London Poor,* 4 vols (1861), II, p. 125

Informal state support for the Jewish ecclesiastical establishment, as noted below, was important in sustaining the authority of the Chief Rabbi.

The Jews in this country are classed as "Portuguese" and "German." Among them are no distinctions of tribes, but there is of rites and ceremonies, . . .

The fundamental laws are equally observed by both sects, but in the ceremonial worship there exists numerous differences. . . . The German Jews are much more numerous than the Portuguese; the chief Rabbi of the German Jews is the Rev. Dr. Nathan Marcus Adler, late Chief Rabbi of Hanover, who wears no beard, and dresses in the German costume. . . . Each chief Rabbi is supported by three other Rabbis, called Dayanim, which signifies in Hebrew 'Judges.' Every Monday and Thursday the Chief Rabbi of the German Jews, Dr. Adler, supported by his three colleagues, sits for two hours in the Rabbinical College (Beth Hamedrash), Smith's-buildings, Leadenhall-street, to attend to all applications from the German Jews, which may be brought before him, and which are decided according to the Jewish law. Many disputes between Jews in religious matters are settled in this manner; and if the Lord Mayor or any other magistrate is told that the matter has already been settled by the Jewish Rabbi he seldom interferes. This applies only to civil and not to criminal cases. The Portuguese Jews have their own hospital and their own schools. Both congregations have their representatives in the Board of Deputies of British Jews, which board is acknowledged by government, and is triennial. Sir Moses Montefiore, a Jew of great wealth, who distinguished himself by his mission to Damascus, during the persecution of the Jews in that place, and also by his mission to Russia, some years ago, is the President of the Board. All political matters, calling for communications with government, are within the province of that useful board.

b) Observations of David Salomons MP on Jewish Marriage Registration, 1867

Source: Report of the Royal Commission on the Laws of Marriage, Parliamentary Papers, [4059] XXXII (1867–8), Appendix No. 16, pp. 10–11

Figure 3   Before the Beth Din, 1901   The Beth Din (Jewish Court), the court of the
Chief Rabbi, dealt with matrimonial disputes and a wide range of civil causes.
Would-be litigants from the immigrant community were frequently referred to it by
policemen, magistrates and judiciary (G.R. Sims, (ed.), *Living London*, 3 vols
(London: Cassell, 1901), II, p. 33).

David Salomons (1797–1873), the first Jew to speak in the House of Commons,
was twice President of the Board of Deputies (1838–40 and 1846) and a
member of the West London Synagogue of British Jews. Here he explains how
the Chief Rabbi's spiritual authority was immensely strengthened by the privileged
position he occupied in the marriage registration process.

1. The Marriage and Registration Acts, as they affect the Jews, seem to
me to require some alteration. By their operation the registration of the
secretaries of synagogues is encumbered with unnecessary formalities, and
the element of thorough religious liberty, granted to all other dissenting
bodies, is in the case of the Jews but imperfectly secured.

2. These Acts present, for persons professing the Jewish religion, a complicated system, alike wanting in the simplicity of a mere civil registration, as enacted for other dissenting bodies, or as affording the solid advantage of that double character of registrar and minister, which the clergyman exercises in all the marriages of churchmen.

3. The Marriage and Registration Acts were intended to afford *civil* registration of every marriage, leaving it to the parties themselves to marry according to their own religious views, without any heed or interference by the State in what may be properly considered as the spiritual element.

4. This principle is abandoned in the case of the Jews, for they, in compliance with these Acts, are required to marry according to their "usages." Marriages so celebrated are to be certified by the secretary of a synagogue, who is to be present at marriages "of persons professing the Jewish religion," and in effect he certifies to their "rites and ceremonies."

5. We here see that Parliament has deviated from the strict principle of civil registration, and has undertaken that in the marriage of Jews, the registrar, who is to be "the secretary of a synagogue," shall superintend and certify such marriages, he being the agent of the State for that purpose, *certifying religious usages, and also rites and ceremonies*. (6 & 7 Will. 4. cap. 86. clause 31. schedule C.)

6. It was the avowed object of Parliament to extend to all religious denominations in Her Majesty's dominions the inestimable privilege of registration of their marriages without interference as to matters of faith. But, as regards the Jews, the position assumed by the State has been of such a mixed character that it enabled the appointment of the registrar secretary to be so managed as to become an especial element of religious discipline. In fact the Acts have been so administered as to make the adhesion of synagogues to an *orthodox* Jewish *ecclesiastical standard* the very *substance* and *condition* of registration.

7. By such means the religious independence which the Legislature proposed conferring on congregations of every denomination of religious worshippers in the United Kingdom in the celebration of their marriages has hardly been extended to the marriages of Jews.

8. This is brought about by the course prescribed in 6 & 7 Will. 4. c. 86. s. 30., as preliminary to the appointment of the registering secretary. By it Parliament has conferred a power which has been so applied, or rather, it may be, as I think, misapplied, not for testing the respectability of the secretary, or of his due election by his congregation, but for judging of the orthodoxy of the worshippers that have made him their secretary, and have put him forward to be certified as such to the Registrar-General.

9. This manifest violation of the true spirit of these Acts for the purpose of enforcing religious conformity, and of establishing ecclesiastical supremacy over Jewish congregations, by the assumed authority of Parliament, has been productive of great bitterness, which, after years of contention, is hardly yet allayed. A somewhat awkward attempt at a remedy has been since made in the 19 & 20 Vict. c. 119; but it neither sets

free Jewish congregations, nor does it relieve the State from being a party in their religious disputes.

10. Apparently nothing seems easier than complying with the plain words of the Registration Act, and certifying of an appointed secretary of a congregation of persons professing the Jewish religion that *he is* the secretary of that synagogue. *That*, in reason, would seem to be a true compliance with the directions of the Legislature. Nothing more can be required according to the plain reading, the evident meaning, and the true spirit of the Marriage and Registration Acts.

11. But ingenuity is seldom at fault when spiritual authority is to be exerted. So when the secretary of a synagogue is presented by a congregation of persons professing the Jewish religion to be certified as such, the question mooted is not, Is he the secretary? but Are they a conforming congregation? Are they an orthodox synagogue? Registration has in this manner been raised into an element of religious discipline, and of sustaining Jewish ecclesiastical authority by the assumed power and action of Parliament; and according as a congregation of worshippers have conformed strictly to the Rabbinical rule, or deviated therefrom, so have secretaries of synagogues been accepted or repudiated. . . .

c)   Certificate denied, 1907

Source: PRO RG 48/190, Chief Rabbi Hermann Adler to Charles Emanuel, Secretary and Solicitor to the Board of Deputies of British Jews, 2 August, 5663 [1907]

In 1898 the Spitalfields Great Synagogue applied to have the building registered for marriage solemnization, and would have succeeded in so doing, but for the opposition of the Chief Rabbi who pointed out that the applicants were not unorthodox Jews and persuaded the Registrar-General that it was very undesirable that registration should take place. A similar issue arose in 1907 with respect to the Russell Street Synagogue, Liverpool. This time, though, the congregation were able to compose their differences with the Chief Rabbi who, it will be seen, possessed considerable leverage in the matter.

Dear Mr Emmanuel,

I was in receipt of your letter of the 29th ult. with reference to the application made by the body styling itself the Great Synagogue Russell Street, Liverpool, to the Registrar-General.

In reply to your enquiry I beg to say that I altogether fail to see what justification this body have for naming themselves Hebrew Dissenters. From communications made to me by members of that body and from trustworthy information which I have received from other quarters, it does not admit of doubt that their form of worship is absolutely identical with that of the Synagogues under my spiritual jurisdiction, and that they will use the form of marriage ritual adopted by all orthodox congregations. They are therefore not justified in describing themselves as Dissenters from orthodox Jews.

The reason why I have not yet granted them my Certificate stating that they constitute a Synagogue is that they have not placed themselves under my spiritual jurisdiction, so that I do not yet possess the necessary guarantee that marriages to be solemnized in connexion with that place of worship will be in strict accord with the marriage law of England.

5.   Irregular Jewish marriage

a)   A subject of gravest importance, 1877

Source: Archives of the United Synagogue, Report of the Executive Committee of the United Synagogue on Wedding Fees, 13 June 1877

The arrival of immigrants from Eastern Europe who followed the Jewish law in regard to marriage and divorce created problems for an Orthodox establishment that sought to mediate relations between the minority and the state. The response of the United Synagogue is illustrated below.

. . . A third subject grew out of the investigations of the Committee – that of the so-called "irregular" marriages. This subject is one of the gravest importance to the Community, in its religious, social, and legal aspects. Though not, therefore, in terms remitted for its consideration, the Committee consider that no apology is necessary for adverting to it in this report. . . .

. . .

The question as to whether the amount of the Wedding Charges is in any way connected with the existence of irregular marriages, is one which was closely pursued by the Committee, and enquiries were addressed to the Rev. the Chief Rabbi on the point. The following observations are extracted from the letter received in reply, and will be found generally to give explicit information on the subject of these irregular marriages:–

"I beg to acknowledge the receipt of your letter of the 28th ult. on the important subject of Clandestine Marriages. As the parties engaged in these proceedings naturally dread exposure, it is difficult to learn the exact reason which prompted them to be married in secret. But I believe that these illegal weddings are caused by one or more of the three following motives:– 1. I find it absolutely necessary to require

satisfactory proof, in the case of foreigners, either that they are single
or that their wife is dead, or that a legal divorce has taken place. And I
believe that, in some few cases, when neither a certificate could be
produced, nor satisfactory evidence be given, the parties have gone
through the ceremony of marriage in secret, the person officiating at
such marriage asking no questions. 2. There are foreigners who,
unfortunately, believe that they are not bound by the law of the land,
and wish to avoid the trouble and expense of civil and religious
registration. It need scarcely be added, that the unqualified person or
persons, who assist at those secret weddings, do not require the
production of a certificate from the Registrar of the Parish. 3. There
have been a few instances, in which I have been informed by the
parties, that the reason for their resorting to a secret wedding was their
inability to pay the fees. I am not in a position to say whether these
allegations were founded on fact. But the evils consequent upon such
clandestine marriages are obviously so great, that every measure should
be adopted to check and prevent them." . . .

. . .

So keenly did the Committee feel the importance of this subject, and so
sharply did they feel the disgrace which attaches to the Community by the
irregular marriage of any of its members, that they have solicited legal
opinion as to the advisability of prosecuting persons who conduct these
irregular services; but find it prudent to wait till some amendment is made
in the Marriage Acts of Parliament, which will probably take place at no
distant date.

The Committee are aware that many of these marriages are contracted
– they cannot say solemnised – for the most nefarious of purposes. They
do not and cannot hope entirely to prevent acts of wickedness and fraud
by their legislation, but through the course hereinafter recommended, they
hope to render these acts more difficult of accomplishment, by bringing
within the knowledge and the means of all, the manner and mode of
legitimate Jewish marriage; a course they believe the Council will endorse,
even though no hardship can be proved to have existed by reason of the
present system among the class hitherto attaching themselves to the
Synagogue by marriage.

As the evidence collected by the sub-Committee has abundantly shown,
the class of persons for whom these enactments are more especially
recommended are, in most instances, satisfied and contented with the
services of any travelling hawker, whose abilities enable him to copy out
the כתובה (marriage contract), and to read the marriage service, and who
carries all the scandal of the Gretna Green marriages of a past age into
the midst of the Jewish community of to-day. In place of this it is
proposed to give to this class of persons all the advantages of a legitimate
marriage, solemnly and decorously conducted by one of the ministers of
the United Synagogue in a building consecrated to Divine worship, and at
the same charge as he would have paid for the irregular service.

b) *Statement of the President of the Board of Deputies, 1912*

Source: Minutes of Evidence taken before the Royal Commission on Divorce and Matrimonial Causes, Parliamentary Papers, [Cd. 6481] XX (1912—13), qq. 41,467—41,468

Unsupervised foreign rabbis who solemnized marriages without due certification or licence and administered Jewish divorces not preceded by a civil divorce, posed a threat to the standing of the minority and the pretensions of its leaders who decided to summon the intervention of the civil power in support of their own authority.

. . . The Board is the recognised medium for communication with the Government, and, during the last 74 years, it has enjoyed Parliamentary recognition, the duty of certifying marriage secretaries for the registration of Jewish marriages being under the Marriage Acts entrusted to the President for the time being of the Board. Under the Marriage Acts of 1836 and 1857, Jews are permitted to solemnize their marriages according to their own usages, provided that due notice to the Superintendent Registrar shall have been given and his certificate or licence shall have been issued for the marriage; and every possible precaution is taken by the Board in conjunction with the Chief Rabbi to ensure a compliance with these statutory conditions and also to prevent the solemnization of marriages, which although allowable by Jewish matrimonial law, are prohibited by English law. Where a person intending marriage has been previously married, the Chief Rabbi always requires strict proof of the death of the former husband or wife (as the case may be), or of the legal dissolution of the previous marriage. To prove such dissolution, he requires in the case of an English domicil, production of a decree absolute of the English Court of Divorce, and in the case of a foreign domicil, production of clear and satisfactory evidence that the previous marriage has been fully dissolved according to the law of the foreign domicil, and he withholds his authorisation until such evidence is produced to him. Moreover, the Chief Rabbi never pronounces a Jewish divorce unless it is preceded by a civil divorce in this country or elsewhere. There are, however, a few foreign Rabbis in this country who presume not only to solemnize Jewish marriages in the absence of the Superintendent Registrar's certificate or licence – which marriages are called "Stille Chuppah" (*i.e.,* clandestine) marriages – but also to grant Jewish divorces not preceded by a civil divorce in this country, and for many years past such irregular proceedings on the part of these foreign Rabbis have been a constant source of trouble to the Board. The Board has taken every available step within its power to put a stop to such marriages and divorces, but I regret to say with little or no success. The position taken up by these rabbis is, that it is their duty to administer the Jewish matrimonial law and that where the English law conflicts with

Jewish law the former must give way. As regards Jewish divorces, these foreign Rabbis still continue to grant them in spite of their knowledge of the want of legality. Every year cases are brought to the attention of the Board and the number of these so-called divorces is decidedly on the increase. . . . The evil consequences of such divorces are extremely serious, for the divorced parties are led to believe that their marriage has been validly dissolved and that they are quite free to contract a fresh marriage. Even when the divorced husband is aware of the want of legality the divorced wife is as a rule ignorant of it, for the bill of divorcement handed to her by her husband purports to give her full power to re-marry. More often than not a Jewish divorce is followed by the re-marriage of one or both of the divorced parties, with the result that the party so re-marrying is guilty of bigamy and adultery. But the mischief does not rest there. Cases frequently come under the notice of the Board in which the divorced husband deserts his second wife, or the divorced wife is deserted by her second husband. In neither case can the woman obtain a maintenance order against the man who has deserted her, and the mischief is naturally accentuated when, as often happens, there are children of such a second marriage, for besides being illegitimate they are as a rule wholly unprovided for and become dependent on charity. Such re-marriages are usually of the Stille Chuppah type but occasionally they take place at a registry office, the divorced party assuming a name slightly different from his or her own, or describing himself or herself as a bachelor or spinster. A further evil arising out of these Jewish divorces is, that unless the divorced wife can prove that she did not consent to the proceedings she can neither obtain a maintenance order against her husband on the ground of his desertion nor a decree of divorce even where he has married again, for, in the absence of such proof, she is taken to have connived at his subsequent marriage and adultery. . . .

. . .

. . . The misery caused in such cases is entirely due to the action of the foreign Rabbis in this country, for without their assistance these irregular divorces could not take place. They invariably charge a fee for the performance of the ceremony, which in many instances induces the parties to believe that he is a person having authority to dissolve their marriage legally. . . .

. . .

. . . Legislation is undoubtedly needed to suppress the irregular proceedings of these foreign Rabbis . . . A severe penalty should be imposed on all persons assisting at or taking part in the pronouncing of a Jewish divorce except after, and on production of a decree absolute of the Divorce Court in England or proof of a previous legal divorce elsewhere. . . .

c) A plea for legislation, 1922

Source: PRO HO 45/2030801/436597/7, Unsigned Memorandum on Jewish Irregular Marriage, August 1922

The attempt to secure religious conformity through state intervention against the background of a resurgent anti-alienism associated with the First World War provoked the demand for rather greater adjustments than the Anglo-Jewish leadership either wished for or thought desirable.

The question at issue is perfectly simple. The Marriages Act 1836 recognises and validates marriages between Jews according to Jewish usage provided a certificate or licence is obtained from the superintending registrar. But the penalty clause (see 39) is so drawn as to exempt Jews (and Quakers) from the penalty inflicted on all other persons who knowingly and wilfully solemnise a marriage without the statutory requirements as to notice and certificate having been first complied with.

The attention of the Secretary of State was called to this matter by the Commissioner of Police, who reported that it is by no means uncommon for East End Jews to go through a form of marriage which is apparently valid according to Jewish religious law but has no binding effect at all in English law. There appear to be two main types of such irregular marriages: (a) where the ceremony is performed in a private house by a Rabbi and a marriage certificate is signed by the parties and witnessed by the Rabbi; (b) where the parties exchange rings before witnesses and sign a form of certificate (to be bought from any Jewish stationer); this is not witnessed or put on record.

It is obvious that serious evils must attend the existence of a system of marriages which have the appearance of validity while being in fact quite invalid in law. Ignorant persons particularly if they are of foreign origin may be put to serious inconvenience and suffering; and unscrupulous persons may take advantage of this state of affairs. The particulars given by the Commissioner indicate that many Jews are quite acute enough to play fast and loose with their religious marriages on occasion. . . .

. . .

It cannot, of course, be supposed that the passing of this Bill would entirely put a stop to irregular Jewish marriages. But it would clearly do something to obviate the worst evils if people who knowingly and wilfully celebrate irregular Jewish marriages were made criminally liable in the same way as people of any other religious persuasion who do the same thing. It is unsatisfactory to find that the Jewish ecclesiastical authorities, seem indisposed to give any help in the matter, and it is not easy to understand their attitude. In 1836 when Jews were still regarded by the law as partially aliens there may have been some justification for giving them special treatment in this matter. But now that they stand on precisely the same legal footing as any other citizen they can have no claim to be treated differently from any one else in respect of offences against the marriage laws. Nor is it obvious what advantage the continuance of the present state of things can be to the Jewish body. I think Mr. Henriques ought to be asked to explain what grounds there are either in the public interest or in the interest of Judaism for continuing to allow Jews knowingly and wilfully to solemnise invalid marriages with impunity when members of all other religious bodies are liable to punishment for doing the same thing.

6. Conscription and conscience

a) Interview with Chief Rabbi Hertz at the Home Office, 1917

Source: PRO HO 45/10819/318095/497, Note of interview with the Chief Rabbi on the question of Jewish ministers of religion in relation to the Military Service Acts, by J.F.H.[enderson], 31 October 1917

Opposition to military service during the First World War was considerable among certain sectors of the non-naturalized Russian Jewish population of East London. Exemptions from military service were sometimes claimed on religious grounds, and it was the role of independent immigrant rabbis in sustaining these claims that concerned both the State and the Chief Rabbi. The two parties looked to one another for mutual support in crushing this challenge to their authority.

There have been a number of cases and there will be still more in which a Russian of military age in this country endeavours to evade military service by alleging that he is a minister of religion and therefore excepted from the operation of the M.S. Acts. On the introduction of Mr. Montefiore, the Chief Rabbi, Dr. Hertz, came to H.O. yesterday to suggest that something should be done to defeat these bogus claims. He saw Mr. Pedder and there were also present Mr. Thompson of the National Service Dept., Mr. Gibbon of the L.G.B., Major Lionel Rothschild, Mr. Montefiore and myself. Dr. Hertz left the enclosed memorandum and in conversation, he explained the position more or less as follows:–

Broadly speaking there are four distinct Jewish religious bodies in this country:– (a) The Portuguese Community, (b) the Liberal Synagogue, (c) the Reformed Synagogues (or the Synagogue of British Jews) and (d) the remainder of the Jewish Community under the Chief Rabbi.

No cases of disputed military liability are likely to arise in regard to persons belonging to the first three of these communities; all disputed cases, broadly speaking, will occur in regard to persons owing allegiance to the Chief Rabbi.

The present arrangement is that the Chief Rabbi issues certificates that a man is a minister of religion after enquiry and that such certificates are accepted by the military authorities as evidence that the holder is a minister of religion and therefore not liable to service. A number of Russian Jews, however, with little or no claim to be regarded as regular ministers of religion apply to the Chief Rabbi for certificates are refused by him and eventually are summoned as absentees. Then they set up a claim to be ministers of religion and assert that they do not recognise the authority of the Chief Rabbi.

Though there will be exceptions it is broadly true to say that every man who puts up a claim in a police court to be a minister of religion, is a man who has already tried to get a certificate from the Chief Rabbi and failed. Dr. Hertz had it in his mind that possibly his opinion on a disputed case could be accepted as final, but it was explained to him that the decision in each case was one for the magistrate to make and that any opinion or evidence from the Chief Rabbi could only be in the nature of expert advice. Dr. Hertz accepted this but suggested that it might be possible to inform the magistrates in the districts where these cases are likely to arise that he will be ready to give expert assistance to them. Mr. Pedder told him that some such communication might perhaps be made to the Courts if S. of S. approved but he could not pledge S. of S. to take such action.

Dr. Hertz seemed genuinely anxious that scandals such as have already occurred in one or two cases should be avoided, but it is obvious that the question of deciding what exactly constitutes a Jewish minister of religion is difficult.

On the whole, it might be a good thing to write to a selected number of courts in the terms of the enclosed draft. The National Service Dept. are interested in the question as it affects recruiting, and concur in the proposal.

b) A note of caution, 1917

Source: PRO HO 45/10819/318095/497, Minute of John Pedder, 1 November 1917

Sir John Pedder (1869–1956) was educated at Oriel College, Oxford and entered the Civil Service in 1892. From the Public Record Office he moved to the Local Government Board and hence to the Home Office where he was Principal Assistant Secretary. He was knighted in 1919 and retired in 1932. In the extract printed below he reveals the limitations of the special relationship with the Jewish ecclesiastical authorities.

There is no doubt of a widespread attempt . . . among Russian Jews to obtain exemption from the Convention . . . There is on the other hand some risk in accepting and promoting the Chief Rabbi's claim to a jurisdiction over sections of Jewish religious opinion which do not readily admit it. That was why I was very cautious in dealing with the Chief Rabbi.

But I think a letter carefully phrased [as below] can do no harm and may be of much assistance to the Courts. It will rest with the Courts to decide the point at issue, after hearing evidence from or on behalf of the Chief Rabbi if they choose. . . .

c) Home Office circular, 1917

Source: PRO HO 45/10819/318095/497, Home Office circular, 12 November 1917

The supremacy of the Chief Rabbi was in no small measure assisted by his prescribed role in the judicial process.

Sir,

I am directed by the Secretary of State to inform you that the Chief Rabbi, Dr. Hertz, called at the Home Office recently with a view to ascertaining what could be done to defeat bogus claims by Russian Jews of military age to be ministers of religion and therefore to be excepted from liability to military service. As the Secretary of State understands the matter, there is an arrangement in existence with the National Service Department by which a certificate from the Chief Rabbi that a particular individual is a minister of religion is accepted by the recruiting authorities as entitling the holder to be regarded as coming within the fourth paragraph of the schedule of exceptions in the first Military Service Act. There is, therefore, generally a presumption that in a disputed case which comes into court, the defendant has already applied to the Chief Rabbi for certificate that he is a minister of religion and has been refused. The Chief Rabbi is satisfied that a number of bogus claims are being made and he expressed himself as ready to render any assistance which the courts may desire by giving or supplying the Court with expert evidence on matters relating to the Jewish ministry.

The Secretary of State thinks that it may be useful to you to have this information so that in any case where you feel doubt as to the validity of a claim by a Russian Jew to be a regular minister of Jewish religion, you may, if so disposed, take advantage of the Chief Rabbi's offer of assistance.

It should be added that in one or two cases which have already come before the Courts, the defendant or his witnesses have repudiated the Chief Rabbi's authority over them. There is some reason to think that this attitude is taken where the defendant either has met with or anticipates no success from an application to the Chief Rabbi for a certificate. In any case it appears that the opinion of the Chief Rabbi on all Jewish matters in this country may be regarded as the highest expert evidence available. . . .

III
THE JEWISH QUARTER

The settlement of large ethnic and religious minorities in Britain has not been a uniform process. The Jewish experience differed from that of non-Christian New Commonwealth immigrants in several respects. The newcomers from Eastern Europe were received into an established community that was well-organized, affluent and well-regarded. In the two and one quarter centuries that separated the re-admission of the minority from the passage of the May Laws, the Jews of Britain had prospered, acquired civil rights and developed an extensive communal support system to manage the adjustment of their immigrant co-religionists. The institutional framework has been discussed in the previous chapter. Here the emphasis is upon the settlement localities, upon spatial relations, family and community.

The newcomers were urban in their orientation. Large communities developed in inner city districts like the Leylands in Leeds, Cheetham Hill in Manchester and the Gorbals in Glasgow. The largest concentration of immigrants, however, was to be found in the East End of London. In an area of less than two square miles lived nine tenths of the Jewish population of late Victorian Britain. A comparison of the accounts of Mayhew at mid-century with that of Mrs Brewer in 1892 illustrates the transformative effects of the immigrant presence upon the spiritual and secular life of the minority (**docs. 1–2**). Orthodox Judaism is presented as more than just a religion. Its rules and rituals are seen to have informed everyday life. Others noted the tendency to turn to the *landsmannschaften*, that support network of religious and voluntary associations that had been transplanted from the same village or district in Eastern Europe from which the newcomers came. The Jewish friendly societies and the *stieblch* with which they were often associated provided for more than just the material requirements of the members; their role in the allocation of social honour was scarcely less important (**doc. 3**).

The immigrants, it was sometimes noted, were anything but an undifferentiated mass. The *landsmannschaften*, while they gave members a dignity and self-respect, also served to sustain certain social divisions based upon place of origin. Was marriage between Polaks and Litvaks, Galizianers and Roumanian immigrants, as rare as the literature suggests? We do not know. Jewish family history is still in its infancy. Myths about the Jewish family exist in place of systematic knowledge on marriage, household structure, kinship relations and residence patterns. On gender roles and on continuities and changes in family behaviour our information is indicative rather than definitive **(docs. 8(a)–8(b))**.

Immigrant living conditions were the subject of much comment. Some was descriptive, some evaluative and much of it was hostile. Contemporary social observation combined all three elements in varying proportions **(doc. 5(a))**. Streets, strewn with decomposing fish-heads and fruit, and lined with litter and rotting vegetables, were automatically classified as 'Jewish' as though there was some necessary connection between faith and filth. The contribution of Jewish landlords and property speculators to the degradation of the environment also received a good deal of exposure. Jewish landlords, however, displayed no particular anti-Christian bias; Jewish tenants were equally oppressed **(doc. 5(b))**. Housing and rent struggles were in fact a major source of tension between host and minority populations.

The extension of the settlement locality was by no means an untroubled process. The influence of inter-communal conflict upon spatial patterning in Jewish East London was pronounced. The assertion of Jewish territoriality was contested street by street by an indigenous population that was alarmed by the inflationary influx on rented accommodation. Peace reigned only in those streets in which the issue had been decided. Here the Jewish and gentile populations developed avoidance strategies to regulate conflict and opposition. In those districts on the edge of the foreign quarter, where street supremacy had not been settled, resistance to Jewish encroachment was most intense. Personal violence and the threat thereof led to the formation of Jewish exclusion zones with long-lasting effects on the political culture of the area. **(docs. 6(a)–6(e))**.

It was the language of the immigrant which in part defined the settlement locality. Shopkeepers with unpronounceable names selling goods advertised in an incomprehensible language, above all the locals gabbling in an unknown tongue, made for a strange sense of isolation. It also made for hostility. Conflict and consternation were unavoidable where English was neither spoken nor understood. Effective policing, too, was impossible where the people spoke little English and the police spoke nothing else.**(docs. 4(a)–4(c))**.

But it was not only the gentile population that was put out by the growth of an extravagant Yiddish culture in the heart of the empire. The political implications of mass immigration and the ways in which the settlement in East London was applied to the creation and definition of a specifically 'Jewish Question' made Anglo-Jewry's acculturated leadership uneasy. From such concerns came a concerted attempt to dissuade would-be emigrants from making a home in these islands coupled with a comprehensive strategy of 'Anglicisation' directed at those who chose to remain. Lay, ecclesiastical, educational and philanthropic resources were mobilised for a crash course in Englishness. Not only was Yiddish to be abandoned, the newcomers were expected to quit the congested quarters in Whitechapel and Spitalfields and remove to the outlying suburbs where cultural resistance was more difficult to sustain. A Jewish Dispersion Committee was appointed in 1902 to organize their departure **(docs. 7(a)–7(b))**.

The culture under attack, though shot through with religion, also possessed a strong secular component. The versatility and creativity of the newcomers was embodied in an assertive ethnically-based popular culture which still awaits its historian. Yiddish newspapers supplied instruction and amusement; serious social and organizational issues rarely occupied more space than the 'romanen', the popular tales, into which the weary immigrant loved to escape. Secular Hebrew culture also found expression in *HaYehudi* (*The Jew*), the long-lived Hebrew weekly which catered for a minority within a minority (**doc. 9(a)**). Self-generated social institutions, too, were numerous. The friendly societies movement was respectable. The same could not be said of the clubs, meeting halls, trade union branches and coffee shops that sprung up. Some were barely disguised gambling dens; others combined politics with entertainment. The pious condemned them; the police were vigilant. At times religious and secular cultures were too close for comfort (**docs. 9(b)–9(d)**).

Clubs, societies, coffee-houses, cafes and restaurants, though they opened and closed with startling rapidity, provided one source of sociability, the streets another. Jewish East London, with its crowded shops and barrows, was full of customers who were as much concerned with the exchange of news and views of family and friends as with the purchase of goods and services. The streets were not only filled with shoppers. On Saturdays, once the Sabbath was over, Whitechapel High Street and Commercial Street were given over to promenading couples courting and displaying, and young people having fun. Those who had saved their coppers might catch a show at one of the local Yiddish playhouses. Musicals and melodramas were the standard fare. But the versatility and artistry of the players was remarkable and some productions were exceptional. Can you imagine Shakespeare or Verdi performed in Yiddish? In Whitechapel seats were 4d. (**doc. 9(c)**).

1. The Jewish Colony, 1851

Source: Henry Mayhew, *London Labour and the London Poor*, 4 vols (1861), II, pp. 117–29

The oldest settled non-Christian minority in Britain, Jews had maintained a distinctive presence in London ever since their re-admission into the Commonwealth in the seventeenth century. The Jewish area of settlement on the eastern fringes of the City, the district to which the East European immigrants would later flock, is described below.

The number of Jews now in England is computed at 35,000. This is the result at which the Chief Rabbi arrived a few years ago, after collecting all the statistical information at his command. Of these 35,000, more than one-half, or about 18,000, reside in London. . . . The foreign Jews who, though a fluctuating body, are always numerous in London, are included in the computation of 18,000; of this population two-thirds reside in the city, or the streets adjacent to the eastern boundaries of the city. . . .

The localities in which these . . . traders reside are mostly at the East-end – indeed the Jews of London, as a congregated body, have been, from the times when their numbers were sufficient to institute a "settlement" or "colony," peculiar to themselves, always resident in the eastern quarter of the metropolis. . . . The quarters of the Jews are not difficult to describe. The trading-class in the capacity of shopkeepers, warehousemen, or manufacturers, are the thickest in Houndsditch, Aldgate, and the Minories, more especially as regards the "swag-shops" and the manufacture and sale of wearing apparel. The wholesale dealers in fruit are in Duke's-place and Pudding-lane (Thames-street), but the superior retail Jew fruiterers -- some of whose shops are remarkable for the beauty of their fruit – are in Cheapside, Oxford-street, Piccadilly, and most of all in Covent-garden market. The inferior jewellers (some of whom deal with the first shops) are also at the East-end, about Whitechapel, Bevis-marks, and Houndsditch; the wealthier goldsmiths and watchmakers having, like other tradesmen of the class, their shops in the superior thoroughfares. . . . The Hebrew dealers in second-hand garments, and second-hand wares generally, are located about Petticoat-lane . . . The manufacturers of such things as cigars, pencils, and sealing-wax; the wholesale importers of sponge, bristles and toys, the dealers in quills and in "looking-glasses," reside in large private-looking houses, when display is not needed for purposes of business, in such parts as Maunsell-street, Great Prescott-street, Great Ailie-street, Leman-street, and other parts of the eastern quarter known as Goodman's-fields. The wholesale dealers in foreign birds and shells, and in the many foreign things known as "curiosities," reside in East Smithfield, Ratcliffe-highway, High-street (Shadwell), or in some of the parts adjacent to the Thames. In the long range of river-side streets, stretching from the Tower to Poplar and Blackwall, are Jews, who fulfil the many capacities of slop-sellers, &c., called into exercise by the requirements of seafaring people on their return from or commencement of a voyage. A few Jews keep boarding-houses for sailors in Shadwell and Wapping. . . .

Concerning the street-trades pursued by the Jews, I believe there is not at present a single one of which they can be said to have a monopoly; nor in any one branch of the street-traffic are there so many of the Jew traders as there were a few years back.

. . .

. . . The greater number of them reside in Portsoken Ward, Houndsditch; and their favourite localities in this district are either Cobb's-yard, Roper's-building, or Wentworth-street. They mostly occupy small houses, about 4s.6d. a week rent, and live with their families. They are generally sober men. It is seldom that a Jew leaves his house and owes his landlord money; and if his goods should be seized the rest of his tribe will go round and collect what is owing.

The rooms occupied by the old-clothes men are far from being so comfortable as those of the English artizans whose earnings are not superior to the gains of these clothes men. Those which I saw had all a littered look; the furniture was old and scant, and the apartment seemed neither shop, parlour, nor bed-room. For domestic and family men, as some of the Jew old-clothes men are, they seem very indifferent to the comforts of a home.

. . .

The Amusements of the Jews – and here I speak more especially of the street or open-air traders – are the theatres and concert-rooms. The City of London Theatre, the Standard Theatre, and other playhouses at the East-end of London, are greatly resorted to by the Jews, and more especially by the younger members of the body, who sometimes constitute a rather obstreperous gallery. The cheap concerts which they patronize are generally of a superior order, for the Jews are fond of music, and among them have been many eminent composers and performers, so that the trash and jingle which delights the costermonger class would not please the street Jew boys; hence their concerts are superior to the general run of cheap concerts, and are almost always "got up" by their own people.

Sussex-hall, in Leadenhall-street, is chiefly supported by Israelites; there the "Jews' and General Literary and Scientific Institution" is established, with reading-rooms and a library; and there lectures, concerts, &c., are given as at similar institutions. Of late, on every Friday evening, Sussex-hall has been thrown open to the general public, without any charge for admission, and lectures have been delivered gratuitously, on literature, science, art, and general subjects, which have attracted crowded audiences. The lecturers are chiefly Jews, but the lectures are neither theological nor sectarian. The lecturers are Mr. M.H. Bresslau, the Rev. B.H. Ascher, Mr. J.L. Levison (of Brighton), and Mr. Clarke, a merchant in the City, a Christian, whose lectures are very popular among the Jews. The behaviour of the Jew attendants, and the others, the Jews being the majority, is decorous. . . .

. . .

The Jews' Hospital, in the Mile-end Road, is an extensive building, into which feeble old men and destitute children of both sexes are admitted. Here the boys are taught trades, and the girls qualified for respectable domestic service. The Widows' Home, in Duke-street, Aldgate, is for poor Hebrew widows. The Orphan Asylum, built at the cost of Mr. A.L. Moses, and supported by subscription, now contains 14 girls and 8 boys; a school is attached to the asylum, which is in the Tenter Ground, Goodman's-fields. The Hand-in-Hand Asylum, for decayed old people,

men and women, is in Duke's-place, Aldgate. There are likewise alms-
houses for the Jews, erected also by Mr. A.L. Moses, at Mile-end, and
other alms-houses, erected by Mr. Joel Emanuel, in Wellclose-square, near
the Tower. There are, further, three institutions for granting marriage
dowers to fatherless children; an institution in Bevis-marks, for the burial
of the poor of the congregation; "Beth Holim;" a house for the reception
of the sick poor, and of poor lying-in women belonging to the
congregation of the Spanish and Portuguese Jews; "Magasim Zobim," for
lending money to aid apprenticeships among boys, to fit girls for good
domestic service, and for helping poor children to proceed to foreign
parts, when it is believed that the change will be advantageous to them;
and "Noten Lebem Larcebim;" to distribute bread to the poor of the
congregation on the day preceding the Sabbath. . . .
The Jews in this country are classed as "Portuguese" and "German."
Among them are no distinctions of tribes, but there is of rites and
ceremonies, . . . Nor are the present ecclesiastical authorities in London of
the two sects the same. The Portuguese Jews have their own Rabbis, and
the Germans have their own. . . .

. . .

The Jews have eight synagogues in London, besides some smaller places
which may perhaps, adopting the language of another church, be called
synagogues of ease. The great synagogue in Duke's-place (a locality of
which I have often had to speak) is the largest, but the new synagogue,
St. Helen's, Bishopsgate, is the one which most betokens the wealth of
the worshippers. It is rich with ornaments, marble, and painted glass; the
pavement is of painted marble, and presents a perfect round, while the
ceiling is a half dome. There are besides these the Hamburg Synagogue,
in Fenchurch-street; the Portuguese Synagogue, in Bevis-marks; two
smaller places, in Cutler-street and Gun-yard, Houndsditch, known as
Polish Synagogues; the Maiden-lane (Covent-garden), Synagogue; the
Western Synagogue, St. Alban's-place, Pall-mall; and the West London
Synagogue of British Jews, Margaret-street, Cavendish-square. The
last-mentioned is the most aristocratic of the synagogues. The service
there is curtailed, the ritual abbreviated, and the days of observance of
the Jewish festival reduced from two to one. This alteration is strongly
protested against by the other Jews, and the practices of this
synagogue seem to show a yielding to the exactions or requirements of
the wealthy. . . .

. . .

There are seven Jewish schools in London, four in the city, and three at
the West-end, all supported by voluntary contributions. The Jews' Free
School, in Bell-lane, Spitalfields, is the largest, and is adapted for the
education of no fewer than 1200 boys and girls. The late Baroness de
Rothschild provided clothing, yearly, for all the pupils in the school. In

the Infant School, Houndsditch, are about 400 little scholars. There are also the Orphan Asylum School, previously mentioned; the Western Jewish schools, for girls, in Dean-street, and, for boys, in Greek-street, Soho, but considered as one establishment; and the West Metropolitan School, for girls, in Little Queen-street, and, for boys, in High Holborn, also considered as one establishment. . . .

. . .

The Loan Societies are three: the Jewish Ladies Visiting and Benevolent Loan Society; the Linusarian Loan Society (why called Linusarian a learned Hebrew scholar could not inform me, although he had asked the question of others); and the Magasim Zobim (the Good Deeds), a Portuguese Jews' Loan Society.

The business of these three societies is conducted on the same principle. Money is lent on personal or any security approved by the managers, and no interest is charged to the borrower. The amount lent yearly is from 600*l.* to 700*l.* by each society, the whole being repaid and with sufficient punctuality; a few weeks' "grace" is occasionally allowed in the event of illness or any unforeseen event. The Loan Societies have not yet found it necessary to proceed against any of their debtors; my informant thought this forbearance extended over six years.

2. Are we in London or Lithuania? 1892

Source: Mrs Brewer, 'The Jewish Colony in London', *The Sunday Magazine,* XXI (1892), pp. 16–20, 119–23

A simple comparison of the previous account with that which follows reveals the impact of mass immigration upon the settlement locality and the people within it.

. . . We Christians could not tell how they would be received by the inhabitants of the Jewish colony, and for the best of all reasons, viz., that we know very little about the colony. . . . They have been neither trouble nor expense to us as citizens; they have not attracted the notice of the public by their appearance in the police courts; they have not intruded themselves on our attention in any way, and hence there has been nothing in their existence to excite our interest or rouse our wrath. . . .

Still it is not entirely our fault that, growing up amongst us as the Jews do, they are yet perfect strangers to the majority of us, for it is a well-known characteristic of theirs that they do not willingly mingle with other peoples; their life, therefore, is an isolated one, and quite apart from ours; they have little or nothing in common with us if we except their love of and loyalty to our Queen, whose land affords them shelter, and which are as genuine among the Jews as with us; their language even is not the same as ours; they neither eat, nor drink, nor pray with us; in fact, there is no common meeting-ground, and the result is that we are ignorant of their home-life, their daily work, their social condition, their religion, and the influence they exercise on those among whom they live, and yet each of these points would form an intensely interesting and profitable study.

Generally, when writing of a people, attention is drawn almost exclusively to what we term the upper classes, for as a rule it is they who appear to make history. This example I cannot follow, because, with one or two exceptions, my acquaintance has been entirely with the *poor Jews*. . . .

It is of my visits to the immigrants and to the poor resident Jews that I desire to speak, having seen them as they are. Too much has hitherto been written from hearsay, and the Jews feel they have suffered from this practice.

My first impression on going among them was that I must be in some far-off country whose people and language I knew not. The names over the shops were foreign, the wares were advertised in an unknown tongue, of which I did not even know the letters, the people in the streets were not of our type, and when I addressed them in English the majority of them shook their heads. This being so, I tried German, which succeeded up to a certain point; but to have reached their hearts and brains I must have had a knowledge of Yiddish, which unfortunately I had not. It is a sort of mixture of Hebrew, Russian, and Polish.

Whitechapel is not attractive either in name or reality, and yet I doubt if there is any place of its size in the wide world that contains so much of intense human interest as this same Whitechapel. To right and left of the high road, in its courts, streets, and alleys, are to be found the dwellings of the poor Jews, special streets and lanes being dear to their hearts, and which please them better than all the grand four-per-cent buildings, with their improved sanitary conditions. Such are Wentworth Street, Petticoat Lane, and Old Montagu Street. The density of population in and about these is fearful, and serves to isolate them almost entirely from the Gentile population.

Wentworth Street in full swing, as it is called, is a sight worth seeing. It is difficult to make one's way. Its shops are crowded, barrows with their wares of every kind fill the road, and are surrounded with busy, picturesque groups. The women would be handsome but for the practice of shaving their heads when they marry, and replacing their hair by ugly brown wigs. The rising generation are rebelling against the habit, which takes greatly from their beauty, and is not so cleanly as keeping their own hair. No woman or girl here ever thinks of wearing a hat or bonnet, but they do sometimes hide their ugly wigs by a bright coloured kerchief.

In Wentworth Street I first saw meat bearing the seal of the shoumier, or watcher. The Jews are very particular about the meat they eat. The animal can only be slaughtered by a Jew, and one duly qualified, and if when opened it is found to be diseased in ever so small a degree it is rejected as unfit for Jews' tables, and sold to the Gentiles. If, on the contrary, it is perfect, a leaden seal is affixed bearing the word "Koscher", right. . . .

Old Montagu Street is almost entirely occupied by Polish and Russian Jew tailors, and we noticed that many of the immigrants had letters to the people living here. It is a long, weary, monotonous street, with the houses all of one pattern, the line broken only by an entrance into some court or alley still poorer than the street itself. Nearly every room is occupied by a separate family, and I was surprised to find how high the rents are considering the accommodation; for example, among those whom I visited was a family of husband, wife, and four children, who paid three shillings and sixpence a week for a dark cellar in this unlovely street.

As you walk along you notice that most of the rooms on the ground floors are occupied by groups of men and women stitching away on men's garments for dear life to the tune of sewing machines; these last are almost exclusively purchased on the hire system and paid for in small weekly instalments. These people work very hard to gain a livelihood, often from seven in the morning till ten or eleven at night. No one works after sunset on Friday, and Saturday and Sunday are free days, so that it is only by long hours on the other days that they are able to earn enough to keep them. Although life is a continued struggle with them, and they enjoy none of what we call the comforts of it, I observed that they were not unhappy.

Living and working as they do in one room, they avoid cooking in it as much as possible; their mid-day meal is often very small. Supposing even they have a little money they cannot afford time to prepare one. It is generally a little fried fish or a cup of weak tea and bread. I stood in the fried-fish shop while the purchases for dinner were made, and it was remarkable how many came in for a halfpennyworth of fish and the same of fried potatoes; the rare customer, one in fifty, perhaps, bought a penny-worth of each, and it was sad to think how many persons would have to partake of this larger quantity. Still what they obtain for their money is superior in the way of cooking to anything we can have, unless we are rich enough to have a French cook. The plaice were cut across, the centre slice being a penny, and those at either end a half-penny.

I took my stand also in the general shop of the neighbourhood, at a little after twelve mid-day, and if you ever have a desire to realise the value of a penny, and that four farthings make a penny, go there and note the purchases and the purchasers – dear little children scarcely able to lisp the language, and whose tiny arms when raised cannot reach the counter, coming in rapidly one after the other with a halfpenny tightly clasped in the hand as if it were of priceless value, asking for a farthing's worth of tea and a farthing out; a farthing's worth of flour, of milk, of soap, and so on, until my heart ached. It might be thought that these little ones were merely playing at keeping shop. Not at all; it was real and sober earnest – the farthing's worth of tea, of milk, of flour, were to help make a dinner for more than one or two people.

During the hot weather there is a trade, peculiar to this quarter, carried on in *boiling water*, which may be had at certain shops from five o'clock in the morning till a certain hour in the evening. It is only a summer trade, but to my mind a very excellent one, and I hear it pays well. A fire in a room on a hot day where people live and work would be a needless cost and an aggravation of the evil of limited space. As it is, the wives may be seen running over to where the boiling water is to be had early in the morning with tea pots or coffee pots in which they have already put some tea or coffee, and for a farthing get it filled. If the husband goes out early to work it is a comfort to him to have a cup of tea or coffee with his bread, even though he may have to drink it without milk or sugar. For a halfpenny they may have the vegetables or stew cooked. Altogether it is a most useful institution, and we wondered no enterprising person had started it in other parts of London.

One of the first things which struck my notice in the Jews' quarter was the reverence bestowed upon a long narrow piece of metal nailed up to the door-post of every house inhabited by Jews. Each person going in or out touched a certain spot on it with his finger and then raised it to his lips.

This was the Mezuzah . . .

However poor a family may be they strive to have a little feast on Friday evenings after the service in the synagogue, and in order to see what the family circle was like on these occasions I made a number of visits to the Jews' quarter on the opposite side of the high-road lying between it and the river.

I rather startled the people, I think, as my guide knocked at the various doors, saying, in German, "Good evening. Are you at the evening meal? May we come in? Some ladies want to know how we Jews live." At first they hesitated – as I certainly should have done in their place – but it was only for a few minutes; courtesy prevailed, and we were made welcome.

In every case I found the husband at home in the midst of his family. The meal consisted of a double portion of white bread, in memory of the manna in the wilderness, a little fish or meat, and a small decanter of raisin wine. These are placed on a clean white tablecloth, which remains on the table till the Sabbath is over. A peculiarity of the supper-table was the number of lighted candles in tall brass candlesticks. On the first I saw three. I asked in my ignorance, "Why do you have candles when the gas is on full?"

The mother answered, "There is no joy without light, and each of these is a thanksgiving for a child."

In another house there were seven burning on the table, and, with my newly-acquired knowledge, I said, "So you have seven children."

"No, we have but four; but we lighted three extra because God has given us a good week."

While the wife lights the candles the man spreads forth his hands, saying, "Blessed art, thou, O Lord our God, King of the Universe! who has sanctified us with thy precepts and commanded us to light the Sabbath lamps."

Figure 4 In the Ghetto Bank, 1901 The Ghetto Bank of Whitechapel, an important institution connecting East and West, remitted nearly one million roubles to Russia and Poland. Situated at the corner of Osborn Street, Whitechapel, its outside walls were covered with long lines of Hebrew characters and other advertisements. Drafts for five roubles upwards were available, and for the convenience of customers, it was open seven days a week till 10 p.m., with the exception of the Jewish Sabbath (G.R. Sims, (ed.), *Living London*, 3 vols (London: Cassell, 1901), I, p. 24).

Immediately on their return from the synagogue, they take their places at the table, and the husband takes in his hand a glass of wine and says grace, then he drinks a little from the glass and presents it to the members of his family.

In some cases I was too late for the meal, but saw the men with the Talmud or the Old Testament in their hands; the poor Jews, as a rule, are great students. . . .

The Jews marry early as a rule, and should they put it off too long they are not thought well of; indeed, they are considered to be living in sin. . . .

In order to learn something of the Jewish children and the way they are trained in London, I made my way to Spitalfields, which is a centre densely populated by the poorest class of Jews, and visited first the Old Castle Street Schools, one of the first built by the London School Board.

There are sixteen hundred children, 95 per cent of whom are Jews. There is no difference made between the Jew and Gentile children, and they agree well together. The Jewish children are remarkably quick and intelligent, and pick up English rapidly, though only a few of them know anything of our language when admitted, for their parents come from distant parts of the world.

Mr. Levi, the superintendent, is very proud of the schools, and delights in the children; he tries to train them morally as well as physically, and, looking on the schools as a miniature world, encourages them to fear social ostracism.

A Sunday-school is held for Jewish children, and here they are taught Hebrew and the Old Testament by paid teachers.

On the girls' side Mr. Levi has instituted a benevolent society, which is managed by the children themselves, one girl as treasurer, another secretary, and a certain number form a committee. The whole school subscribes its farthings or halfpennies, and for each gift receives a special receipt.

If it happens that a child has had no breakfast, or is wretchedly poor and unhappy, her case is looked into, and if found deserving, a committee is called to decide what can be spared, and one or two members are appointed to go marketing for food, clothing, and other necessaries. The society is in a flourishing condition, and Jew and Gentile alike are the recipients of its benefits.

The excellence of these schools was remarkable – they learn cooking and needlework, and their intellectual attainments are marvellous. A child is never refused admission except for want of room. . . .

On leaving Old Castle Street I made my way to Bell Lane, which is close by, to the Jews' Free Schools, the largest in Great Britain; . . . One great privilege enjoyed by the scholars in these schools is that they never need work upon an empty stomach; they can go up-stairs to the kitchen and have a cup of hot milk and a piece of bread for their breakfast. . . . The boys frequently work at some trade between school hours, so as to increase, if possible, the weekly income of the family. . . . In times of sickness or accident the difficulties of the Jews would be great indeed, but for the Rothschild wards in the London Hospital. . . . When more cases arrive than can be accommodated, the Jewish patients are in the emergency placed in the Gentile wards; this gives great offence to the Jews and often retards their recovery. The sick people like the Jewish minister to come and speak to them or pray with them, and when a member of the family dies, the body is stripped and at once removed from the bed on to the bare floor and covered with a sheet. It remains in this state, watched by a Jew or a Jewess, as the case may be, until the ceremony of cleansing by water is performed by special people sent from the synagogue, who also dress the body in linen garments, and place a lighted lamp fed with the purest sweet oil at the head. . . .

The Jews do not use coffins such as ours, but four plain deal boards loosely joined together; they are not even coloured or covered. There is no difference made between the rich and the poor. When the body is laid within these boards, if it be that of a man, his "talleth" with fringes which he used to wear in the synagogue is placed over the linen clothes.

There is no service over the grave; but the nearest relative throws in the first lot of earth; this is often a heard-rending scene. There is an utter absence of pomp and flowers; the mourners rend their clothes, and on their return to the house keep a week of mourning, during which time they sit on low seats, and do nothing, while their friends, rich and poor, visit them and bring them food.

There are two Jewish cemeteries, one at Willesden and the other at West Ham.

And now a word or two about the immigrants. It is a mistake to regard them as of the lowest order of foreign Jews; many of them have held good positions in those towns and districts from which they have been driven, . . .

. . . Of course I am not including the rough element who come here from Amsterdam. I was present at the coming in of a German boat with some forty Jewish immigrants, and stood by while their luggage was examined; there was not much of it, but it was clean and whole. Most of them were met by relations already established here; three only were without addresses, and these were sent to the Jewish Ladies' Association in Tenter Street and to the Jewish shelter in Leman Street by their agent. . . .The poor Jews in London do not stand alone . . .

3. Jewish Friendly societies, 1905

Source: A. Rosenbury, 'Jewish Friendly Societies; A Critical Survey', *The Jewish Chronicle*, 8 September 1905

Jewish friendly societies were *landsmannschaften* par excellence which, apart from the provision of sickness, invalidity and death benefits, played a key role in the allocation of social honour and maintenance of personal identity within the immigrant community. By the beginning of the twentieth century the Jewish friendly society movement had obtained a commanding position among the newcomers. Its progress and prospects are reviewed here.

The Friendly Societies movement enters, to a very large extent, into the life and thought of the Jewish work-a-day world in England. To the immigrant from Eastern Europe, this form of social life is quite a novel experience, which partly accounts for the continually reckless formation of new societies. Two forces may be said to keep the movement growing. One of these attracts the provident rank and file to whom the friendly society is not only an insurance at death and a protection during sickness and distress, but also a social nucleus, calculated to elevate the emotions and enhance the self-respect of every one of its members. The second force attracts those whose chief desire is to rule and influence their fellow-men, at least for a brief period of their life, to wear the insignia of office or regalia, and to be bowed to for one moment a week on the average. Intensely human as this desire may be, it is nevertheless accountable for a large amount of waste, lack of co-operation, and absence of good understanding between the various societies.

Friendly Societies and Trade Unions

Numerically and, of course, financially, the Jewish friendly societies totally eclipse the Jewish trade unions. The reason for this is not far to seek. Modern trade unionism appeals to a sharply defined class of society working for wages. As such, it is based on strenuous agitation and conflict, implying frequent defeat as well as occasional triumph. But although conflict is part and parcel of the system of things the progress of civilisation is ever increasingly tending to diminish its extent and intensity. Hence the masses instinctively prefer avoiding conflict, even if assured that gain would accrue to them as a result of engaging in it. Provident societies, on the other hand, appeal to, and embrace, all classes of society, from the humblest workman to the most successful tradesman or manufacturer. The necessity for conflict being thus entirely eliminated, the friendly societies acquire a more permanent and stable equilibrium.

Friendly Societies and Insurance Companies

The Jewish friendly society is to its members much more than the insurance company to the insured. The industrial branches of the latter make no return during life. In the ordinary branch a return is made, on the completion of the term insured for, of the principal with about seven per cent interest on the lump sum, while the sum insured for is payable if death occurs any time after twelve months. Now, on comparing the expectations of the insured in each case the Jewish friendly society will be found to have an advantage over the insurance company. An illustration in figures will tell its own tale. Let us assume that a man over 30 years of age, able to pay £2 17s. 6d. per quarter (an average of 4s. 5d. per week), takes out an endowment policy for £150, maturing at the end of fifteen years. If he survives, he receives £183 15s. for £172 10s. paid in. Assume, on the other hand, the case of a man able to pay 3s. per week, who joins three societies (this is really the practice to some extent), where the sum payable at death of a member is £50, death of a member's wife £10, sick benefit 15s. per week for 13 weeks, confined mourning allowance £2 2s., a certain sum varying between £3 and £30 or £50 in case of genuine distress, medical aid at all times, incurable and non-suspension allowances, surgical appliances and a physician's fee of £1 1s. in case of accident. When the chief money benefits enumerated come to be trebled, the result will be a sum considerably over £200, for £117 paid in during an assumed period of fifteen years.

Important Social Factor

It might be urged that were it necessary for any friendly society to pay all those benefits to every member it would soon reach a state of insolvency. But precisely the same argument applies to the case of the insurance company. In both cases insurance is a sort of wager. There is, however, an additional advantage on the side of the Jewish friendly society. While the insurance company may be said to have "neither a body to be kicked, nor a soul to be saved," the Jewish friendly society is continually throbbing with sociability, friendship, solace, and all the human emotions without which civilised life would be impossible. Jewish friendly societies do not merely insure against sickness, distress and death. They are also social factors of great importance, which to immigrants from mediæval and benighted countries is not to be despised. Indirectly, they inculcate lessons of co-operation, self-help, discipline, friendly intercourse, bringing together people from many lands and various occupations, and forming them into brothers and friends in need. So that, no individual member, provided he be of the genuine sort and does not neglect his duty, will be utterly forsaken in the hour of misfortune. In many cases, members have indeed been nobly helped into attaining a higher position in life. Insurance companies admittedly lay no claim to any such pretensions.

Some Typical Bodies

The Jewish friendly societies, which are estimated to have a membership of about 15,000, may be divisible into various sections. They include the orders with branches, or lodges, under their control, independent societies named after continental towns, purely trade societies, dividing societies, and nondescript local bodies. To enumerate them all by their respective names (their number is said to be no less than 272) is neither possible nor desirable. I therefore propose to pass under brief review a few typical bodies fairly representing the various sections.

The orders are no doubt of primary importance, for various reasons. They may be described as the first attempt at concentration of power and purpose with a view to self-help. They are governed by central bodies: grand lodges, and executive councils. These have the control of the death endowment fund, formed either from compulsory *per capita* contributions by subordinate lodges, or covered by levies upon all members. They are also invested with general ruling and advisory powers. The orders may be said to comprise the majority of friendly society members. The oldest and most widely known of these is the Order Achei Brith, established in 1888, controlling 30 lodges, having a membership of 2,800, and a capital of £7,000.

Next in numerical, if not financial, importance is the Grand Order of Israel, numbering 26 lodges, including three lodges in South Africa, and a Colonial Grand Lodge in Cape Town, with a membership of 2,639, and total funds amounting to £3,846. This order shows much activity, being engaged in keen competition with all the others, and claiming to give large benefits for a comparatively small weekly contribution. Its report for 1904 reveals a record increase of membership of about 800.

The Hebrew Order of Druids, a distinctively Jewish society with a rather non-Jewish name, numbers 19 lodges, including one in Johannesburg, South Africa, with a membership of 1,120 and a capital of £1,622.

The Order Achei Emeth might be next referred to as one which, through the energetic lead of Mr. David Levy, now its past-Grand President, has distinguished itself in setting its house in order. It has shown a good example in the abolition of vanities and empty ceremonial, introducing reform in the shape of the elective principle. In these matters some of the orders still lag behind with considerable waste of time as the result. The Order Achei Emeth takes a keen interest in what affects the Jewish people. To quote its chief officer's own words from the last annual report, it realises that "a Jewish order forms part of the Jewish community to which it owes certain duties in times of emergency and crisis." During the great influx of Russian Jewish reservists into this country, the Order Achei Emeth rushed to the rescue in forming an "Ahavath Gerim" branch, and contributing a sum of over £30. Twenty lodges are under its control, including three distinct ladies' lodges, with a total membership of 1,118, and a capital of £1,000. Recently, the Hans Herzl Lodge was formed exclusively of Zionists. This branch accepts no member unless he can conscientiously subscribe to the Basle Programme. Both Mr. I. Zangwill and Dr. M. Gaster are honorary members of this Order. Numerous lodges belonging to these various orders are scattered all over the provinces. These have, besides, independent orders of their own, and a number of local societies.

The Ancient Order of Maccabæans is an intensely Jewish national body, devoting much of its activity to the cause of Zionism, and collecting money for its various financial institutions. There are twelve branches or "Beacons" under its control, with a membership of 648. Active spirits would consider their lives mis-spent if they could not succeed in forming some new Order, or lodge of an Order, bearing their own name as a matter of course, or some local society. I met with no success in my endeavour to obtain definite details of the Order Shield of Abraham, Ancient Order of Mount Sinai, Sons of the Covenant of Abraham, and some others. This shows that the list of orders is, as yet, by no means exhausted. The membership of these bodies increases with every year, the competition among them sometimes assuming a serious and rather acrimonious form. On the whole, the Orders, with their signs, passwords, degrees, and forms of ritual, appealing to the emotional side of human nature, are more interesting and attractive than the independent societies.

The Independent Societies

Next in order are those societies bearing the names of Russian and Polish towns in which their founders were born. This is an illustration of the extent to which Jews are attached, mentally, at least, to their birthplaces, which even in a newly-adopted country they still honour and perpetuate in their memory in this dignified manner. The Cracow Jewish Friendly Society is by far the foremost of this group, both numerically (379), and financially (£1,550). Warsaw, Denenburg, Witebsk, Zhitomir, Siedletz,

Plotsk, Radom, Sochechov, and many other insignificant Russian towns are duly honoured by Jewish societies bearing their names. Some of these are closely connected with synagogues. For the present these societies more or less pay their way, strenuously endeavouring to increase their membership and funds, and fiercely competing with each other in the matter of contributions and benefits. It may be said of most of them that they are rather ill-provided against possible future contingencies. Evidently they take it for granted that the future will be the same as the present, although the present is never like the past, and apparently oblivious of the fact that their members are growing older and are likely to become, sooner or later, a great drain on their funds. Some of these are already experiencing this bitter truth. For almost every financial statement issued by some societies reveals a deficit, entailing the necessity to draw upon the reserve fund. The dividing societies also do a good work. They are managed on the principle of dividing their annual surplus funds, generally before Eastertide, after meeting all liabilities, consisting of death and sick claims, and deducting a certain percentage to add to the reserve fund. This form of saving is very popular, relieving many workmen from the anxiety and worry of finding the extra wherewithal requisite to commemorate honourably, and as becomes "princes" (בני מלכים) the deliverance of Israel from the bondage of Egypt. The loan societies may be included in this category, but their activity is confined to issuing loans only, and dividing the principal with the interest obtained from the borrowers at the end of the year.

The Trade Societies
There are also the purely trade societies admitting as members only those connected with their trade. This category includes the Mutual Tailors' Benefit Society, the Mantle Makers' Benefit Society, and the Jewish Cabinet Makers. The latter has a membership of 325, and a reserve fund of £321, and is managed on the annual sharing-out principle. The Cigarette-Makers' and Tobacco-Cutters' Benefit Society, although numerically small (100 members) is financially by far the soundest of this section, having a fund of £607. During eighteen years of its existence it has defied the popular view as to the danger to health arising from tobacco dust. The Cracow Society and several others prohibit the admission of tobacco workers into their ranks, but will not hesitate to admit tailors. Yet, the tailoring trade could be shown to yield more victims to pulmonary tuberculosis. The exceptional health of the members of the Cigarette-Makers' and Tobacco-Cutters' Benefit Society might be illustrated by their accumulation of a large fund, and by the very few deaths occurring among them. This would tend to indicate that workers in this trade are immune from, rather than liable to, life-destroying diseases.

A Labour Benefit Society
A society which must be considered distinct from any of the above groups is the Free Workers' Ring. This is a Jewish labour benefit society, formed

some three years ago, in imitation of the Jewish Workers' Ring of the United States. The latter, like other combinations, assuming there large dimensions, is said to have attained to the gigantic numerical position of 20,000. The London Labour Society, which only the other day opened a new branch in the West End, has been founded on a somewhat novel basis. It admits as members men and women on equal terms, and has morally pledged itself to trade union and labour propaganda. On entering, a member is required to pay the sum of 10s. This is applied towards forming the reserve fund, which is never touched. If by reason of emigration a member desires to leave the society he is entitled to a return of this preliminary fee on giving three days' notice. The benefits are: 15s. per week sick pay, the usual medical aid, £2 2s. confined mourning allowance, and £15 at death. A distress fund is also being instituted. The Society accumulates no fund, and there are no fixed weekly contributions. Whatever the disbursements during any given quarter in the shape of benefits paid or management expenses incurred, the total amount is restored at the end of every quarter by each member paying an equal part thereof. Every member is entitled to benefit after three months' membership, and no member is entitled to benefit unless the preliminary fee, which need not be deposited at once, is paid up.

Immediate Future Problems

The conclusion to be drawn from the above facts and figures may be thus stated: There are two distinctive features observable in the Jewish friendly societies' movement. One, which may be described as co-operation to give effect to the precept, "Love thy neighbour as thyself," cannot be sufficiently encouraged. Concurrently with this laudable aim, there may be noted a competitive spirit prevalent to a dangerous degree, a feature which cannot be sufficiently regretted and deprecated. Not only is the latter feature contradictory of, and tending to destroy the effectiveness of, the former, but also directly responsible for a large amount of waste and inefficiency, and for the bankruptcy which is confronting many societies. If the first feature reveals the cultivation of the noble human emotions, the second feature also reveals the cultivation of personal egotism, and ignoble passions. The immediate future problem, therefore, appears to be, how to preserve and ensure the cultivation of that which is tending to the common good, and to eradicate the disturbing elements, potentially, if not actually, fraught with evil. The movement has now become a permanent factor in the life of the masses. But there is a crying need for the Jewish friendly societies to extend the sphere of their operations, and widen the scope of their usefulness. Is this possible under the present chaotic conditions, when a host of societies with practically one aim and object are yet pursuing different courses in defiance of each other?

Hopes and Prospects

Recently a gleam of hope has appeared on the horizon. The masses are regrettably inert and apathetic. But they are for that reason like "clay in the hands of the potter." Much depends on the desire of the popular and respected leaders to mould the masses into a possible and harmonious unity, or keep them in "blind-folded" isolation, eventually resulting in the harm of many and the good of none. Some leaders are averse to innovations, content to walk in the conventional grooves trodden by their predecessors, while others have, as usual in every movement, their own axes to grind. These naturally constitute a temporary hindrance. Happily, a number of disinterested and earnest-minded workers in the movement are indefatigably labouring to bring about an improvement in the *status quo*.

Some Notable Leaders

Of the men who are devoting time and energy in connection with their particular orders and societies, a few of those occupying the highest positions might be mentioned. Mr. Max Fisher and Mr. H. Bernstein, his colleague, are widely known and esteemed as the founders of the parent body of all the Jewish Orders: The Order Achei Brith. Messrs. S. Ginsburg and H. Comor, of the Grand Order of Israel; Messrs. Appelbaum and Isaacs, of the Hebrew Order of Druids; Mr. J. Becker, of the Order Shield of Abraham; Mr. J. Van Leer, of the St. James's Philanthropic Society; Mr. S. Dancyger, of the Order Sons of the Covenant of Abraham; Mr. I. Berliner, of the Cracow Society; Mr. Grossman, of the Cigarette-Makers' and Tobacco-Cutters', are a few examples of a host of leaders. I may, however, single out for especial mention Messrs. David Levy and A. Lewinstein, of the Order Achei Emeth, whose activity is not confined to their own Order, but extends to the movement as a whole.

Mr. David Levy is justly recognised as a man of many qualities, and as being of the stuff that statesmen are made of. Eloquent, logical, determined, and bristling with original ideas, he has only the disadvantage of having been born in darkest Russia. As an immigrant to this country some years ago, he would, no doubt, have been excluded under the present Alien Act. For, although a skilled tailor, he arrived poor and illiterate. Whatever education he now possesses is due to his own efforts. Mr. Levy was practically the first to endeavour to bring about a good understanding among the principal Jewish friendly societies. Some time ago he drew up a rough scheme that might well form the basis of discussion. He believes in the necessity of the Jewish friendly societies affiliating for certain objects which can never be achieved otherwise. The most important are: (1) Abolition of well-known abuses; (2) creation of new and indispensable institutions; (3) participation with united voice, in communal matters affecting the Jewish people everywhere. A conference to discuss these points has been suggested. Although there are initial difficulties to surmount, one is not without hope that a way will yet be found to obviate them.

The New Spirit

While Mr. D. Levy is breaking up the soil, Mr. A. Lewinstein is sowing the seed. Mr. Lewinstein has rendered the movement a great service in establishing the *Jewish Friendly Societies' Gazette*, a bright monthly publication, conceived in no sectarian spirit. From the tone of most of its contributors and correspondents, it is evident that a new era is dawning. Thoughtful men are everywhere becoming alive to the urgent need of dealing collectively with the vexed questions agitating their minds, which might be referred to as: (1) Present faulty system of medical aid; (2) necessity for meeting-places other than public-houses (a question which the Chief Rabbi emphasised in his letter to the first number of the *Gazette*); (3) improved arrangements with reference to burial; (4) necessity for a convalescent home; (5) protection of funds against fraud and imposition; (6) prevention of undue multiplication of societies; (7) the question of one man joining several societies; (8) eliminating unhealthy competition; (9) advisability of equalising the scale of contributions and benefits; (10) ultimate amalgamation. Even Mr. H. Bernstein, the veteran of the Order Achei Brith, holds that eventually the societies will have to amalgamate. The new spirit is already being manifested within some of the Orders, where, with a view to securing greater efficiency and preventing waste certain lodges are joining forces. This internal movement cannot fail to have an external effect. Prejudice, indifference, and misunderstanding, everywhere bars to human progress, constitute the only obstacles in the way. These the *Jewish Friendly Societies' Gazette* is combating with no uncertain voice. Its motto appears to be the advice given by Mr. Zangwill to the first number: "Organisation is the great need of Jewish life."

A. ROSEBURY

4. Language problems

a) *Policing the Ghetto, 1904*

Source: PRO Mepo 2/733, Report of Superintendant Mulvaney, Leman Street Police Station, H Division, 17 December 1904

It was the language of the immigrant which defined the area of settlement and created an impression of being in some distant territory. Problems arose from the fact that members of the Metropolitan Police were not on the whole Yiddish-speakers while those whom they policed often spoke nothing else.

I beg to bring under the Commissioner's notice the fact that in consequence of the settlement of Aliens in this Division, the resident population consists chiefly of Russians and Poles who speak the Yiddish language.

Bills and circulars in this language are distributed and posted all over the Division but police know nothing of their purport unless the interpreter is employed to translate them. As it is known that a number of these people are members of Continental Revolutionary Societies it would be very desirable to have members of the Service who could speak this language.

If authority were given I should have no difficulty in forming a class of Police for this purpose. A gentleman has volunteered to teach the class without charge.

If the idea is entertained I would respectfully suggest that a grant of say £15.00 be allowed to be given as awards on obtaining certificates of proficiency, say two prizes of £5.00 and two of £2.10.0. each. This would act as an incentive to the men to persevere and, if they were successful in acquiring the language, it would be very beneficial to the Service generally and to this district in particular, although of course, they could not be employed officially as Interpreters.

b) Red tape, 1895

Source: Report of the Chief Inspector of Factories and Workshops for the Year 1894. Parliamentary Papers [C. 7745], XIX (1895), p. 72

It was difficult enough for the indigenous population to supply the information which officialdom required; for those with little English it was impossible.

... H.M. Inspector in Manchester, Mr. Rogers, writes:-

From the way in which the office here is inundated with callers, I think the provision of offices for H.M. Inspectors must have been, as regards the public, one of the most popular and beneficial of the many changes that have recently been brought about in the Factory Department.

The office in Manchester is right in the centre of the city, and every day a number of manufacturers and others call to consult me as to the working of the Acts. As it is now so easy to do so, the occupier who wishes to carry out the Acts calls on the Inspector on meeting with the slightest difficulty. Every Saturday I know to expect half-a-dozen Jewish occupiers (besides those who come on other days) who call to make inquiries, often about the filling up of forms with which they have the greatest difficulty. In fact, it is very seldom that out of the dozens of forms I receive weekly from Jews, one is filled up correctly. In this connection I would submit that they can hardly be expected to fill up the forms properly, many of them have but a very meagre knowledge of English, and the special exception forms are so numerous and complicated. I am strongly of opinion that these forms should be reduced in number and simplified.

Figure 5 Immigrant letter writer, 1901 Professional letter writers, working out of the many local cafe restaurants, provided a service in Russian or Yiddish for those who required it (G.R. Sims, (ed.), *Living London*, 3 vols (London: Cassell, 1901), I, p. 28).

c) An unwanted wedding, 1926

Source: The Law Times, 162 (1926), p. 360

Conflict and consternation were unavoidable where English was neither spoken nor understood as rabbi Hirsch Neuman and Mrs Sarah Greenberg were to discover at Whitechapel Registry Office on 18 March 1925.

An interesting and unusual reason for annulling a marriage arose in the recent case of *Neuman* v. *Neuman* (*otherwise Greenberg*) (reported in The Times, Oct. 15, 1926). The facts in that case were briefly as follows: The petitioner was a Cohen, or member of the race of priests descended from Aaron, the High Priest. Being a Cohen, he was debarred by Jewish law from marrying a divorced woman. The respondent, who was also a member of the Jewish persuasion, was a divorced woman. Both the parties were orthodox Jews, and they intended to marry at a Jewish synagogue in accordance with Jewish law. They had been told, and believed, that the ceremony could be expedited so as to be celebrated

before the first day of Passover if they went to the register office to carry
out some formality as a preliminary to their intended marriage. But they
had no intention of marrying at the register office at all. The petitioner
could speak no English, and the respondent only knew a little of the
language. The parties went to the register office where the ceremony of
marriage was performed. The petitioner stated that he did not understand
that the proceedings at the register office constituted a legal marriage as
no ring was used, and the questions asked at a Jewish ceremony were not
put. The respondent said that she went to the register office to get a
special licence, but had no idea that she was going through a ceremony of
marriage there. Afterwards, when the parties went to the Beth Din (the
Jewish Ecclesiastical Court) to arrange for the Jewish ceremony, the
petitioner then learnt that the respondent was a divorced woman, and the
latter learnt that the petitioner was a Cohen, which facts put the marriage
out of the question. The parties had never lived and cohabited together,
and the learned president granted a decree of nullity.

5. Hearth and home

a) The Polish Jew at home, 1884

Source: 'Report of the Lancet Special Sanitary Commission on the Polish Colony of
Jew Tailors', The Lancet, 3 May 1884, pp. 817–819

The effects of Jewish immigration upon the health and housing of the area of
settlement was first raised by the medical profession. The special investigation,
commissioned by The Lancet is reported below.

The foreign Jews, who for many years have been flocking to the East-end
of London, are so numerous that their presence seriously affects the social
and sanitary condition of this part of the metropolis. Dr. Dorgel, in his
work on the "German Colony in London," estimates the number of his
fellow-countrymen at the East-end at 130,000, the majority of whom are
Jews. But the recent persecutions in Russia have necessitated a further
exodus, and now there are close upon 30,000 Russo-Polish Jews huddled
together in districts that were already overcrowded. Not only are the Jews
from Russia all of Polish origin, but a very large proportion of the
German Jews are also from the Polish provinces. Hence we have to deal
with a large population of Jews in blood and creed, but to a great extent
Poles in their instincts, customs, and predilections. Even in its Jewish
aspect this colony is thoroughly foreign, for the eastern Jew is very
different from the western, who indeed is looked down upon as almost a
heretic. In one respect, however, this is fortunate, as the orthodox Jews
are more likely to observe those regulations affecting diet which have
greatly contributed to maintain the health and vigour of the race. On the

other hand, the rigorous observance of the Sabbath makes it difficult for these men to obtain work in other than Jewish workshops, and this obstacle tends to lower the wages, which at best are not high enough for the maintenance of health. It is needless to say that, with but few exceptions, the members of this Jewish colony are all extremely poor, and it is so difficult for them to obtain the barest subsistence that the Jewish Board of Guardians, and all the eminent and philanthropic Jews who contribute so largely to the charities instituted to relieve their poorer brethren, use every possible influence to prevent any more emigrants from coming to England. It is well known that no assistance is given to any Jew by Poor-law guardians unless he has resided at least six months in England. The Jews themselves recognise that they are overcrowding the labour market, and therefore it is time that the question at issue should be taken into serious consideration by others than the local authorities.

Under these circumstances we have instituted an inquiry among the Jews in the East-end of London, and visited a large number of their homes and workshops. In these explorations we found that all the difficulties attached to the question of the housing of the poor are aggravated by the special habits of this peculiar people.

In Southern Russia the artisan class is composed almost exclusively of Polish Jews; and, unlike their English co-religionists, their first idea is not to trade, but to work. Hence they have created an industrial colony, where the majority are producers, the victims of middlemen rather than middlemen themselves. But those among them who have lived long enough in England to acquire some knowledge of English, and who possess a small capital, are able to profit, in an exceptional manner, by the forlorn condition of their fellow-countrymen. The Polish Jew, refugee or exile, arrives in London penniless, and unable to speak a word of English. He is rarely able to find employment in his own trade, and must go to the Jew "sweater," who alone knows his language, and will not ask him to work on the Sabbath. The market where he can sell his labour is thus restricted to very narrow limits. The employer is master of the situation and can impose any condition. The unfortunate worker greedily accepts starvation wages, and even assists his employer to defy the Factory Act, the Sanitary Act and other laws instituted to protect him, fearing that, by availing himself of our legislature, he may lose the little he is able to earn. Such are the economic circumstances which have brought about a state of affairs that urgently require reform.

The principal grievance to be brought against these Jew tailors of the East-end is that they work in unwholesome, overcrowded houses, where girls and women are kept toiling long after the hours prescribed by the Factory and Workshops Act. These facts are undoubted and undenied by all who live in the neighbourhood; and though in some workshops the stipulations of the Factory Act are observed, their avoidance is very general. After considerable difficulty we obtained the addresses of several "sweating" tailors where women worked beyond the time prescribed by law. The first of these workshops was kept by a Russian Polish Jew. The tailoring was done in a small irregularly-shaped room with a very low ceiling, where, we were assured, no more than six persons worked together, but on counting those present we found no less than ten men and women bent over their tasks at the very moment of our unexpected visit. The whole house was in a ruinous state; a wretched and rickety staircase led past the rooms occupied by lodgers to the workshop in the attic. There was but one closet for all the inhabitants and the work-people, and, as a natural consequence, it was in a foul condition.

In Hanbury-street we found eighteen workers crowded in a small room measuring eight yards by four yards and a half, and not quite eight feet high. The first two floors of this house were let out to lodgers, who were also Jews. Their rooms were clean but damp, as the water was coming through the rotting wall. The doors fitted badly, and the locks would not act. In one room the window-frame was almost falling into the street; in another the floor was broken, and the fireplace giving way. The boards of the stairs were so worn that in some places they were only a quarter of an inch thick, and broke under extra pressure. The sink was not trapped, the kitchen range was falling to pieces, while the closet was a permanent source of trouble. A flushing apparatus had been provided, but this discharged the water *outside* the pan; the water consequently came out under the seat and flowed across the yard to the wall opposite, which was eaten away at its base. There is a drain under the water tap, but the yard naturally inclines towards the wall, where the slops accumulate and emit foul odours. Yet the tailor who hired this miserable abode showed us a receipt for £17 in payment of only one quarter's rent. It seems preposterous that £68 should be charged for a house literally falling to pieces, and containing only six rooms. When, further, we consider that the top room, though the largest, had at times to hold eighteen persons, working in the heat of the gas and the stoves for warming the pressing irons, surrounded by mounds of dust and chips from the cut cloth, breathing an atmosphere full of woollen particles containing more or less injurious dyes, it is not surprising that so large a proportion of working tailors break down from diseases of the respiratory organs. In Wilks-street we went over some workshops recently opened in new houses. The ceilings were more elevated, the surroundings clean, and the printed forms on the walls showed that they had been duly visited by the factory inspector. But, in spite of this, it is impossible to convert one or two rooms of a private house into a good workshop. The ventilation was defective even in the best of these private workrooms. The same may be said of the houses we inspected in Heanage-street. Here great professions were made of respect for the Factory Act; but, on the other hand, even the masters themselves acknowledged that where the Factory Act is applied the women are only paid for three quarters of a day. If a woman wishes to earn a full day's wage, she must work from eight in the morning till eleven or twelve at night. This is freely done even in the workshops visited by the factory inspector; nor do we see any regulation in the law calculated to defeat the practice. The workshops are but rarely inspected either early in the morning or late at night, and our appearance after nine caused quite a panic; the master tailors freely expostulating that visits at such hours were illegal. But at each call we found women still at work. On the appearance of any stranger the women are often distributed throughout the private parts of the house – in the bedrooms, kitchens, and so forth. If any question is asked, there is always a ready reply – the one is a niece, the other is a daughter; and if they are working, it is only for the family, and not in the pursuit of their trade. These explanations are often absolute falsehoods, but the foreign Jew workwomen are, for the reasons we have described, in so dependent a position that they dare not rise and contradict their employer. They will even answer questions falsely, so as to avoid the application of the Factory Act. It is absolutely useless to question the workwomen in the presence of their employers; they cannot say how long they work, how little time is allowed for their meals, unless they feel certain that such revelations will not be brought home to them, entailing the loss of their means of livelihood. The evil cannot be uprooted by official visits paid in the broad daylight; it must be dealt with by the same methods as those employed in the detection of ordinary crime.

Tailoring of the poorest description will be seen more especially in Pelham-street, Spitalfields. This is a peculiar and miserable thoroughfare. Nearly every one of the small low-class houses, on either side of the street, contains one or two workrooms. At all hours of the day and night the street resounds with the rattle and whirr of the inumerable sewing machines, the windows shine with the flare of gas, but the street is comparatively deserted. There are but one or two Christians in the whole of the street, and these are at least as poor and miserable as their Jew neighbours. Here also we entered a large number of the houses, and found none of the closets provided with water. The staircases were extremely small, very dirty, and covered with the dust from the cloth, which apparently no one ever thought of removing. In some cases there was only one closet for two houses, and no one in particular seemed anxious to maintain it in any degree of cleanliness. One room was tenanted by a woman, her husband, and three children. By the window and close to the bed two cripples, who were called assistants, sat huddled together on a tailor's table hard at work, helping this family to manufacture clothes in what was at once the sleeping-room, the nursery, the kitchen, the workshop, and the living-room; and, to make matters worse, the rain had been coming through the roof for the last two winters. Close by, in Hanbury-street, we had occasion to notice that the dustbins of the houses where Jewish tailors work are very often specially offensive. Even the constant and rapid removal of the dust does not suffice to obliterate the evil. The rubbish often becomes so foul that steam is seen rising from the heap. The large quantity of refuse from the fish, which forms a staple of the Jewish diet, mixing with the cloth dust coming from the workrooms may, perhaps, contribute to create this unpleasantness, and under these circumstances we would strongly urge the extensive use of disinfectants.

On questioning the police in this neighbourhood, they testified to the fact that they have often seen women returning from work at 1 o'clock in the morning. One policeman told us he frequently heard the machines as late as 2 o'clock in the morning, and that they began again at 7 o'clock. In one street there was a house where women worked from 7 o'clock in the morning till 1.30 at night; and in another we surprised some young girls working at about 10 at night, though they hid in a back room on our approach. As a natural result the stamina of both the men and women is greatly reduced. When compared with the more prosperous English Jews and the English working-classes, these foreign Jews seem weak in muscle, emaciated in frame, and stunted in growth. Their pale unwholesome complexions and dejected attitudes clearly indicate that the law has failed to protect them from the deteriorating effects of overwork and overcrowding.

Whitechapel has never thoroughly recovered from the overcrowding that arose when, night after night, waggon loads of poor Jews were brought up from the docks, where they had just arrived still panic-stricken from Russia. Starving and penniless, glad to have escaped with their lives, they thronged the poor dwellings of Fashion-street and neighbourhood. The population of the Whitechapel Union has, it is true, decreased to the extent of 6000 persons within the last ten years, but in the parish of Christ Church, Spitalfields, where the Jews mostly congregate, there has been an increase of 1000 inhabitants. About 22,000 persons live in the parish, and the augmentation in their number is a very serious matter, for not only are there no houses vacant to accommodate the new arrivals, but an entire street of old houses was recently pulled down. Thus, though the general population may not be so numerous, the specific overcrowding in a particular class of dwellings is greatly aggravated. One of the poorest of the Jewish quarters is known as Tenter-ground. There is no tailoring done here, but many of the poorer workers live on this spot. . . . In Emely-place, a part of the district, we found five persons living in one room, while in another house we came upon a Jewish potato dealer who kept his wife, five children, and his stock of potatoes all in one room measuring five by six yards. There was but one bed in the room, and probably some of the family slept on the floor. The potato dealer was utterly unaware that such overcrowding was illegal. He seemed very proud of his family, and complained only of a strong smell of drainage which came from a cupboard in the corner of the room, where the damp wall suggested the proximity of a broken pipe. . . .

. . . We visited, . . . Shepherd's-buildings, a large block of dwellings erected some three years ago overlooking Tenter-ground, and consisting of thirty-nine separate tenements, inhabited by about 150 persons. Some of the rooms are so dark that candles have to be lit in the middle of the day, and out of the fifteen waterclosets four were broken and only one clean. Though provided with a waste-preventer and a flush of nine gallons, the whole system was so foreign to the inhabitants that they had not yet learnt to pull the chain so as to flush and clear the pan. In Booth-street there are similar blocks containing 230 rooms with some 700 inhabitants. Here the closets were neglected, soiled and damaged to such an extent that they were ultimately removed to the yard so as to avoid

Figure 6   Jewesses taking the air by their doors, 1901   Spatial relations in the immigrant quarter were more a function of poverty than of planning. Where houses were small and families large the street became as much a communal leisure resource as a means of communication (G.R. Sims, (ed.), *Living London*, 3 vols (London: Cassell, 1901), II, p. 35).

infecting the house. Now, however, the inhabitants, many of them foreign Jews, objecting to descend the stairs, simply throw the soil out of the windows, according to the practice of the Middle Ages.

b)   A Jewish landlord, 1900

Source: C. Russell and H.S. Lewis, *The Jew in London, A Study of Racial Character and Present-day Conditions* (1900), pp. 173–74

House and home were emotive concepts with great resonance in the vocabulary of anti-alienism. Contemporaries, even when they tried, found it difficult to sever economics from ethics and focus upon the operation of the private housing market.

The foreign Jew as landlord is a new and unwelcome figure. The Chief Rabbi, in a recent sermon, tells the story of an East-End Jew who exclaimed to him, 'Thank God I live under a Christian landlord.' This statement illustrates quite fairly the evil reputation that Jewish landlords have acquired amongst their own co-religionists. The condemnation is undoubtedly too sweeping. In East London there are good Jewish landlords, some of whom are foreigners, whose excellent qualities are acknowledged by their tenants. But harshness, oppression and even fraud are too often associated with foreign Jews who have recently invested in house property. Considering this question, at the moment, as illustrating the sense of morality of the offenders, it must be noted that many of them cannot be considered as bad men in the ordinary relations of life, whilst in several notorious instances, they make professions, probably not consciously insincere, of charitable and religious zeal. The root of this inconsistency is the notion, too often entertained, that business stands apart and is governed by different rules from those prevailing in the other relations of life. One of my friends asked a landlord how he came to oppress one of his tenants, a very poor man and a Jew like himself. 'When I go to synagogue,' was the reply, 'I am a Jew; when I come for my rent I am a *goy*.' This inconsistency is, of course, common enough outside the Jewish community; it has been a favourite theme of satirists in all ages. It is, however, peculiarly offensive in the followers of a religion which teaches, above all others, that a man should consecrate all the activities of life to the service of the Supreme.

6. Jew and Gentile

a) No Yids here, please. We're British! 1903

Source: Minutes of Evidence taken before the Royal commission on Alien Immigration, Parliamentary Papers [Cd. 1742] IX (1903), qq. 9675–699

The growth of the immigrant quarter was essentially a negotiated process. The assertion of Jewish territoriality was contested street by street by the indigenous population. Here one such encounter is described by a member of the British Brothers' League.

Mr. J.A. KREAMER

9675. (*Major Evans-Gordon.*) Where do you live? – 55, Exmouth Street, Stepney.

9676. How long have you lived there? – Three and a half years.

9677. And have you lived in the neighbourhood before that? – I was born in High Street, Wapping, in the Parliamentary Division of St. George's.

9678. You are a pianoforte tuner by profession? – Yes, and a pianoforte dealer.

9679.   I think you are, unfortunately, blind? – Yes.

9680.   Have you suffered in your business? – Very much indeed.

9681.   How? – In these last two years alone – I have gone through my books – I can give the names and addresses of over 200 residents in the Borough of Stepney who have been driven out of this parish by the alien immigration. . . .

9686.   The 200 customers that you speak of, have they in all cases been displaced by foreigners? – In all cases they have been displaced. The system by which they have been driven off is much the same system as I am suffering from now. Next door to me there has come a pickled herring yard. I do not know whether you gentlemen know what pickled herrings are – I have never tasted one, but the odour from them is something dreadful. I have even been to the Thames magistrates to ask them to help me to do away with the nuisance, but they tell me I have no redress, and all day on Sunday these pickled herring barrels are being thrown in and out of the shed. I want to live, as I consider myself a decent working man, and I want to live in a respectable neighbourhood. I always thought Exmouth Street was a respectable street, but they are turning the street into one of the worst streets I know of in the neighbourhood.

9687.   Exmouth Street used to be a very respectable street? – Yes.

9688.   With none of that kind of thing going on? – No.

9689.   This fish business has come next to you? – Yes, within the last 18 months.

9690.   And the eventual effect will be to drive you out of it? – Yes.

9691.   That is the process that has been going on amongst your friends? – Yes, my customers have complained of it for some years past.

9692.   These people come and live next to you with some objectionable business? – Yes, and drive them away.

9693.   And the rents are raised? — Yes, I have suffered from that myself.

9694.   How much has your rent been raised? – From £24 to £30 a year.

9695.   You are a yearly tenant? – Yes.

9696.   You are one of many who suffer in this way? – Yes, the whole row, in fact, in which I live has been raised in the same proportion.

9697.   Among your customers are there people who have to come back to London to do their work? – The majority of them, a great many of them, have been shop-keepers who have unfortunately failed in the neighbourhood. . . .

9698.   Who have lost their businesses? – Yes.

9699.   And feel very strongly about it? – Undoubtedly. The feeling is very strong, but there is a place just south of where we are sitting called

Wapping, and south of Old Gravel Lane Bridge, where they will not admit a foreigner. In fact, I lived in Old Gravel Lane for some years myself, and on more than one occasion when the foreigners have come there to live I have seen the native population of that place go and smash the windows and turn the foreigners out. In fact, I feel that way – that it is quite time we did turn them out and do something. . . . I assure you, gentlemen, if you don't do something this time, it will be something more than serious, for only yesterday I was talking to a clergyman in this neighbourbood who expressed himself very very strongly, and said he was an anti-Semitic man, and he would go with the people as hard as he could. I am a member of the British Brothers' League, and at the same time, in going round in my business, I have brought this Brothers' League before the clergy – I work for a number of the clergy – and I have already got five clergymen as members of the British Brothers' League. The object of the British Brothers' League is to stop these pauper aliens coming here.

b) Judenhetze *in Ernest Street, Stepney, 1901*

Source: David Englander, *Landlord and Tenant in Urban Britain, 1838–1918* (Oxford, 1983), p. 121

Housing struggles and the price of accommodation were prime generators of intercommunal conflict. The period of mass immigration coinciding with an intensive burst of street clearances and factory extensions had a devastating effect upon the local housing market. The following report is from the *East London Observer.*

The position in regard to Ernest Street, Stepney, is unique. So strong, indeed, is the local feeling, that at present a number of houses are empty because incoming tenants are seriously threatened if they take the houses at the higher rent their lives won't be worth many years purchase. Some of the houses are already wrecked; windows and doors are broken and burst; the surrounding population is in a general state of ferment, and the evictions which take place daily only tend to fan the flame. In essentials a Judenhetze prevails, and though we do not believe there is anything more than a local significance, it is, of course, quite obvious that such a feeling ought not to be encouraged, because although its beginning may be small, like a rivulet, its ending may be great.

c) *Childhood memories of the 1870s*

Source: Arthur Goldberg, *A Jew Went Roaming* (1937), pp. 3–4

Born and brought up in the Jewish East End, Arthur Goldberg left home in 1876 for an adventurous life in South Africa. He subsequently returned and in old age wrote the revealing autobiography from which the following is taken.

. . . Oh! there was Jew-baiting in the East End then, as now, but in those days it was not considered of sufficient news value to be mentioned in the papers. There was no sort of ceremonial made of it, with banners and crudely worded pamphlets and young men dressing themselves up in quasi-military uniforms. They just did it single-handed, if they felt like it.

My Jew-baiter was a hefty young rascal considerably bigger than I was, who had earned something of a reputation in the neighbourhood as a bully and tormentor of Jewish boys smaller and less muscular than himself. Strangely, up till then he had not set his cap at me. I and some other boys were playing cricket early one evening when this larrikin came swaggering down Duke's Place. He had an elder brother who worked in the fruit market, and that quite possibly filled him with pseudo-importance. One of the boys gave a mighty swipe at the ball with an improvised bat, and it fell at the feet of the tormentor. He picked it up, glanced at the small group who were playing, saw me running towards him, then coolly slipped the ball into his pocket. The ball happened to be my property.

"Give me my ball, please," I said, pulling up in front of him. . . . He stepped up to me menacingly.

"Accusin' me of pinchin' yer ball, eh? You stinking, dirty Jew-kid! Yer better mind what you're saying."

That was more than enough to make me see red. Regardless of the size and strength of him, I shot out a fist which, more by luck than judgment, caught him full on the nose. The next moment we were at it hammer and tongs, with an ever-growing circle of pals urging us on. . . . I realised I was getting the worst of affairs, and felt I must do something about it. This fight was no ordinary scrap. It was Christian versus Jew. I was fighting for the honour of my race! If I let my opponent get the better of me, life would become intolerable not only for me but for all the other Jewish lads around. . . .

d)   A police perspective, 1889

Source: Minutes of Evidence taken before the Select Committee on Emigration and Immigration (Foreigners), Parliamentary Papers, X (1889), qq. 875–909

Thomas Arnold, Superintendent H Division Metropolitan Police, whose experience of the Whitechapel District went back to 1874, describes the response of the indigenous poor to the immigrants from the East.

876. You have, I understand, a return which you wish to hand in to the Committee? – Yes; it is a return for the Whitechapel Division ... showing the total number of persons charged during the years 1881 and 1888 respectively. In the year 1881 the number of British subjects charged in the Whitechapel Division was 4,233, and of foreign subjects 248; in the year 1888 the number of British subjects charged was 3,390, and of foreign subjects 336.

877. That return shows a less percentage of English and a greater percentage of foreigners in the latter period? – Yes, that is so. ...

882. Are whole districts of the town now occupied by foreigners which some years ago when you went there were occupied by the English working class? – Yes, and the area seems to me to be spreading. ...

884. What are the habits of that class of people? – They are generally quiet; we find them more amenable to the Police Regulations than we find in the case of what we should term our English roughs.

885. Are they cleanly? – No.

886. What are their ideas of sanitary law as a body? – Very low I should think.

887. Are they generally sober? – Yes, generally sober. ...

890. What are the charges with generally? – Minor offences, principally ranging from burglary (there are very few cases of burglary) to disorderly conduct; there are a good many assaults.

Mr. Cremer

891. Are the assaults generally upon their own fraternity, or upon British subjects? – Very frequently upon their own fraternity arising out of quarrels. We have a good percentage of aggravated assaults, and some indecent ones, but the majority are what would be termed common assaults, perhaps a street row, or slapping each other's faces, or something of that kind.

892. Do they often come into collision with British workmen or British workwomen; do they quarrel and fight with British workmen or British workwomen? – Not to a very great extent, and I have noticed myself that that is often brought about by British workmen setting upon them first.

893. Then there is bad blood existing between British workmen and Continental workmen? – Yes, amongst those of the lower class.

894. And that results in quarrels and fights? – Yes. ...

Mr. John Talbot

896. Do you think that there is a good deal of common talk amongst the English working classes as to the large number of foreigners in the East-end? – Yes.

897.   And you think it is a source of irritation? – Yes, I think it is.

898.   And that leads to this bad blood of which you have been speaking? – Yes, at different times they have rows, but we can only interfere with them when they are passing through the streets. It is whilst the foreigners are passing that the roughs interfere with them.

899.   Because the foreigners, we have been told, run away, and they interfere with them then? – Yes.

900.   Are there any minor cases; cases of people who commit petty larcenies and things of that kind? – We have had a good many larcenies, and cases of embezzlement and fraud. . . .

903.   I suppose many of them are very destitute? – I should say that they are myself, from the class of food that I see them carrying about in their hands; certainly they would not eat it if they were not nearly destitute. It is a very low class of food.

904.   Have there been, in your experience, many burglaries committed for the sake of food? – No, I do not find that they steal very much food.

Mr. Montagu

905.   You stated that in those seven years, from 1881 to 1888, there had been an increase in the number of foreigners charged with petty crimes? – Yes.

906.   What do you consider, that the increase of foreign residents altogether in Whitechapel would have been in the seven years from 1881 to 1888? – A much larger percentage than that, but I have not figures to go upon.

907.   There is nothing to show in this estimate that foreigners are more frequently charged now, in proportion to their numbers, than they were in 1881? – I should say that it was the contrary. I put it down, that increase myself to the increase of the population.

908.   You mentioned just now that there was bad blood between the British workmen and the foreigners; is there a mutual quarrel, or is it on one side? – It is on one side principally. I do not think that the foreigners entertain much bad blood to other people, on the score of working.

909.   But they are interfered with by the British workmen? – More frequently than otherwise by the lower order of British roughs. . . .

e)   *Mission to the Jews, 1890*

Source: Charles Booth, *Life and Labour of the People in London*, Third Series: Religious Influences (1903) II, pp. 231–232

Figure 7   An open air service in Yiddish (St Mary's, Whitechapel), 1901
Conversionist meetings conducted in Yiddish formed part of the summer spectacle in Whitechapel and Spitalfields, but were more provocative than effective (G.R. Sims (ed.), *Living London*, 3 vols (London: Cassell, 1901), I, p. 213).

Jewish immigration posed a major problem for parish life in the settlement localities. The missionary response, however, did little for reconciliation or inter-faith relations.

We had received a post-card asking us to call on Saturday afternoon, from 3.30 to 5, when 'we should find a full room, and be able to talk after.' The door was opened by a matronly-looking Jewess, who proved to be the wife of the missionary. The room into which I was ushered was a small one, and was, as had been claimed, full, with twenty-five Jewesses and five Jews. I was given a seat at the top of the room, next to a strange-looking individual with a black beard, who is the most important person in this story. The missionary and another man, who acted as chairman, sat also at the upper end of the room. On his legs was a German, who was addressing those present in Yiddish. He spoke fluently, and with a good deal of gesture; but, with the exception of two Jewesses in the front row, all seemed to hear him with complete apathy, mingled with unconcealed signs of boredom. But the two women were evidently following the speaker closely, and constantly nodded their heads, apparently in consent to his arguments. The German having finished, the black-bearded man was asked to say a few words. He was a most extraordinarily grotesque person, and it is not easy to give any, even the most remote, conception of his appearance, his speech, his manner, his gestures. He spoke in English, with a voice something between a rook and a corn-crake; but even more astounding than his voice was his accent, which, if reproduced on the stage, would be described as an absurd burlesque of the vilest type of modern cockney speech. The matter was of the usual street-preaching kind, on the lowest level. The Jews probably did not understand a word of it, and they mainly looked profoundly bored. At the end, we Christians sang a hymn in English, out of Moody and Sankey's collection: "I am trusting, I am trusting, Sweetly trusting in His blood." The Jews had no hymn books, and showed no signs of being able to follow. The proceedings closed with a prayer in Yiddish from the missionary, and the audience trooped out, leaving me with the missionary and his wife, and the bearded man. From the conversation that ensued, I gathered that this man was in truth the founder of the mission, twenty-six years ago, and that the present missionary and his wife, were his converts, having 'loved their Saviour,' respectively, twenty-six and twenty-two years. As to present conversions, they said that all those in the front rows at the meeting were really converts; though, owing to persecution, they were not all 'professing Christians.' 'The persecution is terrible,' said the missionary's wife, adding, 'I have been through it, and know what it is.' Asked about relief, she said 'they were very poor, and that what God sends us we give them.' The mission being in financial difficulties, was about to be transferred to a larger organization. The bearded man said he saw signs of a great movement among the Jews, and asserted that this mission had converted thousands! 'You may report,' he said, at the end, 'that they are coming over in thousands.'

7.   Native and foreign Jews

a)   An outrage against common sense! 1900

Source: Forty Second Annual Report of the Board of Guardians for the Relief of the Jewish Poor (1900), pp. 16–19

Anglo–Jewry, though opposed to formal restrictions on immigration, was equally opposed to an open door policy and did its best to dissuade desperate co-religionists from permanent settlement in these crowded islands.

The denial to our co-religionists in Roumania of the civil and religious liberty guaranteed to them by European treaty has long been to them a source of great unhappiness. During recent years their political and social status has been one of increasing hardship; while of late their hard lot has been aggravated by the material suffering caused by successive bad harvests and the desperate economic condition of their country. Under such extreme circumstances it is not surprising that the public mind should be prone to accept the escape apparently offered by flight, without duly considering the chances of the enterprise. Be that as it may, it is certain that in the past year, from causes it is not possible to define with certainty or precision, the popular imagination in Roumania and in adjacent territories, also afflicted with deficient harvests, became inflamed with the extravagant idea, that Canada was impatiently awaiting an unlimited influx of any and every kind of immigrants; and that these had only to reach London in order to find, either a qualified organization prepared with plans and funds to equip and forward all applicants to the land of promise, or, as an alternative, the prospect of an assured career in England. From the very outset the Board made known, both here and abroad, in the hope of checking the movement, that having regard to the overcrowded condition of the East End and the congested condition of its trades, it could not in justice to the resident poor, and also in the true interests of immigrants themselves, depart from its established custom in dealing with new comers; and that, in the main, the only relief it could offer to applicants arriving here in a helpless condition would be to assist them to return to the countries they had left with such deplorable absence of foresight. The Board, further, on being consulted by other communal authorities, discouraged, as the custodian of the interests of the foreign poor already established here, the formation of a special Roumanian fund for disbursement in England. Such a fund would have attracted here under false impressions of prevailing economic conditions and possibilities, not only those for whom it would have been intended, but also, according to all past experience, applicants from other parts of distressed Jewry. The Board, however, supported a proposal, which was subsequently adopted, to raise a relief fund to be remitted abroad for distribution by the local communal authorities in the afflicted districts. The Board was also successful in consultation with other bodies, in defining in regard to the immigration a common line of action, which in subsequent developments was adhered to as closely as the exigencies of a very difficult position permitted. In securing this desirable accord, the Board was supported by, among others, the President of the Poor Jews' Temporary Shelter, Mr. Landau, to whose energy and influence during the subsequent period of crisis the community is greatly indebted.

Unhappily the untoward immigration continued throughout the summer. Committees in Roumania assisted large batches of emigrants to leave their country without regard to their fitness or chances of success. Communal authorities on the Continent acted, apparently, on the view, that they were discharging their responsibilities towards the wanderers, by assisting to forward them from one city to the other, till on their arrival at the nearest port to London they were shipped thither. Immigrants from Roumania arrived singly, in small parties, and in bands under leaders. The influx was swollen by numbers of Russians and Poles. The prevailing idea that a great scheme of emigration was in progress, caused considerable unrest even among foreigners of various nationalities already resident in London. There was a rapid increase in the number of cases applying in the usual way to the Board for relief; while petitions for assistance to proceed to Canada were presented by leaders on behalf of their bands, and demonstrations were planned and in some instances attempted in order to bring pressure on the Board and other bodies. The presence of these immigrants in the over-crowded East End, where on occasions even the necessary sleeping accommodation was lacking, created a position of danger and anxiety both for the sufferers and the community in general. In the solution of the problem the organization of the Poor Jews' Temporary Shelter rendered considerable assistance. From that centre many of the more eligible cases were assisted to emigrate to Canada by the action of gentlemen acting on behalf of the Jewish Colonization Association, which, in view of the exceptional emergency, intervened with its assistance. But there fell on the Board not only the onerous duty of dealing with the heavy balance of rejected cases, but also of attending to the numerous applications which were made direct to the Board in the ordinary way by new arrivals. It may be as well to record that the Board applied itself to the discharge of its exceptional task without departing from its principles of relief.

The result of the application of these principles in the treatment of the total of 2,903 new cases relieved by the Board in the past year was that 1,399 were repatriated, mainly at their own request, and, naturally, never without their own consent; 375 emigrated to places outside Europe, and 1,129, or 39 per cent. added to the books of the Board. Of this total of new cases, 1,199, (including 493 Roumanians and 613 Russians and Poles) actually arrived during the year under review, and were dealt with as follows:– 883 were repatriated, 91 emigrated, and 225, or about 19 per cent., added to the register. It would be hard to exaggerate the significance and the pathos of these figures. The fruitless journeyings to and fro of the repatriated must have involved in travelling expenses alone an outlay, from start to finish, of at least £8,000, of which sum the Board had to provide some £3,000. But serious as is the waste of such an amount, the expenditure of which can only have benefited the railway and shipping companies, there is an aspect of the case which is even more pitiable: that is the physical and mental suffering of the 1,900 men, women and children, represented by the 1,399 cases. It is an outrage against the dictates of common sense and humanity, that such a senseless and hopeless movement should have ever been directed towards these shores; and the responsibility is heavy of those who encouraged and assisted it.

b)   A filthy beastly lot! 1900

Source: C. Russell and H.S. Lewis, *The Jew in London, A Study of Racial Character and Present-day Conditions* (1900), pp. 24–26, 36–37, 96, 104–106

Y Brifysgol Agored yng Nghymru
24 Heol yr Eglwys Gadeiriol
Caerdydd
CF1 9SA

Ffôn (01222) 397911
24-awr (01222) 397917
Ffacs (01222) 227930

The Open University in Wales
24 Cathedral Road
Cardiff
CF1 9SA

Telephone (01222) 397911
24-hour (01222) 397917
Fax (01222) 227930

gyda chyfarchion

with compliments

Trevor

Differences between native and immigrant Jews were profound. To the former the newcomers seemed uncivilised and barely human; to the latter their co-religionists seemed scarcely Jews at all.

. . . There appears to be almost a stronger line of severance between the English and foreign Jew than between the English Jew and Gentile. In habits, ideas and religion they are fundamentally distinct; and when they come too much into contact there is even mutual hostility and contempt. In Whitechapel the bitterest enemies of the foreign immigrant that I have come across have been English Jews; while the foreigners are commonly shocked and scandalised at the laxity in faith, and the shamelessly 'non-observant' lives of their English co-religionists. Charges of hypocrisy on the one side, and of flagrant impiety on the other, are freely preferred; and in secular, as in religious interests, the two sections appear to have little in common. The same line is drawn very clearly by public opinion among the Gentile population. English Jews I have found to be surprisingly popular. They are pronounced to be good fellows, and 'just like us Christians.' They spend their money freely and 'have the best of everything'; and command respect, especially among the *habitués* of the public-house, by the lordly style in which they take their pleasures. Foreigners, on the other hand, are for the most part, cordially disliked. They are accused of cutting down wages, of displacing British labour, of dealing solely with one another, and generally of being dirty and disreputable members of society. It is true that this ill-feeling is by no means universal, and does not, except under special circumstances, amount to anything like a bitter hostility; but it presents a sufficiently marked contrast to the friendly feeling which is generally entertained towards the English Jews. . . .

. . .

Whether the English Jew is a better man than his foreign parent is open to question, but it can hardly be disputed that he is a better citizen. His secular interests are less bounded by his home and family, and he plays his part in local politics. There is a loss, no doubt, of many of the finer qualities which are bound up with a strong religious feeling; but there is a gain in cleanliness and self-respect. The English Jew, moreover, is often an ardent patriot; he is proud of being an Englishman, and seems generally to regard his foreign co-religionists from the English rather than the Jewish standpoint. Except, perhaps, in business matters, he has quite a different set of virtues and vices. In business he remains a Jew in shrewdness and capacity, and often in unscrupulousness as well though palpable lying and cheating are less characteristic of him than of his foreign brethren. Much of this change of character is, of course, due to emergence from poverty; a fairly prosperous man has little to tempt him into many of the meaner vices.

He acknowledges a standard of respectability which may not be a very lofty one, but none the less acts as a safeguard against certain anti-social tendencies. . . .

. . .

. . . It is generally recognised in Jewish circles that the stronghold of orthodoxy is in the East End where the foreign Jews congregate. And in the East End itself, the division between English and foreign Jews is roughly a division into the lax and the orthodox; . . . apart from the question of orthodoxy, most immigrants are moved with the ambition to become Englishmen; and seven or eight years' residence in this country is often enough to fill them with contempt for 'foreigners.' English Jews have a higher social standing; and, naturally, it is the *parvenu* of the East End who most despises the Yiddish-speaking part of the community. Now a part of the effect which must be produced by this schism in the congregation, will be to emphasise the association of extreme orthodoxy with the speech, habits and general social inferiority of foreigners. That is to say, in a majority of the community, and especially in the rising generation, it will serve to hasten the process of alienation from strict Judaism.

In many quarters, indeed, orthodoxy has already fallen into contempt through being associated with foreigners of the lowest social grade. I have met an English Jew who assured me, with a grave countenance, that orthodoxy and dirt always went together; and that the former was invariably found to vanish under the influence of soap and water. This is an epigrammatic statement of the case, but it has a remote basis of truth, and it certainly indicates the sort of feelings which the newly 'Anglicised' Jew is apt to entertain on the subject of his religion. The contempt, however, which the 'Englishman' of the Jewish community entertains for the 'foreigner' is heartily reciprocated. Each, in his own eyes, stands on a pinnacle above the other. They recognise totally different standards of human worth, and despise each other respectively for dirt and irreligion. . . .

8.   The Jewish family

a)   Image and reality, 1900

Source: C. Russell and H.S. Lewis, *The Jew in London, A Study of Racial Character and Present-day Conditions* (1900), pp. 186–191

The effects of immigration upon family stability, though reduced by the growth of *landsmannschaften*, were nevertheless significant as the following document suggests.

... The Jew is a born critic, but he seldom finds fault with his wife, and he is, as a rule, blessed with domestic happiness. The Jewish husband spends most of his leisure at home, and, possibly owing to this fact, his wife's advice and influence count for much with him. ... Jewish women are seldom allowed by their husbands to go out to work, although, if the family has a shop, much of its management devolves on the wife, and interferes very little with the performance of ordinary home duties. The Jewish husband is generous to his wife so far as his means will allow, and he does not retain a large proportion of his wages as pocket-money. So far as household expenses are concerned, the wife is chancellor of the exchequer. The result is that the husband seems often more liberal in his ideas of money than the wife, who is weighted with the responsibility of avoiding a deficit in the family budget. Poverty necessarily makes home life more difficult, and the absence of privacy for members of a family who have only one or two rooms of their own must often tempt them to seek distraction elsewhere. It is all the more remarkable that foreign Jews, whose houses are so often overcrowded, are able to conquer adverse influences and to set such an example of happy and contented home life. ... the question of wife-desertion ... is an evil sufficiently common amongst foreign Jews to detract from the almost completely favourable judgment which one would otherwise pronounce on their conjugal relations. The evil is one dating far back in Jewish history; it was ... caused by the husband's necessity and not his choice.

. . .

... It still, however, continues true that the absent husband has often left in search of work and intends to return or to send for his wife in his new home when circumstances become more favourable. The Jewish Board of Guardians finds at times, in alleged cases of desertion, that there is collusion between husband and wife, and that they are in regular communication with each other. It may happen also that a man is compelled to leave England by a doctor's orders and that his wife has to remain behind until he has established himself in America or South Africa. Undoubtedly, however, there are cases where a Jewish husband loses his work and tries to escape his responsibilities by flight. The excuse which he sometimes makes is that he cannot bear to see his wife and children starving, and perhaps he imagines that, if he goes, charitable assistance will be forthcoming on their behalf. The Jewish Board of Guardians has frequently the painful duty of refusing such relief, which, if freely given, would encourage desertion in other cases. As an explanation of the worst type of cases of wife-desertion, it must be remembered that foreign Jews have been accustomed to a greater facility of divorce than is permitted in England, and the unscrupulous amongst their number wish to evade the provisions of English law. Cases of wife-desertion, as opposed to those of temporary absence, are, however, comparatively few in number. ...

b) Poles and Litvaks, 1899

Source: J. Smith, 'The Jewish Immigrant', Contemporary Review, LXXVI (1899), p. 433

Status distinctions based upon place of origin were an important source of social differentiation among immigrant Jews which may well have affected the choice of marriage partner. The extent of such differentiation and its persistence, however, remain to be established.

. . . There exists a strong jealousy between Polish and Russian Jews much like the traditionally bad feeling between a Yorkshireman and the cockney. Their language or dialect is different, the Litvock speaking a more gruff and gurgling sort of *patois* than the Polak. The Polak is the Pole, and the Litvock comes from some Russian rural district. The Polak imagines himself superior to the Litvock, and their antipathy is so great that a Polish swain will never be found paying court to a *Litvotchshki* (sister or daughter to a *Litvock*). The *Polaken* are ostentatious and boastful, not to say prevaricating, and are concerned more with appearance and show than with substantial reality. Many of them are effeminate and garrulous to a degree, almost childish in their credulity, with an utter absence of knowledge of the world and its ways, having come directly from a backward Russian province to a slum in Soho. Some are here more than twenty years and cannot speak a dozen sentences of English. They will buy jewellery for themselves and leave their homes bare and mean. . . .

9. Children of the Ghetto

a) HaYehudi, manifesto from the editor, 1897

Source: Risa Domb, 'A Hebrew Island in the British Isles' Hayehudi and its editor I. Suwalski in Ada Rapoport – Albert and Steven J. Zipperstien (eds), Jewish History: Essays in Honour of Chimen Abramsky (1988) p. 131

Isaac Suwalski (1863–1913) came from Poland to London in 1896, and for seventeen years edited and published the only Hebrew weekly in England. The manifesto, printed below, is from the first issue of 28 October 1897.

The journal is open to everyone, so long as what they have to say is worthy of being heard . . . We shall supervise only the technical layout of the articles, improve the style and translate from other languages if the author's Hebrew is not good enough . . . The responsibility for the contents is the author's, not my own . . . I shall publish the following: 1) Literary materials . . . to strengthen our impoverished literature in this country. 2) News and current affairs of the Jewish world. 3) Scientific articles – only specialists will contribute here. 4) Feuilletons – to entertain the readers. 5) Stories and sketches – this section will be devoted totally to [pieces written originally in] Hebrew, and should reflect the lives of our people both in the present and in the past. 6) Book reviews and literary criticism – this hardly exists in our literature . . . We shall not concern ourselves with the personalities of the authors but only with the books themselves.

Figure 8 In an East End Russian restaurant, 1901 Cafe restaurants not only supplied *heimishe* foods, but were also the focus of radical politics and Jewish sociability (G.R. Sims (ed.), *Living London*, 3 vols (London: Cassell, 1901), I, p. 28).

b) Club life, 1918

Source: PRO HO 45/10819/318095/529, Special Branch report on Russian Revolutionary Matters, 3 January 1918

Special Branch kept Jewish East London under close surveillance during the First World War. Its reports on the location of political dissidence are as interesting as its policy analysis and recommendations.

With reference to Russian revolutionary matters in the Metropolis: I beg to submit the following details received through an Informant. . . .

A considerable number of . . . absentees can be found at the New Home Restaurant, 3 Great Garden Street, E. (first floor); Ladies Tailors Trade Union, 10 Great Garden Street, E; The Local No. 9 of the I.W.W., No. 76 Great Tongue Yard, Whitechapel; The Communist Club, 107 Charlotte Street, W; The New York Restaurant, 128 Whitechapel Road; The Parisien Restaurant, 162 Whitechapel Road, E. No. 3 Great Garden Street is best attended on Saturdays and Sundays from 2 to 10 p.m., and at 10 Great Garden Street, Saturdays and Sundays between 3 and 8 p.m. The other addresses any evening.

c) Rigoletto in Whitechapel, 1912

Source: Jewish Chronicle, 19 April 1912

The secular culture of the immigrant quarter found its most popular form in the Yiddish theatre. The 'Judisch–Deutsch' productions of the Garrick Theatre, Leman Street, noted by the Annual Register in 1880, were but a harbinger of still greater triumphs.

We are becoming so accustomed to the remarkable enterprise of the authorities of the Temple, East End Jewry's playhouse in Commercial Road, that we cease to wonder at anything they now attempt in order to entertain a fastidious public. But it was, however, with more than a feeling of indifference, that we accepted the invitation to witness the performance of "Rigoletto" last week. It was an ambitious project, this "doing into" Yiddish of Verdi's great opera, and the successful accomplishment of so great a task reflects all the greater credit upon those who had undertaken it. Mr. S. Alman, the musical director, once again showed his remarkable versatility, for to him was entrusted the difficult work of translating the libretto into Yiddish, a work which was beset with no ordinary difficulties, but which he accomplished with surprisingly successful results. His version appeared to fit the musical accent admirably and to run easily.

This represents the first occasion upon which "Rigoletto" has been produced in the jargon, and little did Verdi imagine, when his work was first produced in Venice in 1851, that 61 years later it would delight the denizens of the East End in their own tongue. But such is the march of time, and all opera lovers in search of new and refreshing experiences may be recommended to pay a visit to the Yiddish theatre in our midst. . . .

Taking all things into consideration, it is hardly surprising that the general press are so enthusiastic over the production, and we cannot help culling the following from the Daily Chronicle, which in the course of its critique remarks: "Nowhere, except in grand opera at Covent Garden, could one hear, in England, a company of such brilliant talent as in this Yiddish Theatre, in the very heart of the East End, which has been founded by the subscriptions of rich and poor Jews, and has been built to fulfil a great racial ideal among those people who have come from all parts of the world, refugees from persecution and direst poverty, to the Ghetto in London, where they are bound together by the same faith, the same tragic history, and by that mixed language spoken by all the Jews of Europe. The performance of 'Rigoletto' in Yiddish stands by itself as one of the most notable operatic triumphs in this country." . . .

d) When two worlds collide, 1904

Source: 'Jewish Riot in the East-End', The Times, 20 September 1904

Religion played a key role in the formation of immigrant settlement localities. Its position, though was contested. The clash between the secular and spiritual sometimes provoked disturbances of the peace.

Religious differences which have for a week past been disturbing the Jews of Spitalfields culminated yesterday afternoon in a riot in the neighbourhood of Brick-lane and Princelet-street, necessitating the drafting of large bodies of police from every station in the H Division. The orthodox Jews were observing the religious fasts in connexion with the Day of Atonement. Between 3 and 4 o'clock large numbers were walking along the streets when a body of Socialist Jews drove a van containing food through the crowded streets. The orthodox Jews resented this and drove the Socialists into their club, from the windows of which glass bottles were thrown. Several small injuries were inflicted, and one man received a severe cut on the face. The disorder thus started quickly spread, and within half an hour the whole neighbourhood around Princelet-street was in a state of great agitation. Stones were thrown at the houses of several prominent Socialists, and the police had to clear the streets and, by forming cordons, shut off the quarter where the disturbance had been most acute. Several arrests were made during the evening. It was 10 o'clock before the police were able to withdraw. The Socialists are accused of pelting a synagogue which stands adjacent to their club, and of arranging for a concert on the day of the fast and sending invitations to the Rabbis.

IV
GETTING A LIVING

Immigrant Jews were primarily wage labourers. The East European immigrants who, for example, came to Manchester in increasing numbers from the late 1840s, and who by 1875 accounted for between one-half and two-thirds of the city's estimated 7,000 Jews, were not solitary pedlars cum shopkeepers or master craftsmen grasping at a precarious independence. Quite the contrary; they were quickly absorbed into the industrial workforce, principally in cabinet-making and the garment trade, working in domestic workshops with uniform conditions and uniform rates of pay. In London, too, there developed a Jewish working class. Increasingly, the street trades gave way to paid employment in clothing, tobacco, furniture and footwear as the characteristic occupations of the Jewish minority. Jewish industry was located in trades in which capital and skill requirements were minimal and cheap labour plentiful, and in which homework, the application of simple hand-driven machinery and subdivision of labour, made it possible for London employers to compete effectively with provincial factory production. 'Sweating' is simply the term which historians now use to describe this particular industrial strategy.

The trades which the immigrants entered reflected their previous industrial experience but was also influenced by considerations of language and religion, particularly facilities for Sabbath observance, and by the expectation of a greater sense of security and well-being among *landsleit* and fellow co-religionists than among the indigenous population. It is possible, too, that the narrow occupational base of the immigrant community was sustained by discrimination and popular prejudice. In some sectors of the riverside trades, for example, job protection seems to have relied upon a racially exclusive vigilantism comparable with that encountered in the housing market. But there was also a random element at work determined by the port of debarkation and the character of the local labour market into which the newcomer was received (**docs. 1(a)–1(d)**).

The immigrant community, though industrious and peaceable, regarded the state and its officials with some suspicion. Policemen, local administrators and factory inspectors were often seen less as agents of progress making for a safer and healthier environment and more as interfering busybodies making it difficult for traders and small masters to earn a living.

Only with great difficulty could tight-lipped employers, large or small, be persuaded to unburden themselves. Charles Booth and his associates were, in this respect, more successful than most. The unpublished notebooks of the Life and Labour Inquiry provide a unique insight into productive and social relations in the workshop trades of Jewish East London. Not only are we given a careful description of industrial processes and work organization in one of the largest sweatshops, the report assaults the senses even more than it stirs the intellect. The account of the fetid cramped environment with combined smells of scorched materials, perspiring workers and insanitary lavatories is, indeed, almost overpowering (**doc. 2**). Conditions in the furniture trade were different but hardly better. Our informant here, a non-Jewish trade unionist, presents an equally evocative account of conditions in what, after the ready-made clothing industry, was the largest of the immigrant trades (**doc. 4**).

These trades were notorious for their defiance of the regulations and statutes concerning health and safety at work. The factory inspectors, however, had to contend with more than the opposition of employers. Worker resistance was equally pronounced. The collusive arrangements into which both parties entered frustrated the efforts of the under-resourced inspectorate arrayed against them (**doc. 3**).

Immigrant workers and their representatives, questioned by social and parliamentary investigators, sometimes provide vivid accounts of their work experiences, values and expectations. These testimonies bring us closer to the everyday concerns of an immigrant working class and suggest possibilities for further historical inquiry (**docs. 5(a)–5(e)**). Contemporary curiosity about the standard of living of the Jewish Worker, for example, has not been converted into systematic historical knowledge. Immigrant living standards were thought to be massively inferior to those of the general population. Polish Jews, fortified by faith alone, were said to exist on wurst, bagles, potatoes and soup. They didn't drink but gambled their earnings in places of low repute and lived like beasts. The truth is difficult to establish. We know little about the pattern of expenditure and the calculation of earnings is problematic. Wage payment systems were extraordinarily complex. Take tailoring. Apart from the variable skill content, workers in the same shop might be paid hourly or weekly or by output in an industry notorious for short-time working and seasonal fluctuations (**doc. 6**). And when all allowances have been made we only possess a snapshot of wages and earnings rather than the moving picture that is required. A historian's lot is not an unhappy one; it's just difficult!

1.   The Jewish labour market

a)   No Jews need apply! 1867

Source: J.H. Stallard, *London Pauperism amongst Jews and Christians* (1867), pp. 8–9

Jewish concentration in a limited number of trades was primarily, though not exclusively, a function of previous industrial experience. Discrimination also played a role.

The occupations of the Jews are undoubtedly influenced, to a certain extent, by the prejudices which still prevent them from working on comfortable terms with the English and Irish labourers. If a Jew gets work at the Docks, he is so jeered and chaffed that he is obliged to give it up. He is not rough enough to retaliate, for the Dock labourers are the very lowest of their class; and for the same reasons day labour is impossible on railways and public works. But the grand difficulty in the way of the Jewish poor is the restraint of the Mosaic ritual. It is almost impossible for a Jew to be bound apprentice to a master who is not of the same persuasion; being interdicted from partaking of his food, from working part of every Friday and the whole of every Saturday throughout the year, besides the festivals and periods of mourning, when no Jew can work. This loss of time no Christian master can afford, so that there is no possibility of acquiring a trade or of being employed at day-work more than four days and a half per week. No Jews can be employed in Christian factories, shipyards, engine-works, or shops. There are no Jew carpenters, builders, plumbers, or workers in iron. They are excluded from all kinds of labour in which association with Christians is involved, and so are necessarily driven to occupations in which they work at home or in connection exclusively with members of their own community. The Jew therefore obtains his living by trade and barter; and although the cry of "Old Clo" is much less common than it used to be, an extensive business in wearing apparel is still carried on. It is, however, less profitable than formerly, and the Jew has a liking only for trades which return a high profit. The chief industrial occupations of the Jews are tailoring, cigar making, fish and fruit selling, and glaziering, and for the women, tailoring, shirtmaking, and umbrella and parasol making. Cap and slipper making is largely in their hands, whilst in common with many English they deal in a variety of goods which are not always obtained from legitimate sources.

b)   A moral antipathy to Jewish employment! 1898

Source: J.A. Dyche, 'The Jewish Workman', Contemporary Review, LXIII (1898), pp. 35, 46

The previous document emphasised worker opposition to Jewish employment; the autobiographical fragment printed below identifies employers as no less discriminatory.

... I am, I think, entitled to style myself a typical alien immigrant. I am a Jew, born in Russia, landed in this country some nine years ago with threepence in my pocket. I learned the trade of a tailors' machinist, and have worked in the ready-made, bespoke, and ladies' mantle trades, mostly in Leeds. ...

. . .

Most of the Jewish immigrants who are engaged in the clothing trade in Leeds have followed different trades and occupations in their native country; but they could not get the same employment here, as English employers as a rule have a "moral antipathy to employing Jews," as one of them expressed himself. I know many Jewish engineers, painters, brushmakers, etc., who were compelled to take to tailoring because they are Jews and foreigners. The Jew, being excluded from the means of livelihood in ordinary trades, has created industries for himself.

c)   Que sera, sera! 1899

Source: J. Smith, 'The Jewish Immigrant', Contemporary Review, LXXXVI (1899), p. 426

The constraints of skill, capital, language, religion and culture served no doubt to limit the occupational base of the immigrant community, but contingency, too, exerted some influence upon the choice of employment.

... Strange as it may appear, the immigrant's future is more or less determined by the sort of trade done at the town where he lands or arrives. He may become a tanner or a dyer in Hull, and have a different ambition from what he would have if he landed at, say, Liverpool, Glasgow, or London. A party landing at Hull would probably separate and disperse in different directions, some to Leeds, Leicester, Manchester, Nottingham, Bristol, Birmingham, and the North. Those who land in London would in most cases stay there. Their choice of a domicile depends on the friends or *lanzlard* (fellow townsmen) they expect to see, and to whom they had probably previously written. They are in the great majority of cases very poor alike in wealth, intellect, and capacity. Not ten per cent. of them know any trade; not half of them can read or write their own or any other language. The only reading they know at all is the Hebrew scripture, and most of that they cannot write, through the peculiar grammatical or rather want of grammatical form it is in. Coming here with no knowledge of any trade, they are extremely anxious to find something to do that will bring them in a living, no matter how poor or mean it may be. These "greeners" will accept with equal avidity and impartiality the offer to work with a barber, tinker, tailor, furrier, hawker, or what not, so long as the offer comes from a co-religionist. . . .

d) A census of immigrant occupations, 1885

Source: Poor Jews' Temporary Shelter, First Annual Report, (1885–86)

The Poor Jews' Temporary Shelter not only provided helpless immigrants with their first bed, it also pointed them towards their first job. Its annual reports, which include information on the previous industrial experience of the inmates, supplies the basis for an occupational profile of the newcomers, and are key documents in the recreation of the immigrant experience.

Although the Preamble which heads the accompanying copy of the Constitution may be regarded as sufficiently explaining the aim and purpose of this Charity, the Committee deem it desirable to direct attention to the circumstances which called it into existence.

Their object in so doing is to remove any erroneous impressions that may still be lingering in the minds of many would-be supporters, that this Institution is a mis-chievous innovation calculated to encourage, rather than to check, the unhappily continuous immigration of destitute foreign Jews. So far is this from being the case, that, as may be seen from the annexed Tabular Statement, the number of Inmates in the Shelter has of late visibly diminished.

Further it will be clearly shown that the Shelter was established to supersede, and has effectually superseded, an objectionable and long-existing Refuge, and has subsequently led to the closing of private resorts that were beyond question a scandal to the Community.

Long prior to that intensified Russian persecution of the Jews which led to the formation of the Mansion House Relief Committee, the stress of foreign oppression had led to a constant flooding of the East End of London with our poor foreign co-religionists.

These were harboured by their humble brethren in miserable hovels, and even crowded for the night into dingy places of worship belonging to the Chevras that abound in the District – not to speak of the many whose only refuge was the open street. Scraps of food collected by some of the poorest residents, in those districts where Jewish penury abounds, supplemented by occasional gifts of money and in kind, served but inadequately to feed and clothe these helpless, wandering outcasts.

Foremost amongst those whose exertions were unremittingly employed in this primitive fashion was Mr. Simon Cohen, who, about six years ago, allowed an unoccupied portion of his premises in Church Lane, Whitechapel, to be resorted to as a Refuge, which gradually absorbed within its precincts a considerable proportion of the homeless foreign Jews.

Figure 9 In the Poor Jews' Temporary Shelter, 1901 Penniless arrivals taken from the dockside not only received shelter here, but were also found employment and accommodation (G.R. Sims (ed.), *Living London*, 3 vols (London: Cassell, 1901), I, p. 53).

This well intentioned work would not have come to the notice of the general public, had it not broken down through the circumstances that the local sanitary inspector condemned, as utterly unfit for the purpose, the building in which these immigrants were housed.

The well known philanthropist, Mr. F.D. Mocatta, visited the place, and on his confirming the inspector's report, a few gentlemen in the West End came to the rescue. Having satisfied themselves of the imperative necessity for continuing the work, they combined with the old Committee of Management, and raised a building fund.

Premises were then engaged ad interim at 12, Great Garden Street, where Mr. M. Berlinger, to whom the thanks of the Committee are due, gratuitously discharged the functions of superintendent until the present excellent site was secured. The house there standing, under the kind supervision of our honorary architect, Mr. Lewis Solomon, was adapted to the special requirements of a Shelter, and was opened on April 11th,

Tabulated statement showing the number and description of the inmates, and the number of meals dispensed during each month

1885–86	Number of inmates	Single	Married	Widowers	With a calling	Without a calling	Meals	Age of the youngest inmate	Age of the oldest inmate
November	36	26	10	—	27	9	1020	15	48
December	81	45	33	3	66	15	1406	16	51
January	49	24	24	1	33	16	1045	18	49
February	71	42	29	—	57	14	1234	15	54
March	55	36	17	2	42	13	1111	14	52
April	59	42	16	1	36	23	1374	11	56
May	101	51	49	1	71	30	1357	16	48
June	125	65	58	2	81	44	1743	16	57
July	131	61	70	—	78	53	2458	16	82
August	122	53	69	—	77	45	1878	16	65
September	115	48	67	—	67	48	1818	16	68
October	85	38	47	—	60	25	4000	16	65

Note: The above figures of meals supplied include the following served on behalf of the Sabbath Meals Society: July 159, August 183, September 169, October 2798.

The following is a description of the occupations of some of the inmates who followed a 'calling'

Amber turners	2	Jeweller	1
Bakers	22	Ladies' tailors	2
Barbers	11	Lithographers	2
Bookbinders	13	Locksmiths	6
Bootmakers	101	Looking glass maker	1
Brassfinishers	2	Machinists	14
Brassfounders	4	Millers	3
Bricklayers	4	Mineral water makers	2
Bristlesorters	2	Painter	1
Butchers	11	Paperhangers	2
Cabinet makers	31	Pipe maker	1
Cap makers	15	Pouch makers	3
Carmen	2	Pressers	10
Carpenters	2	Potter	1
Carriage builder	1	Printers	2
Carriage painter	1	Rabbis	2
Carver	1	Readers (Chazonim)	2
Chimney-sweeper	1	Rope makers	2
Cigar & cigarette makers	22	Saddlers	2
Clerks	22	Schochetim	11
Comb maker	1	Seaman	1
Confectioners	2	Sign writer	1
Cooper	1	Smiths	18
Coppersmiths	2	Soap-boilers	3
Coral worker	1	Sopher (Scribe)	1
Cutlers	2	Stewards	2
Distiller	1	Stick makers	6
Driver	1	Surgeon	1
Dyers	4	Tallowchandler	1
Embroiderers	2	Tanners	9
Engineers	2	Teachers	6
Farm labourers	12	Tinkers	19
Flower maker	1	Tobacco cutters	4
Frame maker	1	Traders	6
Furriers	6	Turners	6
Galvanizer	1	Umbrella maker	1
Gas fitter	1	Upholsterers	4
General workmen	3	Varnisher	1
Glaziers	12	Waiter	1
Glovers	2	Watchmakers	10
Goldsmiths	6	Waterproofers	2
Gruel makers	2	Weavers	6
Hawkers	20	Wood cutter	1
Interpreters	3		

1886, with a Consecration Service by the Delegate Chief Rabbi, under the presidency of the Treasurer, Mr. Samuel Montagu, M.P.

A generous response having been made to an appeal for contributions, forty-one beds were fitted up, and arrangements completed for the supply of simple yet substantial food, to be served on the premises.

. . .

The Committee having been fortunate in obtaining the services as manager and house-steward of Mr. A. Hirschowitz, a native of Russia, who, with the assistance of his wife as matron, not only keeps the house and its inmates in good order, but also exercises the most valuable moral influence upon them.

. . .

In conclusion, the Committee beg to announce that, with a view to provide a further wholesome check to the immigration of any pauper adventurers who might be attracted hither from a misapprehension of the character of the Shelter, as well as in order to discourage habits of indolence amongst those already here, it is in contemplation to institute a Labour Test of such a character as not to interfere with the already overstocked labour market.

. . .

e)   Hard times, 1904

Source: PRO Mepo 2/260, Report by Inspector J. Hewison, Commercial Road Police Station, 5 December 1904

The report printed below presents a poignant comment on the sources of Jewish immigration, the condition of the immigrants and the implications for the policing of the community.

I beg to report that at 12.20 pm 5th inst. about 300 aliens of Russian nationality assembled outside the Synagogue at Fournier St. Spitalfields and demanded relief. On being informed by the caretaker, Wooly Ospeter, that no relief could be given, they threatened to force the doors. P.S. 19 Burt with 6 P.C.'s were at once sent to the Synagogue and immediately dispersed the crowd and patrolled the vicinity until 1 pm all then being quiet, three P.C.'s were withdrawn. A P[olice] S[ergeant] with 3 P.C.'s remaining in the vicinity until 2.45 pm and as there appears no likelihood of them re-assembling the P.S. and 2 P.C.'s were withdrawn. I being left to patrol to prevent any damage being done to the premises. A P.C. has also been sent to patrol in the vicinity of Booth Street Synagogue for a similar purpose and subject to approval I have arranged for this to continue for the present. There has been a great increase of Aliens to this district recently, several have been found in the streets at night by police without money or a place to sleep and there is no doubt that a large number of them are at the present time in a starving condition.

The reason given by many of these people is that they have left Russia to evade Military Service and there is little doubt but that the increase of Aliens is due to the Russo Japanese war. The special attention of all ranks has been called to the Synagogues in the district and every thing possible will be done to prevent damage.

Submitted it is necessary to continue special patrols in the vicinity of the Synagogues at present. There are hundreds of these people arriving and walking about practically without means of any sort.

Mulvaney, Superintendant.

2.   Interview with a sweater, 1893

Source: Charles Booth Collection, British Library of Political and Economic Science, Booth Notebooks, B96 fos. 47–48, 75–81

Koenigsberg, described as the man with 'the unenviable distinction as the worst sweater in the fur trade', was interviewed for Charles Booth's inquiry into the Life and Labour of the People in London on 14 September and 16 October 1893. The report is revealing as much for the perspective as for the substance.

Koenigsberg: Furrier, dealer, sewer, cutter, blocker. Commercial Street, Whitechapel on a letter of introduction from Canon Barnett.

He is reputed to be the greatest sweater in the Trade, is a Jew, small evil-looking. They say that he works his men and women beyond regulation hours and the factory inspectors have found much fault with him. He was angry at my coming and told me to go in a mixture of German, Yiddish and English.

The son was rather more amenable; said the 'Governor' was rather put out because he had had Factory inspectors round 3–6 times in the last fortnight. Business was very bad and he had been told to make many alterations in his workshops.

They employ Germans, English and French. They all work on piece.

When they are busy they take on new hands and when they are slack discharge them at once.

They are usually very busy at this time but this year is abnormally slack. They expect to be busy in a fortnights time and if I can wait till then they will send me a card and I can go round the works.

Women earn 37/- in busy times and men £6.00.0 on valuable fur (sable) work.

There is a sick club among the men; young K said he had tried to start one in which the firm could join but the men would have nothing to do with it.

Koenigsberg: 25 Commercial Street (makers of furs and cloth caps)

Miss Koenigsberg a lady of any age between 30 and 45 years was told to show and explain everything to me, she apologised for her Father's rudeness on a former occasion, said he had been a bit out of temper and had thought I was another Factory Inspector.

This lady contradicted herself a very great many times during the interview, the different members of her family who looked in from time to time made statements directly contradictory, so that the following interview is only an attempt at the exact truth. They have the following classes employed: Cutters; Sewers; Blockers; Liners; Salters and Packers.

Blockers is the Trade name for Nailers. The wages of cutters were given variously as £2.15.0; 44/-; £3.00.0 throughout the year. They seem from the actual wages taken down from the wage book to be really £1.5.0. to £2.10.0.

In busy times they employ 200 men and women and about half that number in slack. They take on and dismiss as occasion arises, but persisted in saying that they had no seasons and that everyone had regular employment throughout the year.

May to the end of October is the busiest time.

Nailers become cutters when they can.

1891 was good

1892 nicely

1893 middling; began very well indeed in the early part of the year but the late season has only just begun.

There is no shifting, each one takes his own work and sticks to it.

Fifty per cent of the people employed are foreigners but very few Jewesses; said there were not 40 Jewesses working in the London Trade. She is herself a Jewess, her father is very strict and never worked or allowed any of his people to work from sunset on Friday though a few came in on Sunday.

The girls employed were very quiet in the factory but a wild lot outside especially the 'Thomas's machinists', these are the girls who work the machines (made by one Thomas) used in sewing caps together.

One of the cutters on being asked said that the fluff got on to his chest and into his eyes, it depends on the quality of the skins. Sometimes a great deal flies about if the skins are poor. He also said that all his family and relations were employed in the Fur line and that it ran more in families than any other trade that he could think of.

The fur work was all done on the top floor which was a large and fairly airy room and I calculated that there was about 60 men and women working; the women on forms running down and across the room at their machines.

The second floor was of about the same shape but not so light or airy as there was no skylight as in the top room.

The cutters in this department were cutters of stuff for caps. Men and women were here very much crowded, there was not very much ventilation and a good deal of the 'pazza del prossimo!' The men working machines were very small-looking foreigners with sunken pale cheeks. Of the women, some looked ill and others tired, and all were working as if their very lives depended on it, as indeed they probably did. There was no looking up as one passed and the scowls and evident dislike of Miss K[oenigsberg] when we passed and she asked to see the work were ill concealed. Never have I seen machinists work so fast or such hopeless faces. There was no talking and very little giggling even when Miss K was called away and I was left to walk around by myself. They seemed mostly too tired.

Downstairs there were four girls measuring the caps and pasting in or rather licking and sticking in the small tickets of their different sizes.

Underground was the place where the furs were stretched and nailed on boards and the cap blocks and the felt hats with a fur rim made.

Here there was no daylight. At one end of a long room there was a small grating on a level with the pavement and at the back there was another dark opening in the ceiling which might lead up to a passage. Calculated that there were about 30 men working in the room which was hot from the gas jets and steam cap blocking place and the gas presses for the felt hats.

Ladies felt flat hats with a fur rim are made as follows: the felt is only stuff and not felt at all parted tightly on either side of a piece of pasted buckram to give it stiffness. These are hung up to dry as stiff pieces and are then taken to a press containing the mould of the exact shape of the hat. The piece[?] is then pressed and the gas jets turned on to heat the outside of the press to make the buckram and stuff more pliable. The edges are then trimmed with a pair of scissors and the fur sewn on by hand.

The man who does this work takes out so much at a certain price, employs other men to help him and gets as much out of it as he can.

Caps after being machine made must be given some shape so they are stretched over blocks and then put into a steam chamber and then allowed to stiffen and dry.

Miss K gave the exact wages paid out to the men and women in the fur department in a given busy and slack week. She read out and I copied. In the first instance she seemed to choose the higher amounts only and shut up the book when I attempted to look but was somewhat ashamed and in the end allowed me to copy down directly.

Was anxious to give all information she could and would let me come again or write any further questions. Also would give introduction to small Jewish drapers.

Old K produced cakes and wine in a medicine bottle to end up with.

3.   An inspector calls, 1895

Source: Report of the Chief Inspector of Factories and Workshops for the Year 1894, Parliamentary Papers [C.7745] XIX (1895), pp. 46–47

John B. Lakeman, Superintendant Inspector of Workshops in London, explains the difficulties confronting his under-resourced staff in the enforcement of the factory acts.

. . . The East End and West End have each its own methods of avoiding detection, which may be worth knowing.

As regards the East End coat makers I have to report that their capabilities to resort to sundry new expedients consequent upon the more frequent inspection during meal times, after hours not overtime, upon overtime, after 10 o'clock at night, and on Saturdays and Sundays, are versatile and divergent, there is no more respect for the law shown by the Jews now than there was 18 years ago, when I began to inspect them. Morality does not enter into their thought, for the love of gain shuts out every other consideration, working to 9 p.m. instead of Sunday labour has been resolved on by many, who work on Thursdays or Fridays to 10 p.m., but in the morning some of them begin at 6.30 or 7 a.m. several of them have been caught, on Sundays they have employed men. Many have taken on girls from 13 to 14 years of age without school certificates, well knowing they have not procured them, or being foreigners cannot produce them. Cribbing time from dinner hour by altering the clock, no tea time given, and if insisted upon by the workers, dismissal is threatened. On Thursdays the tea is provided by the occupier who gives it at the most convenient time to himself, without any regard to the time named on his abstract, and without any cessation from work, stating on his overtime form that he ceases work at 9.30 p.m., but continues till 10 o'clock, many of them have worked from 7 a.m. to 9, 10, and 12 o'clock at night, allowing 20 minutes for dinner, no tea half-hour and right on to midnight, overtime notices not sent, but filled up, no record made, working all through Friday night to dinner time on Saturday, then go home, and resume on Sundays at 8 or 9 a.m. to 4 o'clock. In another coat maker's, on door being opened to inspectors at 10.15 p.m., four knocks were made upon the door and a whistle was blown from the street, six men and a boy said to be 18 years old were only in the workshop, on leaving the inspectors were met by a crowd of about 80 people laughing and making fun of them.

In another tailor's, on same night, a woman was seen at work from the opposite pavement, inspectors knocked, but whilst waiting, three girls shouted 'Inspectors!' On entering, three females were met coming down stairs, two of whom said they were wives of the master, and the third a girl of 16, admitted she had been working when the knock was given. Another man was known to bring home work from a warehouse, where he and the females had been at work all day, and at 9 p.m. several females start work in a kitchen till the small hours of the morning, no work is done here in the day time. Inspectors saw him enter with a bundle, and three females also went in, the inspectors then left and returned at 11 o'clock nearly, when they found the man, his wife, and daughter in the kitchen, where also was a machine, two women were found coming out of a bedroom, they said they were daughters; in the bedroom were six bundles of cloth, and on the floor were litters of cloth cuttings, on leaving, a man stopped the inspectors and asked them if they had seen his daughter who was kept from home by the occupier, they returned and found her hidden in the water-closet. Again, they have lately employed Gentiles and Jewesses in equal numbers, so that they work the former on Saturdays and the Jewesses on Sundays, giving the excuse that they only work each for half a day on the half-holiday, although the form 18 is duly affixed and signed by the occupier, which distinctly forbids labour to be undertaken on the Saturdays. A man puts his head out of window upon the knock of inspectors, he is told who are below and replies that he will go down at once and let them in, but in the meantime all the females and young persons are sent into bedrooms, water-closets, and kitchens, the clothes of the workers are left undisturbed. On one occasion the inspectors made a second visit, waiting until they found the door opened and caught them all at work; on another occasion when a visit to the kitchen was made the wife of occupier had a pack of cards dealing out to the girls who were seated around the table, she cleverly joked with them and asked them to join the party, but when the inspectors left work would be resumed. . . .

4.   Up and down the Curtain Road, 1892

Source: Minutes of Evidence taken before the Royal Commission on Labour Group "C", Parliamentary Papers [C.6795–VI] XXXVI (1892), qq. 19,736–19,965

Harry Ham, Secretary of the Alliance Cabinet Makers' Association, here provides a vivid description of the immigrant cabinet maker *shlepping* along the Curtain Road in search of a living.

19,736.   What is the numerical strength of your Association? – 6,500 members.

19,737.   Are those all engaged in cabinet making or in the various branches of the furniture trade? – Various branches, such as cabinet makers, chair makers, carvers, shop fitters, and turners.

19,738.   What is the number of your branches? – There are 68 branches; 60 in England, 5 in Scotland, and 3 in Ireland.

19,739.   What number of those branches are in London and the district? – 16.

19,740.   What is the proportion of the men in union to the members who are non-unionists, those outside the Union? – Roughly speaking we consider in the United Kingdom there are between 70,000 and 80,000 cabinet makers. Out of that number there are less than 15,000 in union.

19,741.   About 15 per cent? – Yes. In London we estimate there are from 20,000 to 25,000 cabinet makers. Out of that number there are under 3,000 in any union.

19,742.   How do you account for the fact that the proportion of unionists to non-unionists is so small? – It is chiefly apathy on the part of the workmen.

19,743.   How long has your Society been established? – Since 1865.

19,744.   Is it growing in numbers? – Six years ago, when I took the office of general secretary, it was only just over a thousand strong.

19,745.   And now you have 6,500? – And now we have 6,500.

19,746.   And you say there are 2,500 members in London? – Under that.

19,747.   That is about 10 per cent of the whole in London? – In London that would be about it. . . .

. . .

19,950.   What do you mean by the lower class in the trade? – The Jewish workmen as a rule.

19,951.   Under what system do they work? – The greater proportion of them pick the trade up, as we call it. They come over here as greeners, pauper aliens, and they go into a shop and they are given a bit of wood to plane up. They learn to do that. Then they are given a bit to saw up; they learn to do that, and they get at it by degrees, so that they can make a little job on their own account. In no sense of the word are they competent cabinet makers; they cannot take a job and do it all right out, but can only do a small portion.

19,952.   Do they work in shops? – They work in shops mainly, if you can term them shops; perhaps an ordinary dwelling with a little bit of a shanty at the back. Of course they are allowed to work all the hours that God gives them, and there is no one to interfere with them.

19,953.   What wages do they get? – A young lad would get not more than 8s. or 9s. a week. Then he would get up to 15s. or 16s., and there are scores and hundreds of men who would think themselves lucky to have a sovereign for a week's work.

19,954.   Of what average hours? – 60 or 70 hours a week.

19,955. Would there be a large proportion of those in the East End engaged in the trade? – A large number.

19,956. So that when you mentioned that the London rate was 8½d. to 9d. an hour you did not include that class of workmen? – No.

19,957. When you mentioned that there were thousands in London getting 7½d. only, you did not intend that to include the lowest? – No.

19,958. These others are much lower? – Yes.

19,959. When they have done their work, what becomes of it; where do they take it? – If you have never been down Curtain Road it would be well worth your while to go down there on Saturday morning. You will see them come down there with their trucks in dozens. No one would think they were cabinet makers. What with the red ochre, the chalk, and the glue, they look more like Red Indians. Of course they go to the shops and ask so much for the work. They are told: "We do not require it." They take it somewhere else. They know they can get a certain price, and then they get there in time to get a cheque, so as to rush to the bank. They are generally paid in small cheques. Perhaps they do not get the cheque until 2 o'clock, when it is too late to go to the bank. Then they go to a second salesman, and for a small commission he cashes the cheque. That is the system adopted in many of the East End shops; so that although a man might perhaps get a cheque for 3l. for his job, he will only get 2l.17s.0d., the other 3s. going to the second salesman who cashes it.

19,960. Is there any institution known as the pawnshop there? – Unfortunately, there are places where they can put the work in pawn. There is a place in Curtain Road. If a man is not fortunate enough to sell his job at 2 o'clock; of course he wants to sell it before 2 o'clock if he can, because he has to go to the timber yard to get a supply for Monday morning, but if he has not been fortunate enough to get a cheque, then he will leave the job at this place, with the understanding that it is sold at the best price that can be obtained, and that he will have that with the commission knocked off.

19,961. Then does he get something advanced upon it? – I expect so.

19,962. Have you any hope of being able to stamp out lump-work? – We are gradually doing it. In several shops we have introduced day-work recently. . . .

19,965. What effect has that had upon the men; has it increased the wages? – They work under better conditions, I think, in a day-work shop. A man has to slave his life out to get anything like a decent living at this lump-work.

5.   Jewish voices

a)   *God bless the man who discovered Formica! 1913*

Sources: Press cuttings, London Museum of Jewish Life, 59/1988/1

Mrs Mary Silverberg, a remarkable lady and long-time resident at the Rokefield Home for the Jewish Blind, was the subject of newspaper profiles on her 93rd and 100th birthdays from which the following has been created.

Mary Silverberg was born in Poland and when she was only 14 married her widowed brother-in-law.

He already had three young children and Mary spent her teenage years bringing them up. She had six more children of her own and when one of her daughters died she took two of her grandchildren into her home.

Not content with bringing up 11 children Mrs Silverberg helped her husband run a baker's shop. She used to start work at 5 o'clock every morning and bake three lots of bread shifting 120 lbs of flour with each batch. Her experience came in useful when the cook at Rokefield was on holiday.

Mrs Silverberg stepped into the breach and baked bread for the 50 people at the home . . .

What was it like baking again after so long? 'Once you know how to do a thing you can always remember how to do it again', she said . . .

But Mrs Silverberg agreed that modern day living makes things easier. 'God bless the man who discovered Formica', she said. 'In my day we had to scrub hard . . .

Mrs Silverberg left Poland in about 1913 – she had sent her son and husband to England to avoid being drafted into the army.

And when her husband wrote to say he was homesick and wanted to come back to Poland, she packed up everything and brought the whole family over.

b)   *How did your mother manage? 1917–23*

Source: London Museum of Jewish Life, Oral Histories, Tape 67

The following text is transcribed from an interview with the children of immigrant parents recorded in the spring of 1986. In this remarkable retrospect the three respondents recall the vicissitudes of their parents in the First World War and its aftermath with an immediacy and a variability that is engaging and instructive. The names of the speakers have been altered.

3 May 1986 – X Family
RX – his son
LX – his daughter
EX – eldest daughter

(re father)

LX: He had the most splendid personality, let's be fair.

EX: Exactly.

LX: He had the most tremendous personality. He left home when he was 11 – or 13 –. He was born in Russia and he went from Russia right away across – I don't know any geography –

EX: To everywhere.

LX: To Turkey. And there he apprenticed himself to a baker and became a very expert baker. Then he came to England and stayed with Rabbi Fraenkel who was my grandfather, *olav hasholem*, and met and married my late and unlamented mother . . .

EX: That's a terrible thing. It's not necessary!

LX: My mother was Rabbi Fraenkel's daughter. And then he worked as the manager for Cadbury Hall, for the bakery (?) in Cadbury Hall and then he became a menshevist . . .

EX: You know, they never had birthdays. They had those registration cards. What were they called those cards?

RX: It was roughly 1912 when he came over.

LX: That's right. I reckon he must have been in his mid 20s then.

Interviewer: Why did he leave home?

EX: Because there was nothing there.

LX: He left home because he was in a *yeshiva* which was being run by his uncle who was the person in charge of the *yeshiva* and he was reading from the *Gemora*, but he – being my father – wanted to learn Russian and he had a little Russian book inside the *Gemora* and he was reading that and his uncle caught him.

RX: And took his ear off

LX: And beat him, so he hopped it . . .

RX: He must have been a character, to leave at eleven.

EX: His father was a *shochet*. His father died when he was young and his
        mother brought him and his sisters up. I know that – but when he
        got here . . . he'd forgotten the address or something (garbled)

LX: Didn't he have a brother, Esther?

RX: Yes, in America.

EX: He did not have a brother in America. He had two sisters and I
        remember my mother used to write to his mother – *bube*, as we
        knew of her – and the two sisters: aunt Zippe and . . . I can't
        remember the name. In Russia

LX: All that we know are the things that he told us and probably what
        each of us know is slightly different; either because we've forgotten
        or because he might have told . . .

EX: Yes, he always embroidered his stories . . .

LX: My father was the gift of the song par excellence. When he was a
        very old man and was dying from emphysemia and he was senile
        . . . I went to visit him with my eldest son and when we came out
        Peter said 'Mom, he's a fantastic man' He had him absolutely
        enthralled. He was an old, old man.

RX: He had an education.

EX: Self-taught, from reading books

RX: And also, he was a socialist.

LX: A menshevist.

RX: He went back to Russia. He opened a business in Southampton,
        after he'd been to camp and the [First World] War and all that

EX: He never had a business! he went to work. He worked for Slater's
        because when he'd come back from Russia . . . he used to go on his
        bike, and he used to come back with loaves and loaves, I can see it
        now in front of me. He used to sell to shops . . . for supplementary
        income. And as soon as he came back from Russia, while he was at
        this job, he said to our mother 'we're going to open a shop' she said

'open a shop?'. We lived in 2 rooms, they never had tuppence, let alone a shop. So he said 'well, we gotta borrow' So he borrowed money from wherever he could. But they didn't <u>buy</u> a shop, they rented it.

LX: When he went back to Russia, because he was a menshevist he went back to fight the revolution and we were all supposed to be going with him. I was only a few months old. 1917.

EX: I told you, he left our mother with three children, I was the eldest. I was four. She (i.e. LX) was six months.

RX: Because that's when the Russian revolution really got it strong. He believed in the socialist theory, that the world <u>could</u> be much better if everybody did the right thing. When he got back over there, too many people started saying 'no, we're gonna do this and we're gonna do that' and he ended up in Siberia in prison. The white Russians put him in prison. And the Bolsheviks. He was very lucky; the man in charge of that prison was an old friend of his so your father and Tagorsky (?) and a few other, another baker, got . . . he said 'right, see you, get going' and they got out and came back

EX: Escaped

RX: From Siberia, right through Russia and everything, to get back to London.

EX: How did they get over the border? – they swam under the river – over the border, till he got out of Russia. He had to swim. And gradually he made his way back out.

RX: When he was in Russia, they pushed his face in the burning sand and burned his eyebrows

LX: And he had no eyelashes.

RX: It shows his will. He led them all the way back. Because he was, he was a leader, no question about that, and as I say, he got back to England, 1922 he came back . . .

RX's wife: How did your mother manage?

EX: That's a good question, Hanna, how did my mother live with three children? I remember, they don't. My mother, with three children, used to take us all and she used to sell tea. Do you know what that means? She used to buy quarter pound of tea at tuppence or whatever it is, and sell it for tuppence-ha'penny. To all her friends, acquaintances, people she knew . . . to make a few coppers other than the allowance that they got . . . So then, the war was on 1917, and you know, by that time the zepplins came over so she took the three of us to Swansea and we lived in Swansea till the war was over, and then we came back to the East End, (did she hear from him during these years?) I don't think so. She must have done, because he know where to come.

LX: She had a basket full of letters, I remember that basket very very well, yes I do indeed, she had a cane basket, square, with a lid and there were all the letters that she had from him . . . when he came back –

EX: My mother had a very good character, and people took a chance, (indecipherable) we lived above the shop. Charles street, then

RX: The second shop was in Charles Street, we had three rooms there, then we got the next shop, in Commercial Road, we lived there.

LX: And that was posh, that.

EX: I told you, seven rooms . . . it was absolutely marvellous

c)   A costermonger, 1905

Source: Minutes of Evidence taken before the Select Committee of the House of Lords on the Sunday Closing (Shops) Bill, Parliamentary Papers [344], VIII (1905), q. 2047

The Whitechapel and Spitalfields Male and Female Costermongers' Union was formed in 1894. Here Benjamin Davis, its secretary, explains the difficulties created by the enforcement of Sunday trading legislation.

. . . The number of members of my union (most of them Jews) is nearly 500, and there are a vast number of Jewish costermongers who are not members of the above union. I should say that the aggregate number of Jewish costermongers trading in the neighbourhood which I represent are nearly 2,000; this is only one portion of the East End. There are many others in other markets such as Crisp Street, Poplar, Salmons Lane, Limehouse, Brick Lane, Bethnal Green, Great Street, Bethnal Green, and various portions of London. Assuming each costermonger had to keep four in family this would amount to at least 10,000 persons in this district alone, depending for support on the earnings of the costermongers, and the principal earnings of breadwinners are on Sunday. Many of these costermongers work at their trades during the week and cannot earn enough to maintain their wife and family with, and they are therefore compelled through no fault of their own to come into the markets on Sunday morning where, by selling miscellaneous wares, it at least enables them to earn an honest livelihood and to further bring their children up as respectable citizens to take their position among His Majesty's subjects. The customers are almost all, if not all, Jewish persons. I am of opinion that if the Jewish costermongers were prevented from so trading it would nothing less than starvation to thousands of little children; there are sufficient children at present who are going to school improperly fed, and I do not think it would be advisable to bring any further starvation among the infantile class. I am perfectly agreeable to a six day working week, but I cannot agree and must strongly oppose a two and three quarter days working week, which certainly would be the case, if the present Sunday closing of Shops Bill became law. Let us for one moment take the following figures and see how impossible it would be to expect any person to earn a livelihood in a little more than six months in a year which the following figures will prove. We first of all lose 52 Saturdays, next we lose 52 halves of Fridays, 26 days, we also lose all Jewish holidays, 13 days, or a total of 91 days. Now sir, I go further than that, for we lose 52 ½ days by the early closing of shops as a result of the Early Closing of Shops Bill which your Lordship introduced, making 26 more days, and if we were compelled to close on Sundays that will bring the number of days we lose to, 169, or an average of 3 ¼ days per week. I agree that a six days working week is sufficient for any man to work, but it would be impossible for any individual person to earn a livelihood in two and three quarter days which according to figures remain. No one deprecates more than myself, any person working seven days a week. But I sincerely hope that no endeavour will be made to interfere with the religious liberties for so many years enjoyed by His Majesty's Jewish subjects, who would be compelled to work on their Sabbath to save their families from want if this Bill became law. I feel sure that this would not improve us either as Jews or citizens. . . .

d)   My father and mother were both cigarette makers

Source: London Museum of Jewish Life Oral History Transcripts

The following extract, made by the Age Exchange Theatre Company for a projected oral history of the Jewish community of London, is one of a series of interviews recorded at the North East London Jewish Day Centre on 29 October 1986. The speaker recalls the life of his parents who came from Poland to East London around the turn of the century.

My father and mother were both cigarette makers and they worked in the West End. Her father was also a cigarette maker, and they worked in the West End. Markovitch I think the name of the cigarette people were called, and they used to make hand made cigarettes there. And they used to work so hard because to make a living when they came home they had to bring what they called cases – which is the case for the cigarettes – and he said that to make a living they had to make a load at night, to take back in the morning to compensate . . .

Did the children ever help with that?

Well yeah, we used to be more of a nuisance than a help. Then you didn't buy a box of twenty cigarettes. There was a little scale, they used to weigh them and you had to pay by weight, you know. The papers were already stuck round like and they had a long stick and a thing they called 468 paper. They used to put the tobacco under that, push it in and then with a stick they used to push it through. And it used to be more flat than round. And they had special scissors with curved ends.

And on top of that, if you were wealthy enough, you could have your own name on the cigarettes you know. The papers were printed. They can't have earn't lots of money. They used to bring the tobacco home and used to make it and take it back in the morning. You worked in the factory and in the evening they used to make so many to take back to make their money up. Neither of them smoked. And none of my brothers smoke, even today.

But not only that I remember my mother showed me a ticket which she used to go on the horse bus to work – they had horse buses then – and it was like a metal ticket and you pay your ticket to the driver like that and as you got off you were supposed to hand the ticket back but somehow my mother got one back. How she got it I don't know.

Who did the cooking while your mother was doing all that?

She used to do everything. Father wouldn't do anything it was below him. . . .

And another thing about the cigarette making – my father and mother had to follow the jobs around because it wasn't easy to get a job so one time she was in Scotland and one of my brothers was born in Scotland. And then my father, the job was going bad, and he went over to France, but my mother never went across and then gradually when that job was over he came back again. And they came down to London. So they lived in Scotland, when the job was there they had to move. There was quite a community up in Scotland, quite a community. And another thing there was no assistance or anything. You had to do it all yourself you see. They came over here and if they had enough money they'd go on to America. If they didn't have enough money they'd stay here.

e) *I had two mothers you could say – a milliner's daughter*

Source: London Museum of Jewish Life, Oral History Transcripts

Interviewed by the Age Exchange Theatre Company, an aged East Ender recalls the difficulties of her early life. The untimely death of her father left the respondent's Roumanian-born mother with an eleven-month old child to care for. Here she explains how her mother made ends meet.

. . . I had an aunt living with us, one of her sisters. She had the most unhappy marriage too because she had a husband who was a drunk and a gambler. Mind you he was good to her if you know what I mean but she couldn't stand this awful way he used to carry on, you know. In the end she left him and she came to live with my Mother. Oh but she was wonderful . . . I had two mothers you could say. She was the wonderful mother ever.

So you had two mothers. So what did your Father do before he died?

He was a tailor. Yes he was in tailoring. But he had such a short life. And it was ended so quickly. I'll tell you what happened. After my Father died she had to find some means of making a living and she couldn't do it tailoring because that involved so many different people like her. You had to have someone to do one part of a garment and someone to do another. You know what I mean. So she had to find a means of making a living. Well she had the other sister, the older one, they've both gone now, she had a daughter and this daughter had just not long gone in to . . . you know she found a job, earning as a milliner. So she was with my mother, she was really desperate you see. So she said to her sister, "would she come and work for me?" So her sister said "well if she does that she'll have to give up her job won't she, I don't know if she'll want to". Anyway . . . out of pity you could say . . . they persuaded her too. And she used to sit and make hats and my Mother watched her. In those days they used to wear hats with big brims; shawland lace. And they were always wired edges you know. I used to make those hats and picked it up. And she didn't know how to start . . . they lived in this block, a tenement block it was and they had a little flat, not in the same block but in another (part of the building). They used to get this big fat woman coming in – she put hats in the window. They never wore a hat, only when there was a holy day. So they used to come in and she used to say to them, "ooh this is a lovely hat, would you like to see how it looks on me". Of course she looked wonderful in it. And they'd say, "oh yes but it won't look like that on us". At least they had the sense to know that. So anyway that was how she started.

In this tenement block, there were five blocks. One was the one where she had the shop window like . . . a shop and parlour they called it. There was a little parlour beyond the shop with two rooms. No bathroom, nothing. Just two rooms.

. . .

My Aunty Netty used to help my Mother. She worked her way up gradually, got a little bit of money. It was a boom time. People used to say, "ooh you're doing so well in the wholesale". So she thought, "oh you know she'd do anything to try". So that's how we started and do you know what I'll never forget this – because I did it – we used to make up a lot of hats and there was no money for the rent see. So we used to load up . . . we used to make her throw up the bags purposefully for that job . . . big tall bags, stuff the hats in them, and we used to go out in the West End, Oxford St. and side turnings, trying to sell those hats. Sometimes she'd go on her own. And I hated it because when we went on the train everybody looked at us, you know they were so conspicuous, great big bags almost as big as we were. Still we didn't take much notice. You know business is business and she had such poor beginnings you know. She used to go and they'd look over the whole blessed bagful and they said, "Oh I'll take one or two or three", you know. Well anyway she worked her way up, gradually. In the end she employed about six, eight, or sometimes even more. All lived at the back of the shop and she worked her way up. And anyway that's how we went on and I used to sit with the others and after work I used to go out with the girls. Course I had no life of my own so I looked at the employee girls as friends. And they said, "oh they'll take advantage of you, impose upon you". But I didn't care so we used to go for long walks. Do you know it was so lovely we used to take the long walks through the city. We'd walk and walk, especially one girl – Millie – who was a particular friend of mine.

6. Wages in the tailoring trade, 1888

Source: Second Report from the Select Committee of the House of Lords on the Sweating System, Parliamentary Papers, [448], XXI (1888), Appendix H, pp. 584–589

Accurate data on wages in the immigrant trades is hard to come by. The following, compiled by John Burnett, the Labour Correspondent to the Board of Trade, are more reliable than most.

Kind of work	Time or Piece	Men's wages, daily Maximum	Minimum	Average	No. of Cases
		s d	s d	s d	
Presser	time	9 0	2 6	6 5	108
Presser	piece	7 0	4 6	5 6	4
Machinist	time	10 0	2 6	6 0	188
Machinist	piece	10 0	3 4	7 0	10
General tailor	time	10 0	4 0	7 3	23
Baster	time	9 0	3 0	6 2	89
Baster	piece	7 0	3 0	5 5	5
Feller	time	6 0	3 0	4 8	12
Apprentice	time	1 2	4	8	4
Apprentice	time, per week	13 0	5 6	8 6	5
					448

		Women's wages, daily*			
Machinist	time	6 0	1 8	4 0	17
Baster	time	4 6	6	2 9	12
Feller	time	5 0	6	2 7	243
Feller	time, per week	22 0	9 9	14 1	10
Buttonholing	time	6 0	1 8	4 0	12
Buttonholing	piece	6 6	1 6	3 9	94
Less deductions for gimp and materials		1 3	4½	9½	
Apprentices	time	1 6	3	10	14
Apprentices	time, per week	10 0	3 0	6 10	5
					407

---

* Excludes ten cases with board and lodging. In seven of these cases the daily wage ranged from a maximum of 1s. 8d. to a minimum of 1s. 2d. with an average of 1s. 5d.; in the remaining cases, where the women were paid by the week, the maximum received was 10s., the minimum 9s., with an average of 9s. 4d.

V

PROTEST AND POLITICS

The failure of Jewish trades unionism was one of the most striking features of late-Victorian social observation. Numerous, small and sickly, Jewish trade unions had an exceptionally high mortality. Only four or five of the thirty-two unions enumerated in the Halpern survey of 1902 had been in existence six years earlier. Jewish workers in London were particularly resistant to permanent organization. Strike, they would; organize, they wouldn't. They could be brought together by a strike or lockout, but once the object of industrial action had been achieved they seemed to lack the cohesive power necessary to sustain continuous organization. The reasons for this lay in the structure of the workshop trades, the division of labour within them and the character of the product markets they served. A simple comparison of the East End of London with the strength of Jewish labour organization in Leeds, or, better still, with the lower East Side of New York, underscores the variability of the immigrant experience. The Victorians did not see it like this. The dominant explanation relied upon an ethnically-determined concept called 'the Jewish worker'. Shaped by the Old Testament and the Talmud into a perfect money-making machine, and indifferent by experience towards those outwith the faith, immigrant Jews were untiring, unceasing and unstoppable in their relentless ascent through the social scale (docs. 1(a)–1(c)). It was this innate individualism that made the immigrant an impossible trade unionist. The Polish Jew in London thus appeared as the exemplary worker conforming to the precepts of political economy. He – it is a gendered concept – abstains from personal consumption, eschews alcoholic liquor, works every hour that God gives, has an ambition to become an entrepreneur and employer of labour, saves to realise it, and believes in competition. The immigrant Jew, in short, was programmed for profit. The belief in a specific achievement-centred Jewish ethos, the product of race and religion, formed part of the intellectual baggage of the period. The resort to cultural rather than structural explanations to account for the upward mobility of the immigrant was, in fact, common to Jew and Gentile alike (docs. 2(a)–2(b)).

An exception, and not much noticed at the time, came from Rosenbaum, who argued before the Royal Statistical Society that the secret of Jewish success lay in demography rather than culture, and that the superior market position of the immigrant population had more to do with its age structure, sex composition and civil condition than was usually allowed (**doc. 3**).

Labour organizers faced an uphill task. Operating in an overstocked labour market in which outwork and instability were widespread, they found neither the material nor the moral basis for effective trade unions. Isolated and with low bargaining power, workers in the immigrant trades lacked the confidence and the cash to develop permanent organization capable of enforcing agreements in workshops that were periodically replenished with fresh supplies of 'greeners', and diminished by the departure of more experienced hands seeking to set up on their own account. Indeed, masters and workmen, moving backwards and forwards, seemed to change places as readily as children in a game of musical chairs. (**docs. 4(a)–4(c)**) Immigrant workers also looked to the *landsmannschaften* rather than the union for important 'friendly' services and resisted demands for additional dues. (See **doc. III.3**).

Trade union activity tended to pick up during periods of high employment and fall away with the economic downswing. The dramatic strike among the London Jewish tailors of 27 August to 2 October 1889 reveals both the oppressive environment in which the immigrants spent their working lives and their desire for something better (**docs. 5(a)–5(b)**). The strikes of 1889 also showed that poor labour organization was not a peculiarity of the immigrants. Native workers, erroneously presented as model trade unionists, displayed similar weakness.

Jewish socialism provided the immigrant labour movement with much of its energy and enthusiasm. Social Democrats like Philip Kranz, Morris Winchevsky Benjamin Feigenbaum and Moyshe Baranov supplied not only the trade union leadership; they established a Yiddish press, organised lectures, clubs and public meetings, represented the workers and ran their strikes. The Russian revolutionary tradition in which many had been reared also explains the appeal and persistence of anarchism among the immigrant intelligentsia. The movement they created was internationalist in outlook and secular in tone with a deep commitment to science and progress. By contrast, the immigrant masses to whom they appealed, were attached to their religion and their rabbis and were particularist rather than internationalist. Jewish workers, even when unobservant, had no desire to discredit Judaism or the institutions that depended upon it. Its libertarian life-style, Yom Kippur balls and the presentation of the ancestral faith as outmoded, backward and harmful were deeply offensive and made it easy for opponents to confuse socialism with conversionism (**docs. 6(a)–6(c)**).

What was the role of Jewish women in all of this? Did they occupy a more prominent position than their sisters in the national labour movement? We do not know. At present immigrant Jewish women remain hidden from history. They were certainly noticed in their own day. The female members of the Jewish cap makers' union, held at the 'Duke of Clarence', in Commercial Road, for example, made an impression on Booth's research assistant who recorded them in his notebook. In the tailors' strike of May 1890 masters and workers both tried to mobilise the women on their behalf, and in 1906 the refusal of the immigrant housewives to buy bread except that stamped with the union label was critical to the successful outcome of the strike organized by the Jewish Bakers' Union. Jewish women were also particularly active in anarchist politics. Millie Sabel, 'Red' Rose Robins and Milly Witkop were all closely involved with Rudolf Rocker and his circle (**doc. 7**). The *Arbeiter Fraint* group owed much to their contribution. Jewish immigrant women, then, were not passive observers. Nor were their native sisters whose militant campaigning for the right to vote upset the service of the synagogue on more than one occasion (**doc. 8**). The links between immigrant and native women require extended study, as do most aspects of the experience of Jewish women.

1. The Jewish worker

a) The secret of Jewish success, 1889

Source: Beatrice Potter, 'The Jewish Community' in Charles Booth, *Life and Labour of the People in London*, First Series, Poverty (1889), III, pp. 180–92

Between 1886 and 1889 Beatrice Potter (1858–1943) undertook a number of carefully conducted studies into the Jewish community for the Booth survey of life and labour in London. The coverage, which was both wide and deep, embraced the customs, beliefs and institutions of the minority and a close scrutiny of its principal source of employment. Her ethnically-determined concept of the Jewish worker, presented below, was influential and enduring.

. . . Alone among the great nations of Europe, Russia has resolutely refused political and industrial freedom to her Jewish subjects. Under the Russian Government oppression and restriction have assumed every conceivable form. . . .

. . . Robbed, outraged, in fear of death and physical torture, the chosen people have swarmed across the Russian frontier, bearing with them, not borrowed "jewels of silver, and jewels of gold, and raiment," but a capacity for the silent evasion of the law, a faculty for secretive and illicit dealing, and mingled feelings of contempt and fear for the Christians amongst whom they have dwelt and under whose government they have lived for successive generations.

These have been the outward circumstances forming the Polish or Russian Jew. The inner life of the small Hebrew communities bound together by common suffering and mutual helpfulness has developed other qualities, but has also tended in its own way to destroy all friendly and honourable intercourse with surrounding peoples. Social isolation has perfected home life; persecution has intensified religious fervour, an existence of unremitting toil, and a rigid observance of the moral precepts and sanitary and dietary regulations of the Jewish religion have favoured the growth of sobriety, personal purity, and a consequent power of physical endurance. But living among an half-civilized people, and carefully preserved by the Government from the advantages of secular instruction, the Polish and Russian Jews have centred their thoughts and feelings in the literature of their race – in the Old Testament, with its magnificent promise of universal dominion; in the Talmud, with its minute instructions as to the means of gaining it. The child, on its mother's lap, lisps passages from the Talmud; the old man, tottering to the grave, is still searching for the secret of life in "that stupendous labyrinth of fact, thought and fancy." For in those ten volumes of Talmudical lore the orthodox Polish Jew finds not only a store-house of information and a training-ground for his intellectual and emotional faculties, but the key to all the varied perplexities and manifold troubles of his daily existence. To quote the words of Deutsch, the Talmud, besides comprising the poetry and the science of the people, is "emphatically a *Corpus juris*: an encyclopædia of law, civil and penal, ecclesiastical and international, human and divine." Beyond this law the pious Israelite recognizes no obligations; the laws and customs of the Christians are so many regulations to be obeyed, evaded, set at naught, or used according to the possibilities and expediencies of the hour.

In these facts of past training we see an explanation of the present mental and physical qualities of the majority of East End Jews. The Polish or Russian Jew represents to some extent the concentrated essence of Jewish virtue and Jewish vice; for he has, in his individual experience, epitomized the history of his race in the Christian world. . . .

. . .

They are set down in an already over-stocked and demoralised labour market; they are surrounded by the drunkenness, immorality, and gambling of the East-End streets; they are, in fact, placed in the midst of the very refuse of our civilization, and yet (to quote from a former chapter), whether they become bootmakers, tailors, cabinet-makers, glaziers, or dealers, the Jewish inhabitants of East London rise in the social scale; "as a mass they shift upwards, leaving to the new-comers from foreign lands and to the small section of habitual gamblers the worst-paid work, the most dilapidated workshops, and the dirtiest lodgings." But this is not all. Originally engaged in the most unskilled branch of the lowest section of each trade, Jewish mechanics (whether we regard them individually or as a class) slowly but surely invade the higher provinces of production, bringing in their train a system of employment and a method of dealing with masters, men, and fellow-workers which arouses the antagonism of English workmen. The East End Jewish problem therefore resolves itself into two central questions:– (1) What are the reasons of the Jews' success? (2) Why is that success resented by that part of the Christian community with whom the Jew comes in daily contact? I venture to end this chapter with a few suggestions touching this double-faced enigma of Jewish life.

First we must realize (in comparing the Polish Jew with the English labourer) that the poorest Jew has inherited through the medium of his religion a trained intellect. For within the Judaic Theocracy there are no sharp lines dividing the people into distinct classes with definite economic characteristics such as exist in most Christian nations: viz. a leisure class of landowners, a capitalist class of brain-workers, and a mass of labouring people who up to late years have been considered a lower order, fit only for manual work.

The children of Israel are a nation of priests. Each male child, rich or poor, is a student of the literature of his race. In his earliest childhood he is taught by picturesque rites and ceremonies the history, the laws, and the poetry of his people; in boyhood he masters the long passages in an ancient tongue; and in the more pious and rigid communities of Russian Poland the full-grown man spends his leisure in striving to interpret the subtle reasoning and strange fantasies of that great classic of the Hebrew, the Talmud. I do not wish to imply that the bigotted Jew is a "cultured" being, if we mean by culture a wide experience of the thoughts and feelings of other times and other races. Far from it. The intellectual vision and the emotional sympathies of the great majority of Polish Jews are narrowed down to the past history and present prospects of their own race. But the mechanical faculties of the intellect – memory, the power of sustained reasoning, and the capacity for elaborate calculation have been persistently cultivated (in orthodox communities) among all classes, and there has resulted a striking equality, and a high though narrow level of intellectual training.

This oneness of type and uniformity of chances, originating in the influence of a unique religion, have been strengthened and maintained by the industrial and political disabilities under which the Jews have laboured through the greater part of the Christian era, and which still exist in Russian Poland. The brutal persecution of the Middle Ages weeded out the inapt and incompetent. Injustice and social isolation, pressing on poor and rich alike, sharpened and narrowed the intellect of Israel, regarded as a whole, to an instrument for grasping by mental agility the good things withheld from them by the brute force of the Christian peoples.

In the Jewish inhabitants of East London we see therefore a race of brain-workers competing with a class of manual labourers. The Polish Jew regards manual work[1] as the first rung of the social ladder, to be superseded or supplanted on the first opportunity by the estimates of the profit maker, the transactions of the dealer, or the calculations of the

---

[1] It is a mistake to suppose that the Jew is physically unfit for manual work. On the contrary, he is better fitted than the Anglo-Saxon for those trades which require quickness of perception rather than artistic skill, and he will compete successfully with the Englishman in forms of manual labour needing physical endurance, and not actual strength of muscle. Hence the Jew's success in the machine-made coat and Boot and Shoe Trades.

money lender; and he is only tempted from a life of continual acquisition by that vice of the intellect, gambling.

Besides the possession of a trained intellect, admirably adapted to commerce and finance, there is another, and I am inclined to think a more important factor in the Jew's success. From birth upwards, the pious Israelite (male and female) is subjected to a moral and physical regimen, which, while it favours the full development of the bodily organs, protects them from abuse and disease, and stimulates the growth of physical self-control and mental endurance.[2] For the rites and regulations of the Mosaic law and the more detailed instructions of tradition are in no way similar to the ascetic exercises of the Christian or Buddhist saint seeking spiritual exaltation through the mortification or annihilation of physical instinct. On the contrary, the religious ordinances and sanitary laws of the Jewish religion accentuate the physical aspect of life; they are (as M. Rénan has observed) not a preparation for another world, but a course of training adapted to prolong the life of the individual and to multiply the number of his descendants.

Moreover, the moral precepts of Judaism are centred in the perfection of family life, in obedience towards parents, in self-devotion for children, in the chastity of the girl, in the support and protection of the wife. The poorest Jew cherishes as sacred the maternity of the women, and seldom degrades her to the position of a worker upon whose exertions he depends for subsistence. Thus Jewish morality, instead of diverting feeling from the service of the body, combines with physical training to develop exclusively that side of man's emotional nature which is inextricably interwoven with the healthful and pleasurable exercise of physical instinct. Hence in the rigidly conforming Jew we have a being at once moral and sensual; a creature endowed with the power of physical endurance, but gifted with a highly-trained and well-regulated appetite for sensuous enjoyment. And with the emotions directed into the well-regulated channels of domestic feeling, the mind remains passionless. Anger, pride, and self-consciousness, with their counterparts of indignation, personal dignity, and sensitiveness, play a small part in the character of the Polish Jew. He suffers oppression and bears ridicule with imperturbable good humour; in the face of insult and abuse he remains silent. For why resent when your object is to overcome? Why bluster and fight when you may manipulate or control in secret?

The result is twofold. As an individual competitor the Polish Jew is fettered by no definite standard of life; it rises and falls with his opportunities; he is not depressed by penury, and he is not demoralized by gain. As a citizen of our many-sided metropolis he is unmoved by

---

[2] From a psychological as well as from an ethical point of view, a detailed study of the sanitary observances of the Jewish religion (more especially those relative to sexual functions) would be extremely interesting. The musical talent which distinguishes the Hebrew race has been ascribed by psychologists to the effect of these observances on successive generations.

those gusts of passion which lead to drunkenness and crime; whilst on the other hand he pursues the main purposes of personal existence, undistracted by the humours, illusions, and aspirations arising from the unsatisfied emotions of our more complicated and less disciplined natures. Is it surprising, therefore, that in this nineteenth century, with its ideal of physical health, intellectual acquisition, and material prosperity, the chosen people, with three thousand years of training, should in some instances realize the promise made by Moses to their forefathers: "Thou shalt drive out nations mightier than thyself, and thou shalt take their land as an inheritance"?

Such, I imagine, are the chief causes of the Jew's success. We need not seek far for the origin of the antagonistic feelings with which the Gentile inhabitants of East London regard Jewish labour and Jewish trade. For the reader will have already perceived that the immigrant Jew, though possessed of many first-class virtues, is deficient in that highest and latest development of human sentiment – social morality.

I do not wish to imply by this that East End Jews resist the laws and defy the conventions of social and commercial life. On the contrary, no one will deny that the children of Israel are the most law-abiding inhabitants of East London. They keep the peace, they pay their debts, and they abide by their contracts; practices in which they are undoubtedly superior to the English and Irish casual labourers among whom they dwell. For the Jew is quick to perceive that "law and order" and the "sanctity of contract" are the *sine qua non* of a full and free competition in the open market. And it is by competition, and by competition alone, that the Jew seeks success. But in the case of the foreign Jews, it is a competition unrestricted by the personal dignity of a definite standard of life, and unchecked by the social feelings of class loyalty and trade integrity. The small manufacturer injures the trade through which he rises to the rank of a capitalist by bad and dishonest production. The petty dealer or small money lender, imbued with the economic precept of buying in the cheapest and selling in the dearest market, suits his wares and his terms to the weakness, the ignorance, and the vice of his customers; the mechanic, indifferent to the interests of the class to which he temporarily belongs, and intent only on becoming a small master, acknowledges no limit to the process of underbidding fellow-workers, except the exhaustion of his own strength. In short, the foreign Jew totally ignores all social obligations other than keeping the law of the land, the maintenance of his own family, and the charitable relief of co-religionists.

Thus the immigrant Jew, fresh from the sorrowful experiences typical of the history of his race, seems to justify by his existence those strange assumptions which figured for *man* in the political economy of Ricardo – an Always Enlightened Selfishness, seeking employment or profit with an absolute mobility of body and mind, without pride, without preference, without interests outside the struggle for the existence and welfare of the individual and the family. We see these assumptions verified in the Jewish inhabitants of Whitechapel; and in the Jewish East End trades we may

watch the prophetic deduction of the Hebrew economist actually fulfilled
– in a perpetually recurring bare subsistence wage for the great majority
of manual workers.

b)   From greener to guv'nor, 1888

Source: Beatrice Potter, 'East London Labour', *The Nineteenth Century*, XXIV
(1888), pp. 176–77

Jewish social mobility is explained here not in relation to the environment but as a
function of an achievement-centred ethos, the product of race and religion.

. . . two circumstances tend to an indefinite multiplication of small
masters in the Jewish coat trade, competing vigorously with each other,
not only for the work of the shops, but for the services of the most skilled
hands: the ease with which a man becomes a master, coupled with the
strongest impelling motive of the Jewish race – the love of *profit* as
distinct from other forms of money-earning. The ease with which a man
may become a master is proverbial at the East End. His living-room
becomes his workshop, his landlord or his butcher his security; round the
corner he finds a brother Israelite whose trade is to supply pattern
garments to take as samples of work to the wholesale house; with a small
deposit he secures on the hire system both sewing machines and presser's
table. Altogether it is estimated that with 1*l*. in his pocket any man may
rise to the dignity of a sweater. At first the new master will live on 'green'
labour, will, with the help of his wife or some other relative, do all the
skilled work that is needed. Presently, if the quantity of his work
increases, or if the quality improves, he will engage a machinist, then a
presser. His earnings are scanty, probably less than those of either of the
skilled hands to whom he pays wages, and he works all hours of the day
and night. But the chances of the trade are open to him; with
indefatigable energy and with a certain measure of organising power he
may press forward into the ranks of the large employers, and if he be
successful, day by day, year by year, his profit increases and his labour
decreases relatively to the wage and the labour of his hands. It is this
passion for the chances of a successful 'deal' which tempts the East End
Jew into his only vice – gambling. For the machinist may be passing his
slack time in a gambling den, while the master of the workshop slaves day
and night for profit, the presser buys and renovates old clothes for the
Petticoat Lane market, and the greener hoards his hard-earned pence to
buy cheap the coveted watch of the unemployed Gentile. And it is rare
for an East End Jewish worker to be content with his nominal profession:
hours and days of enforced idleness, like the unspent farthings of the
scanty income, are turned to profit, unless both alike be dedicated to that
vice characteristic of the profit-seeker – gambling. The out-o'-work Jews

are the dealers and financiers of the East End. All alike try to supplement the income made in actual labour by the turnover of money by the wise use of the talent entrusted to their care. It is this dominant race impulse that has peopled our Stock Exchange with Israelites; it is the same instinct that has made the Rothschilds the leaders of European finance and the bankers of emperors and kings.

At the East End this characteristic of the Jewish race has a two-fold tendency; to raise the workers as a mass of individuals, and to depress the productive industry through which they rise. Contractors and workers alike ascend in the social scale; taken as a mass they shift upwards, leaving to the new-comer from foreign lands the worst paid work, the most dilapidated workshop, and the dirtiest lodgings. For the Jewish community at the East End is like a reservoir fed from beneath: the bottommost layer of excessive poverty is always present, but the constant influx of destitute foreigners is compensated by a continual overflow of settlers and natives into more well-to-do districts and into richer classes. Hence a Jew may begin in Backchurch Lane, but he may end in Bayswater. On the other hand, the prices at which work is taken are constantly reduced by a race of workers who have neither the desire nor the capacity for labour or trade combination, and who are endowed with a standard of life that admits of an almost indefinite amount of work in the worst possible conditions.

c) The Jew as workman, 1891

Source: David F. Schloss, 'The Jew as a Workman', *The Nineteenth Century*, XXIX (1891), pp. 99–108

David F. Schloss (1850–1912) was a senior civil servant in the Board of Trade, Director of the Census of Production of 1907–08, a member of the Jewish Board of Guardians and an important contributor to Charles Booth's *Life and Labour of the People in London*. Although critical of Beatrice Potter's analysis, Schloss's refutation tends to substitute one variety of culturalist explanation for another.

The most serious allegation made against the Jewish workman is his supposed willingness to work at a lower wage and for longer hours than the Gentile. The Jew who is working at fourpence per hour or less will almost invariably be found to be of foreign birth. Possessing in many cases, when he lands on our shores, little or no skill in any form of handicraft, he is, in order to learn a trade, forced to work, at first for his keep, and then for a few shillings a week. By-and-by his earnings increase, until they reach the level of those of our English casual labourers at the docks, or our chain- and nail makers, of our Sheffield knife-blade-grinders, and so on. Very often the average wages received by the Jew of this type, taking one week with another, will, even when he has been here twenty years, amount to only fifteen shillings a week. The reason is not far to seek. In trades so greatly affected by seasonal variations and by spasmodic pressure of orders as are those in which most of these men are engaged, an income sufficient to support a family could not be earned by so incompetent a worker, except by working, when the trade is busy, for from fourteen to eighteen hours or even more out of twenty-four. . . .

. . .

While I am inclined to admit that the Jewish workman is, in many cases, less unwilling to work long hours than his Gentile neighbours, the idea that the Jews are willing to work for an inadequate remuneration appears to me totally without foundation. Of course, the very unskilled workman, be he Jew or Gentile, is often, unfortunately, obliged to take whatever wages he can get, however low. But there are plenty of Jewish working men who possess a high degree of skill, and who insist upon receiving a rate of pay as high as that of the Gentile workers engaged in the same industry. It is all very well to sneer at the Jewish tailor because he has no skill with his needle, and cannot 'make a coat right out.' But these Jews are, as I heard a Gentile manufacturer call them, 'true artists with the machine,' and the pressers work marvels with the iron. As to the rate of remuneration prevalent in the Jewish workshops, no one acquainted with the facts will deny that the best class of Jewish workmen can earn quite as good money as the Gentile tailors in receipt of the full wages fixed by the 'log' of the Amalgamated Society. Indeed, it is in a large measure to the recognition of this fact that what little ill-feeling exists among our working classes in regard to the competition of Jewish labour is due. . . .

The chief objection to their Jewish fellow-workmen that has hitherto been taken by the leaders of the English industrial classes is the alleged incapacity of the Jews for trade combination. From this reproach, however, the Jews have of late years done much to redeem themselves. Of the development of trade-unionism among the Jewish tailors, who both in Leeds, in Manchester, and in London have struck for, and have obtained, not unimportant concessions, there is no need to speak; but the story of the organisation of the Jews in the metropolitan boot trade is, in some respects, so remarkable as to demand a brief exposition. The manner in which the work has been given out by the manufacturers to 'middlemen,' or 'sweaters,' who themselves employed subordinate workmen, is well known. Now, the absolutely unique feature of the recent trade-union movement among the Jews is that, for some three years past, the unions both of the sweaters and of the sweatees have been engaged in a combination having for its aim the abolition of the sweating system. The middlemen have conspired to effect the extinction of the middleman. In all the history of labour I know of no parallel to this singular fact. Why were these 'sweating-masters' so anxious to abandon their relatively lucrative position as small employers, and to relapse into the ranks of ordinary workmen? . . .

A . . . reason given to me for the action of the sweating-masters was their desire to avoid the stigma with which they found themselves branded by the public, by whom they were held up to scorn as the cause of that deplorable oppression of the workers upon which the sweating inquiry cast so lurid a light. . . . When, in April last, the great boot strike, in which some 10,000 men took part, broke out in East London, one of these sub-contractors went to the manufacturer by whom he was employed (also a Jew), and begged him to yield to the demand of the unions for the abolition of the sweating system. 'I am convinced, sir,' said this sweating-master to his employer, 'that the maintenance of the sweating system is *Chillul Hashem* – a disgrace to the ineffable name of the God of Israel. Now, I am determined that this disgrace shall no longer rest on my head: on yours be it, if our attempt to put down this system shall fail.' The strike succeeded; the manufacturers were forced to agree to provide workshops of their own, in which all the men should be in their own direct employment. It is beyond question that one factor, which largely contributed to secure this victory, was the good faith and energy of the Jewish sub-contractors.

Of the part played in this strike by the trade union of the 'sweatees' it remains to speak. From the first, in all the preliminary skirmishes, the Jewish journeymen had shown the most marvellous constancy; and when the final struggle began in earnest, the unsavoury purlieus of Spitalfields and Bethnal Green witnessed a sight strange indeed. At the rendezvous in Brick Lane there gathered together the most curious set of human beings that it has ever been my fortune to look upon – sallow, blear-eyed, stunted forms, clad in all manner of quaint varieties of the most piteous shabbiness. At mid-day these poor wretches fell in; their calico banners were proudly unfurled; their band struck up; and some six hundred members of the Jewish Journeymen's Union started on their march through the slums. Singly, in twos, and in threes – like the rats of Hamelin – from all sorts of cellars, garrets, and hutches, the finishers still at work came forth, and joined the ranks amid the cheers of their comrades, until, after a few days, no less than a thousand was the tale of the insurgents. The 100*l.* which, with how great self-denial may be imagined, the members of this trade-union had scraped together out of their most meagre earnings was soon spent, the more so, since in its distribution they generously invited the non-unionist workmen to participate. The public was appealed to for funds with very trifling success. But the Jewish tradesmen supplied food on credit to the value of 200*l.* Towards the end of the strike, indeed, everything – cash and credit alike – was exhausted. Still, these Jews fought on with the courage of the Maccabees; fought on, and at last won. Possessing some little personal acquaintance with strikers and strikes in many trades, I declare without hesitation that a better stand was never made by any body of workmen than by these unjustly despised scions of the Jewish race.

. . .

. . . 'He, who does not teach his son a trade, virtually teaches him to steal,' says the Talmud; and the first and last thought of the Jew is, how to find for his son a suitable occupation; if possible, an occupation far more advantageous than his own. The consequence is that . . . in the lowest forms of Jewish industry it is comparatively rare to find any but foreign-born workmen. There are, of course, many English-bred Jews in the tailoring trade; but these will usually be found to be men who learned their trade thoroughly in early youth, and are now skilled workmen, earning a day-wage of from seven to ten shillings. As to the boot-finishers, I remember asking the members of the Strike Committee of the Jewish journeymen if any one of them was born in this country: they were all foreigners. The son of their chairman is as sturdy a little Englishman as can be found between the Land's End and John o'Groat's. He did well at the Chicksand Street Board School, and says he intends to enter the Civil Service. The secretary of this trade-union has to support a wife and seven children on sixteen shillings a week; his eldest boy, educated at the excellent Jews' Free School in Bell Lane, is a clerk in a commercial house. I know of a poor fellow who earned a scanty living by attending prayers in Jewish families – it is usual to make up the number of the congregation to ten by employing very needy Israelites in this manner; this *Minyan-man* had four sons, of whom one took his B.A. degree, and is a master at one of the most important Jewish schools in the metropolis, while his brothers occupy well-remunerated positions in the City. Instances almost without number could be given of similar circumstances, proving the extraordinary faculty, which the Jewish race possesses, of emerging scatheless and with renewed vigour from the most terrible adversity. Here, indeed, lies the true *cachet* of the Jewish nature. . . .

2.   The Jew as trade unionist

a)   An inveterate individualist, 1900

Source: C. Russell and H.S. Lewis, *The Jew in London, A Study of Racial Character and Present-day Conditions* (1900), pp. 80–85

The weakness of Jewish trades unionism relied in no small part upon a false comparison with a native trade union movement modelled upon the cotton workers and miners. Contemporaries too easily forgot that in London strong trade unions were exceptional as Charles Russell's analysis for the Toynbee Hall Inquiry shows.

It must be remembered that trade-unionism is a new thing to the Polish Jew; and it is natural that he should hold aloof from it until he has been educated into some form of sympathy with English ideas upon the subject. And from the number of Jewish unions which have sprung into existence in the last few years, it is evident that English ideas are not wholly thrown away upon him. In the *Jewish Year Book* there is published a list of fifteen Jewish unions in London. Those in the mantlemaking, cabinetmaking, and cigar and cigarette-making trades are in a fairly flourishing condition. None of the others, however, seem to be of much account; and the number of organisations in itself is in part a sign of weakness. The presence of rival unions in the same trade indicates a disunited state; and possibly points to a radical incapacity for organisation on a large scale. Thus in the cabinet trade only half of the Jewish unionists belong to the Hebrew branch of the Alliance Cabinet-makers' Association, which is the principal organisation in the trade and has branches all over the kingdom; the other half were unwilling to submit to the control of a central executive and founded an 'Independent' union of their own. Similarly in the tailoring trade there are only about forty members of the Hebrew branch of the Amalgamated Society of Tailors,* and the Jewish 'London Tailors', Machinists' and Pressers' Union,' in which the 'Independent' and 'International' unions were merged has quite recently again divided its ranks. That the state of Jewish unions is generally unstable is an inference which is unmistakably forced upon anyone who has tried to gather information by visiting their secretaries or going the round of their meeting places, . . . Even out of the list given in the *Jewish Year Book* (published in August 1898), three had disappeared before November 1898, or were at least untraceable, one had had a 'split' and one was reduced in membership to the secretary and treasurer. The truth appears to be that the foreign Jew is easily roused to enthusiasm upon the subject, but is at once too quarrelsome and too impatient for results to be a 'good unionist.' He does not like paying so many pence a week without any prospect of a prompt or substantial return; and he seems to have a shrewd distrust both of fellow-unionists and officials. Each is too bent on playing for his own hand, and efforts at organisation are not backed by any real feeling of solidarity. As, however, the foreigner becomes thoroughly Anglicised, he seems generally to grow into sympathy with English ideas, and is able to shake off this reproach. It must also be remembered that the Jew has a genius for individual bargain-driving which goes far to counterbalance the lowering effect which his incapacity for organisation might have upon the rate of wages. Nor would it be quite fair to say that this cuts both ways when the employers are Jewish; since it means that master and men can already deal with one another upon tolerably even terms – a condition which English workmen can only assure by combination.

---

* This branch, by the way, is not included in the *Jewish Year Book*'s list.

b)   Landsmann v proletarian, 1900

Source: C. Russell and H.S. Lewis, *The Jew in London, A Study in Racial Character and Present-day Conditions* (1900), pp. 191–95

The weakness of Jewish trade unionism in London was bound up with the absence of factory production and instability of employment. The space which class-based forms of industrial and political organization might have occupied were in consequence taken by the *landsmannschaften* and by the claims of family and kin. On the whole, though, contemporary observers, even when sympathetic, tended to present the weakness of trades unionism among immigrants as a Jewish personality defect and as a cause rather than a consequence of the workshop trades in which it was formed.

The masterly picture, drawn by Mr Russell, of the Jew as workman may be accepted as substantially correct. Undoubtedly he is industrious, sober and, in a sense, reliable; but, on the other hand, an inveterate individualist, whose ambition is usually for himself rather than for his class. He desires almost invariably to become ultimately a small master, a dealer or a shop-keeper; to live, in short, on profits rather than on wages. This fact diminishes his powers of combination, and few permanent successes can be recorded in the history of Trade Unionism amongst the foreign Jews resident in England. The prevalence of the 'sweating system' in such specifically Jewish trades as tailoring, bootmaking, cabinetmaking, arises largely from these peculiarities of character, although trade conditions have, of course, a most important influence on methods of production. I only propose to consider how far social life and the 'sweating system' are mutually interdependent.

One important aspect of the case must not be forgotten. In the small workshop there is practically no class distinction between master and man. They are usually also united by a common religion and by numerous associations, which tend to humanise even business relations. It will often be found that the master, in selecting his hands, gives a preference to his 'landsmann' who hailed originally from the same town in Poland. This will not always prevent the master from imposing hard or even unfair terms, but it remains true that, in the small workshop, there usually exist far more kindliness and good feeling than in the large factory. Journeymen out of work often receive much assistance from their former employers, and many small acts of kindness, which do so much to sweeten human relations, are some set-off to the criticisms which can be justly levelled against the 'sweating system.'

There is another special peculiarity of the foreign Jew which has tended to create and to perpetuate this method of production. Whilst possessing undoubted industry and powers of endurance, he is with difficulty disciplined into the orderly regularity and steady methods which are essential to the large factory. The long hours for which tailors and bootmakers work are not quite so exhausting as they seem. The pressure is by no means equal. At certain times it is undoubtedly very intense – Thursday evening, for example, often brings with it a great press of work. But there are intervals also in which very little is done; when cigarettes are smoked and topics are discussed in the workshop which would surprise those who have not been initiated into the vigorous intellectuality that often lurks behind the unpromising exterior of the Polish Jew. It might be much better for his health to work steadily for ten hours a day in a factory, but not only are his powers as an industrial machine undoubtedly greater under the present system, but he finds life fuller and richer in interest. It must be noted also that the difficulties of Sabbath observance are lessened for those who work for small masters.

3. The Jewish worker: a demographic perspective, 1905

Source: S. Rosenbaum, 'A Contribution to the Study of the Vital and other Statistics of the Jews in the United Kingdom', *Journal of the Royal Statistical Society*, LXVIII (1905), pp. 535–36

Never mind all the talk about the immigrant's defective sense of social morality or his innate profit-making propensities, said S. Rosenbaum, the pioneering Jewish demographer. In the sex composition and age structure of the immigrant community lay the true source of Jewish industrial competitiveness.

. . . The wide divergencies between the general and Jewish population are undoubtedly due to the fact that the Jewish community is not a settled one, subject only or mainly to growth by natural increase (*i.e.*, by excess of births over deaths). It is constantly and continuously being fed by immigration from abroad, and especially from the countries in Eastern Europe (Russia, Russian Poland, and Roumania). These immigrants consist mainly of adults, a large excess being males. They include a small proportion of children and of old people. This may be seen from an examination of the census figures for foreigners in London in 1901.

Proportion of Foreigners and Russians in London at Three Groups of Ages, and Comparison with Age-Distribution for England and Wales (Census 1901).

	Foreigners		Russians*		England and Wales	
	Males	Females	Males	Females	Males	Females
0–	82	121	135	158	335	314
15–	744	702	745	713	477	483
45–	174	177	120	129	188	203
	1,000	1,000	1,000	1,000	1,,000	1,000

* Including Russian Poles.

The Russian population, which may be regarded as resembling most closely the foreign section of the Jewish community, contains, according to the last census, 745 males and 713 females at ages 15 to 45, per 1,000 of all ages. The remainder is nearly equally divided between those under 15 and those at and over 45. The number of children under 15 is appreciably larger, and the number of old people over 45 is correspondingly smaller than for foreigners generally. Indeed, if Russians and Russian Poles are excluded, the remaining foreigners are found to contain only 53 males and 89 females under 15 per 1,000 at all ages. This fact has some connection with the transitory character of the residence of the alien population other than those born in Russia, Russian Poland, Galicia, &c. The proportions at ages 45 and upwards are much larger – 204 for males and 218 for females. The proportion at the middle-group of ages work out to 743 for the males and 693 for the females respectively. Compare these figures with those for England and Wales, where, roughly, one-third of the population is under 15 and one-half between the ages of 15 and 45. Incidentally it may be remarked that these figures suggest an explanation for the abnormally low rates at which the foreigner, and especially the newly arrived Jew, is willing to work. His dependents are considerably fewer, and his expenses necessarily smaller. The absence of any large number of dependents makes it also less frequently necessary for the wife to go out to work to supplement her husband's income. It would be difficult to say how much of the traditional restraint exercised by Jewish husbands in this respect is accounted for by the absence of this important economic factor. Among the Russian foreigners the males between 15 and 45 constitute nearly 40 per cent. of the total Russian-born population, male and female. This compares with the proportion of 24 per cent. among the general population in England and Wales. Thus whereas the Russian on arrival here has to provide for an average of 1½ mouths besides his own, the native has to provide for an average addition of 3⅙ mouths. Even when allowance is made for the difference in age and the consequent needs of the average dependent, and also for the number of dependent parents, wives and children left behind, who have to be more or less provided for, the handicap is considerably in favour of the foreigner. It is a potent factor in mitigating the pressure of the earlier years of his sojourn here, and increasing his competitive power in the labour market.

4. Interviews with trade unionists

a) *Secretary of the Hebrew Cabinet Makers' Association, 1888*

Source: Charles Booth Collection, British Library of Political and Economic Science, Booth Notebooks B81, fo. 41, Notes of Interview with the Secretary, 14 March 1888

The need for organisation among immigrant workers, the Booth Inquiry noted, was made more pressing by the want of English.

The Society had only been in existence about 12 months. It had about 50 members of whom 40 were free for benefit. The subscription is 4d. per week. The benefits were 18/- a week for sick pay and 10/- a week when out of work. A man when out of work would have to sign the register daily. If a man is out of work as a result of neglect or through any fault of his own, he would not be paid. The only expenses the Society had to meet besides payments to members was an allowance of £3.00 per annum to the Secretary for all expenses, etc.

The Society was formed to protect the men many of whom were unable to speak the English language and consequently were imposed on by the masters. Now, when there was a dispute between the masters and the men, the Secretary would undertake to look after the men's interest. Had had two cases of this sort.

The Society was not strong enough to influence the trade yet and was disliked by the masters. Men had been discharged for belonging to the Society.

b) *Secretary of the Jewish Tailors' Trade Society, 1889*

Source: Minutes of Evidence taken before the Select Committee of the House of Lords on the Sweating System Parliamentary Papers [331], XIV (1889), qq. 30184–386

James Sweeney, the Leeds labour leader, was a non-Jewish bootmaker by trade and the President of the Boot and Shoe Operatives. A committed socialist, he became involved with the organisation of the garment industry and the unpaid Secretary of the Jewish Tailors' Trade Society. He lead the local tailors' strike of 1885 and continued to act as an important intermediary between the Jewish unions and the Leeds Trades Council.

30189.   When was that society formed?
It has been formed on several occasions; but the one that I formed will be as far back as seven years ago, between seven and eight.

30190.   And that is lasting still, is it?
No, it lasted up to the last dispute, and I am sorry to say they were compelled to close it.

30191.   By "the last dispute" you mean the strike last year?
Yes.

30192.   And your society has broken up since then?
Yes.

30193.   Altogether?
Altogether, with the exception that a week or two ago it has been re-organised.

30194.   How do you account for its breaking up?
By the manner in which the middlemen used their force against the workpeople that belonged to those branches in connection with the society. They would not engage a society man under any circumstances if they could help it. When they found a society man they used all force and pressure to remove him from such shops as they had, and under no circumstances could we get men to join or stick to their various branches on account of expecting to be turned out of the shops which they were getting a living from.

30195.   Do you mean before the strike or after the strike?
After the strike. Before we had such a thing as a strike, we were 1,000 strong; eight months after we had about 150; about a month or six weeks ago we diminished down to two members, that was the chairman and one of the committee-men of a branch; and under no reasonable persuasion would they take notice of joining, on account of the masters, and the way in which the middlemen used to manage the men and threaten what they would do if they belonged to the branches.

. . .

30202.   How long have you been in Leeds?
I may say for about 23 years.

30203.   I suppose you know nothing about the tailoring trade; I need not ask you any questions as to that?
Well, I have as much experience and more than some brought up in it.

30204.   How so?
Through investigating certain branches of it years back; and I have taken great interest in it since, as far as the various branches are concerned, and the various systems we have for getting those ready-made clothes up to be sent back direct to the warehouse. I have taken a great interest in this, and I have pointed out certain grievances

connected with it, and have drawn the attention of the warehouse firms more than once to the system which is carried on by the middlemen, the tyranny and blasphemy in the shops which they are over, with no respect for females any more than males, no respect for the smallest child that is under their control, no more than for the largest workman; and we have not only spoken of it in the branches, but we have had it mentioned in the Press.

30205.   What was the object of the strike last year?
The object of the strike was to try and get less hours, and to make the middleman have better arrangements in his shop, and more respect for those that work under them.

30206.   How is the ready-made clothing trade carried on?
Well, it is carried on to a great extent by a system of nothing but bribery, and it is not practical men that get this work from the warehouses.

30207.   First of all there are large warehouses?
First of all there are large warehouses, such as Messrs. Barran and Sons, a Member of the present House of Commons. He is one of the leading ones that employ people in that way.

30208.   And there are several large warehouses.
Yes.

30209.   How do they get the work done?
By cutting them out and putting them together in large bundles, and giving them out to the middleman, and letting the middleman take them home to his large workshops and so on; and he, in return, gives them out to a fitter-up; from the fitter-up he hands them to the machiner; from the machiner, in some particular branches, it goes to the under presser; some other parts of the garment go to the tailor, what they call a tailor, that is, a baster out, and a baster under him; then they go back again to the machiner, what they call a piecerup; then there is the lining maker that pieces linings before they are put into a garment, to be stitched together and made up ready to be sent to the presser. Then the presser presses the garments off, and that is calling pressing-off, and they have to go through the finishers, feller hands and button-hole hands, and then they come to, what they term, a brusher off; the garments then being all ready for going to the warehouse.

30210.   You said that he sends it to the machinists, and sends it to these different people; is not all the work carried on in the one shop?
Yes.

30211.   They are all different branches, and they have all a certain amount of work to do?
One does not make a garment through; one makes a certain part of it; there are certain parts made by certain individuals; not one who makes it all through.

30212. How does the middleman get paid by the warehouse?
So much from the warehouse, 1s., 1s.6d., 1s.9d., and upwards, according
to the quality and to the workmanship they have got to put in it.

30213. How does he pay for the work?
He pays so much a day; from a girl, a small basting puller, at 6d a day up
to a feller hand that will take 1s., 1s.6d., and 2s. a day, a finisher that will
take from 2s. a day to 2s.6d. a day, a machinist whose wages run very
irregular, some might take 2s. a day, 2s. 6d., and 3s., and 4s., a day, and
some 5s. a day, both male and female. The majority are male; there are
exceptional cases where females get them.

30214. Do you mean that most of the machining is done by men?
Yes.

30215. And the master finds all the thread, and so on?
He finds such things as thread and various materials, barring certain
quantities of frilling, such as binding, stay tape, linen, and shoulder
padding; that is found by the firm.

30216. The hands do not have to find anything?
No, the hands do not; with the exception of the button-hole hands where
they are pieced.

30217. And the general custom is to pay by time?
Yes; the general custom is to pay so much per day.

30218. Then you said a little while ago that you were going to say
something about the system of bribery; what do you mean by that?
I mean that the system of bribery which extends to the majority of
warehouses, and to one warehouse in particular, is a system that brings
on this great evil which is connected with sweating in Leeds; and I have
this on good authority from one who was a middleman for a large
number of years. I wish to give his name if it is advisable.

30219. I do not want the name.
He was a large middleman for a number of years, and he worked in this
particular warehouse, and he publicly stated this; and it has been publicly
exposed in the Press on the 9th of May last, 1888, that this system of
bribery did exist in those warehouses; a system of bribing the managers
and certain foremen to get work out of those warehouses, by those who
in the majority of cases are unpractical tradesmen. The great majority of
those that get this work from the warehouses are not practical men.

30220. That is another thing altogether is it not. What I understand you
to say, so far, is that these middlemen bribe the foremen of the warehouses in order to get work?
Yes, that is the case.

30221. And supposing they do, you say that that is the cause of the evils
which exist in what you call the sweating system?
Yes.

30222. Why?
Because they have to take out so much more profit than what they would if they were to get it by legitimate means. If they were to get it by fair and honest means they would not have to leave the amount of profit they do. I have known, in certain instances, middlemen that have been small middlemen, and could not afford to adopt this system of bribery, say that if they could bribe managers in the way others do they would be able to get more work out. And in the majority of warehouses there is this connected with it: a few men can get the quantities, and the others have to keep their shops closed, and cannot get any work, while the first-named are pretty regular in work.

30223. I understand you to say that it is difficult for the middleman to get work without bribing, and that if they do bribe, they have to take it out of the wages that ought to go to the hands?
Undoubtedly; because they have no capital to start with, and it must come out of the labour of the hands.

30224. Now as to the hours of work in these shops; is all the work done by the middlemen carried on in shops of some considerable size?
Some of them, and they lately are of larger proportions than what they used to be some years back to my knowledge.

30225. They all would come under the Factory and Workshops Act?
I would like to speak of that a little later on in reference to the sanitary and factory inspectors' duties in those shops.

30226. But you can tell me now whether this work is carried on in shops that come under the Factory Act or in the people's own homes?
It is carried on in shops under the Factory Act, and the great proportion of it is in domestic workshops, as I term them, that is, taking work home.

30227. This is all the ready-made trade that you are speaking of?
Yes, I am speaking of the ready-made trade.

30228. What about these workshops, are they in a proper condition?
I may state that we denounced them something like 12 months ago as being in a very unhealthy state and in a very filthy state, the majority of them, and we also drew the attention of our borough authorities, the sanitary authority, to the matter: and on many occasions have notified the inspector, both the factory inspector and the sanitary inspector of things that we thought were not right.

30229. What do you mean by "We," the society?
Yes; the representatives of the society and the men belonging to it. And we also had a commissioner from the "Lancet," Mr. Smith, that investigated into a lot of those sweating shops, as we claim them to be, with regard to their sanitary condition; and I might state myself, the same as Mr. Smith reported, that the filthy condition of those shops should not have been allowed then; but I must state this, that since then there has been a great alteration. But our sanitary authorities at Leeds at that time

tried to whitewash the thing over that did exist, and make the public believe that we were simply getting up those cases; but still at the same time they must have known that such things did exist in Leeds.

30230.   What was the matter with the shops?
Filthy and unclean, and bad accommodation for males and females. In many of the shops where there have been 30 and 40 male and female hands, I have known only one accommodation; and in one particular case, the Ship Inn yard in Briggate, where there is such a thing as three or four shops, and each shop having only one accommodation for males and females.

30231.   How many hands would there be in the shop?
In one shop I should say there were 40 males and females, from small girls up to grown women and men; and the condition in which those places were kept was really a cruel one; and there were many more besides that in the various parts of the borough.

30232.   These places you visited yourself?
I have seen those places myself on more occasions than one.

30233.   And you say that formerly they were very bad, but now they are getting better?
In some cases; but still there are some great nuisances yet.

30234.   What are the hours of work in these shops?
The present hours of work for the under-presser, that is, a man learning his trade, and who has not been in the country very long, are as a rule from 6 o'clock or 7, to 8 o'clock at night, with an hour and a-half for meals, and getting his breakfast the best way he can. The presser works from 8 to 8, with an hour and a-half, and sometimes they allow him, but very rarely, to get a little breakfast in the shop. The tailors work from 7 to 8 o'clock at night, with the same hours for meals as the pressers. The machinist (a woman) and the machiner (that is the male) work from 8 to 8, with an hour and a-half for meals. The feller hands and finishers also those same hours and an hour and a-half for meals, and button-hole hands the same.

30235.   Button-holers, I presume, are paid by piece?
Yes, in the majority of cases, I believe.

30236.   All the others by time?
Yes, all the others by time, with the exception of a few shops, I am given to understand, where they are on piece.

30237.   Those are the regular hours; do they work overtime often?
Very often; in some shops all night; and some shops have begun to make a system of all night work, that is, the latter part of the week, such as Wednesday and Thursday; they allow the men to do nothing on either Sunday or Monday in the majority of cases, and they get it out of them in the latter end of the week.

30238. What object can it be to them to crowd the work into the latter part of the week?
The only object I can see, in many cases I have had my attention drawn to, is this, that when they go to the warehouses and see that there is not sufficient work to run them through the three or four days, they allow that work in many cases to stand till another cutting comes out and they get sufficient work to carry on for three days or for three and a-half days, and instead of taking that cutting on the Saturday and allowing it to be fitted up and partly done of a Sunday so that the pressers could start on the Monday morning, it is not taken away from the firms until the Monday, and many times they do not allow the presser to start, or the tailors, till the Tuesday morning or Tuesday dinner-time; and then by cutting another lot of work out they try to rush this work through so that they will be able to get it in by Friday noon or Friday before their Sabbath comes on.

30239. What do you mean by "cutting"?
The garments, they come out in so many garments to a cutting.

30240. How many?
Some cuttings run different from others. And they are put then in bundles, as I have stated before, and given out.

30241. But I do not understand now what object it is to the middleman to wait till another cutting comes out, and rush the work through in the last few days of the week?
If they take work out for two days and give the hands two days' work, and then cease and close the shop for a day and start again, they lose a lot of time, and it is very inconvenient to them; whereas, if they can get the work to go through with, without any break off, then they can get more quantity of work put through their hands.

30242. What do they pay when working overtime?
The same as the ordinary time, the tailors.

30243. When you say that they work overtime very frequently, do you mean that they work more frequently than they are allowed to under the Act?
I mean as far as the men are employed, not the women; my statement does not apply to the women; it is the males that work those long hours, the overtime.

30244. If the men work these long hours of overtime, how is that part of the work done, which is done by the women?
It is taken home at night and done at home. They leave off at eight o'clock, their ordinary hours, and I have known them to work till 12 or one o'clock, before they would be able to get to bed, owing to the quantity of work they have taken home; and I have known women to object to this, and they have been given to understand that if they did not take this work home, as it was wanted for the presser on the following

morning to take it into the warehouse, they must find another shop; I have known several women to protest, both married and single.

30245.   How do the women who take it home get paid?
Threepence or fourpence; so much a garment according to the amount of work.

30246.   A woman is paid by time, you mean, when working in the shop, and piece-work when she takes it home?
Yes.

30247.   And that when the men are working overtime in the shop the women are working in their own houses?
Yes.

30248.   So that, as far as the women are concerned, they might just as well be working in the shop?
Undoubtedly; and far better in one sense, I should say.

30249.   In what sense?
Because I believe that the houses of the people would be kept a great deal cleaner. Allowing the work to stop in the shops, I consider, would prevent a lot of the disease that in many cases is caused by taking work into houses where there are great diseases, and I have known it myself in more cases than one . By taking the quantity that they do I hold that there is a tendency to create disease and spread it more than otherwise.

. . .

30283.   When you speak of the middleman being "tyrannical" what do you mean?
I mean because of the system he pursues in his workshop of taking neither male nor female into consideration, and the foul and filthy language which he uses. I must say that I could not for a moment think you would believe half of what I have seen myself (and no man would believe it without he saw it), the filthy language which these men use; I might say which nine out of every 10 of them use towards all, even from the smallest little girl up to the principal hand in the shops; and the way in which these men go up and down the workshop is nothing more nor less than like a wild beast, raising up their hair with their hands, as though they were not right in their heads, and taking nobody that is under their control into their consideration.

30284.   You think the masters ill-treat the hands?
They do in many cases.

30285.   And drive them too hard?
And drive them too hard indeed for any man to be driven; not only a girl.

30286.   Why do the people put up with it?
Because they cannot help it. We have tried to cure it by organisation, and

we have succeeded in many cases; we have lowered the hours in many cases, and have brought middlemen to understand what they should do to the work hands, and have compelled them in many cases to do away with a lot of the tyranny; but so soon as they get any power they are always prepared to exercise that power and break down any movement that the working man may attempt to carry out.

30287.   Does your society object at all to the employment of female labour?
It is impossible to object to the employment of female labour, because the majority of the trade is carried on by females.

30288.   Then I do not exactly understand what the strike is about?
I may state that the late strike, 12 months ago, was for the purpose of protesting against the tyranny that existed in the shops, and for shortening the hours, and for the better understanding of man and master, that is, to make society shops.

. . .

30308.   Can you give us the prices that a middleman gets paid for the various garments?
There are some I know that get paid as low as 1s., and then for others they get 1s.3d., 1s.6d., 1s.9d., 2s., 2s.3d., and upwards, I might say to 3s., or 3s.3d.

30309.   What are these?
Some are coats, some are what they call double-stitched.

30310.   But they are all coats?
Yes, they are all coats, different sizes and different qualities; some youths, some for grown-up men.

30311.   Do you know what they pay for vests?
I have no knowledge what they pay for vests; our department is simply the coat department.

30312.   Do you know what the hands get paid?
I have told what they average by the day.

30313.   Do you know what they get paid by piece-work?
I have no knowledge, because it is only in a few isolated cases that this piece-work has got in. Since the last dispute, they have tried to introduce this system, and a lot of the men are bound to accept the system, whereas if they had the privilege to go in for day-work, they would not accept it. Some feel inclined to work piece-work, but the great majority would not.

. . .

30335.   Earl of *Derby*. Did I not understand you to say that the men would invariably prefer to work by time either than by piece if they had their choice?
Yes, the majority of them.

30336.   Why is that; what is the advantage of working by time?
We hold that piece-work has a tendency to reduce prices to a level, such that a man cannot get a proper subsistence in the time, and also that he submits himself to work many hours over the time that he really would work providing he were working by day-work; and where I hold that the evil of the system of piece-work comes in is that it gives power to those that employ them to pull off certain prices; that it brings the prices down many a time to starvation.

30337.   Does it not come to this, that piece-work gives a greater opportunity than day-work does to the good workman to get better wages than an inferior workman?
It holds that way; but in return we have it through experience, that if an employer of labour, Jewish or Christian, finds a man a practical tradesman, and a clever or exceptional man earning a good wage by piece-work, he then steps in and wishes to reduce the prices (and in many instances they do) and brings that man down so that he really is driven more into slavery than he would be if he were on day-work.

30338.   Do I understand you to put it in this way, that if men were paid by time, they would be paid at a uniform rate, and it would therefore be less easy for the employer to reduce the rate?
I mean that if the men were paid by time, that is, by the day, so that they had better arrangements, it would be more healthy for them and more convenient than it would be by being paid by piece.

. . .

30345.   Lord *Thring*. You tell us that when this strike began you had 1,000 men on your books?
Close upon 1,000.

30346.   Then I cannot understand why 1,000 men did not resist; they could have resisted surely?
Our funds were not sufficiently strong to support them; while the funds lasted those men held out, but when the funds were done, the men could not stand any longer; and when we adopted the system of assisting them in small grocery shops (which to-day we have to pay for), the middlemen took upon themselves, on many occasions, to tell those small shop owners to give no more stuff to their Jewish workmen, or otherwise it would be worse for them.

30347.   On credit you mean?
Yes, and we had to be security; in fact I had to be securities myself; there were 12 of us in number, for 20*l.* When the fund was done we signed our

hands for 20*l.* for provisions, and we have had to pay it out of our own pockets, with no assistance from anybody.

30348. Earl of *Derby.* What you mean, I suppose, is that the shop-keepers were warned that the men would not be able to pay for what they bought?
That is so.

30349. And that was the fact, they were not able?
No.

30350. Lord *Clifford of Chudleigh.* You mentioned, I think, that you made some representations to the sanitary inspectors about the shops?
Yes.

30351. Did they proceed to alter the individual shops to which you alluded?
I may state this, that when we denounced the sanitary conditions they tried to ignore our statement, and made believe that such things did not exist, and I know of one man in particular, a member of the committee, sending a letter to one of the sanitary authorities and telling him that such things existed in such and such a shop, and he saw him personally, or wrote a letter, I would not like to say which, and he told him he would drop a letter to this particular shop, and if such things did exist he would see into it. Now as far as I am given to understand, this state of affairs went on for a long while before it was seen into. They also said that such statements as we made were wrong. If they were wrong then I should like to draw attention to this, that to-day there are a lot of accommodations that there were not 12 or even six months ago, as far as accommodations for males and females are concerned; and also there has been a difference in the cleanliness of the shops as well as in the election of additional sanitary inspectors; and if what we stated was untrue I hold that they had no right to elect those sanitary inspectors, because in that case the work they were elected to do was not there for them to do it.

30352. Your experience is that they did do a great deal?
At this present time they are doing it, but up to the time of the agitation they were not doing it.

30353. They did it unwillingly you mean, when they did it?
Yes, they did it unwillingly, I must hold; nothing else.

. . .

30380. Is there anything more you wish to say?
I would like to make a statement, if you will permit me to do so, in reference to what not only I, but the Jewish working men of Leeds, and certain gentlemen who have taken an interest in this inquiry, consider an injustice. We consider that there has been some mistake or some gross injustice done somewhere or another by cutting off certain important

evidence and witnesses from attending before this Committee. I may make this statement; there is a gentleman, Mr. Marsden, president of the Leeds Trades Council, who has taken an active part in this inquiry, and assisted Mr. Oram while in Leeds; and he holds in his possession certain facts and figures connected with the way in which our borough authorities contract for their police clothing with firms in London, and those firms sublet them out to certain sweaters in London; he has got certain statements that I, for one, would have liked him to have stated.

30381.   How do you know all this?
He has told me, and begged me to draw your Lordships' attention to it. And the Jewish workmen have also other witnesses who would have liked to attend this Committee with me and tell you certain facts that I am not prepared to handle direct, workmen who have held positions in this society, such as the present president and the late president.

30382.   Why did they not come?
They have not been notified to come.

30383.   Why did they not write and ask?
They were ignorant of the fact that they could get here without being notified.

30384.   You did not know that you could write and ask to come?
We did not. I was asked last Saturday; I told them I thought your Lordships would not give your permission, but I am sorry (and I must state it) that those men have not been called, and I have no doubt but what they would have made a great impression upon the minds of the Committee by proving certain facts which they hold in their possession.

30385.   It is difficult for the Committee to know by instinct that a certain man at Leeds would like to give evidence?
I do not mean that.

30386.   I understand from you that certain men would have asked to give evidence if they had known that they might have been asked?
Yes, they would, and be only too glad to come.

c)   Secretary of the Mantle Makers' Union, 1903

Source: Minutes of Evidence taken before the Royal Commission on Alien Immigration, Parliamentary Papers, [Cd. 174] IX (1903), qq. 20257–281

Joseph Fine (1860–1946), was a capable and energetic trade unionist whose many contributions to the Yiddish socialist press display a shrewd understanding of the productive relations of the immigrant worker and the problems of labour organisation arising therefrom. Here he considers the division of labour and its effects on worker solidarity.

20257.   *Lord Rothschild.* You were born in Russian Poland? – Yes.

20258.   You arrived here 23 years ago without an occupation? – Yes.

20259.   Perhaps you will read your own evidence and explain it? – Is it necessary that I should read my biography, and give the details of how I came here?

20260.   *Chairman.* You had better state what your experience has been. You worked in tailors' shops for eight years in the United States? – Yes, and for six years in Leeds.

20261.   In 1893 you came to London and took a position as paid secretary of the Mantle Makers' Union for two years? – Yes.

20262.   You were in the centre of the foreign Jewish labour movement? – Yes.

20263.   Since then you have been in business, but you say you have been in continuous touch with the foreign and Jewish labour movement, auditing books, lecturing, and so on? – Yes.

20264.   Now will you go on with your statement? – First I deal with the classification of Jewish immigrants. In order to refute the ridiculous statement made by Mr Arnold White that many Jews are induced to come here by the charities of the Jewish Board of Guardians and some Jewish philanthropists, I will to the best of my knowledge classify them.

(1) The first Jewish immigrants were young men of 21 who escaped military service. This might sound unpatriotic, but when we take into consideration the status of the Jew in Russia, that, however capable he might be, he cannot become an officer, and, what is worse, that he is not allowed to live in the country for which he is asked to shed his last drop of blood – when we take these facts into consideration he is more than justified in trying to escape military service. These young men very often bring over their sisters and their sweethearts after a year or two.

(2) When the Russian Government imposed a fine of 300 roubles on the father whose son escaped, many for whom the payment of such a fine would have been a great blow sold out all their belongings and came over. Such people generally bring a little capital with them.

20265. That fine of 300 roubles is a fine with regard to escaping the military service, I suppose? – Yes, my Lord. Then, (3) artisans and small traders, who in Russian Poland owing to the limited area of settlement, in Galicia owing to clerical and anti-Semitic agitations, and in Roumania owing to the special laws, are unable to earn a living, emigrate to America and England.

(4) Political offenders – Of these the largest percentage are workmen who simply took part in the new trade union movement, which in Russia is a political offence. These four classes constitute at least 90 per cent of the

Jewish immigrants. When we take into consideration the cost to come to England, and the natural reluctance to leave one's native place for a strange country, no reasonable person will believe that the few shillings from the Board of Guardians will over-balance these difficulties. . . .

. . .

20269. . . . It has been said that we, the foreigners, are taking the bread out of the English working-man's mouth. We foreigners are not merely machines. We take work, and we give work; all that we earn by our labour we spend in this country. We – the Jewish work-men especially – have not come here to work for several years and to live like pigs during the time in order to hoard up a certain sum and return to our native place; we spend the greatest part of what we earn, and what we manage to save is either kept for a rainy day or as a stepping-stone to a higher step on the social ladder. My experience among the Jewish working-men enables me to prove that, far from taking bread out of English working-men's mouths, we have put bread in them.

. . .

20271. . . . I will now consider each industry separately and point out the part we, the foreign Jews, played in their development. The ladies' costume and mantle trade. From 1893 to 1895 I was secretary to the Mantle Makers' Union, and during that time I acquired some knowledge about the trade. I came in contact with most of the workmen, their masters, and some City firms. The number of workmen in this trade at that time was about 1,500; from 600 to 700 were organised; now the number of workmen in the trade is about double, but the number of organised about the same. The reason of the weakness of the organisation is partly due to the lack of efficient leaders and organisers – this holds good for all Jewish organisations – and partly to the intimacy between Jewish masters and men. The masters of to-day have been workers yesterday, and even strong and devout members of the Union, and many workmen of to-day will be masters to-morrow. Some, after having been masters and failed to succeed, become workmen again. This state of affairs will last so long as the trade will be in a transitory period, and until it will develop to the factory system proper, like the ready-made clothing trade developed in Leeds. A third reason for the weakness of the organisation is the antagonistic interests of the workmen themselves. The machiners and pressers are working by piece, the basters by week, the under presser is employed by the presser, and the plain machiner by the principal machiner. We have here five different working men, each one having a natural grudge against the other. The machiner works by piece, hence it is for his interest to hurry up. In order to keep pace with him the baster must hurry also although it is not for his interest to do so, as he is working by the day. The presser has a grudge against the baster because the latter gives him the coat to press in a state not to his liking; for instance, the edges are not straight enough, the shape is not well worked out; the baster leaves these finishing touches to the presser, to which the latter objects, as he is working by the piece, and therefore, objects to all labour which he considers not his duty to do. The plain machiners and under pressers have complaints against the chief machiners and head pressers. It therefore follows that when people are working under such conditions natural unity is impossible; they can be united artificially, so as to say, when proper organisers and good speakers take them in hand, but these are at present lacking. I entered into these details to show how shallow are the reasonings of some people who, seeing that at times the Jewish Unions are weak, blame the character of the men for it. These philosophers did not take the trouble to study the matter in detail; they do not even know the secret, that some English Unions are strong, not because the English working man is of a more fraternal disposition, but because the trades they are engaged in have developed to the factory system proper, namely large numbers of workmen are working under one roof, they are all working under one system – by the day or hour; they, therefore, have all one interest in common. That my reasoning is based on facts can be proved by Leeds. There the ready-made and part of the second-class order trade, employing foreigners, have developed to the factory system proper; they all work by the day, from eight to eight; they are all directly employed by the masters, and their Union is, therefore, as good and as strong as any English Union. I will return to the development of the trade and show the rôle played by the Jewish workmen. I am speaking now of the mantle trade. I will quote a part of a circular which when secretary of the Mantle Makers' Union, I addressed to the firms in the City: "Germany and France, though behind England in the evolution of other trades, were ahead of her in the mantle trade. They have created a new branch of the trade in question. They have combined the style and workmanship of the bespoke tailor-made with nearly the cheapness of the cheap ready-made. How did they do it? By applying to the bespoke tailor-made garment the present mode of capitalistic manufacture – that is, production on a large scale, use of machinery, and division of labour. Thus England has been a market for Germany and France. Some years ago certain English manufacturers realised that the same class of garments could be made in this country. Circumstances brought to England the class of workers, experts in that work; the trade is now rapidly growing". This quotation gives some idea as to the part the Jewish workman played in the development of the mantle trade. The truth of my statement is confirmed in an article in a German periodical, the "Neue Zeit", no. 39, of the year 1893, where the writer points out to his countrymen the cause of the diminution of the mantle trade in Germany. He says: "The cause is the transference of the trade to England by the Russian and Polish Jews". . . . The middleman also played, and does now, an important part in the development of the trade, inasmuch as he relieves the capitalists in the trade of many hardships, and so induces people with capital to enter into the business. I will illustrate the point. If

Figure 10   Jewish Sweatshop, East London, 1892   Factory production was exceptional in the East End garment trade; stitching and sewing operations were usually conducted in the groundfloor rooms of private houses as shown here in Old Montague Street, Whitechapel. (Mrs Brewer, 'The Jewish Colony in London', *The Sunday Magazine* XXI (1892), p. 16).

someone would be good enough to give me a couple of thousand pounds I would enter the mantle business.

20272.   This is very detailed, and you are getting away from the question of the aliens and talking about the middleman coming in. We must keep to the aliens? – The middleman is an alien, and I only want to point out the part which he plays, because he relieves the capitalist proper from many works which the capitalists in other industries are bound to set up.

20273.   You are dealing with the alien middleman? – Yes, I want simply to show the way the trade is carried on is this: Instead of a man going into the mantle trade and taking a factory, employing hands and managers and machinery, and all that, he only needs to have an office in the City somewhere about St. Paul's Church-yard, and he advertises for mantle makers. All he gets is simply samples of some cloth. Those middlemen from the East End will come in answer to the advertisement with samples of jackets of their own invention. By invention I mean their own style – a different lapel or a different sleeve, according as the fashion might be. He looks at the garment, and he asks him what he wants for the making of it, and when they have agreed upon the price he sends out his travellers to take orders. So he has no trouble at all. It is the alien Jewish middleman who does for the garment those things which in other industries is done, or ought to be done, by the manufacturer – and all the business man in the mantle trade has to do is to get the ready-made garment and send out his travellers and get orders for it.

20274. *Mr Vallance.* The alien has captured the mantle trade from Germany? – Yes.

. . .

20280. . . . The men's clothing trade can be divided into three principal divisions and two sub-divisions: (1) The ready-made, (2) The second-class order work, (3) The high-class bespoke. No. 1 can be sub-divided into: (a) the better-quality men's coats and youths' coats of the higher sizes; (b) the commoner class of men's and youths' and the juvenile. (a) Is made mostly by foreign Jewish workers in large Jewish workshops. When I speak of this sub-division, I have in view chiefly Leeds, because it is the classical city of the ready-made clothing trade. (b) Is made mostly by English women in factories. Many of the Jewish workshops are real factories. In such workshops are employed from 100 to 200 hands. The hours of labour are from eight to eight, with an hour for dinner and half an hour for tea; closed on Saturdays. Sundays, the hours are from eight to six. Winter-time, when it is busy, and the hands are employed the whole week, they work on Friday only till the Sabbath sets in, which makes the day a very short one. Sub-division of labour has reached there the highest point. The machinery part alone is divided into five or six parts. £2 per week is the maximum wage foreign, and 30s, the minimum for machiners, basters, and pressers; for under-machiners and under-pressers, about 25s. the maximum; and from 12s. to 15s. the minimum. The latter are only learners, and do not remain long in this position. English women are also employed in these workshops, mostly as finishers and button-hole hands. The former earn from 8s. to 14s. per week; the latter from 20s. to 30s. They also work as machinists, and they receive equal wages with men for equal work. Besides sub-division (b), which is made most by English women inside the warehouses, they are gradually encroaching upon sub-division (a); so much so, that some firms are making all their work inside with English women. Such firms at first employ inside a set of Jewish workers, or a Jewish foreman, who teaches the women the Jewish system. As a result, the greater part of the tailoring trade in Leeds is really in the hands of English women, and that the Jews have only enough work now left them to average from three to four days a week the year round. A comparison: In the Jewish workshops, English women get the same wages as men for the same work. Inside the English warehouses they are making the garments for less than half the price that would have to be paid to Jewish tailors. In the Jewish workshops the employers supply the silk cotton; in the English warehouses the women have to buy it from the firm, paying 50 per cent more than they could get it outside. In the Jewish workshops, when there is not enough work to keep them going for the day, they can go home, and come back when work is prepared. In the English warehouses they are actually locked in from morning till noon and from noon till 6 p.m. whether there is work or not. Whilst division (1) was being transferred from the Jew to the English woman, the former began to develop a new trade – division (2). Twenty or 30 years ago a suit made to order was unknown to a working man; such a suit cost £5 or £6. To-day a suit made to order can be had for £2, and only an expert can tell the difference between the one worn by the working man for £2 and the one worn by the capitalist for six or eight guineas. The classical city for this division is London, and the greatest number of all the Jewish tailors in the East End are employed in this trade. All these kinds of garments are issued from shops and not from warehouses, and each shopkeeper prefers to have a tailor to himself, it consequently follows that the workshops in which they are made are small. As people order for themselves suits only in certain seasons and not regularly the whole year round, consequently, the workmen have an abnormal busy season and abnormal slack season. Considering the facts, that if the workman will not earn enough in the busy time to pull him through the slack, he will starve, and that all the work given out by the shopkeeper must be ready in a given time, it is easy to understand the reason for the long working hours. The machiner and presser work by the piece and the baster by the day. The machiner gets 1s.2d. per coat, the presser 1s. In a busy week they can earn £3, and more; it all depends upon the number of hours they are working. The talk about 18 and 20 hours a day regularly is a ridiculous exaggeration. About the hours, I will say something later on. The baster is being paid from 8s. to 10s. a day, from 7 a.m. till about 9 p.m. As a rule, he eats his breakfast in the workshop, has an hour for dinner, and no specified length of time for tea. When he works longer he gets paid extra. The foreign Jewish tailors in the West End are employed in the upper part of division 2 and the lower part of division 3.

20281. *Chairman*. You really must compress this statement. We are going into details which do not assist us in the least . . .

5. Strikes and lockouts

a) To tailors and tailoresses, 1889

Source: *Commonweal*, 7 September 1889

The Tailors' Strike of 1889 lasted for nearly six weeks and affected some 10,000 garment workers in London. The following manifesto was issued after the public meeting of 26 August at which the decision to strike was adopted.

TO TAILORS AND TAILORESSES

Great Strike of London Tailors and Sweaters' Victims

Fellow Workers – You are well aware that a Commission of Lords have been appointed to enquire into the evils of the sweating system in the tailoring trade. The revelations made before the Commission by witnesses engaged in the tailoring trade are a disgrace to a civilised country. The sweaters' victims had hoped that this Commission would have come to some satisfactory conclusion as to an alteration in the condition of the sweated tailors. Finding they have just put off their deliberations until next session, we have decided to take immediate action.

It is too long for us to wait until next session, because the hardships inflicted on us by the sweater are unbearable. We have, therefore, decided to join in *the general demand for increased comfort and shorter hours of labour*. Our hours at present being in an average from fourteen to eighteen per day, in unhealthy and dirty dens, we demand:–

1. That the hours be reduced to twelve, with an interval of one hour for dinner and half an hour for tea.
2. All meals to be had off the premises.
3. Government contractors to pay wages at trade union rates.
4. Government contractors and sweaters not to give work home at night after working hours.

We now appeal for the support of all tailors to join us and thus enable us to successfully enforce our demands, which are reasonable. Tailors and tailoresses support in joining this General Strike.

We appeal to all tailors, machinists, pressers, basters, etc to meet *en masse* on Thursday, Friday and Saturday morning at ten o'clock (outside the Bells) Goulston Street, Whitechapel, E.

Piece workers finish up, week workers give notice at once. All work to cease on Saturday afternoon, when the strike will be declared.

(Sgd) Strike Committee
W. Wess. Secretary

Tailors Strike Committee Room,
'White Hart', Greenfield St,
Commercial Rd, E.
Aug. 27th 1889.

b) Tailors' strike, 1889

Source: *Jewish Chronicle*, 4 October 1889

What were the causes of the strike? The answer, said one communal commentator, lay not in the realities of work and the work environment, but in agitation and malevolence.

The strike of Jewish tailors in the East End of London affords material for serious reflection . . .

The grievance on the part of the men is that they are compelled to work 15 to 16 hours consecutively for a day's wage. For the first three days of the week they are mostly idle. It is generally on Thursday mornings that the men are taken on to work. They are then compelled to labour "nearly every hour that the Almighty gives them" during Thursday and Friday, and are paid two days' wages. Having nothing whatsoever to do on the early days of the week, it can easily be understood that their lives become demoralised. Satan can always find plenty of work for idle hands to do. The homes of the Jewish tailors – generally consisting of one or perhaps two dirty and ill-ventilated rooms, with the usual large number of small children which mostly falls to the lot of the poor man – offer no attraction to them, and the workers loaf about the street-corners. In course of time they find their way into some gambling-den, too many of which now exist in the East End of London, or are seduced into the more congenial premises of the Berners Street Club. It is here they hear repeatedly dinned into their ears the hardships which they have to undergo, and are assured that the only panacea for the ills from which they suffer is Socialism. Is it any wonder that they are an easy prey for the Socialist agitator? While the hand of every man is against them in the battle of life, the Socialist puts forth the hand of fellowship, and shows them an easy way out of their servitude. Bodily pain or pecuniary distress make men an easy victim to the sophistry of the professional agitator. And in this way the Jewish Socialists of Berner Street multiply, and become, if not a danger to themselves, a source of annoyance to the whole community.

6.   Socialism and the Jews

a)   Manifesto of the Hebrew Socialist Union, 1876

Source: W.J. Fishman, East End Jewish Radicals, 1870–1914 (1975), pp. 104–05

The Hebrew Socialist Union, the first attempt to organise the Jewish proletariat on revolutionary lines, was formed in East London on the initiative of Aaron Lieberman (1845–80) and its manifesto was presented to the second meeting on 27 May 1876. The following is translated from the original Yiddish–Hebrew text by W.J. Fishman.

The system, everywhere, is no more than oppression and injustice; the capitalists, the rulers and their satellites, have usurped all men's rights for their own profit and through the power of money have made workers their slaves. As long as there is private ownership, economic misery will not cease. As long as men are divided into nations and classes, there will be no peace between them. And as long as the clergy hold dominion over their emotions, there will be religious strife.

Redemption for all mankind can only be attained by a universal political, social and economic upheaval which will destroy the *status quo*, and replace it with a society based on Socialist principles, which will end injustice with the domination of capital, together with parasitism and the system of 'mine' and 'thine'. That all peoples should have equal rights and rid themselves of religion; to retain only one's own free will by ending superstition for the peace of mankind. While we Jews are part of humanity, we cannot achieve personal liberation except through that of all men.

The emancipation of all mankind from oppression and slavery can only be brought about by the workers themselves, in their united efforts to wage war against their exploiters; first to destroy the existing order and then to replace it by workers' control, justice, freedom and the brotherhood of man.

And as the workers of Europe and America have already joined together in various organisations to rouse the dispossessed and dedicate themselves to revolution for the victory of workers' Socialism, so we Jewish sons bind ourselves to this noble alliance and to this end we have created a Jewish Socialist Union.

This our comrades understand to be true and correct, the supreme arbiter of their relationship with each other and other people, notwithstanding colour, race or creed, and undertake to accept the following:

1. The Union's aim to spread Socialism among the Jews as well as non-Jews; to support organisations recognised by it and to unite all workers in the fight against their oppressors.
2. The Union's undertaking, in brotherly fashion, to unite with workers organisations from other nations.
3. Any worker can join the Union on the recommendation of two members.
4. All members are equal; all must pay a weekly subscription of 2*d.* a week or 8*d.* a month.
5. Meetings will be held every Saturday evening. Each meeting will elect its President and resolutions will be passed by vocal majority.
6. A secretary and treasurer will be elected for six months, but can be replaced before then.
7. Any member whose behaviour does not accord with these statutes will be expelled.

b) Socialism and the shuls, 1889

Source: Jewish Chronicle, 22 March 1889

The unremitting hostility of the Anglo–Jewish establishment towards the immigrant labour movement provoked Jewish socialists as their march to the Great Synagogue on the Sabbath of 16 March 1889 reveals.

The approaches to the Great Synagogue presented a scene on Sabbath afternoon last quite unparalleled in the history of the Jews of London. At the beginning of February, Messrs. Lewis Lyons and Phillip Krantz communicated with the Rev. Dr. H. Adler informing him that it was intended to organise a "synagogue parade" of Jewish sweaters' victims and the unemployed, and asking him to address them on the subject of their grievances. . . . Dr. Adler informed them that he would preach in the Great Synagogue on the 16th February. Our readers are aware that a goodly number of the class on behalf of whom Messrs. Lyons and Phillip Krantz profess to speak, attended on that occasion, when Dr. Adler gave them some wholesome advice with respect to their daily work, and persuaded them not to be deluded by the false socialistic and revolu-tionary doctrines which a few noisy agitators were desirous of propagating.

Last week Dr. Adler received a further communication from Messrs. Lyons and Krantz, stating that they had organised a procession with flags and a band of music, and asking him to deliver a sermon to the unemployed on the Sabbath, At the same time they sent a handbill containing an announcement that the Chief Rabbi would preach a sermon. Dr. Adler replied at once, expressing his great regret that they did not follow his advice. He also stated that they were not justified in circulating the announcement that he would preach for, in accordance with a long standing engagement, the Rev. I.S. Meisels had arranged to preach on that day.

The comparatively small but persistent body of Jewish socialists in the East End, although baffled in their attempts to create a sensation at the service held a month ago, were determined not to be outdone upon Sabbath last, and the proposed "Synagogue Parade" had been for some days extensively advertised throughout the district by handbills in the Judisch-Deutsch jargon. The handbills bore the following announcement: "Synagogue parade – A procession of Jewish unemployed and sweaters' victims will be held on Saturday, March 16, 1889, and will proceed to the Great Synagogue, where the Chief Rabbi will deliver a sermon to the unemployed and sweaters' victims. The procession will start at half-past twelve from 40 Berners Street, Commercial Road, E. We demand work to buy bread, and the hours of labour to be eight per day."

The processionists numbering between some three and four hundred, were headed by a German band, and proceeded through Commercial

Road and Whitechapel. . . . The procession was led by a black banner, on one side of which was in letters of white, "Jewish Unemployed, and Sweaters' Victims."

The approaches to the synagogue on Duke Street and St. James's Place were kept clear, but not without some difficulty, by a large body of police, whilst in the room used by the choristers for robing there was a reserve force of 50 men. When the procession reached the synagogue, which at that time was more than half filled, they found the entrances well guarded by a strong cordon of police. A deputation of four demanded an interview with Dr. Hermann Adler, and when they, much to their disappointment, learned that the Delegate Chief Rabbi was not in attendance, left the synagogue. The procession was again marshalled into order, and made their way, headed by the band playing the "Marseillaise," to the "Waste" in Mile End Road, where an "indignation meeting" was held.

The following resolution, written both in Hebrew and English, was circulated: "That this meeting of unemployed and sweated London Jewish workers of both sexes, strongly condemns the Delegate Chief Rabbi, Dr Hermann Adler, for refusing to comply with the courteous request of the Committee of the Jewish unemployed to preach a sermon at the Great Synagogue, having special reference to our position and prospects; further, we render our protest against the practice of labour sweating indulged in by certain members of the Jewish community. In consequence of the indifference of the rich Jews in not telling us, through the Chief Rabbi, how to improve our miserable condition, we clearly see that they are unwilling to assist us in ameliorating our position; we, therefore, call upon our fellow-workmen not to depend upon the rich classes, but to organise in a strong body to strike for the abolition of the capitalistic ruling." When the resolution was put to the meeting there were not many hands held up for it, and some were held up against it, but it was declared carried. The meeting broke up quietly, but the leaders were followed to Berners Street by a large crowd, where a disturbance occurred in which it was said several persons were more or less injured, and that two or three arrests were made.

c)   Socialism and atheism, 1900

Source: C. Russell and H.S. Lewis, The Jew in London, A Study of Racial Character and Present-day Conditions (1900), pp. 127–28

The appeal of socialism to the immigrant community was to some extent blunted by its identification with a militant atheism that was too far in advance of the traditionalist masses.

. . . Socialism deserves to be briefly noticed as one of the disruptive forces with which East End Judaism has to reckon. Jewish Socialists are for the most part Freethinkers; and as the leaders of Jewish Socialism have generally been also the pioneers of trade-unionism, they have obtained a certain amount of influence over a fairly large section of the Jewish workmen. Still the spread of Socialism among the foreign community does not seem to have been considerable. The Jew is an individualist by nature; and though he is enough of a dreamer to be attracted by almost any remote ideal, there seems to be peculiarly little in the programme and promised Utopia of Socialism that is really congenial to him. Even those who have been Socialists in Russia do not seem to find much that is to their taste in the Socialism of English workmen; it is not flamboyant or revolutionary enough to kindle their enthusiasm. Moreover, in Jewish circles, it is the correct thing to disapprove of Socialism; it is vaguely associated with Atheism, and the word 'Socialist' is perhaps most commonly employed as a term of abuse.

7.   Milly Witkop (1877–1955)

Source: Rudolf Rocker, *The London Years*, Translated by Joseph Leftwich (1956), pp. 98–103

Milly Witkop came from Zlatopol in the Ukraine and settled in East London and became involved in revolutionary politics. Rudolf Rocker (1873–1958), the non-Jewish leader of the East End Jewish radical movement, provides a moving portrait of his partner as she breaks with the *shtetl* culture in which she had been reared.

I continued my visits to the Jewish comrades in Whitechapel . . .

It was in that circle I really got to know Milly Witkop, who afterwards became my life's partner. She was one of the most devoted members of the "Arbeter Fraint" group. I had met her before in the West End, among the German comrades. She used to go there to sell papers and pamphlets, and to collect funds for the activities of her movement. She was 18 or 19, a slim young girl, simple and unaffected, with thick black hair and deep, large eyes, earnest and eager and zealous for our cause. Everybody held her in high regard. But it was only when I came to live in the ghetto that I got to know her rare and beautiful character. We became close friends.

I had met a girl at home in Germany, who followed me to Paris. We had a child, my son Rudolf. We lived together in Paris, and afterwards in London, but without ever discovering any spiritual bond between us. We parted. She insisted on keeping the child. Later, when she married another man, the child was in his way, and Milly and I took him. He was six at the time. Milly and I had meanwhile found our way to each other. She was a good mother to my son.

Milly and I have been together for a very long time now. Our union has withstood all the blows and buffettings of fate. We have been happy together. We have never regretted our choice. Our companionship has brought out certain qualities in me that could never have developed under less favourable conditions. A man who has stood as I have from his earliest youth in the crush and throng of a movement must have a place where he can find inner peace, and another human being who is not only his wife, but his friend and comrade, to whom he can open his heart and trust her with everything.

Not even the freest and most emancipated ideas about the relationship of the sexes can alter this fact. I know there is no golden rule in these matters, that human beings are very different in their nature, and that one can't lay down any general principle that will apply to everybody. I realise that I have been a very lucky man in this regard. We have gathered no worldly treasures on our life's road. We have been richly acquainted with hardships and dangers. But we have carried the burden together; we have lived and worked and fought as good comrades; we never had reason to reproach each other, for our cause was the same for both of us. But in return we have had much joy, such as is given only to people for whom the struggle for a great cause has become a vital need. We did not have to go searching for the blue bird. He was always with us.

Milly was born in Zlatapol, a small town in the Ukraine. She had a hard childhood. Her parents were very poor. Her father was a tailor, who made and repaired clothes for the estate owners round about. However hard he worked there was always want in the house.

Her mother was a deeply religious Jewess, a fine woman, who in spite of her own poverty was always helping others poorer than herself. She did the same afterwards in London. She devoted herself to the relief of the poorest of her Jewish fellow-beings. Her reward was that she was venerated in her own circle as almost a saint. She was always looking for something to do for others. And she was so modest and unassuming about it that everybody had to respect her.

Milly had been very religious as a child. The family was proud of her piety. She game to London in 1894, hardly more than a child. She went to work in the tailoring sweatshops of the East End, and for years grudged herself a bite of bread to save up the fare to bring her parents and sisters to London and provide a home for them.

But meanwhile she had undergone a change. At home, in the small town in the Ukraine, her world had been one of simple folk, who held strictly to the traditions of their Jewish faith and practice. In London she found people for whom religion had become a dead ritual. The conditions under which she lived and worked forced her to draw conclusions which she could not reconcile with her old beliefs. Her young spirit was tormented by doubts. Milly was one of those natures who cannot accept anything by halves. She always looked for a whole. It must have been agony to her to be a divided being.

She came upon a strike meeting of Jewish bakery workers in the East End. The speeches made a tremendous impression on her. She felt that she must join the fight against injustice. She had started on the road that led her to the meetings of the Jewish Anarchists at the "Sugar Loaf" public house. The rest followed. Milly read our literature, attended our meetings regularly. She had lost her old religion, but she had replaced it with a new faith.

When her parents at last arrived in London with the other children they no longer found the daughter they had known before. She was a grown, mature person, standing on her own feet. She was still devoted to them, helpful, affectionate.

But one could hardly expect these old people, completely untouched by modern ideas, to understand the inner transformation in their daughter. They showed the same love to her as always, but they felt they had lost her. The father could not help reproaching her sometimes. The mother never did. She kept her grief hidden in her heart. To her, utterly absorbed in her religion, the calamity that had struck her was God-ordained, something against which man must not complain, but must accept and make the best of it. The three other daughters, Polly, Fanny and Rose later went the same road as Milly. It was a heavy blow for their parents.

When I first got to know her Milly was living with her parents and her three sisters. There is no doubt that she felt and was moved by the grief of her parents, but what could she do? Should she hide her real beliefs, and play a game of pretence? That her nature would not allow. She had to be completely, wholly herself. She could give her parents everything in her power, but she could no longer think as they thought.

In December 1897 I had a letter from an old friend in New York, proposing that I should come to America. . . .

Of course I spoke about it to Milly. We were not living together yet. We had no relationship as man and wife. But we had now been close and intimate friends for over a year. She agreed at once to go to America with me. . . .

The "Chester" was an old tub, that had been hastily got ready for the purpose. Our cabin, which was between-decks, was tiny and gloomy, without any comfort at all. Yet we did not mind, for we were two young people about to step over the threshold into our new life together. . . .

It was not till late in the afternoon that we reached the landing pier. After the first formalities were over we were driven like a herd of cattle on to a small boat that took us to an island. That was the place where the immigrants were put through their examination. . . .

. . .

The official who dealt with us asked me several questions. I answered briefly. Then he asked for our marriage papers.

We hadn't any. He noted this down, and told us to go. The next day we were taken to another room, where four high officials and an elderly lady sat round a table. We were offered two chairs. One of the officials addressed me in German: "You say you have forgotten your marriage certificate. People don't forget such things when they come on a journey like this."

"I didn't say that," I answered. "I said we have no marriage certificate. Our bond is one of free agreement between my wife and myself. It is a purely private matter that concerns only ourselves, and it needs no confirmation from the law."

The old lady looked straight at Milly, and said to her: "But you can't as a woman agree with that. Don't you see the danger you are in? Your husband can leave you whenever he pleases, and you have no legal hold on him."

"Do you suggest," Milly answered, "that I would consider it dignified as a woman and a human being to want to keep a husband who doesn't want me, only by using the powers of the law? How can the law keep a man's love?"

"This is the first time I have heard a woman speak like that," the old lady said reproachfully. "If everyone ignored the law in respect of marriage, we should have free love."

"Love is always free," Milly answered. "When love ceases to be free it is prostitution."

The old lady bit her lip, and said no more.

8. Suffragettes at the Synagogue, 1913

Source: Jewish Chronicle, 17 October 1913

Jewish women were not unaffected by the growing radicalism of their gentile sisters in the campaign for female suffrage. The following report, first published in the *Jewish World*, was subsequently carried by the self-proclaimed 'organ of Anglo–Jewry'.

On the afternoon of the Day of Atonement, towards the close of the Musaf Service, the worshippers at the New West End Synagogue were startled by hearing three women in the gallery exclaim: "May God forgive Herbert Samuel and Sir Rufus Isaacs for denying freedom to women; may God forgive them for consenting to the torture of women." The words were uttered in unison as though they had been rehearsed. . . . As they left the Synagogue their names and addresses were taken by the police. All three are Jewesses, though they are said not to be members of the New West End Synagogue. Their names were given as the Misses Phoebe and Esther Rickards (sisters) and Miss Russell.

In view of the wretchedly bad behaviour, to say nothing of the dastardly crimes, of which suffragettes have been guilty, the exploit of the "ladies" who interrupted the service . . . with some hysterical insensate shouts, does not surprise us. If, as is said, however, these syrens were Jewesses, their outburst on the occasion referred to gives striking proof of the fact which has frequently been observed, that there are really no lengths – or depths – to which these quasi-demented creatures will not go in their madness. They do not, of course, see that they form the strongest possible argument against giving votes to women. Woman suffrage has much argument in its favour. It is when men look at the first fruits of the agitation and observe such blackguards in bonnets as those who interrupted the Atonement Service . . . that wise men hesitate to confer the franchise on women. They object to making a concession to crime, outrage, blasphemy – and bad conduct.

VI
RELIGION

No account of Jews in Britain during the Victorian era can fail to note the impact of the English establishment upon the Anglo-Jewish establishment. The Church of England supplied a model of authority and respectability which the leaders of Anglo-Jewry, lay and ecclesiastical, sought to emulate – even to the extent of seeking state recognition of the United Synagogue. The transformation of the Jewish ministry during the Queen's reign reflected the changing social composition of the Jewish population. Anglo-Jewry was increasingly middle class both in occupation and outlook. To the acculturated bourgeois who constituted the mainstay of the congregation, comparisons with the Church and its clergy appeared odious and demeaning. Ashkenazic prayer, by comparison with Christian worship, seemed ill-disciplined and incomprehensible. Long before the mass immigration of the 1880s, steps had been taken to beautify synagogue worship, curb congregational excess and generally render it more acceptable to an Anglican audience.

The services of the preacher too came under scrutiny. What was required was a cultured and cultivated gentleman of a type thought to be common in the Church of England, who spoke with an engaging fluency and could deliver learned and uplifting sermons with grace and refinement. These ambitions found expression in Jews' College, a seminary founded in 1855 to recruit and train gentlemen preachers. The Jewish minister was also expected to undertake the full range of duties performed by his peers in other denominations, particularly in the sphere of pastoral care. Not only was he expected to perform like his Christian counterpart; he was also expected to be like him in designation and dress. The newcomers from Eastern Europe, accustomed to non-uniformed rabbis and teachers, were startled by the Anglicisation of the Jewish ministry. Native Jewry itself began to wonder whether the transformation of the rabbinical role had gone too far (**doc. 1(b)**).

Equally shocking was the low level of *Yiddishkeit* to be found among English Jews. By the beginning of the nineteenth century religion occupied but part of the life of the well-to-do Jew and a very small part of that of his co-religionists. Mayhew may well have overdrawn the exotic and curious in his portrait of London Jewry, but his observations on the religious life of the community remain worthy of note (**doc. 1(a)**). Fears that the immigrants would go the same way were a recurrent theme of contemporary Jewish social observation. (**docs 1(d) and 3**).

Anglo-Jewry was singularly free from the communal convulsions unleashed by the progress of Reform Judaism throughout Central Europe. In Britain, where social acceptance preceded emancipation, pressures to modernize the faith were less urgent than elsewhere. The Anglo-Jewish elite, unlike its German counterpart, was not persuaded of the need to abandon the ritual and nationalistic features of the faith as proof of its fitness for civil and political equality. The secessionists who formed the West London Reform Synagogue of British Jews in 1842 were themselves hardly revolutionaries. The differences that separated them from the mainstream were small and in most respects bridgeable (**doc. 4(a)**). They were in fact very English in attitudes and outlook. The curious combination of liturgical conservatism and militant anti-rabbinism that characterised the Reform movement in these islands was, indeed, without parallel in either Germany or the United States.

The prospects for Reform Judaism were sharply curtailed by the newcomers from Eastern Europe whose antagonism to anything that smacked of the Science of Judaism made any further accommodation by the Chief Rabbinate and the United Synagogue impossible. The challenge to his authority posed by the immigrants from the East was the major preoccupation of the Chief Rabbi in the generation before the First World War. Immigrants accustomed to commune with unrestrained zeal and passionate self-abandonment found the sober service and board-room ethos of the United Synagogue singularly deficient and the Christian character of the Anglo-Jewish ministry suspect. The immigrant poor found the cost of the United Synagogue prohibitive and also resented the monopolisation of its status-bearing rituals and ceremonies by a native elite who made them feel worse than *schnorrers*. The *chevra*, by contrast, represented a self-creating, self-supporting and self-governing alternative which gave participants dignity, independence and scope for the acquisition of social honour. Its role as a social, spiritual and cultural shock absorber was well understood (**docs. 2 and 4(b)**).

The spectre of a separatist immigrant community, organised around an autonomous federation of small synagogues posed a threat to the unity of Anglo-Jewry and the authority of its leaders. The Federation of Synagogues, formed on the initiative of Samuel Montague, the observant bullion broker, was more than a simple attempt to prevent schism, however. The integration of the *chevroth* with mainstream Jewry, it was hoped, might also serve to revitalize a somewhat somnolent Orthodox establishment (**doc. 4(c)**). Apart from the provision of special overflow services for the High Days and Holy Days (**doc. 1(c)**), the United Synagogue considered meeting immigrant needs through the East End Scheme. This, essentially an attempt to create an Anglicised version of the *chevra* within the jurisdiction of the Chief Rabbi, was first proposed in 1889, debated for fourteen years and dropped in 1894, by which time the Anglo-Jewish establishment had concluded that dispersal and Anglicisation were the only solutions to the problems posed by the people from the Pale (**doc. 7**).

Dissatisfaction with the compromised latitudinarian practices of the United Synagogue culminated in the formation of the *Machzike Hadath* (Upholders of Religion), an ultra-orthodox association of German and East European Jews, that was founded in 1891–92. To be free of the 'West end goy', as Dr Adler was irreverently known, and his deficient supervision of *shechitah*, and to fortify themselves against Sabbath desecrators, required the formation of an independent synagogue-community in which traditional standards of piety and learning would be maintained. The magnificent Huguenot church in Brick Lane, that was acquired shortly afterwards, quickly became the most popular of East London synagogues (**docs. 6(a)–6(d)**). It set a standard which Anglo-Jewry might not follow but dare not ignore.

The experience of the Second World War and the foundation of the State of Israel made Zionism the civil religion of British Jews. Before the First World War, however, Zionism was less a secular faith and more an additional source of differentiation between the native and immigrant Jews. To the grandees, the idea of a Jewish national home appeared dangerous and divisive and inconsistent with their self-image as Englishmen of the Jewish persuasion; to the immigrants, by contrast, Zionism seemed as the saviour of a Judaism threatened by assimilation. As with Reform Judaism, so with Zionism – it was the peculiarities of the environment which separated the Jewish experience in Britain from that of Germany or the United States (**doc. 8**).

1. *Yiddishkeit* in London

a) *Never even heard of Dr Adler! 1851*

Source: Henry Mayhew, *London Labour and the London Poor*, 4 vols (1861), II, pp. 120–27

The Jewish poor interviewed by Mayhew provide a striking illustration of the moral and spiritual dangers confronting the faithful in a liberal environment.

. . . A Jew clothes man is seldom or never seen in liquor. They gamble for money, either at their own homes or at public-houses. The favourite games are tossing, dominoes, and cards. . . . On a Saturday, some gamble away the morning and the greater part of the afternoon. . . . They meet in some secret back place about ten, and begin playing for 'one a time' – that is, tossing up three halfpence, and staking 1*s.* on the result. Other Jews, and a few Christians, will gather round and bet. . . . The play lasts till the Sabbath is nearly over, and then they go to business or the theatre. . . . They seldom go to synagogue, and on a Sunday evening have card parties at their own houses. . . .

. . .

"When they return from their day's work they have mostly some stew ready, prepared by their parents or wife. If they are not family men they go to an eating-house. This is sometimes a Jewish house, but if no one is looking they creep into a Christian 'cook-shop,' not being particular about eating 'tryfer' – that is, meat which has been killed by a Christian. Those that are single generally go to a neighbour and agree with him to be boarded on the Sabbath; and for this the charge is generally about 2s. 6d. On a Saturday there's cold fish for breakfast and supper; indeed, a Jew would pawn the shirt off his back sooner than go without fish then; and in holiday-time he *will* have it, if he has to get it out of the stones. It is not reckoned a holiday unless there's fish."

. . .

On the subject of the street-Jew boys, a Hebrew gentleman said to me: "When we speak of street-Jew boys, it should be understood, that the great majority of them are but little more conversant with or interested in the religion of their fathers, than are the costermonger boys of whom you have written. They are Jews by the accident of their birth, as others in the same way, with equal ignorance of the assumed faith, are Christians."
I received from a Jew boy the following account of his trading pursuits and individual aspirations. There was somewhat of a thickness in his utterance, otherwise his speech was but little distinguishable from that of an English street-boy. His physiognomy was decidedly Jewish, but not of the handsomer type. His hair was light coloured, but clean, and apparently well brushed, without being oiled, or, as I heard a street-boy style it, "greased"; it was long, and he said his aunt told him it "wanted cutting sadly;" but he "liked it that way;" indeed, he kept dashing his curls from his eyes, and back from his temples, as he was conversing, as if he were somewhat vain of doing so. He was dressed in a corduroy suit, old but not ragged, and wore a tolerably clean, very coarse, and altogether buttonless shirt, which he said "was made for one bigger than me, sir." He had bought it for 9½d. in Petticoat-lane, and accounted it a bargain, as its wear would be durable. He was selling sponges when I saw him, . . . The Jew boy said – "I believe I'm twelve. I've been to school, but it's long since, and my mother was very ill then, and I was forced to go out in the streets to have a chance. I never was kept at school. I can't read; I've forgot all about it. . . . I could keep myself now, and do sometimes, but my father – I live with him (my mother's dead) is often laid up. . . . Can I speak Hebrew? Well, I know what you mean. O, no, I can't. I don't go to synagogue; I haven't time. My father goes, but only sometimes; so he says, and he tells me to look out, for we must both go by-and-by." [I began to ask him what he knew of Joseph, and others recorded in the Old Testament, but he bristled up, and asked if I wanted to make a Meshumet (a convert) of him?]
. . . I don't know what's the difference between a Jew and Christian,

and I don't want to talk about it. The Meshumets are never any good. Anybody will tell you that. Yes, I like music and can sing a bit. I get to a penny and sometimes a two-penny concert. No, I haven't been to Sussex Hall – I know where it is – I shouldn't understand it. You get in for nothing, that's one thing. I've heard of Baron Rothschild. He has more money than I could count in shillings in a year. I don't know about his wanting to get into parliament, or what it means; but he's sure to do it or anything else, with his money. . . . I only wish he was my uncle . . . I buy what I eat about Petticoat-lane. . . . Pork! Ah! No, I never touched it; I'd as soon eat a cat; so would my father. No, sir, I don't think pork smells nice in a cook-shop, but some Jew boys, as I know, thinks it does. I don't know why it shouldn't be eaten, only that it's wrong to eat it. No, I never touched a ham-sandwich, but other Jew boys have, and laughed at it, I know.

. . .

Of the street Jewesses and street Jew-girls

I have mentioned that the Jewesses and the young Jew girls, compared with the adult Jews and Jew boys, are not street-traders in anything like the proportion which the females were found to bear to the males among the Irish street-folk and the English costermongers. There are, however, a few Jewish females who are itinerant street-sellers as well as stall keepers, in the proportion, perhaps, of one female to seven or eight males. The majority of the street Jew-girls whom I saw on a round were accompanied by boys who were represented to be their brothers, and I have little doubt such was the facts, for these young Jewesses, although often pert and ignorant, are not unchaste. Of this I was assured by a medical gentleman who could speak with sufficient positiveness on the subject.

Fruit is generally sold by these boys and girls together, the lad driving the barrow, and the girl inviting custom and handling the purchases to the buyers. In tending a little stall or a basket at a regular pitch, with such things as cherries or strawberries, the little Jewess differs only from her street-selling sisters in being a brisker trader. The stalls, with a few old knives or scissors, or odds and ends of laces, that are tended by the Jew girls in the streets in the Jewish quarters (I am told there are not above a dozen of them) are generally near the shops and within sight of their parents or friends. One little Jewess, with whom I had some conversation, had not even heard the name of the Chief Rabbi, the Rev. Dr. Adler, and knew nothing of any distinction between German and Portuguese Jews; she had, I am inclined to believe, never heard of either.

. . .

The Jews have eight synagogues in London, besides some smaller places which may perhaps, adopting the language of another church, be called synagogues of ease. . . .

The synagogues are not well attended, the congregations being smaller in proportion to the population than those of the Church of England. Neither, during the observance of the Jewish worship, is there any especial manifestation of the service being regarded as of a sacred and divinely-ordained character. There is a buzzing talk among the attendants during the ceremony, and an absence of seriousness and attention. Some of the Jews, however, show the greatest devotion, and the same may be said of the Jewesses, who sit apart in the synagogues, and are not required to attend so regularly as the men.

I should not have alluded to this absence of the solemnities of devotion, as regards the congregations of the Hebrews, had I not heard it regretted by Hebrews themselves. "It is shocking," one said. Another remarked, "To attend the synagogue is looked upon too much as a matter of *business*; but perhaps there is the same spirit in some of the Christian churches."

As to the street-Jews, religion is little known among them, or little cared for. They are indifferent to it – not to such a degree, indeed, as the costermongers, for they are not so ignorant a class – but yet contrasting strongly in their neglect with the religious intensity of the majority of the Roman Catholic Irish of the streets. In common justice I must give the remark of a Hebrew merchant with whom I had some conversation on the subject:– "I can't say much about street-Jews, for my engagements lead me away from them, and I don't know much about street-Christians. But if out of a hundred Jews you find that only ten of them care for their religion, how many out of a hundred Christians of any sort will care about theirs? Will ten of them care? If you answer, but they are only nominal Christians, my reply is, the Jews are only nominal Jews – Jews by birth, and not by faith."

Among the Jews I conversed with – and of course only the more intelligent understood, or were at all interested in, the question – I heard the most contemptuous denunciation of all converts from Judaism. One learned informant, who was by no means blind to the short-comings of his own people, expressed his conviction that no Jew had ever been really *converted*. He had abandoned his faith from interested motives. On this subject I am not called upon to express any opinion, and merely mention it to show a prevalent feeling among the class I am describing. . . .

I was told by a Hebrew gentleman (a professional man) that so little did the Jews themselves care for "Jewish emancipation," that he questioned if one man in ten, actuated solely by his own feelings, would trouble himself to walk the length of the street in which he lived to secure Baron Rothschild's admission into the House of Commons. This apathy, my informant urged with perfect truth, in nowise affected the merits of the question, though he was convinced it formed a great obstacle to Baron Rothschild's success; "for governments," he said, "won't give boons to people who don't care for them; and, though this is called a boon, I look upon it as only a *right*."

When such is the feeling of the comparatively wealthier Jews, no one can wonder that I found among the Jewish street-sellers and old-clothes men with whom I talked on the subject – and their more influential brethren gave me every facility to prosecute my inquiry among them – a perfect indifference to, and nearly as perfect an ignorance of, politics. Perhaps no men buy so few newspapers, and read them so little, as the Jews generally. The street-traders, when I alluded to the subject, said they read little but the "Police Reports." . . .

b) Wanted a rabbi, 1910

Source: Augustus Kahn, 'The Status and Training of Jewish Ministers', Jewish Review, I (1910–11), pp. 501–09

The redefinition of the role of the rabbi and replacement of the traditional chazan by a 'minister' who performed pastoral, teaching and preaching roles similar to those of the Anglican clergy, created problems of leadership and legitimacy in a community transformed by immigration.

The Conference of Jewish "Ministers," held last year, included Preachers and Readers. Both are Ministers – and it is difficult to draw a hard and fast line between the one and the other. The Preacher is, indeed, as a rule also a Reader, and the Reader may, at any rate in a provincial synagogue, easily extend his "ministration" from the Almemar to the Pulpit. Why should not he? He has learned "Hebrew and Religion," and has taken lessons in Elocution. This want of differentiation of office is illustrated by the nomenclature employed by the United Synagogue; for instance, the Hambro Synagogue has a "First Reader," and a "Minister, Second Reader, and Secretary"; the Central Synagogue has a "Preacher and Reader," and a "First Reader"; and St. John's Wood Synagogue possesses, in addition to its "Minister," a Reader and Secretary, who also preaches, and is styled "Junior Minister and Secretary."

The combination of the offices of Preacher, Second Reader, and Secretary is quite peculiar to this country; and at the same time Anglo-Jewry is distinguished unenviably by the low standard of qualifications of its Ministers and the practical non-existence (except in the case of Chevrahs and congregations of foreign Jews) of Rabbis. There is, indeed, no recognised minimum standard of qualifications. . . .

The community appears to be awakening from its complacent slumber. One hears the question put: "What is to happen if the Chief Rabbi should, after his many years of labour, seek retirement or release from some portion of his duties?" How many men are there among all the "Ministers, Second Readers, and Secretaries" who could possibly be considered eligible for the Delegate Chief Rabbinate?

The centralisation of Rabbinical functions is no doubt largely responsible for the present state of affairs. With a "Chief Rabbi of the United Congregations of the British Empire" there was no demand for

Rabbis, and Jews' College was limited in its aims to the imparting of a modicum of Jewish learning, ancillary to such secular knowledge as was required by the B.A. pass degree of the University of London. It was only in the year 1900 that the Rabbinical Diploma was opened up to students of the College. Since that time the Diploma has been granted to one student and one ex-student. There is still therefore no very strong demand for "Rabbis." The ex-student is the learned "Minister and Reader" of the Brondesbury Synagogue, and his stipend, according to the last Report of the United Synagogue, is £250 per annum, exactly one-third of the salary of the United Synagogue Secretary. This scarcely looks like a substantial recognition of the Rabbinical Diploma.

. . . Not that learning is despised . . . But it is nevertheless regarded in leading Anglo-Jewish circles as a sort of a luxury, a non-essential, or even as antagonistic to the discharge of ministerial functions, which are to preach simply, decently, and in good English and not above the heads of the congregants, to read the Law correctly, to assist in the reading of prayers, to engage in charitable work, to keep books (account books), render synagogue bills, and to be all things to all men.

Now, the supply of Ministers is necessarily conditioned by the demand, and the force of demand depends obviously not only upon the number of pulpits to be filled per annum, but also upon the nature of the work, the emoluments and the status of the Minister. It would be a mistake, however, to suppose that status is involved entirely in emoluments. There is a small independent congregation in the north of London whose Rabbi is remunerated on a considerably lower scale than almost any Minister or Reader of the United Synagogue. But no Minister or Reader has a status comparable to his, if his status may be measured by the respect and even homage which is paid to him. And why? Because, in the first place, his congregants are of the type of Jews who honour the Jewish scholar; but in the second place also, because their Rabbi's learning is a living and inspiring force exerting its influence in the synagogue, classroom, and ordinary intercourse.

The improvement of the status of our Ministers can be effected only by a change of attitude in regard to the Minister's functions, and at the same time an improvement of the Minister's qualifications. As long as congregations insist upon their Preachers being Secretaries and second-rate Readers, we shall keep the doors of the ministry closed against some of the best material available, we shall discourage even the pick of the students from submitting themselves to a long and arduous course of training, and we shall damp the enthusiasm of those who have already entered the profession. . . .

Now, what are the needs of the community which are to be met by the Minister-Rabbi? Firstly, under a system of decentralised ecclesiastical administration – which in the future can be the only effective system – we shall require Rabbis capable of deciding questions of Jewish Law and supervising Jewish rites and institutions. We require Rabbis also as religious guides and teachers, Rabbis qualified by their knowledge of Judaism and modern thought of presenting Judaism, and of spreading by speech and writing the understanding of Judaism and the love of Judaism; capable of representing Jewry in its religious aspect to the outer world; and lastly, able and willing to co-operate with laymen in the various branches of our communal activity.

We have not many such men at present. And those we have are made to fritter away much of their energies in sterile labour. If any evidence were needed of the lack of men, and lack of opportunity, it would be sufficient to point to the insignificance of the contributions on the part of Ministers to Anglo-Jewish literature. The recent edition of the Festival Prayers was the work of laymen; portions of our liturgy are still without an English translation; we have no popular Jewish Bible, no Jewish Bible Commentary in English, scarcely any text-books for our Religion classes or standard works for teachers. How little, moreover, is, and can be done by our London Ministers – in the work of religious education! Some there are who are actually called "Honorary Superintendents"! Honorary, forsooth! What a conception of the functions of the Minister, who teaches, or, without teaching, supervises in an *honorary* capacity!

There is now hope that the vicious circle, in which interaction of supply and demand moves, will be broken. A Sub-Committee of the Conference of Anglo-Jewish Ministers has just issued a "scheme for the District Organisation of Provincial Congregations" so far-reaching, that it will assuredly make history. The scheme recommends the division of the United Kingdom into nine districts, each with a Council of Rabbis and Preachers (with the power of co-opting Chazanim and laymen). The Council of each district is to "deal with such religious questions as may be delegated to it by the Chief Rabbi and Beth Din"; to control and supervise religious education; to co-ordinate charitable relief; to arbitrate on matters of difference in congregations; to obtain from congregations the acceptance of a recognised standard of qualifications on the part of candidates for clerical office; and to offer assistance in the selection of candidates.

This scheme of decentralisation appears to be entirely on the right lines. We have at last definite Rabbinical duties assigned, which must tend to raise immeasurably the status of the Minister. Unfortunately, the men are wanting to give reality to the scheme. No doubt co-operation will be sought with the foreign-trained Rabbis of congregations of recent immigrants; and this is the right plan to adopt. But on these Rabbinical Councils the English-trained Minister will needs have to play a subordinate part. And this is not merely a question of *amour-propre*. What comes home to us now is that the English ministry is unprepared for the great opportunity of galvanising the religious life of the community. The Rabbi, born and bred and trained in Russia, can exert no great influence on the younger generation; and the English Minister – subordinated in learning and rank to the Rabbi – must fail to inspire confidence in the foreign Jew, who, to his credit be it said, requires his religious guide to be first and foremost a "Ben Torah." The scheme of the Sub-Committee is nevertheless a very great step, even though it can be but imperfectly realised at present. . . .

c) A Happy New Year, 1893

Source: Jewish Chronicle, 15 September 1893

The popularity of special services on High Days and Holydays for Jews without any synagogue affiliation reflects the strength of Jewish identity and the weakness of the United Synagogue in East London.

The New Year services which have been held under the auspices of the United Synagogue for the Jewish poor of East London will deserve to rank as gatherings of historical importance, for never, perhaps, in the history of Judaism has so vast a throng been collected in a single building for the purpose of religious worship.

In modern times, the largest synagogues are in Russia and Galicia. The Brody Synagogue holds 3,000 people; that at Warsaw about 3,600. The Warsaw temple holds 4,000, and the new temple which has been constructed at St. Petersburg will accommodate over 4,000. These numbers are dwarfed into insignificance beside the attendances at The Great Assembly Hall at Mile End on Monday and Tuesday, the first and second days of the New Year. The hall has seating accommodation for 5,500 people. On the first day of the festival, about this number were admitted, and several thousands were turned away. On the second day, admission was granted to some 7,000 or more. The whole of the vast edifice was literally packed from floor to ceiling. The ground floor, the two galleries and a smaller upper gallery, both platforms up into the organ loft, the steps leading thereto, the vestibule, every nook and cranny, in fact, were taken possession of by the crowd from about the hour of commencement. The men occupied the ground floor, the women the first gallery, and the men again the second and third galleries. Finding, however, that many women were unable to obtain seating accommodation, the men were requested to make *place aux dames* and resign the topmost gallery to the gentler sex, which they readily did. . . . The order and decorum, the piety and devotion of this enormous throng of men and women, most of them hailing from the despised ghettoes of Russia and Galicia, were such as to redound to the credit of the foreign immigrant, whom it is customary to describe as wanting in the elements of order and decency. Two large placards on either side of the platform enjoined silence, but they appeared to be hardly necessary. On the contrary, for an object lesson in genuine devotion, and religious fervour which rises at times to the white heat of passion, some of us might do worse than pay a visit during the Ten Penitential Days to Charrington's Assembly Hall. . . .

I am most concerned to speak of the sublime religious fervour which characterised this seething mass of humanity; the deafening din, as of the tumultuous sea, which 7,000 lungs, all exerted at one time, gave forth; the talith-covered heads of the men, the bodies of the devout swaying to and fro, the sobs of the women, particularly before the blowing of the Shofar and during that sublime prayer preceding Musaf.

d) *Spiritual life in London, 1900*

Source: C. Russell and H.S. Lewis, *The Jew in London, A Study of Racial Character and Present-day Conditions* (1900), pp. 199–213

The absence of restraint in state and society that was a marked feature of the English-speaking world made for a rapid acculturation and a gloomy prognosis as to the survival of Judaism in these islands. Orthodox immigrants, though fearful of the future, were unwilling to abandon their faith without a struggle.

. . . I must admit that . . .
. . . Sabbath observance and synagogue attendance are both diminishing, . . . In such specifically Jewish trades as tailoring and bootmaking, it seems clear that over half of those employed abstain from work on the Sabbath. . . .

. . .

. . . In the various branches of the furniture trade – cabinet-making, upholstering, polishing – there is much desecration of the Sabbath. In many cases also where a Jew engages in trades in which the bulk of those employed are Christians, he finds it difficult to observe a day of rest different from that of his fellow-workmen. . . .

. . .

Jewish shopkeepers in the by-streets of the Jewish districts nearly all close their shops on the Sabbath. Wentworth Street – which has inherited the name and traditions of the old 'Petticoat Lane' – enjoys a Sabbatical calm and quiet which is unknown to it during the remainder of the week. On the other hand, many Jewish shopkeepers, in main thoroughfares such as the Whitechapel Road, carry on business on the Sabbath; and the same is true of Jewish costermongers who are dependent on Gentile custom. . . .
. . . the wilful desecration of the Sabbath practised by those who frequent places of amusement on that day . . . is generally condemned by Jewish public opinion, and it is practised by a comparatively small section of the community. . . .
. . . It is certain that the number of foreign Jewish workmen attending synagogue is far greater than that of churchgoers amongst any sections of Christians other than the Catholics. Again, whilst in most church congregations there is a large preponderance of women and children, they

are in a minority in the East-End synagogue. Judaism does not, in spite of all assertions to the contrary, regard women as inferior, but there has certainly been a tendency amongst Jews to consider that the proper sphere of female influence is rather the home than the synagogue. At any rate, the wife of the East-End orthodox Jew does not attend synagogue very often. . . .

East-End synagogues are perhaps not calculated to impress favourably a casual visitor to whom the whole service is unintelligible. There is no decorum, and during parts of the service there is much talking and noisy movement. But, none the less, the little synagogue, sometimes insanitary and built with unlovely surroundings, is the seat of deep devotion – a devotion full of self-abandonment, supplying the worshipper with an inspiration which transfigures his life and makes him feel that he too has a share in the traditions and in the hopes of the chosen race. It is indeed difficult to realise how strong is the affection which the Jewish liturgy excites amongst those who have grown up under its influence. The ground-work of the service is almost without exception simple and sublime; even in a translation its beauty can be appreciated. On the festivals and chief Sabbaths this is supplemented by a number of poetical compositions, sometimes beautiful, sometimes quaint and curious, occasionally absurd, often endeared to the worshippers by familiar and touching melodies. And we must note that none of the activities of life are considered common and secular. The Jewish poet dares to praise God, on occasion, for instructing us in the weights and measures; . . .

A large majority of Jews understand their liturgy very imperfectly. Many of the poems contained in it were written by the learned for the learned, and presuppose some degree of familiarity with allusions to Talmud and Midrash. The simple-minded orthodox Jew of modern times will read them without understanding them very much, and perhaps associating them chiefly with the tunes to which they are chanted. At the same time, he is in full sympathy with the spirit of the service, and he feels a spiritual glow as he repeats the words which his father taught him, and which link him with so many past generations of Jewish worshippers. Where the meaning of the words is hidden his imagination will supply the gap. It may not be the highest form of worship, but it is better than the attitude of the cold critic who does not worship at all. . . .

Jewish history has always been marked by much controversy but no abiding division. This principle will probably be exemplified again by the future history of the *Mahazike Haddath*. The secession of these 'upholders of the law' was, at bottom, a protest against undue centralisation – against the government of the foreign Jews, who are the most numerous section of the community, by English Jews, who are in imperfect sympathy with them. The leaders of the movement wished to have an ecclesiastical head of their own, independent of the Chief Rabbi, who has done wonders in holding the community together, but has naturally offended many extremists. The foreign Jew complains that his native-born co-religionist preaches to him constantly about the duties of English

citizenship, but is deplorably lacking in 'Yiddish-keit' – Jewish observances and Jewish feeling. He speaks contemptuously, in moments of
bitterness, of the 'West-End *goy*,' and desires to be independent of him in
religious matters. . . .

. . . Some of the orthodox have expressed distrust with the precautions
taken by the ecclesiastical authorities to ensure the proper method of
slaughter and to remove forbidden fat from the carcases exposed for sale.
None of the questions that have arisen would excuse a prolonged breach.
The healing influence of time will lessen divergence of sentiment and
enable native-born and foreigner to cultivate a better understanding. The
practical grievances of the secessionists will probably be ultimately
remedied by the recognition of their rights and that of their Rabbi to
exercise a defined measure of independent control.

Whilst giving every credit to the earnestness of many who have
identified themselves with the *Mahazike Haddath*, and to the enthusiasm
which enabled them, during the autumn of 1898, to open a large
synagogue in Spitalfields, it cannot be doubted that there are other
elements in the movement besides religious zeal. An independent foreign
community, if created, would give scope to the ambitions of many men
who feel themselves now unappreciated. The size and importance of the
new synagogue have attracted new members who had hitherto held aloof.
It must be added that the past record of some prominent leaders in the
movement is far from inspiring confidence.

2.   Mrs Levy goes to Shul, 1887

Source: British Library of Political and Economic Science, Passfield Papers, VII.8,
'Wholesale Clothing Trade', 22 October 1887

Mrs Levy, an English Jewess married to a Dutch Jewish cigar maker, lived in
Katherine Buildings, Royal Mint Street, before moving to Wentworth Dwellings
in the heart of the immigrant quarter. The Levys were well known to Beatrice
Potter and played a significant role in her education as a social investigator.
Mr Levy provided her with introductions to various garment workers, Mrs
Levy's mother showed her how to sew a pair of trousers while Mrs Levy
herself was equally informative on a whole range of matters connected with
the Jewish East End. Beatrice Potter's considered account, as published in
Charles Booth's *Life and Labour of the People in London*, is given below (see
4(b) pp. 197–99). The interview notes from which it was taken are scarcely
less informative.

Oct 22 went to synagogue in low quarter with Mrs Levy. Narrow Street,
with entrance as if into an ordinary house. Upstairs into ladies gallery
with treliss in fronts. Looking down into square hall with raised & draped
platform in the midst. At one end of the hall, steps leading to sanctuary,

at that time the curtains drawn. Underneath the gallery pews raised one above the other. Scattered in these pews, low-class but apparently comfortably-off Jews. Flung across their shoulders, cashmere or silken scarfs. They were all sitting as if at ease, some in twos and some in three chatting in undertones, one now again wd offer his neighbour snuff. The function was proceeding. For on the platform, a group of men took turns at chanting in loud wailing tones the Law of Moses, which lay on the reading desk facing the sanctuary. Presently a boy, with top hat & heavy gold watch chain stepped up to the platform & taking his place at the reading desk, recited his confirmation with musical intonation (Mrs Levy explained that parents are proud if their son can show sufficient education to recite the Hebrew scripture & prayers to allow of his public recitation as a full-grown Jew). This finished the elaborately bound Law of Moses was rolled up, & dressed in rich embroidery – the boy being initiated into the ceremony 'dressing the law'. At the conclusion of the service the law, dressed up & ornamented with bell like mettle nobs, was carried by the men up the steps of the sanctuary. The curtain was drawn disclosing the different editions of the law . . . for the various seasons or festivals of the year.

With the exception of an occasional burst of monotonous chanting from the congregation, there was little sign of attention, & to my mind, in the whole service there was no suspicion of devotional feeling. Even the boy, received into the church of his fathers, left the reading desk with an air of satisfied achievement – as if he had just passed the sixth-standard.

Walking away, Mrs Levy, who seemed very ignorant of the meaning of the various acts of the service, explained that women were held of no account until they married. In the lowest-class synagogues, no places were provided for them. Their only religious duty in the say of attending services, after their confinements. The poor foreign Jews, male & female, seldom went to the synagogue, tho' they were scrupulous in their attention to the law of Moses, as regards the sabbath etc. Mrs Levy herself thought it a mockery to go to Synagogue, when she intended to break the law the following noon by lighting her fire & cooking their dinner.

The Levys live at the top of a block of artizans dwellings. They have four or five children; the eldest of whom, a boy, is a little scamp. The old Irish woman, dirty & incapable, looks after the home, while Mrs Levy is out working. Levy is a gentle-natured man (a cigar-maker) earning little from the badness of his trade. He & his wife have been lovers since they were children. Indeed according to Mrs Levy's account, their respective parents had to chastise them, because as mere children 'they would not leave one another alone'. Apparently the chastisement had not much effect, for at fifteen the young woman had to be married to her lover, for fear that the coming child shd not be born in wedlock. Mrs Levy has had one child after another, losing about half of them. Levy treats his wife with courtesy, & is a fond but unwise parent. The joint earnings of the two come to about 30/- a week.

Figure 11   A Jewish wedding, 1901   The service included the reading of the marriage contract or *ketubah* in which the groom promised the bride 'to work for thee, honour thee, support and provide for thee, according to the manner of Jewish husbands, who work for their wives, honour, support and provide for them'. In fashionable Jewish weddings the canopy or *chuppah* was richly ornamented with white flowers (G.R. Sims (ed.), *Living London,* 3 vols (London: Cassell, 1901), I, p. 23).

Their home is dirty & untidy & all the money is spent – but Mrs Levy says she must have plenty of food, for her work is heavy. Levy is intelligent & glad to read books or newspapers. He has many friends of a respectable character & willingly talks on religion & social questions. His judgment is singularly free from bias – & I was . . . to see that in taking me to see sweaters & workers, he warned me not to take their account as accurate.

After we had watched Mrs Levy prepare the chickens for the Sabbath dinner, we walked to Rupert Street to see a sweater Cohen by name. Mrs Cohen was at home: a small gentle polish jewess, with musical voice and pathetic accent. She claimed me as a compatriot & to her my appearance was evidently 'sympatique'! The house was damp & comfortless & the little parlour into which we were shewn untidy & without ornament or even sufficient furniture.

3.   Six days shalt thou labour, 1895

Source: Report of the Chief Inspector of Factories and Workshops for the Year 1894, Parliamentary Papers [C.7745] XIX (1895), p. 48

The relegation of religion to the margins of everyday life owed more to the way people lived than to any considered alternative as the following suggests.

The East End Jew is going westward and the West End employer is sending his garments to the East End to be made up. So pronounced is the migration that Saturday labour is done by the East and West End tailors alike, the observance of the Sabbath, once so rigidly observed, is now quite neglected by the majority of the Jewish tailors who say that, 'their living is more to them than their religion.' Mr. Mackie who has charge of the West End remarks in his report to me that a considerable change is taking place in the personnel of the West End outworking tailor, 'the foreign Jew is slowly but surely establishing himself in Soho, Golden Square, and neighbourhood, and where new workshops are erected, I find that a Jew becomes the occupier, employing from 8 to 12 females with two men pressers, who make coats and trousers for the best West End shops at prices considerably below that paid to the ordinary West End journeyman.' Mr. Bineham who has charge of the East End, reports: 'I am sorry to chronicle the fact that many Jews who, 12 months ago, were strictly orthodox in their religion have been compelled under penalty of losing their trade, to work during their Sabbath, because the Christian (*i.e.*, the West End) employer requires his work to be completed not later than 4 o'clock on Saturdays.' . . .

It is evident from the statements made by these East and West End observers that a difference is being made between the value of male and female labour, and that there is a growing disposition and intention of the large manufacturers in the clothing trade to encourage work by outworkers, the West End bespoke tailors who send their orders down to the East End tailor drives him to complete his task by a certain time, especially before bank holidays, during August and September, and in order to keep his promise, which is so important to him, he will work on Friday night and Saturday night, through the Sabbath, preferring as I said, his work to his faith, and it seems to me very probable that in time the modern Jew will ignore his Sabbath day regulations altogether just as so many so-called Christians ignore theirs.

4.   Secessionists: native and foreign

a)   *The West London Synagogue of British Jews, 1841*

Source: M. Margoliouth, *The History of the Jews in Great Britain*, 3 vols. (1851), III, pp. 78–86

The 'Great Secession', as the events which culminated in the formation of an independent reform congregation are inappropriately known, was the product of frustration and faction within Bevis Marks, the principal Sephardi synagogue. Most of the amendments introduced into the service of the reform congregation were not different in kind from those which were subsequently incorporated into Orthodox practice. The dissidents thought of themselves as reformers rather than schismatics.

The Seceding Members of the Spanish and Portuguese Synagogue to the [Elders]

7th Elul 5601 – 24th August, 1841

Gentlemen,

Having so often expressed our sentiments both to your respected body, and to the meetings of the Yehidim, on the important subject of the improvements, which, in our opinion, were so much required in our form of public worship, as well as on some other points, and having on so many occasions ascertained your total disinclination to attend to our suggestions, or even to consider our views, we cannot entertain the idea, that our present communication will excite any surprise in your minds. In fact, we intimated at the meeting of Yehidim, in 5599, (on the proposition being made for the abrogation of Law, No. 1, of the Yehidim), that our object was to establish a new synagogue, on the principles we had so long advocated, and that we adopted this as the best, if not the only course for satisfying our own conscientious scruples, and for avoiding the repetition of discussions tending to excite and foster ill feelings.

In conformity with these views, and with this avowal, we have, in concert with gentlemen of other congregations, adopted the measures requisite to fulfil our intentions, and having made considerable progress, we thought it right before actually opening the intended place of worship, to lay before you a written statement of the principles on which it is to be conducted. We take this course, not only out of respect to the congregation of which we are members, but also for the purpose of removing any misapprehension that might otherwise have been entertained respecting our views. In order to preserve proper decorum during the performance of Divine Worship, it is essential that the whole congregation should assemble before the commencement of prayer, and remain until its conclusion. To secure the observance of this regulation, and at the same time to obtain a full attendance of members, as well as of their wives and children, we have determined that the service shall commence at a more convenient hour, viz., on Sabbaths and Holidays, at half-past nine, in summer, and at ten in winter; also, that the service shall be limited to a moderate length, for otherwise the mind will, in most instances, be unable to maintain, during the entire period, that solemn and devout attention without which, prayer is unavailing. Hence the service, including the reading of the portions of scripture and a religious discourse, will, on no occasion, except on the day of atonement, exceed in duration two hours and-a-half. To bring the service within this limit, and yet to afford time for its distinct and solemn performance, it became necessary to abridge the existing forms of prayer, whilst it also afforded the opportunity of removing those portions which are not strictly of a devotional character. A careful revision on this plan of the daily and Sabbath Prayer-book, has been already completed, and considerable progress has been made with the Festival prayers. We confidently anticipate that little objection can be raised to these revised forms of service, since they consist, almost without exception, of portions of the existing Prayer-book, together, with passages of scripture. An impartial consideration will convince you that by omitting the less impressive and restraining and blending the more beautiful portions of the Portuguese and German Liturgies, an improved ritual has been formed. The effect of solemn song, in inspired devotional feeling is generally admitted, we have, therefore, determined that the service shall be assisted by a choir.

To familiarize the rising generation, with a knowledge of the great principles of our holy faith – to teach them their duty as Israelites, and as men, must be considered one of the primary objects of public worship. To accomplish these important purposes, religious discourses delivered in the English language, will form part of the morning service on every Sabbath and Holiday. Offerings may be requisite for the maintenance of the synagogue, but as they do not form an integral part of the service, it is considered desirable that they should interfere as little as possible with the devotional character of the place, and that they should not, by occasioning interruptions to the reading of the law, mar its effect. We have, therefore, decided on discontinuing the custom of calling up, as it has long ceased to maintain its original objects, viz., that of enabling individuals to read portions of the law. At present, however, it merely affords the opportunity of making offerings, since those called up do not themselves read the law, but only hear it read in common with the rest of the congregation. We have appointed the three great festivals for the offering of the congregation, which with the voluntary offerings on other occasions, will be made on the return of the law to the Ark; they are to be un-accompanied with personal compliments, and limited to two essential objects; the relief of the poor, and the support of the establishment. It is not the intention of the body, of which we form part, to recognize as sacred, days which are evidently not ordained as such in scripture, and they have consequently appointed the service for holy convocations, to be read on those days only thus designated.

We have already stated, that to effect our object, we have associated ourselves with gentlemen of other congregations, thus rendering it requisite to decide, whether the Hebrew should be pronounced after the manner of the Portuguese, or Germans, and under the conviction that the former is the more correct, we have adopted it.

One of the benefits anticipated by us from the establishment we are forming is, that the junction of members of different congregations to which we have already adverted, will lead to the abolition of the useless distinction now existing in relation to those who are termed Portuguese and German Jews, but who, in fact, are neither Portuguese nor Germans, but natives, and in many instances descendants of natives of the British Empire, and we have, accordingly given the intended place of worship, the designation of 'West London Synagogue of British Jews'.

Such are the views we have endeavoured to carry into effect, and we earnestly assure you, they have not been suggested by any desire of schism, or separation . . . but through a sincere conviction that substantial improvements in the public worship are essential to the weal of our sacred religion, and that they will be the means of handing down to our children, and to our children's children, our holy faith in all its purity and integrity. Indeed, we are firmly convinced, that their tendency will be to arrest, and prevent *secession from Judaism – an overwhelming* evil, which has at various times so widely spread among many of the most respectable families of our communities. Most fervently do we cherish the hope that the effect of these improvements will be to inspire a deeper interest, and a stronger feeling towards our holy religion, and that their influence on the minds of the youth of either sex, will be calculated to restrain them from traversing in their faith, or contemplating for a moment the fearful step of forsaking their religion, so that henceforth no 'Israelite born', may cease to exclaim, 'Hear, O! Israel, the Lord our God, the Lord is one!'

In thus establishing a new Synagogue, on the principles hitherto not recognized or approved by your body, we may possibly encounter a considerable difference of opinion, and a strong prejudice against our proceedings; but, having been actuated solely by a conscientious sense of duty, we venture to hope that on further consideration, our intentions and our motives will be duly appreciated, and that those kindly feelings, which ought to exist between every community of Jews will be maintained . . .

b) East End Chevroth, 1888

Source: Beatrice Potter, 'The Jewish Community' in Charles Booth, *Life and Labour of the People in London*, First Series, Poverty (1889), III, pp. 169–72

Immigrant Jews, for all their poverty, were not commonly identified with the rootless disorganised and residual elements of the population. The role of the *chevroth* in the resettlement process explains why.

. . . the East End Jews of the working class rarely attend the larger synagogues. . . . For the most part the religious-minded form themselves into associations (Chevras), which combine the functions of a benefit club for death, sickness, and the solemn rites of mourning with that of public worship and the study of the Talmud. Thirty or forty of these Chevras are scattered throughout the Jewish quarters; they are of varying size as congregations, of different degrees of solvency as friendly societies, and of doubtful comfort and sanitation as places of public worship. Usually each Chevras is named after the town or district in Russia or Poland from which the majority of its members have emigrated: it is, in fact, from old associations – from ties of relationship or friendship, or, at least, from the memory of a common home – that the new association springs.

Here, early in the morning, or late at night, the devout members meet to recite the morning and evening prayers, or to decipher the sacred books of the Talmud. And it is a curious and touching sight to enter one of the poorer and more wretched of these places on a Sabbath morning. Probably the one you choose will be situated in a small alley or narrow court, or it may be built out in a back-yard. To reach the entrance you stumble over broken pavement and household debris; possibly you pick your way over the rickety bridge connecting it with the cottage property fronting the street. From the outside it appears a long wooden building surmounted by a skylight, very similar in construction to the ordinary sweater's workshop. You enter; the heat and odour convince you that the skylight is not used for ventilation. From behind the trellis of the "ladies' gallery" you see at the far end of the room the richly curtained Ark of the Covenant, wherein are laid attired in gorgeous vestments, the sacred scrolls of the Law. Slightly elevated on a platform in the midst of the congregation, stands the reader or minister, surrounded by the seven who are called up to the reading of the Law from among the congregation. Scarves of white cashmere or silk, softly bordered and fringed, are thrown across the shoulders of the men, and relieve the dusty hue and disguise the Western cut of the clothes they wear. A low, monotonous, but musical-toned recital of Hebrew prayers, each man praying for himself to the God of his fathers, rises from the congregation, whilst the reader intones, with a somewhat louder voice, the recognized portion of the Pentateuch. Add to this rhythmical cadence of numerous voices, the swaying to and fro of the bodies of the worshippers – expressive of the words of personal adoration: "All my bones exclaim, Oh! Lord, who is like unto Thee!" – and you may imagine yourself in a far-off Eastern land. But you are roused from your dreams. Your eye wanders from the men, who form the congregation, to the small body of women who watch behind the trellis. Here, certainly, you have the Western world, in the bright-coloured ostrich feathers, large bustles, and tight-fitting coats of cotton velvet or brocaded satinette. At last you step out, stifled by the heat and dazed by the strange contrast of the old-world memories of a majestic religion and the squalid vulgarity of an East End slum.

And, perchance, if it were permissible to stay after Divine service is over, and if you could follow the quick spoken Jüdisch, you would be still more bewildered by these "destitute foreigners," whose condition, according to Mr. Arnold White, "resembles that of animals." The women have left; the men are scattered over the benches (may-be there are several who are still muttering their prayers), or they are gathered together in knots, sharpening their intellects with the ingenious points and subtle logic of the Talmudical argument, refreshing their minds from the rich stories of Talmudical wit, or listening with ready helpfulness to the tale of distress of a new-comer from the foreign home.

These Chevras supply the social and religious needs of some 12,000 to 15,000 foreign Jews. Up to late years their status within the Jewish community has been very similar to that of dissenting bodies in face of a State Church, always excepting nonconformity of creed. No marriages could be celebrated within their precincts, and they were in no way represented on the central council of the . . . United Synagogue. And owing to the unsanitary and overcrowded state of the poorest Chevras, some among the leaders of the Anglo-Jewish community have thought to discourage the spontaneous multiplication of these small bodies, and to erect a large East End synagogue endowed by the charity of the West. I venture to think that wiser counsels have prevailed. The evils of bad sanitation and overcrowding are easily noted, and still more frequently exaggerated. Philanthropists are apt to forget that different degrees of sanitation and space, like all the other conditions of human existence, are good, bad, or indifferent relatively to the habits and constitutions of those who submit to them. The close and odorous atmosphere of the ordinary Chevras is clearly a matter of choice; there is not even the ghost of a "sweater" to enforce it. In truth, the family occupying one room, the presser or machinist at work day and night close to a coke fire, would find, in all probability, a palace to worship in draughty and uncomfortable, and out of all harmony and proportion with the rest of existence. On the other hand, it is easy to overlook the unseen influence for good of self-creating, self-supporting, and self-governing communities; small enough to generate public opinion and the practical supervision of private morals, and large enough to stimulate charity, worship, and study by communion and example. These and other arguments have led to the federation of minor synagogues and their partial recognition by the communal authorities. And probably it is only a question of time before the East End Chevras are admitted to full representation in the religious organization of the Ashkenazite community in return for a more responsible attitude with regard to the safety and sanitation of the premises they occupy.

c) The Federation of Synagogues, 1887

Source: Federation of Synagogues, *Laws and Bye Laws* (London: N.P. Valentine, 1895), in Charles Booth Collection, British Library of Political and Economic Science, Booth Notebooks B197, fo. 33

The Federation of Synagogues was formed by Samuel Montagu, Liberal Member of Parliament for Whitechapel, in 1887, and consisted initially of sixteen *chevroth* located in the East End of London. Devoted to the traditional rites and customs of East European Jewry, it quickly established itself as a significant force within the Jewish community in Britain.

Laws

Name – The name of the Federation shall be the Federation of Synagogues . . . and shall consist of the following Synagogues:– "Bikhur Cholim," Spital Square, "Bikhur Cholim, Sons of Lodz," New Castle Street; "Crawcour," Fieldgate Street; "Holy Calling Benefit Society," [New Street] Fashion Street; "House of David United Brethren," Fieldgate Street; "Jerusalem," Union Street; "Kindness and Truth," Sandys Row; "Kovna," Catherine Wheel Alley; "Love and Kindness," Prescot Street; "Mile End New Town," Dunk Street; "Mikrah," Fashion Street; "New Dalston," Birkbeck Road; "Peace and Tranquility," Mansell Street; "Peace and Truth," Old Castle Street; Princes Street "Polish," Cutler Street; "Righteous Path No. 2," Windsor Street; Scarborough Street; "Sons of Covenant Friendly Society," Hope Street; "United Brethren of Konin," Hanbury Street; "United Kalisher," St Mark's Street; "Voice of Jacob," Pelham Street; and such others as may from time to time be admitted.

Objects

I. To provide or render available to the members of the Federation the services of a Minister or Dayan certified, as holding orthodox opinions, by the Ecclesiastical Authorities.
II. To endeavour to lessen the number of Charity Funerals by negotiating with the United Synagogue, or with others, for Burials at moderate cost.
III. To obtain and maintain direct representation at the Board of Shechita.
IV. To obtain and maintain direct representation at the Board of Deputies.
V. To obtain and maintain direct representation at the Board of Guardians.
VI. To promote by other means the interests of the Federation of Synagogues.

Constitution – The Federation shall be managed by a Board. The Board shall consist of the following: The President and one elected Member of each of the Federation Synagogues, and in addition also one elected Representative for every complete number of fifty contributing adult male members of each of such Synagogues. The members of the Board shall be elected at a meeting of the respective members of the Synagogues in the Federation to be held at each of such Synagogues in each alternate year. The Board shall also include a number of Elders, not exceeding seven, who need not necessarily be members of Synagogues in the Federation.

Officers – The Board shall elect such Officers, honorary or salaried, as it may deem necessary.

Bye Laws – The Board when constituted shall frame such Bye Laws as it may deem necessary.

Admissions into federation – Synagogues not at present included in the Federation shall be admitted only by a special resolution of the Board. . .

Withdrawals from federation – Any of the Federated Synagogues desiring to withdraw from the Federation, shall only do so with the consent of two thirds of the members of each of such Synagogues at a meeting specially called for the purpose. . .

Alteration of laws – The above Laws shall not be altered, rescinded or increased in number except with the consent of two thirds of the members of the Board at a meeting specially convened for that purpose. . .

Bye-laws

I. Election of representatives – The Board of Federate Synagogues shall consist of the following:–

(a) The President for the time being of each Synagogue in the Federation.

(b) Male persons of the age of twenty-one years and upwards who shall during the whole of one year immediately preceding the date of the election have been full members of one of the Synagogues of the Federation.

(c) The Elders shall be elected at a General Meeting of the Board, and shall hold office for two years, or until such period as the next election of members of the Board shall be held.

There shall, in the year 5649, and in every alternate year thereafter . . . be held a meeting at each of the Synagogues for the time being in the Federation, and at such meeting there shall be elected the President of the Synagogue and one member, and in addition one person (being at the time of election a member of such Synagogue) for every complete number of fifty members.

The persons entitled to vote at the meeting shall be all persons of the age of eighteen years and upwards, who shall, during the whole of the six months immediately preceding the date thereof, have been members . . .

3. Election of executive committee – The Board shall at its first monthly meeting elect an Executive Committee, consisting of the Presidents of all the Synagogues in the Federation, with the President, Vice-President and Treasurers of the Federation and any others not exceeding seven, selected by the Board, whose duty shall be to transact all the ordinary business of the Federation . . .

7. Meeting of the board – The Board shall meet once in every month from October to July (inclusive) . . . The ordinary meetings of the Board shall be held on the third Tuesday in the month, and shall commence not later than 7.30 o'clock . . .; or, if it be deemed expedient on the second or third Sunday in the month, and shall commence not later than 4 o'clock . . .

27. Exclusion of members – It shall be within the power of the Board to exclude any member who shall be deemed objectionable, such exclusion to take effect only by a resolution carried by a two-thirds majority at a meeting specially called to consider such exclusion, and on the resolution being subsequently confirmed.

As the Federation has no right to interfere in any way with the internal management of the Federated Synagogues, it is earnestly hoped that the representatives of the Board will use their influence to ensure that the spirit of the foregoing Rules and Bye-Laws be maintained in their respective Synagogues.

6. Machzike Hadath

a)   Here in London faith is easily forgotten, 1891

Source: Bernard Homa, A Fortress in Anglo Jewry, The Story of the Machzike Hadath (1954), pp. 15–16

The formation of the Machzike Hadath in 1891–92 arose out of a growing dissatisfaction with the lax standards of kashrut sanctioned by the Chief Rabbi but, as the following letter to rabbi Spector of Kovno suggests, the causes of unrest were much wider.

. . . Has it ever been heard of in Israel that one man should make religious pronouncements for the whole Kingdom of England and all the countries under her domain, Africa, Australia, Asia, Canada, and appoint only one expert Rabbinic authority, an old and very feeble man, viz Rabbi Ya'acov Reinowitz (although there is another but he is not acceptable to strictly orthodox Jews), so that there is almost no one of whom to ask any question in Jewish law. The words of the Prophet, as interpreted by our Sages of blessed memory, have certainly come to pass in our case, "When a man shall take hold of his brother in the house of his father, saying, thou hast clothing, be thou our ruler, etc."

'Jewish women have long forgotten the laws of the home; the mikvah is not in accordance with the Din – Here, in London, under the leadership of Rabbi Dr. Adler, it is very easy for our Faith to be forgotten by our children. But He who dwells in Heaven has seen all this and has inspired us with this Holy idea to set up an organisation so as to raise the standard of our Faith.

'It is now some ten months since we approached Rabbi Dr. Adler with a request that he should institute rules that are essential for the strengthening of religious observance. We went to him two or three times, but did not achieve anything. We advanced reasoned arguments, but he replied with trifling words, and made light of everything, until we realised that there was no other course for us but to act on the advice of Hillel, who said, "If I am not for myself, who will be for me?" Moreover, when there is a desecration of God's laws, the honour of any Rabbi does not come into account, even when a Rabbi bears the title of Doctor.

'We have therefore chosen our own expert Rabbinic authority, Rabbi Avraham Aba Werner . . . particularly as the Dayan now in London, Rabbi Ya'acov Reinowitz, is not even appointed by the Kehilla. For Dr. Adler pays him £2 weekly from his own purse, lest the question of a *get, chalitza*, proselytization, or the like should arise, when this Dayan advises Dr. Adler as to the sources of the Din; and the Russian and Polish Jews are obliged to pay him a further £1.

'Now when we showed this same Dayan all the terrible things that were happening, he himself stopped eating meat, and gave us advice on how to be saved from the snare that was spread at our feet; but he was afraid to come out in the open for fear lest it might affect his livelihood. . . . We are, therefore, justly proud that this Holy idea came to us to take up the battle of the Lord of Hosts, so that the Faith of Israel shall not be forgotten by all . . .'

b) *Machzike Hadath and Shomrei Shabbat, 1895?*

Source: Bernard Homa, *A Fortress in Anglo Jewry, The Story of Machzike Hadath* (1954), pp. 109–10

The kind of synagogue community envisaged by the secessionists is embodied in the opening passages of the *pinkes* as given below.

At a General Meeting of our Members held at the Synagogue on 17th Shebat, 5653, it was resolved unanimously, that the Synagogue should join the Machzike Hadath Community and in the place of its old name 'Machzike Shomrei Shabbat', it shall henceforth be known by the name 'Machzike Hadath and Shomrei Shabbat' and shall be governed by the following rules:

I   The aim and object of the Synagogue is, as hitherto, to strengthen the observance of the Jewish Religion and to maintain the Holy Law by the strict adherence to the Bible, Oral Law and all traditions.

  (*a*) to keep the Synagogue open from daybreak until midnight free for anyone wishing to read Prayers, Study the Law, or recite Psalms,

  (*b*) to encourage the constant presence in the Synagogue of Learned Men (לומדי תורה) studying the Torah, as well as to fix special hours for Talmudic Courses,

  (*c*) to regard it as a duty to support as far as is possible, necessitous Learned Men and specially for the Leaders to uphold the dignity of the Torah,

  (*d*) to be incumbent upon the leaders and also upon all members to give all their support to the Machzike Hadath Kehilla, in monetary gifts as well as by personal service, but above all that their Religious mode of life and the observance of the dietary laws in their homes be strictly in accord with the guidance of our Rav.

II   The rituals of the Synagogue Services must be strictly in accord with the Shulchan Aruch and with the customs of the communities of Russia and Poland.

   (a)   The Reader's Desk עמוד where prayers are chanted by the Reader, must be close to the Ark, except that in special circumstances after having received the Rav's special sanction, the Reader may officiate from the Bemah,

   (b)   the Bemah must be in the centre of the Synagogue,

   (c)   the Rav, Preacher, Reader or Shammas may not wear such Canonicals which may appear as if in imitation of non-Jewish Clergy.

III   Conditions under which members are admitted:

   (a)   Every Jew observing the Sabbath according to the Din, may join the Synagogue as a Member.

c)   Hermann Adler looks to the east, 1891

Source: Bernard Homa, A Fortress in Anglo Jewry, The Story of Machzike Hadath (1954), pp. 104–05

It was not only the secessionists who appealed to the heartlands of Orthodoxy for support in their struggle against the Anglo Jewish ecclesiastical establishment. The Chief Rabbi, sensing that his own authority was at issue, was equally keen to secure an endorsement from the learned ones of the east. The text of the following is from Hermann Adler to Yitzchak Elchanan Spector (1819–96), the revered Rabbi of Kovno, 20 November 1891.

May the Lord ordain peace to my dear friend, the truly great Rabbi Yitzchak Elchanan, Ab Beth Din of Kovno.

I should not have troubled him, but I desire briefly to inform his Eminence that some Russian and Polish Jews have risen up, calling themselves Chevrath Machzike Hadath, have taken as their Rabbi a certain man named Avraham Aba Werner from the town of Tels, and have appointed for themselves a Shochet and opened shops to sell ritually slaughtered meat; and thereby they have breached the fence which the great Rabbis of former years had set up. We have already forbidden this Shechita.

His Eminence will realise, in his wisdom, the serious situation which may develop, God forbid, if some Russian and Polish Jews separate themselves from the Kehilla. For it is known to his Eminence how much the practice of charity has advanced among us, and should the dispute spread, the members of the Community would turn away from them and would no longer work on their behalf nor for the benefit of our unfortunate co-religionists.

Would his Eminence, therefore, be pleased to write me a few lines to approve the interdict issued by me and by my Beth Din, and that no man in England should dare to perform Shechita without my permission and that of my Beth Din, viz. our esteemed Rabbis, Jacob Reinowitz and Bernard Spiers. Furthermore, should any wicked persons dare to libel the Shechita here, would he please not believe nor listen to them. For just as the Shechita was carried out in the days of my esteemed father, of blessed memory, so it is now, and we watch with open eyes over everything that is done. In addition, we have a supervisor, the Rosh Hashochtim, Reb Nahum Lipman; and all our aims are to strengthen the prestige of the Torah and religion.

d) Memories are made of this! 1910

Source: Bernard Homa, *A Fortress in Anglo-Jewry, The Story of Machzike Hadath* (1954), pp. 77–80.

Bernard Homa (1900–1991), physician, local councillor, former president and historian of the *Machzike Hadath*, was the grandson of its spiritual guide and teacher, the distinguished and immensely popular Rabbi Avraham Aba Werner. Here he remembers its place in the life of the immigrant community before the First World War.

My earliest recollections of the Machzike Hadath Synagogue go back to my boyhood. What a magnificent appearance it presented during the High Festivals! What a splendid array of Talmudic scholars along the honoured Eastern Wall! The *Shool* overcrowded with extra chairs all round the *Bemah*, and, in front of these, personal 'Prayer-stands' suitably covered, with everybody keyed up to the importance of the occasion. One just felt the holiness of the place. And with what fervour were the prayers uttered! When the moment came for the Congregation to recite a prayer, they could hardly wait for the Chazan to finish his part before they would burst out in one loud accord impatient to show their devotion. How strange was the auctioning of the *Mitzvot* before the Reading of the Law! (A practice long since discarded by the Machzike Hadath in favour of calling up those suitable, irrespective of their ability to make offerings.) And when the *Sepharim* were carried to the Bemah, how all thronged to kiss them! And when the Reading took place, how clearly and beautifully each word was pronounced! This applied to the *Haftarah* as well as to the *Sidra*, for the former, too, was always read by the *Ba'al K'riah* from a Scroll and in the more plaintive tune of Eastern European tradition. And the occasional banging by the *Shammas* on a heavy *Machzor* often accompanied by a loud 'Shah' to silence the more audible women-folk in the galleries hidden from view behind lace curtains, how effective it was, if only for a few seconds!

I shall never forget the great number that ascended before the Ark for *Birchat Cohanim*. There were so many Cohanim in the School, that some could not find enough room on the large platform, and had to stand on the steps leading to it. Worshippers, whose seats were along the *Mizrach* wall or in its proximity, would leave their places to stand at the foot of the stairs in front of the Ark, in order to receive the Priestly benediction. Unlike most other Ashkenazi Synagogues in this country, Birchat Cohanim is not omitted in the Machzike Hadath when a Festival coincides with the Sabbath, and the Service proceeds as it would elsewhere on *Yom Kippur*, in similar circumstances. This accords with the *Minhag* of the Vilna Gaon.

The large number of *Lulavim* on *Succot* was most impressive. Almost everyone present seemed to have one, and the circuit had to be extended into the Beth Hamedrash. Very interesting was the way many congregants proudly demonstrated, after the Service, the special merits of their particular *Ethrogim* both as to shape and appearance, to show that they were, in fact, פרי עץ הדר.

Simchat Torah was a day of great spiritual happiness. In the evening, the Synagogue was densely packed with hundreds of visitors who crowded even the gangways until there was hardly any room to move. And it was always a marvel to me how the processions of the Scrolls could proceed at all. As many as thirty Sepharim were carried round in what seemed an endless succession of circuits, after each of which there was singing and dancing. Finally, before the Sepharim were returned to the Ark, there was a formal reading of the Law, only three persons being called up. In the morning, the Shool was again full, although the crowds were not nearly so numerous. Everyone present was called to the Reading of the Law which appeared to go on indefinitely. The Rav was always *Chatan Torah*. I remember Ya'acov Zinkin as *Chatan Bereshith* standing on the Bemah together with my grandfather, both showing expressions of joy, derived only from spiritual exultation.

Another outstanding annual occasion in the Machzike Hadath Synagogue was the Evening of Purim, when a particularly large number of the children of the surrounding district were attracted to the Reading of the *Megilla*. Many were armed with *Greggers* or with nothing more than their boots with which to demonstrate their contempt for Haman. The loud din which greeted each mention of his name was like a miniature earthquake, and would last for well over a minute. The noise, usually started by a few adults would grow in volume like a mounting wave, till the whole building literally shook from the clatter of the rattles and the heavy stamping of hundreds of feet. Sometimes the Reader ingeniously contrived to rush through an odd Haman without being interrupted, but such manoeuvres were more than compensated by some additional unauthorised clatterings which would hold up the proceedings for even longer.

In the early days, soon after the Synagogue was opened, when the East End was crowded with recently arrived immigrants from Eastern Europe, there were many women worshippers on weekdays, even during *Mincha* and *Ma'ariv*. It was an interesting sight to see women who had hurried in specially to join in a *Kedusha*, and who would even stand for this purpose on the steps leading up to the Ladies' Gallery.

My grandfather's house was a hive of constant activity. Practically all day long there was a succession of callers, each with his or her problem of a religious or general character. One would come with an abstruse question of Talmudic lore, another would bring a chicken which raised doubt from the ritual point of view – and what a sigh of relief when the chicken was declared kosher! And if not, my grandfather would frequently pay the cost of another. Some people came to have a chat over a glass of tea with lemon or merely to sit and listen. Others were newly arrived immigrants who had been referred to Reb Aba for advice. Rabbis or other persons of significance in the orthodox world coming to England either for a short stay or in order to settle would, as a matter of course, first visit the Machzike Hadath and call upon Rabbi Werner, who gave all a cordial welcome and sound advice which many were to remember with gratitude.

Among the distinguished visitors who stayed with my grandfather in 1910, I vividly remember the *Ridvaz* from Safed, a very imposing personality, and I recall the stir that was caused when he ventured into the street wearing his *Streimel*, a form of headgear I had not previously seen.

It is perhaps of interest to mention here the statement inscribed in the Synagogue Pinkes by this world-famous Rabbi (grandfather of the wife of Rabbi Abramsky), who naturally frequented the Machzike Hadath Shool whilst he was in London. A reproduction of the original statement is shown . . . [in] . . . translation:

22 Adar 5670, London

Fellow Jews! All that is written here, have I confirmed with my own eyes. I have prayed in this Holy Synagogue for more than a week and nigh on two. I did not feel that I was in the capital City of London but I thought that I was in the Jewish Community of Eisheshok, Wolozin or the like, a place where our forefathers would stand to pour out their words in prayer and in the song of the Torah at the same time. May ye be truly happy, ye sons of this Holy Congregation. All must be indebted to the founders and to those who support and actively assist in strengthening this edifice. Not in vain have ye sown in tears, but so that ye may reap in joy.

Signed: Ya'acov David, 'Ridvaz'
Rabbi of the Holy City of Safed

7. The Chief Rabbi speaks, 1897

Source: Charles Booth Collection, Booth Notebooks, *British Library of Political and Economic Science* B197 fos. 5–15

Chief Rabbi Dr Hermann Adler (1839–1911) was born in Hanover but brought up in England. He was educated at University College, London and received his PhD from the University of Leipzig. He became Minister of Bayswater Synagogue in 1864 and delegate Chief Rabbi in 1879 in which office he succeeded his father twelve years later. In 1897 he gave a revealing interview to Charles Booth's inquiry into the life and labour of the people in London from which the following is taken.

. . . On the general character of the Jewish population in different parts of London Dr Adler gave the following enumeration.

. . .

Asked as to the movement towards securing the diffusion of the Jews, Dr Adler said that there was a very earnest desire on the part of the leaders of the community to secure this. The only place in which there is congestion is in East London, and the only class congested is the foreigner. They keep together because of a natural gregariousness and because they want to be near the shops for which or in which they work.

Reasons for wishing diffusion are: the avoidance of the overcrowding and high rents and permanency of the vernacular that comes from congestion. In the country foreign Jews became anglicised much more rapidly than in London, and it is desired to make London approximate to country conditions as much as possible. The organization that is most active in this connexion is the Russo-Jewish Committee. Movements are at present on foot to plant synagogues in West Ham, Poplar, Peckham etc. as aids to migration. [Dr Adler did not mention it, but I believe that one reason why it is desired that the foreign Jews should not crowd together, is that they are less noticed if they are mixed up with other people. It is felt to be inexpedient, whenever an agitation is started for an Alien Emigration Bill, that streets should be on evidence filled with none but the foreigner. The motive thus caused, and the strong desire to anglicise are I believe the two great reasons why the Jewish leaders dislike congestion].

The English Jews diffuse naturally, and there is a regular movement often of individual families, from Middlesex Street, to Dalston, and then by way of Highbury, Maida Vale, and Bayswater, to Hyde Park.

On the general organization of the Jewish Church in London and the responsibility of local congregations Dr Adler said that the spiritual government of Jews in London [as also of the British Empire] had been vested by a Council in the Chief Rabbi. An elaborate schedule of his powers, duties and responsibilities has been printed and he mentioned the following: visitation of Jewish schools, the enforcement of their responsibilities upon foreigners, as regards education, general social observances etc; the settlement of disputes as regards the management, ritual etc. of synagogues etc. An obligation of the office is to have a residence in the East and every . . . alternate Sabbath as well as on certain Feast and other days Dr Adler and his family live at Finsbury Square. It was not thought desirable that the Chief Rabbi should leave the West End and the surroundings of the more cultured section, but that he should be able to be also near the poorer part of the community and always with the object, and he emphasized and asked me to note the phrase, of making them 'loyal subjects and steadfast Jews'. On these and any other matters, including powers of suspension, see the 'laws of the United Synagogue' which Dr Adler will lend us.

8. Zionism in England, 1900

Source: C. Russell and H.S. Lewis, *The Jew in England, A Study in Racial Character and Present-day Conditions* (1900), pp. 106–17

The environment in which Jews have found themselves has, ever since Biblical times, influenced their spiritual and social development. The rather different place which Zionism occupied in Britain by comparison with its position in Central and Eastern Europe is discussed below.

. . . A somewhat similar testimony to the strength of the forces which make for assimilation, is afforded by the Zionist party. For it seems fairly plain that in England Zionism is in its essence a revolt against this tendency; and it appears to differ widely in aim and motive from the Zionism of the Continent. Emigration to Palestine and the foundation of a Jewish State is there regarded principally as an answer to Anti-Semitism, and the only possible refuge from an intolerable state of things. Whereas in England the state of things is not intolerable; and accordingly the movement has here awakened a comparatively feeble response. Among English Jews proper, in fact, there can hardly be said to be any Zionism at all. It has been estimated that there are ten thousand Zionists in England; but practically all of them seem to be foreign immigrants. English Jews are for the most part either indifferent or hostile; and those in authority have generally set their faces against it. The Chief Rabbi, for instance, has declared the movement to be 'an egregious blunder'; and it is generally deprecated as chimerical and extravagant. The Zionists, however, attach little importance to such expressions of Anglo-Jewish opinion, and look to the Continent for their lead, without apparently recognising that within their own ranks there is any divergence of ideas. Yet on the question of assimilation there is a significant difference of tone in the utterances of English and Continental Zionists. Thus Dr Herzl, at the Basle Congress, spoke of 'our efforts of assimilation, the unsuccess of which has brought us again together'; whereas to the *Jewish World*, the organ of the English Zionists, it is the glory of Zionism, that 'it has called a halt to the assimilators.'* It should be said in fairness that the contradiction is probably not so sharp as might appear, because the word 'assimilation' is somewhat ambiguous; but there is, undoubtedly, a broad difference of attitude. It is significant that the same word should, in England, stand for an imminent disaster to Judaism, and on the Continent for a heaven out of reach. Similarly, it appears that in England Zionism is closely identified with extreme orthodoxy; the Chief Rabbi of the *Mahazike Haddath* is one of the prominent figures in the movement; and at Basle it was Dr Gaster, the Chacham** of the Spanish and Portuguese congregation in England, who insisted that 'the religious element lies at the very foundation of the movement,' and moved a resolution to the effect that 'Zionism will not undertake anything which would be contrary to Jewish religious law.' On the Continent the religious aspect of the movement (so far, at any rate, as its leaders are concerned) is quite overshadowed by the political; and neither Dr Herzl nor Dr Nordau are supposed to be very specially concerned about the survival of orthodoxy. An attempt, indeed, was made at a recent meeting of Zionists in East London, to criticise Dr Herzl for his lack of reference to religion; and although the speaker failed to obtain a hearing, he undoubtedly touched a point of difference which is likely to become more acute as the movement develops, and ceases to be a matter of mere enthusiasm. Here, however, the peculiar character of English Zionism is of interest mainly as evidence of the progress which the English Jewry has made towards assimilation; it shows that in the opinion, at least, of a section, this process has reached a point at which it becomes a menace to Judaism. Zionism and the cult of the 'National Idea,' are here proclaimed as a refuge against absorption among the Gentiles. Assimilation, it is held, must in the long run prove fatal to Judaism, and would be an ignoble end of Jewish history. . . .

. . .

To discuss the probable future of Zionism would take us too far afield, but it is worth while to emphasise one or two points in which it illustrates the main contention of this essay. English Zionism is at bottom a religious rather than a political movement, and appears to be mainly the outcome of a conviction that, in the long run, 'Anglicisation' is not compatible with the preservation of Judaism. The Religious Idea and the National Idea, it is said, are one and inseparable, as the body and soul of

---

* *Jewish World*, September 2, 1898, p. 241
** Chacham (*lit.* wise man), the official title of the Chief Rabbi of the Spanish and Portuguese congregation.

Judaism, and the one can only be maintained by a revival of the other. Zionism is offered as the sole alternative to complete absorption. And it is remarkable that this line of argument seems never to have been fairly met by the Anti-Zionists. The movement has been abundantly denounced 'on prophetical, political and financial grounds.' It has been decried as impracticable and as alien to the true 'mission of Israel.' But this particular argument, either because it is unanswerable or for some other reason, appears to have been passed over in silence.

. . .

Zionism appears so far to corroborate the testimony of the decay of orthodoxy which was furnished by the *Mahazike Haddath*. Both are witnesses crying out against the de-Judaising influence of English life; and if they are right, the comparative weakness of the Zionist movement in England, and its almost exclusively foreign character show that the danger to Judaism is a very serious one. The apathy and aloofness of the great body of English Jews is a sign that they have lost both national and religious enthusiasm. In a word, they have become Englishmen at the cost of their Judaism.

VII
EDUCATION AND IMPROVEMENT

Native and immigrant Jews agreed that education was central to Jewish identity, but possessed conflicting ideas as to the kind of Jewish life it was meant to sustain. In the first half of the nineteenth century the Anglo-Jewish elite had developed an extensive Jewish school system primarily to improve the character of their poorer co-religionists and transform them into disciplined, self-reliant and useful members of society equipped with the marketable skills that would enable them to quit the street trades and secure wholesome employment as industrious artizans. The best known of their initiatives, the Jews' Free School in Bell Lane, was founded by Joshua Van Oven in 1817. At its peak it had 3,000 pupils and was the largest elementary school in the world (**doc. 1**). Similar, if less renowned, Jewish day schools were established in the early 1840s in Birmingham, Liverpool and Manchester. The provision of free non-denominational education by the board schools after 1870 made the further development of a Jewish voluntary school system unnecessary. The London School Board which showed itself sensitive and responsive to Jewish requirements meant that, for Anglo-Jewry, state involvement in elementary education was not experienced as a trauma comparable with that of Anglo-Christianity. Schooling, so far as the Anglo-Jewish elite was concerned, came to be viewed increasingly in non-denominational terms – as an aid to Anglicisation rather than a source of separatism.

Apart from the denominational day schools, the Jewish school system included a large number of traditional *Talumdei Torahs* (schools for the study of Hebrew, Bible, Talmud and other rabbinic texts) and *chedarim*. These latter institutions, concerned solely with religious education, represented the least acculturated forms of organized Judaism. The *chedarim* in particular were an affront to native Jewry. The long hours of after-school instruction given in Yiddish allegedly undermined the health of the student, diminished his academic performance and impeded his ability to adjust to the habits and customs of the host society (**doc. 2**). Neither the Catholic Parochial School nor the Protestant Sunday School supplied an appropriate alternative, however. The former, it was feared, fostered a sectarian self-regarding outlook while the latter was inconsistent with the tradition of family-centred Sabbath worship. Both were rejected in favour of a supplementary system of weekday religious instruction, organized by the Jewish Religious Education Board, and given after hours in the secular state schools which the majority of immigrant children attended. The informal understanding whereby state schools in the Jewish East End were largely run by the Jewish community with the assent of the London School Board (and later the London County Council), produced that unique hybrid the 'Jewish Board School' (doc. 3) and made it unnecessary to expand the voluntary sector or enter the political cockpit in its defence. There was a good deal of contemporary criticism of the policies of the London School Board and a fair amount of popular hostility by Gentile parents who felt that their children were seriously disadvantaged in the competition for scholarships by the constant breaks in the autumn term caused by the observance of the Jewish holidays and festivals. But for all that, Anglicisation on the rates never had quite the same resonance as Anglicanism on the rates (doc. 6).

About the politics of Jewish education and the purpose of Jewish education we know a good deal; about the experience of schooling we know comparatively little. Most of our information comes from teachers, either in evidence given to official inquiries or from personal retrospects in newspapers or book-length memoirs. In general these accounts suggest that immigrant children were industrious, attentive, quick to learn and remarkable in their ability to overcome the poverty and deprivation of their environment (docs. 4–5 and 7(b)). School reports and prizes, too, often reveal the values, goals and curious character of the 'Jewish Board School' as an Anglicising agent (doc. 7(a)). The reception of education and its diffusion throughout the immigrant family will also bear closer scrutiny.

What the *Jewish Encyclopaedia* described as 'a somewhat higher grade of educational effort' was provided by the various social clubs and improving institutions that were intended to connect the juvenile and young adult populations of the immigrant community. The Jewish Working Men's Club in Great Alie Street, founded by Samuel Montague in 1872, was the principal body. Preparatory work was undertaken by the various social and athletic clubs that were founded in the generation before the Great War. Chief among them was the Brady Street Boys' Club, founded in 1896 (doc. 7(c)). Similar provision for girls, included the Leman Street Girls' Club (1883), the Jewish Girls' Club (1886) and the West Central Jewish Girls' Club (1887). The boys' clubs were social and sporty; the girls', which combined recreation with the cultivation of the spirit and the intellect, were also concerned to safeguard their members from vice and impurity (doc. 7(d)). The Education Act of 1902 boosted the membership. Like the legislation of 1870, it transferred the cost of provision from the community to the taxpayer and so enabled English-language instruction to be given in the clubs as part of their continuing education programmes. Directed and controlled by members of the Anglo-Jewish elite – Lady Magnus at Leman Street, Lady Sassoon at Butler Street, Basil Henriques at Oxford and St George's – Jewish youth clubs sought to build character, encourage good citizenship and loyalty to king and country. No doubt the clubs did do much to foster Englishness without loss of Jewishness, but their popularity was genuine. Clubs were fun; they would not have succeeded otherwise.

Non-Jewish philanthropy also played a significant role in the Anglicisation of the Jewish immigrant. The contribution of Toynbee Hall in particular requires attention. The Victoria Working Boys' Club, formed in 1901, was, for example, the outcome of a Toynbee Hall initiative. Not only were its lectures, discussion groups, clubs and societies patronized by large numbers of young Jews; it also encouraged the active involvement of communal representatives in its social work. The role of the Toynbee Hall Settlement as an Anglicising agent should not be underestimated (**doc. 7(e)**).

1.   Jews' Free School, 1864

Source: W. Gilbert, 'The London Jews', *Good Words* V (1864), pp. 923–24

The Jews' Free School, the largest and most famous school of its kind, played an important role in the socialisation of the immigrant East Enders. The Jews' Free School in Bell Lane was founded in 1817; its subsidiary, the Jews' Infant School in Commercial Street, opened its doors in 1841. The kind of education that awaited the newcomers from Eastern Europe is described below.

. . . The magnitude of these two schools will perhaps astonish many of our readers. The first – the Infant School – accommodates 700 pupils. The building, built solely by charitable contributions, is the largest and best adapted for an infant school we have seen. Better ventilation or more perfect arrangements it would be impossible to devise. The rooms are very spacious and lofty, and the play-grounds, both covered and open, are astonishingly large, when the enormous value of ground in Commercial Street is taken into consideration. The whole establishment, both as to building and arrangements, is of a description which shows that the greatest liberality has been shown in every respect.

This institution arose indirectly from the exertions and example of one individual, and is another proof how valuable in many works of public benefit is the assistance of an amiable, energetic, and intelligent woman.

Some years since a Miss Miriam Harris, a member of a highly respectable but not affluent Jewish family, employed herself, gratuitously, in instructing some half-a-dozen children under eight years of age in a small room in a low neighbourhood. By degrees her pupils increased in number, and two or three other ladies joined her in the good work. The results of genuine philanthropy are generally cumulative, and Miss Harris found her pupils increasing in a ratio far higher than either her own finances or the exertions of herself and friends could meet, and they appealed to others of their acquaintance for assistance. By the wealthy Jews, after they have investigated cautiously the merits of an undertaking, an appeal appears to be in general favourably answered; and so Miss Harris was enabled gradually to enlarge the sphere of her usefulness, till at last it culminated in the Jewish Infant Schools in Commercial Street.

Figure 12 Domestic economy class, Jews' Free School, 1908 Prescribed gendered roles were an essential part of the curriculum; the boys received manly and manual training; the girls were made ready to perform as carers and home-makers (Courtesy London Musuem of Jewish Life).

Miss Harris is still the lady superintendent of the establishment, and admirably is it conducted. Her staff of assistants are ladies of talent and energy, and the whole machinery seems in capital working order. On the day of our visit, there was, on account of the cold weather, a scanty muster of infants, still their numbers must have exceeded 500. All were scrupulously clean, although the majority lived in dwellings where it was no easy matter to observe cleanliness; and their clothes, though in many instances miserably poor, were, on the whole, well-mended and tidy. Indeed it is a stringent rule of the establishment, that cleanliness and neatness must be maintained. They went through their lessons remarkably well, and the singing appeared to be their favourite task. They sang several little hymns with great energy, and we were not a little pleased to find that "God save the Queen" was among their favourite performances. On mentioning it to Miss Harris, she informed us that it was one great object with the school committee to inculcate at the earliest age in the minds of the children a pride in their English nationality. We were also exceedingly pleased to notice the absence of fear or restraint in the behaviour of the pupils to Miss Harris. They, on the contrary, seemed to look upon her as their friend, and were evidently pleased when she appeared among them. The parents of the children are expected to pay, when able, one penny per week for the instruction of each child, but there is great irregularity in the payments, arising not from want of integrity but from dense poverty. Notwithstanding this, the children receive in the winter two dinners a week, humble, it is true, but in quality wholesome and amply sufficient. When the children are of sufficient age to be removed, they are drafted into the celebrated Jewish Free Schools in Bell Lane, which, with the exception of a small Government grant of 167*l*. a year and about 200*l*. a year from the children's pence, are also a charitable institution.

These schools are situated in a densely populated district, nearly at the back of the infant schools. They were founded by some wealthy Jews in the year 1817, when the system of education adopted was that of mutual instruction on the monitorial system, and 276 boys were taught by one master Hebrew, English, reading, writing, and the rudiments of arithmetic.

It soon, however, became evident, in consequence of the great number of applications for admission, that the building was much too small, and the necessity of a similar school for girls was also felt. The building was therefore enlarged to accommodate 600 boys, and a separate wing added for girls, of whom 300 were instructed in the same branches of knowledge as the boys, as well as in plain needlework.

The system of education has been changed from the monitorial to that of masters and pupil teachers only. The boys receive a far more extended course of education, while the girls' course has also been improved; and with the intention of increasing their usefulness, the duties of the laundry have been introduced. In the year 1853 these schools were for the first time visited by the government inspector, who expressed himself highly pleased, not only with the curriculum of study, and the general proficiency of the children, but with the sanitary arrangements and ventilation of the building as well.

It has been found necessary to enlarge the school accommodation from time to time, until the Jewish Free Schools in Bell Lane have attained such magnitude as entitles them to rank among the largest educational institutions in the country, accommodating and instructing 2000 children. Still, however, their numbers go on increasing, and the present building, vast as it is, will soon be incapable of receiving the number of pupils that are congregating in the neighbourhood. But additional ground has lately been purchased for further enlargement, and when the new buildings are completed the schools will be capable of receiving at least 3000 children. A visit to them would amply repay any philanthropist. We of course have not the power of giving an invitation, but from the extreme courtesy we received from the head master, Mr. Angell, on the occasion of our visit, we are led to believe that similar kindness would be shown to others. The inspection of the building alone might gratify a visitor. In respect to completeness, every department is especially adapted for its peculiar purpose. Galleries are provided for simultaneous teaching, several groups of parallel desks are set apart for individual instruction, spacious and even elegant classrooms are appropriated for those higher branches which demand isolation and fixity of purpose. There is also a good library for reference and circulation, as well as an amply furnished museum to illustrate lessons on art, science and manufacture. Text-books and class-books, selected with the greatest care, drawing copies and models, maps, diagrams – every article, in short, that was formerly regarded as a luxury of school life, has here been considered as a necessity, and has been copiously supplied. All are taught Hebrew, and among the more intelligent boys that language is most carefully studied. Besides reading, writing, and arithmetic, the more advanced pupils are instructed in Euclid, mensuration, algebra, and natural science. Physiology as applied to health is also taught to the highest class, which is likewise instructed in vocal music, and in drawing.

In the girls' school, of course, less attention is devoted to the higher branches of intellectual cultivation, in order to afford time for instruction in duties more especially useful to females. Needlework in all its applications to domestic or ornamental purposes; washing, ironing, and other household economies are sedulously taught, while care is taken that every girl shall acquire a knowledge of her prayers, not only in the Hebrew, but in the vernacular as well. Altogether the organisation of the female branch of the school does the highest honour both to the ladies who superintend it and the intelligent head-mistress, Mrs. Phillips.

Among other Jewish schools, the Free Schools in Greek Street, Soho, deserve a visit. They instruct about 240 children. A feature worthy of notice in these is the superior dress and appearance of the West End poor, arising from their living immediately under the eye of the wealthier Jews. These schools are models of excellence in their arrangements, and do immense credit to the committee superintending them, and the care of the master and mistress. The girls' school, under the instruction of Mrs. Forty, the head-mistress, is one of the best we have ever had the pleasure of visiting. Another in Red Lion Square is also admirably conducted. There are also several Sabbath schools in different parts of the metropolis, in which the Old Testament is studied in Hebrew and in English. Some of their industrial schools, especially those in which Jewish girls are taught the elements of domestic management, are especially worthy of praise. . . .

2. Education and Jewish identity, 1900

Source: C. Russell and H.S. Lewis, *The Jew in London, A Study in Racial Character and Present-day Conditions* (1900), pp. 214–25

Immigrant Jews from Eastern Europe had their own ideas on what constituted a sound education for their sons, and these were not in accord with the views of their more Anglicised and enlightened co-religionists. The *chedarim* and *Talmudei*

Torah were scattered across the immigrant quarter. The former existed anywhere
— a parlour, front room, small synagogue would do; the latter first made their
appearance at Great Garden Street in 1881 and spread rapidly through Jewish
East London.

. . . One of the most striking feature in the foreign Jew is his anxiety that
his children should receive sufficient instruction in Hebrew. Quite poor
parents frequently pay a shilling a week for each of their sons to the
melammid, or teacher, who instructs them in the Hebrew school or *cheder*.
The boy attends there from the time when he is six years old, or earlier;
and he nearly always leaves at the age of thirteen, when Jewish law
regards him as responsible for his actions and bound to perform all
Mosaic commands. During this time he learns in succession Hebrew
reading, the translation of the Pentateuch, and easy passages in the
commentary on the Pentateuch, written by Rashi, an illustrious French
Rabbi of the eleventh century. He also gains familiarity with the
fundamental portions of the liturgy, although, unfortunately, he is
sometimes taught to 'daven,' or repeat his prayers, without understanding
them. In some of the better *chedarim* Hebrew grammar is taught, and the
more advanced pupils study the elements of ritual law. Moral instruction
is given by the more enlightened teachers, but is often neglected. The
teaching given is usually very earnest and effective; boys attending *cheder*
acquire a far greater knowledge of Hebrew than those whose training in
that subject is only derived from Jewish voluntary schools or from the
religious classes attached to those Board schools which are principally
attended by Jewish children.

. . .

The chief complaints made against the *cheder* are that Yiddish is used as
the medium of instruction, that the rooms used are insanitary, and that
the hours are too long. A few remarks on each of these points may be
desirable.

It is complained that the use of Yiddish in the *cheder* arrests the
process of Anglicisation. Now it is perfectly true that in only a few
chedarim is instruction given in English.* This arises chiefly through the
lack of suitable teachers who can speak English, and partly, doubtless,
through the preference of the parents. Parents, who themselves speak
Yiddish only, like to hear their boys repeat on Saturday what has been
learnt during the week. Many of them, too, entertain the prejudice that
Hebrew can be better taught through the medium of Yiddish, or even
imagine that this jargon has more holiness than English. A prejudice of

* Five such *chedarim* are known to me in Whitechapel, besides others in outlying
districts. The average number of pupils in each is 50, whilst a large majority of
children, taught in Yiddish, attend *chedarim* conducted on a much smaller scale.

Figure 13   A cheder (Jewish school) in Whitechapel, 1901   In bare, humble
schoolrooms all over the area of Jewish settlement ill-paid teachers, the *melammdim*,
hammered Hebrew instruction into the jaded heads of the Children of the Ghetto
(G.R. Sims (ed.), *Living London*, 3 vols (London: Cassell, 1901), II, p. 31).

this kind tends, however, to cure itself, and quite equally foolish is the
idea of the West-End Jew that instruction in Yiddish will arrest the
inevitable process of Anglicisation. It stands to reason that the boy
brought up in this country, and attending an English school, will grow up
an Englishman. . . .

. . .

    With regard to the alleged insanitary condition of *chedarim*, after
having visited many, I believe that the case against them breaks down
almost entirely. The larger *cheder* is fitted up with desks as a schoolroom;
it is not used for living purposes, and is seldom overcrowded or badly
ventilated. The objectionable *chedarim* are those established on a small
scale by 'greeners,' who arrive in England without any means of
livelihood, and supplement a precarious living as hawkers, or sellers of
foreign lottery tickets, by teaching a few children sent to them from
charitable motives by their neighbours and friends. A *cheder* of this kind
is held in a living-room, sometimes in an underground kitchen. . . . A
very small proportion, however, of the children attending *chedarim* are
educated under these conditions, . . . As to the general charge that

children suffer in health through attendance at *cheder*, I would repeat an argument used by Mr Cohenlask, president of the society of *cheder* teachers, in a letter addressed by him to the *Jewish Chronicle*. Foreign Jews do not send their daughters to *cheder*, yet there is no reason to suppose that East-End girls enjoy better health than their brothers. It is eminently desirable to improve the health and physique of the East-End Jew, but the abolition of the *cheder* is not one of the methods to be attempted.

Besides the children attending *cheder*, a considerable number are taught by visiting masters. Collectors of East-End provident and philanthropic societies often supplement their earnings by taking a few such pupils.

Side by side with the *cheder* there exists the *Talmud Torah*,** or institution for teaching Hebrew and religion, supported partly by pupils' fees and partly by subscriptions, and managed by a committee of subscribers. The two principal institutions of the kind are situated in Whitechapel. The larger of the two is now closely connected with the *Mahazike Haddath*. There are about a thousand pupils, and instruction is given in Yiddish. The other has over six hundred pupils and instruction is given in English. Both institutions are quite full and children have to be refused admission for want of room. The fees paid vary according to the circumstances of the parents, but average about twopence per child. The children attend for about two hours each evening. Classes at the *Talmud Torah* are much larger than at a *cheder*. A single master has often to teach forty pupils, and of course cannot give much individual attention. The teaching given, however, is very efficient, and has met with the approval of many educational experts. The results of the instruction, as measured by the progress made by the scholars, must be pronounced satisfactory. The subscriptions obtained for the support of both institutions are derived almost exclusively from the East End.

I have perhaps given details of the *cheder* and *Talmud Torah* in too minute an extent, but these facts are instructive as showing the sacrifices which the foreign Jew is willing to make for his children. It is quite true that complex motives are at work. Even when the Polish Jew is not religious he wishes to see his child grow up amongst Jewish surroundings. Quite unobservant persons frequently send their children to *cheder*. In one instance which has come under my notice, a child at *cheder* was rebuked by his master for not wearing *tsitsith*.† On the next day the father called and stated that he was an atheist who did not wish his boy to become religious, but sent him to *cheder* for the sake of the knowledge which he acquired there. This is an extreme case, but

---

** *Talmud Torah*, a Hebrew phrase meaning 'Study of the Law.'
† *Tsitsith*, *i.e.*, fringes worn in accordance with the Mosaic precept in Numb. xv. 38–39. They are attached to the *tallith* or praying shawl worn in the synagogue, and to the *arba canfoth*, or garment of four corners, worn under the ordinary clothing.

undoubtedly many children sent to *cheder* witness much laxity of religious practice in their homes. . . . Remembering what they see at home, some children, on being told that Judaism requires them to say their prayers and to keep the Sabbath, will retort, 'Is my father not a Jew?' On the other hand, many boys remain faithful to the lessons which they have learnt at *cheder*, especially when home influences have tended in the same direction. A *cheder* teacher has told me that one of his old pupils, on going to a remote part of Australia, was able to organise the religious life of the community there and to establish public worship. In some cases an irreligious parent is brought back to orthodoxy by his child's example.

3.   The first Jewish Board School, 1899

Source: Abraham Levy, 'Twenty-five Years Headmaster at the Old Castle Street Board School', *Jewish Chronicle*, 10 November 1899

Abraham Levy moved from the Jews' Free School where he had been a pupil teacher to become head of the boys' department at the Old Castle Street Board School from which he retired as headmaster in 1899 having developed the prototype of the Jewish Board School.

Last week's *Jewish Chronicle* referred to the completion by Mr. Abraham Levy of twenty-five years' service as Headmaster of the Old Castle Street Schools. The event is one of considerably more than local significance. It possesses a communal interest in that it marks the growth of a movement, initiated by Mr. Levy, which may be said to have given an entirely new direction to the religious education of East End Jews. Mr. Levy is not only the headmaster of what has become, under his direction, one of the most flourishing Board Schools in London, but he has been the pioneer of that system of religious instruction from which between 5,000 and 6,000 children are benefiting to-day, and which is destined in the future to embrace an ever-increasing number. Mr. Levy's services to Jewish education deserve to be recorded in full at the present moment, when he can look back over a quarter-of-a-century's strenuous activity. And the record is the more valuable because those services have been rendered in a spirit of perfect devotion to the communal interests, without a thought of self-aggrandisement, with a modesty, indeed, from which many public workers might take example.

   Mr. Abraham Levy, who commenced his educational career as a pupil teacher of the Jews' Free School, left that institution to become Head Master of the Portuguese "Gates of Hope" Schools. He had not held this position long when, on the suggestion of his old teacher, Mr. Angel, Sir Edmund Hay Currie, the then Member of Parliament for the Tower Hamlets and a leading member of the London School Board, invited him to accept the head-mastership of the Boys' Department of Old Castle Street Board School. This was one of the earliest establishments of the London School Board. Placed as it was in the centre of a large Jewish population, it had entirely failed to gain the confidence of the Jewish poor. In those early days, for a Jewish child to attend a Board School was regarded as a first step on the road to conversion. Mr. Levy accepted the post, and, as he had but just married, he had to interrupt his honeymoon in order to take up his new duties. Hence it happens that Mr. and Mrs. Levy are celebrating their silver wedding concurrently with what may be described as Mr. Levy's official silver wedding.

Mr. Levy justified his appointment by proving himself a Headmaster of exceptional ability. He at once converted failure into success. From 70, the number of boys on the muster rose until it reached 500. And having manifested such efficiency in the boys' department, after a time he was entrusted with the superintendence of the girls' department as well. This was an unusual combination at the time, but the plan has worked so well at Old Castle Street and elsewhere that there are now a great many "mixed" Board Schools, and some of the best under the Board are of this character. At the present time Mr. Levy has charge of over 1,000 children, and there have passed through his hands since 1874 about 7,000 boys and 5,000 girls.

Indeed, the entire history of the school for the past quarter of a century has been a history of uninterrupted successes. In the old days, when the Government assessed schools by percentages of passes, Old Castle Street was among the highest. When the system of payment by result was changed and schools were divided into grades – fair, good and excellent – Mr. Levy's school invariably obtained "excellent." The boys and girls never once lost the maximum marks. And when this classification was abolished, and inspection without examination took its place, the maximum grants continued to be obtained, Now, in the County Council and other scholarship examinations, Old Castle Street takes a very high position among the schools that obtain notable successes. At the examinations held last May, it earned between £500 and £600 in scholarships. The Board School authorities have several times, and in various ways, testified to their appreciation of Mr. Levy's labours. On one occasion, for instance, at the special request of the School Management Committee, they quadrupled in his case the annual increase by which teachers rise to their maximum salary.

Let it not be supposed that Mr. Levy is a mere forcing machine for obtaining examinational successes. He appeals to the hearts of his pupils as well as their intelligences. He has ever been at great pains to inculcate a sound morality, and a virtue upon which he lays special stress is benevolence. Some years ago he funded a benevolent society among the scholars. The better-off children contribute a farthing or a halfpenny per week, and with the money so collected the poorer children are helped. Many thousands of "penny dinners" have been paid for out of this fund. Clothes and boots have been bought. Even some of the children's parents have been temporarily helped by the payment of their rent in cases of disablement or loss of work. A Committee of Teachers and Managers administer this fund, but the children themselves act as collectors and take their part in it.

Another virtue taught at Old Castle Street is thrift. Mr. Levy has instituted a Penny Bank, which now has 700 depositors. This is strictly a bank for the children, and not for the parents. No sum above a shilling is received in any week. When the amount of a deposit reaches a sovereign the depositor is drafted on to the Post Office Savings' Bank. And thrift is encouraged not as an end in itself, but as leading to the exercise of higher virtues. Children are encouraged to save in order that they may have the means at their command to make some return to their parents for what they have received.

But it is in the field of Jewish religious education that Mr. Levy has done most notable work, and deserves the special thanks of the Jewish community. When he came to Old Castle Street in 1874, there was absolutely no provision in Board Schools for specific religious instruction. Dogmatic instruction was not allowed, and he was only empowered to teach Scripture. All that he could do without infringement of the rules was to teach Hebrew *as a language*, and for this purpose he obtained a grant of Hebrew Pentateuchs from the Board. This was only satisfactory as far as it went. Mr. Levy saw at once the necessity of supplementing it with specific religious instruction to be given after school hours unofficially. He communicated his ideas to Mr. F.D. Mocatta, who, with characteristic generosity, undertook to be responsible for the financial cost of such teaching. But then it occurred to Mr. Levy that this extra instruction might be introduced with advantage into other Board Schools as well, and if that were done it ought to be undertaken by some official body. He suggested it to the Jewish Association for the Diffusion of Religious Knowledge. Dr Adler and other leading members favoured the proposition, but in other quarters it was violently opposed. For 18 months the question was debated, and eventually Mr. Levy carried his point. In 1876 the Association started Religion Classes at Old Castle Street, with Mr. Levy, who declined a paid appointment, as their Honorary Superintendent.

The new work in which the Association engaged really proved its own salvation, for at the time it was in almost a moribund condition. Its old activities had grown obsolete, and it sadly wanted fresh ones to take their place. The provision of religious instruction for the Jewish scholars attending the East End Board Schools was destined to infuse new life into the old institution, which ultimately became transformed into the Religious Education Board. The progress of this institution has been phenomenal. It started in 1876 with 400 pupils at one school. Today it has ten or twelve schools under its control, and its 400 pupils have grown into at least 5,400! Perhaps the most gratifying feature in this growth and development is the instruction given to girls. While the foreign poor exhibit an almost pathetic anxiety to obtain religious instruction for their boys, strange to say they quite overlook the necessity of educating their girls. But for the classes of the Religious Education Board, many thousands of girls who have passed through them would have been absolutely untrained in the tenets of their religion.

As a member of the Executive Committee, first of the old Association and afterwards of the Religious Education Board, Mr. Levy has rendered this body infinite service for more than twenty years. In spite of his heavy duties at Old Castle Street, he has been indefatigable in his attendance at all its meetings, while his advice has constantly been sought upon the numberless educational questions with which the Board has had to deal. Provincial bodies, too, have invoked his assistance, and he has been instrumental in helping the Jews of Hull, Sheffield and Bristol to get the same free use of the Board Schools for religious instruction that he had obtained for the Association in London.

Mr. Levy has been a prime mover in the latest development of the Religious Education Board – the Teachers' Training College Committee, the object of which is to assist Jewish teachers to obtain a collegiate training. Hitherto Jewish teachers were under the disadvantage of not having been regularly trained for their profession at a college, and the want of this training acted as a bar to their promotion outside of Jewish schools. This movement has been munificently helped by Mr. Claude G. Montefiore and his mother, Mrs. Nathaniel Montefiore, but for whom it never could have achieved its present valuable results.

4. A schoolmaster glances back, 1909

Source: C.F. Nathan, *A Schoolmaster Glances Back* (Liverpool, 1946), pp. 133–157

C.F. Nathan, the long-serving non-Jewish schoolmaster at the Liverpool Hebrew School (1909–23), was the author of an amusing memoir which provides an illuminating portrait of Jewish schooling outside of London.

I found the interior of this three storeyed building to be far more comfortable than its exterior gave promise of.

There were two class rooms; and glass screens of moveable types divided the large room into three more complete class rooms; the centre one being heated by a gas radiator, and the others by large coal fires. This school, as I saw it, had an air of homeliness about it which I failed to find in my other schools. . . .

. . .

The Hebrew Schools were heavily endowed. All the prizes were 'money' prizes. The prize of one hundred pounds was awarded annually to the top girl. The fortunate winner drew the interest each year until her wedding day, when she received the hundred pounds as a marriage dowry. Should she remain a spinster she drew the interest only. Perhaps as husbands are such 'doubtful blessings' the loss of the hundred pounds was not noticed. I don't think I was quite in order when I said the 'top girl'. There were three 'top girls' and the hundred pounds was drawn for, in the presence of the whole school. The two losers were compensated for their bad luck by smaller money prizes of five pounds each, I think.

I always found the Jewish children most anxious to learn. They had quick perception, lively imagination, but, in my opinion, not very retentive memories.

Never once during the whole fourteen years I spent at that school did I experience the slightest difficulty in maintaining discipline. The Jewish children were most biddable and gave their teachers far more respect than is customary in other schools.

One excellent characteristic of the Jewish boy is his imperviousness to ridicule. I have seen Jewish children standing in front of their classes to recite, sing, or even to dance, and, should the class criticism be harsh (and children can be very cruel to each other) they could take it, without allowing it in any way to interfere with their particular display. In direct opposition to this 'mind concentration' I remember in another Liverpool school, seeing a boy of thirteen sobbing his heart out because another boy had called him a 'stiff'.

Of course, it must be remembered that a Jewish boy, with the completion of his thirteenth year becomes of age, in reference to the fulfilment of all religious duties. On the Sabbath following his thirteenth birthday, the "Barmitsvah", he publicly acknowledges God as the Giver of the Law. So you see, a Jewish boy of thirteen years and over is responsible for his own actions, wise or foolish. Indeed I found it convenient at times to say "I thought you had turned thirteen". This was quite sufficient as a reprimand. . . .

. . .

The first important task facing the headmaster at the beginning of each school year was that of fixing the holidays. Let me explain.

The Board of Education has laid it down that all elementary schools must open for not less than four hundred times in each year. Of course the scholars at some schools put in four hundred and twenty attendances. The Head of the Hebrew Schools knows he will have difficulty in complying with the four hundred minimum. So it rarely happens that the Hebrew children work more than two hundred days out of the three hundred and sixty five. While on this subject of working days, I don't think any other school makes better use of its 'minimum' attendances.

The Jews never allow religion to interfere, in any way, with the instruction given in secular subjects, – no, not even by lesson overlapping.

They have solved this weary educational problem in a really practical way. (They are a practical people). The Jewish managers pay their teachers for teaching scripture. I am unable to quote the amount, but I know that in some months, each teacher had two pay days, one by the Education Committee, the other by the School Managers.

. . .

The Hebrew School, was, in my opinion, in 1909, the best staffed school in the City of Liverpool.

The Boys' Department:

Principal, Mr. M. Kaye, M.Sc., Jewish

First Assistant, Male, Certificated, Standard VII, Jewish.

Assistant, Male, Certificated, Standard VI, Christian.

Assistant, Male, Certificated, Standard V, Jewish.

Assistant, Male, Certificated, B.Sc., Lon., Standard IV, Jewish.

Assistant, Male, Certificated, B.Sc., Lon., Standard III, Jewish.

Assistant, Male, Certificated, Standard II, Christian.

There was no female assistant on the staff of the Boys' Department.

. . .

I don't think I will ever forget my first Monday morning at this school.

Naturally, everything was fresh and new to me, but to my surprise and delight I was presented with a key by the principal and advised to fasten this key securely to my key ring. Nothing wonderful in a new teacher being handed a key by the headmaster. But there was something very wonderful in this presentation.

I had taught in six schools and had not been entrusted with the custody of so important a key. Three of these former schools were Higher Grade Schools. So what was the important key, the key of the stock room? No! It was the key of the teachers' lavatory. *The most important key in any school.* The younger generation of teachers may laugh at the emphasis laid on this presentation, but they don't know what agonising times the older teachers were forced to pass through, owing to the lack of foresight on behalf of the former City Fathers – I fancy the 'City Mothers' would have made a better showing in the preservation of the teachers' health.

The advice I received about class teaching was to me sound, but strange.

1. *Don't* remain in front of your class as if you were on guard; walk about the school; exchange ideas with other members of the staff, but on no account warn the children. Simply walk out of your room as if it were the right thing to do. What do I hear the reader say "You should see my class, I'd like to see those young blackguards working quietly if no teacher were in the room".

"Poor little beggars! So should I."

"Who is at fault?" Not the class! Not the teacher! The fault is entirely that of the headmaster of the school, and the sooner some of the 'Heads' realise this, the better for everybody concerned. The free style will make for better citizens.

Another piece of advice was:–

Don't tear up new exercise books when you want writing paper for your class. Tear up any untidy books, use the clean pages and destroy the used ones. A new clean book will often have a beneficial effect on a boy's future work, and I wouldn't like my school to be let down by a dirty book – I don't mind, but for some reason best known to themselves, the inspectors do mind.

Lastly I was told *not to worry about stock*. "Take what you want, the stock is there to be used, and no one has abused the privilege so far."

The feeling I cherished for this, my one and only *"Non-Christian School"* was a most *"Christianlike"* feeling.

The school opened with a prayer. A desk bell would be rung by the teacher taking the prayer – any one of the Jewish teachers took the prayer with no sign of formality. Hats or caps were donned by the staff and the boys, and the prayer would be said in unison. I thought the prayer an excellent one. So much so, that I have ventured to set it down from memory (later I found my copy to be correct.)

In our Christian family prayer we ask that we be not led into temptation, whereas in their prayer, the Jews ask for strength to enable them to resist temptation; taking it for granted I suppose, that while they are on this earth, they will always be in temptation.

The school prayer

"Almighty God! We humbly offer unto Thee our praise for all Thy goodness. We thank Thee for the health of body, and of mind, which Thou hast mercifully granted us. We thank Thee for the lessons that improve us and for the knowledge we gain from day to day.

Lead us, O God, in Thy ways, so that we may increase in goodness as we increase in knowledge. Keep pure our hearts so that we may think no evil. Guard our lips from falsehood, and our hands from wrong-doing.

Help us, O God, to obey Thy law, and strengthen us to resist temptation.

Help us O God to do our duty to all about us so that we may work Thy will on earth, and earn Thy heavenly reward. *Amen.*

At the conclusion of this prayer the class settled down to their daily tasks. The secular work began promptly at 9 a.m. and all registers were marked immediately the prayer ended.

. . .

Talks to children

I always considered the Jewish children to be particularly fortunate in that the 'grown ups' who came to address them were of the broadminded type.

The usual run of speakers at prize distributions, and other equally depressing 'entertainments', either lay stress on the obvious fact that the children of to-day are the men and women of tomorrow (what else did they expect them to be – 'elephants?') or worse still they annoy their youthful audiences by the distressing news that their school days are the happiest days of their lives. What a hopeless outlook for many children.

It was my privilege to hear an address given to the children of the Hebrew School by the Jewish Rabbi, Dr. Hertz. His opening words caught and held the attention of the whole school. "Now children I want you to tell me what you can do, that your *teacher* cannot do, *I* cannot do! Your *headmaster* cannot do! Even the *King* cannot do it, and yet every boy and girl in this room can do it".

Don't you think that an ideal introduction for a speech to the 'growing' generation. Yes! As you will have guessed, the answer was 'grow' – a child can 'grow'. The address, founded on this simple word, was on a par with the brilliant introduction. (This happened over a quarter of a century ago). If only some of the 'prize distributors' of the present day would endeavour to recall the days of their childhood it would save children the untold agonies of listening to platitudes as unwelcome as they are annoying.

Chess

The game of chess was taken very seriously at the Hebrew Institute. This was probably owing to the fact that the principal of the school, Mr. Kaye, was a member of the Liverpool Chess Club. . . .

In the Hebrew school, one class would play against another class, with the aid of a large chess board with 'eight inch' squares. This board rested in a vertical position on an easel, and, near the top of every square were driven brass nails from which were suspended the chessmen – also cut out of quarter inch wood by the boys.

. . .

School dinners

In the basement of the Hebrew School was a large well-lighted and well-appointed kitchen. This kitchen formed part of the caretaker's apartments – all underground. The basement flat must have been healthy, for each caretaker I heard of, or know, lived to be in the "nineties".

There were four long tables and some really good soup was dished out. The staff took it in turns to act as waiters. I believe the children paid a trifle towards the dinners – whatever they could afford. Yes, the Jewish managers had the well-being of the children at heart.

During one of my spells on duty Mrs. Louis Cohen (Lewis's) called to see how the children were faring. It happened to be 'Buns and Cocoa' day. The most enjoyed of all the dinner days. The buns were disappearing like magic. Mrs. Cohen looked at the empty plates, looked at me, looked at the children and then disappeared like magic herself. When she next made her appearance she was accompanied by three or four extra large

Figure 14 School trip, 1914 Pupils were required to bring a can with a lid for collecting specimens, an orange and threepence-ha'penny; spades were optional (C.F. Nathan, *A Schoolmaster Glances Back* (Liverpool: Robert Duncan 1946)).

bags full of buns. She had been across to the nearest 'bun shop' – Kirklands in Hardman Street. All the plates were filled and all the children were happy. . . .

The school treat

I have never seen a school treat run on better lines. From first to last the outing did not cost the school children one penny. In addition, many valuable prizes were given for successes in sports events. Nothing that could have in any way added to the enjoyment of the children was overlooked.

During my time, the treat was held at a farm in Maghull, near Liverpool. Well over four hundred children, all dressed up in their best, accompanied by their teachers in their second best, walked from the school down Bold Street, Liverpool, to the Central Station. Here a special train was in readiness to take them by way of Garston, Childwall and Walton, to Sefton Maghull Station, next to the treat field. Two large marquees provided shelter from rain and sun. The children 'ran off' their races, and received their prizes before setting about their refreshments. We did our best to see that each child received a prize of some kind. The teachers had an elaborate spread, fresh salmon with vegetables, followed by apricots and cream. For tea it was always strawberries and cream in large quantities and a good assortment of cakes. The managers provided the money, I don't think there could have been much change out of one hundred pounds – if any. The children spent the whole day in the country and their special train conveyed them back to Liverpool.

5. Polite, tractable and anxious to learn, 1903

Source: Minutes of Evidence taken before the Royal Commission on Alien Immigration, Parliamentary Papers, [Cd. 1742] IX (1903), qq. 18866–888

Joseph W.P. Rawlen, headmaster of Deal Street Board School, one of the seventeen Jewish Board Schools in East London, stated that both parents and children were extraordinarily responsive to the academic and civic curriculum and had no fears at all as to their ultimate absorption into the community as true-blue Britons.

18867. You have prepared a statement for the information of the Commission, and perhaps you had better read it to us? – Yes. The Deal Street Board School, Mile End New Town, having on the roll at present 335 Jewish boys out of a total of 340, was opened in February, 1896. During the first year 252 boys were admitted. Of these about 100 were foreigners quite ignorant of the English language; 80 were admitted from a neighbouring infant department. Not one of those lads was placed in the class above Standard I. Yet now there are – this refers to last year, because I made the statement out last year – 25 boys, including 11 foreigners, working in Standard VII; 18 boys, including 6 foreigners, working in Standard Ex VII.

18868. *Chairman*. Which is your highest standard? – Ex VII.; several of these boys worked through the seven standards in 5½ years, the remainder taking 6¼ to do the seven years' work. This work would have been completed in five and six years respectively; the extra months are due to the lengthening of the school year by the London School Board to establish an uniform educational year for all the Board schools. Lest it may be thought that the work suffered in quality in consequence of this repeated advance, I may state here that I have, during a period of over 30 years, never seen better work than has been done by these boys. The average of these classes is as follows:– Ex. VII., 12.4 years; Standard VII., 12.5 years; Standard VI., 12.4 years. Last year (that would be 1901) one lad gained a Junior County Council Scholarship. The school had been opened then about five years. This year (that is, 1902), six boys, three of whom were foreign-born, sat, and all passed the Preliminary Examination. The final result is not yet known. Five boys also sat for the Shakespeare Walk Scholarship. Result not yet published. We have no special facilities for preparing lads for these scholarships as exist in many schools. Whatever the result obtained it will be largely due to the intelligence of the boys, and to their continued application to study. Occasionally the older lads visit public places of interest, such as Kew Gardens, The Tower of London, and the various Museums. They regard these visits not merely as a pleasant outing, but taking an intelligent interest in what they see, freely asking questions of those in charge of them. I am frequently told by the ladies who kindly accompany our lads on these visits, that it is a pleasure to go with them, they are so intelligent and appreciative. The curator of the Whitechapel Museum informs me that some of our lads often visit the museum, and converse with her on objects that interest them. The foreign Jewish boys are excellent workers in school. Under the guidance of a capable teacher they apply themselves to their lessons in a manner worthy of the highest commendation. His Majesty's Inspector of Schools, who was quite new to the district, noted this quality in the lads, and stated in his report last year, "that not the least interesting feature was the painstaking efforts of the boys in all their lessons." Another point worthy of note is the almost perfect regularity of attendance. The percentage of average attendance for the past year was 97.5. I attribute this largely to the great interest taken by the parents in the education of their children. On leaving school the boys are carefully looked after by the managers. Many are apprenticed by the Jewish Board of Guardians to the various trades, and become skilled workers. As Deal Street was so recently opened none of my old boys have yet grown to manhood, but several are giving every satisfaction to their employers as capable apprentices, and I doubt not will ultimately develop into intelligent, capable, and patriotic English citizens, giving of their best to their adopted country, and becoming, as Lord Kitchener recently said of the Boers, a valuable asset to the Empire. That was written under the excitement of the peace declaration last year, but still I adhere to it in my cooler moments. During the past six years two pupil teachers, both foreign-born, have served an apprenticeship here; one is now a student at King's College, has passed the Intermediate Examination for B.Sc., and will, in all probability, obtain the full degree next year. The other has matriculated in the 1st Division of London University, has obtained a First Class King's Scholarship, and after the summer vacation will take up his residence as a student at the Borough Road College, Isleworth.

18869. What age would he be? – About 18.

18870. Where does he go after leaving you? – One went to King's College.

18871. At what age did he go to King's College? – About 18.

18872. He does not remain in your school till that age? – As a pupil teacher.

18873. Are they aliens? – Both aliens. The ability and knowledge of both of these youths will eventually be at the disposal of their adopted country. Jewish boys soon become Anglicised, and cease to be foreigners. My first four classes contain 175 boys; of these 108 were born in England, and 67 were born abroad. The parents of 170 of these lads were born abroad, so that practically the whole of these children are of foreign parentage. Notwithstanding this fact, the lads have become thoroughly English. They have acquired our language. They take a keen and intelligent interest in all that concerns the welfare of our country. During the late war no English followed the course of events more closely than they did. They were most enthusiastic over our successes, and they regretted our reverses. One could not but feel that their rejoicings over the relief of the beseiged towns and the proclamation of peace were as sincere as they were hearty. The Coronation of King Edward VII. is the crowning of their King; they are proud to be considered English boys. They are not lacking in benevolence. I do not think I need go into that. They enter heartily into our English games. Swimming, cricket and football are all adopted with enthusiasm. Ninety boys voluntarily go to the baths every week to learn to swim. The absence of open spaces in the East End is a great drawback to the proper development of cricket and football. The boys make the most of the limited space in our school playground, and will often go to the Tower Moat and even to Victoria Park, to indulge in these ever-favourite games. Many of our lads are members of the Jewish Lads Brigade, an admirable movement for developing the physique, for cultivating habits of obedience and self restraint, and for fostering a spirit of true patriotism. One of our old boys, foreign born, volunteered for the front in the late war, and faithfully served his adopted country. In conclusion, I am firmly convinced that the Jewish lads who pass through our school will grow up to be intelligent, industrious, temperate, and law-abiding citizens, and I think will add to the wealth and stability of the British Empire.

18874.   Can you give us any proportionate number of aliens and native born at present in the school? – This was last year. I should say they would be about the same.

18875.   You have given us evidence here during the first year, that would be in 1896, and you gave us the proportion. Your proportion related to boys working in certain standards now, as regards the whole? – Yes.

18876.   You have only three Christian boys altogether? – That is all.

18877.   What is the proportion of the population around your school? – There are a good many Christians at the north of my school. Immediately at the back there is a block of buildings occupied by Christians.

18878.   What becomes of those Christians' children? – They go to the National Schools generally; the Church schools.

18879.   Is it not what Lord Rothschild was trying to obtain from another witnesses, that these Jewish children do keep to the schools which are ear-marked as Jewish schools, which yours is? – They certainly prefer to do so, undoubtedly.

18880.   They know that they will have nothing offensive, as it were, to their religion said, and, therefore, their parents have confidence in sending them? – I do not know that that is the motive. I suppose they feel that they are among their own people.

18881.   With their own feelings and sentiments? – Yes.

18882.   Do the Christian parents for that reason take their children away in another direction? – I should not say so. I have had very few applications from them.

18883.   Why do not the Christian children come to your school? – I cannot say for an absolute certainty why not. They have never applied for admission there. Those who do come remain. I have three who have been with me some years. That is three out of about 300.

18884.   *Mr. Vallance.* Have you any denominational schools in your district? – Yes. They prefer to go there, I suppose.

18885.   *Chairman.* They prefer to go to the schools of their own denomination, and the Jewish parents treat your school as one they prefer sending their children to? – Yes.

18886.   *Lord Rothschild.* It is probably the fact that the Christian children are educated in the older schools that existed before? – Yes.

18887.   The Jewish children come to the newest schools, and the Christian people send theirs to the oldest schools? – Yes.

18888.   There is no racial hatred between them? – Not at all.

6.   Judaism on the rates! 1903

Source: Parliamentary Debates, 5th Series, Vol. 121, 29 April 1903, cols 831–36

T.P. O'Connor (1848–1929), Irish journalist and politician and biographer of Disraeli, he founded a series of radical newspapers and sat for many years as Member of Parliament for the Scotland Division of Liverpool. His criticisms of the London School Board in connection with the endowment of denominated schools came on the second reading of the London Education Bill.

I speak on behalf of the Irish people of this country. Further, I would say that inasmuch as this country assumes to govern Ireland according to her ideas, if at times Irish Members intervene in matters relating to this country Parliament cannot complain. There was a very expressive passage in the speech delivered by the Secretary to the Board of Education last night. The hon. Gentleman spoke of the position of the children of the poor in our public schools. He pictured in a few words how these children often came to the schools hungry, already tired by work they had done, and from squalid homes. I wish I could bring home to the House as clearly as it is in my own mind the position of the Irish people as it is in this country, because the vice of the system from their point of view is this – From circumstances which would be avoidable at home, Irish men in this country are to a large extent the drudges of the country, doing the hardest and the worst work; they are the poorest of the poor. And this extraordinary thing existed under the Education Acts of this country until modified last year, and it exists in London now, and will till modified by this Bill, that the poorest of the poor are most heavily taxed for education. That is to say, the Irish parent, who is the typical poor parent in this country, has to pay the school rate of the school he is opposed to religiously, and pays the voluntary tax to the school of his own Church. I must say I was surprised that the action of these Irish Catholics in refusing to allow their children to go to the richly-endowed and well-equipped schools of the nation, rather preferring them to go to the tumbledown and badly-equipped schools of their own faith for conscience sake, did not appeal to the reformers of this country. We have 30,000 Irish Roman Catholic children in the schools of London, and 106 elementary schools.

This Bill, like all others, consists of two things, the principle, and the machinery by which the principle is to be carried out. The principle of the Bill is the application of the principle of the Act of last year to London. That principle means that the voluntary schools shall have a right to rate aid, and that being so this Bill contains a principle which neither I nor any man of the Party to which I belong are prepared to give a hostile vote. But when I come to the machinery I must speak with considerable hesitation. It abolishes the School Board, and with it the cumulative vote, and the cumulative vote has been in the past the best protection to the minority of this country, especially the religious minority. It must be remembered that in any observation I make on this matter I represent those who by this Bill are compelled to give up what has been the best method of safeguarding their religious rights. I deplore the fact that the case of the voluntary schools has been brought into collision with the School Board system, and I say that if it had not been for the zealots and extremists on both sides it would have been possible to have made an eirenicon under which the rights of the School Board would have been maintained as well as the rights of the minority. . . . The rights of the Roman Catholics will be extirpated under this Bill, as they have been in many parts of the country by the Act of 1902.

. . .

What I have always desired to see is a combination of the School Board system – that is, popular control – with the system of rate aid to voluntary schools. We actually have that system in London already in the case of the Jewish community. In the East End there are several Jewish schools, one of which is the largest voluntary school in the world, and there are also Jewish Board schools, the buildings of which have been erected at the cost of the rates, the teachers in which are paid out of the rates, and the teaching in which is thoroughly Jewish and as denominational as the teaching in any Catholic school. The School Board gets over the difficulty of giving rate aid to sectarian schools in this way. The Jewish schools teach only the Old Testament, therefore they do not teach any Christian formula or definite Christian doctrine; and the Jewish teacher is appointed, not because he is a Jew – that would be sectarianism – but because he knows Yiddish, and can teach Yiddish to the children. By this subtlety the School Board, swearing it will never give a penny to denominationalism, grants money for the teaching of the Jewish religion by Jewish teachers to Jewish children. I do not blame them for it, but what I do contend is, that if you endow the maximum of Jewish dogma, you have no right to refuse to endow a minimum of Christian doctrine. If zealots on both sides had kept out of the way that is how the question might have been dealt with. If, on the one hand, Catholics had declared, as they were ready to do, that they invited every form of control and investigation by public authority, and, on the other hand, the public authority had been willing to deal only with the secular education for which they paid, leaving to the schools the question of the particular religious doctrine they should teach, we should not now be face to face with the religious war which I believe is seriously threatening the voluntary school system. . . .

7. Jews into Englishmen and women

a) *School is out, 1923*

Source: Chicksand Street School, Report on Eva Amdur, and Scripture Prize

Jacob Amdur of Kovno who became a naturalised British citizen in 1903 (**see doc. I.9**) had six children, all of whom were educated locally. His youngest child, Eva, left school at 13 years of age. Her final report is printed below. She also received the Holy Bible (Genesis to Malachi) — distributed by the British and Foreign Bible Society — as the Scripture prize for 1923.

London County Council

Whitechapel & St George's:
Chicksand Street L.C.C. (e) School.
E.I.

25 July 1923

Eva Amdur, born 27th July 1909, has been a scholar in this school for 6¾ years. Her record for conduct, work, regularity and punctuality is an excellent one. As one of the senior scholars she has proved herself most loyal and helpful, with a very good influence over the others in her class. Her books have always been kept neatly and well. Her needlework is excellent.

F.L. Shaff
Head Mistress

b) *Superior Englishmen, 1903*

Source: *Minutes of Evidence taken before the Royal Commission on Alien Immigration*, Parliamentary Papers, [Cd. 1742] IX (1903), qq. 18811—866

F.H. Butcher, headmaster of Christian Street Board School in St George's-in-the-East, like so many of his colleagues, spoke of the immigrant children in glowing terms. The impact of the Cowper-Temple clause is also noteworthy.

18811. *Chairman.* How is it that you have nothing but Jewish children in your school? — It is an absolutely new school. The whole of that district is congested with foreign Jews. As soon as the children arrive here they get into the school. They built my school for the purpose of these children entering, and consequently all the children I have got are the children of those foreigners who are in the district.

18812.   *Lord Rothschild.* There are Christians in the district, too, quite independently of these children? – Yes.

18813.   Where do these children go to school? – They are already in the schools. . . .

18830.   Then you also say you know very little about their parents, except that they are anxious that their children should attend school regularly and punctually, and get on well. Is that so? – I know very little about their parents, except that they are as eager for their children to attend school as we teachers are to see them regular and punctual. . . .

18836.   *Lord Rothschild.* You do not think these children will become a discredit to the country? – Certainly not. I think they will become a credit. I think – I will put it provisionally – if their parents take the same interest in their welfare after leaving school as they do while attending school.

18837.   You say that the parents take a genuine interest in having their children well educated? – Yes, undoubtedly.

18838.   And their attendance is remarkably high? – It is.

18839.   Can you tell the Commission something about the cleanliness of these children? You say in your statement: "The children of foreign parents in my school are as clean as the children in other schools, but the quality of cleanliness depends a great deal on the master in charge; if he insists on a high standard he gets it, as the foreign children readily take to habits of cleanliness"? – That is perfectly true. . . .

18840.   Your opinion is that the cleanliness of the children depends entirely on the master of the school? – I do not think you can say entirely. There are other circumstances. There is the possibility in some of the homes that they have not soap.

18841.   You say that your children take to all games, and if they had the same privileges they would possibly be equally qualified, and you also say you are proud of your lads, and have good reason to be proud of them? – Yes.

18842.   I suppose you are not in a position to give the Commission any account of their parents? – No, I cannot say anything about their parents, except that they take an abnormal interest in their children's education. There is no doubt about these people taking a very great interest in everything that concerns them; their clothing they look after; they look after their cleanliness, and they are most particular about their attendance at school.

18843.   You do not know anything about the condition of the parents at all? – No, I do not.

18844. Would you say, judging from the children, that the parents' condition was a fairly good one? Are the children well fed? – I think the children are certainly well fed. They look remarkably well. Perhaps you would like to see photographs of them. I have brought these photographs in order that you may judge of their cleanliness. (*Producing some photographs.*) I think they are splendid boys.

18845. I suppose they never attend in Jewish holidays? – Never. Ours is a Jewish school. We close on the Jewish holidays.

18846. For religious instruction they go to their own schools? – No, we give them Bible instruction and stories from the Old Testament only, and then for their Hebrew they go to their own Hebrew schools.

18847. For their Hebrew they go to the Chedarim? – Yes.

18848. Do you find their attendance at the Chedarim interferes much with you? – I know nothing about that. It does not interfere with me.

18849. Have the children a tired appearance when they come to you? – No.

18850. *Chairman.* You teach them from the Old Testament? – Yes.

18851. You are a Christian yourself? – Yes, an English churchman.

18852. How do you manage to draw the distinction between your views on religion and the views of the Hebrew children? – We do not draw any distinction at all. We simply teach them stories that have some moral.

18853. You take care to make them neutral as regards doctrine? – Yes, and if a man cannot keep it neutral he has to stop teaching, and somebody has to be put there who can.

18854. You can manage it so that no practical difficulty arises? – There has never been any difficulty at all.

18855. *Major Evans-Gordon.* Do you know the hours that are kept in the Chedarim now? – I do not.

18856. You do not know whether complaints were formerly made of the hours being too long in the Chedarim? – No, I know nothing about it.

18857. You saw no signs of fatigue? – No, not the slightest.

18858. What do you mean when you say through no fault of their own they do not have the same privileges? – I was accounting for my boys not comparing favourably with the British boys in sport. You know what English sport is – these children have not had the same advantages in learning cricket, swimming, football, and pastimes of that sort. Consequently they do not excel.

18859. They begin pretty young here, and do pretty well, and you would say they are superior intellectually, if not quite physically? – I am afraid you are running away with the wrong idea. My comparison has been all the time between the British child of St. George's in the East and the Jewish child.

18860.   I am talking of that? – I am not talking of the rural children at all.

18861.   It is the only thing you can compare – the children in this neighbourhood. You would say, which I am disposed to entirely agree with, that these children that you are dealing with now are superior intellectually, quicker, and more diligent, and show more application, and are more regular in their attendances? – Undoubtedly.

18862.   They are easier to deal with? – Yes.

18863.   And intellectually superior, if not quite so strong physically as the others? – Yes, undoubtedly.

18864.   That is your general result? – Yes.

18865.   Good educational material, you would call it? – Yes.

c)   Brady Boys' Club, 1897

Source: Brady Street Club for Working Boys, First Annual Report, (1896–97)

Brady Boys' Club, the first of its kind, was for the thousands of immigrant children who passed through it, a source of Jewish companionship and pleasure. Most would have been surprised to learn that they were also being taught to become good citizens with wholesome thoughts and manly ideas. But they were.

In submitting the following Report, the Committee would ask leave to preface the actual record of the first year's work, by setting forth, firstly the causes which have called the Club into being, secondly the main objects which it has in view.

For some time prior to the Club's foundation, a few people, interested in the East End Problem, had noted with some surprise that, whereas various institutions had long existed to minister to the needs of Jewish working men and women, no steps had been hitherto taken to meet the equally, if not more, urgent wants of young working lads. For some unaccountable reason the interests of the rising generation of our working classes from the time of their leaving school to the age of early manhood had been practically overlooked. At the most critical stage in a boy's life, when the undeveloped character is most readily susceptible to external influences, good or bad, he was left to shift for himself, and thrown entirely on his own resources. His leisure hours were spent in aimless loafing about the streets, or occasional visits to low places of entertainment, proper facilities for passing his spare time

Figure 15   Lads' Brigade, Jews' Hospital and Orphan Asylum, West Norwood, 1901
The Jewish Lads' Brigade, organised on strictly military lines, was created as an instrument of social conformity and Jewish integration (G.R. Sims (ed.), *Living London*, 3 vols (London: Cassell, 1901), II, p. 34).

in a healthy and rational manner, being virtually non-existent. To supply this pressing want, to establish a social and recreational centre for working lads fresh from school, to improve their stunted physique, raise their general tone and bearing, inculcate into them habits of manliness, straightforwardness and self-respect; with these ambitious aims the Brady Street Club opened its doors. We say advisedly "ambitious," since it would be idle to deny that the programme of work thus briefly sketched, covers a very wide field. If our first year's record, however, can show that we are on a fair way to realize but a tithe of our projects, we venture to think we may claim the sympathy and goodwill of the whole community in our future efforts.

It should here be mentioned that, though from the beginning boys of all denominations have been eligible for membership, and the Committee do their best to encourage the mingling of Jewish and non-Jewish lads, yet at the present moment the Jewish element so largely preponderates, that the Club may be looked upon as Jewish in all but name.

Opened in April, 1896, the Club has been open throughout the year on five nights a week, on Mondays, Tuesdays and Wednesdays from 7.30 to 10 p.m., on Saturdays and Sundays half-an-hour earlier. On Thursdays the Club remains closed, the Committee fearing lest its attractions might prove inimical to the success of the Gymnastic Class which meets on that night. In addition to the Club Superintendent, at least two members of the Committee are present every night on which the Club is open. The average attendance has of course somewhat fluctuated, ranging from an average of 45 on the first three nights of the week, to 70 on Saturdays and Sundays. On certain evenings a total attendance of 100 has been recorded, as many as the Club can adequately accommodate.

The number of active paying members on the books has likewise fluctuated, at times rising to about 160, on one occasion dropping as low as 90. As had been expected, in the opening weeks of the Club there was a great influx of would be members, so that the Committee were compelled to temporarily limit the number admissible. Once the charm of novelty had worn off many of the boys drifted away, leaving a nucleus of tried, regular members, who have ever since proved the backbone of the Club. It is doubtful whether the Club will ever succeed in checking the nomadic tendencies of the average East End boy, despite the efforts of the Committee to discourage its floating population by putting obstacles in the way of re-admission to membership.

The conduct of the boys while at the Club has been, with but few exceptions, eminently satisfactory. The task of maintaining order, even among new, untried members, proved unexpectedly light, not a single serious disturbance having taken place. Something still remains to be done towards checking a slight propensity to quarrel and wrangle while playing games. In this respect, however, matters have greatly improved since the early days of the Club, and further intercourse between managers and boys must tend to eradicate the failing altogether.

The ordinary attractions of the Club comprise a well stocked library, an assortment of papers and illustrated magazines, games such as bagatelle, chess, draughts, dominoes, etc., and facilities for boxing, etc. . . .

In the direction of physical recreation, classes have been started for gymnastics, musical drill and swimming. . . .

. . .

The Club opened too late in the year to allow of the organisation of a Cricket Club; however, a few of the elder boys used to meet once a week at the Victoria Park for practice among themselves. Not being desirous of officially countenancing Saturday play the Committee made every endeavour to hire a ground, where both cricket and football might be played on Sundays. Unfortunately their efforts were fruitless, and seem likely to remain so. This state of things is much to be deplored, as the benefit accruing to the boys from taking part in such healthy out-door games would be incalculable. The feeling of *esprit de corps* would be promoted, and the birth of a "true sportsman-like spirit," which – as understood in its best sense – is practically non-existent among East End Jewish lads, would react as beneficially on their characters as the actual exercise on their bodies.

. . .

Before referring to the modest record of educational work accomplished during the year, the Committee wish to emphasize the fact that the Club claims to be first and foremost a recreational centre; further, that they are anxious not to compete in any way with the educational work carried on at other institutions, founded *ad hoc*. Moreover, the Club's sphere of usefulness is sufficiently wide, without being extended into provinces, where, in the absence of proper equipment, its labours might be of doubtful value.

. . .

To sum up, without wishing to appear unduly optimistic, the Committee are of the opinion that the Club may fairly congratulate itself on having made a successful début, and established a future claim on the kindly sympathy of all those who have at heart the social improvement of our East End poor. The opening year's work has been necessarily somewhat in the nature of an experiment. As pioneers we have had perforce to feel our way slowly and cautiously; . . . Within another year, the personal relations between "managers" and boys will have grown more intimate; the Club's hold on the affections of its members will have acquired additional strength, and its influence as an agency for good be even more effectively demonstrated.

d) *Oxford and St George's Girls' Club, 1915*

Source: Basil L.Q. Henriques, *The Indiscretions of a Warden* (1937), p. 86

Sir Basil Lucas Quixano Henriques (1890–1961) was born into an old-established Jewish family and educated at Harrow and Oxford. An active figure in the liberal Jewish movement, he was a magistrate and club leader, best remembered for the foundation of the Oxford and St George's Jewish Boys' Club in 1914. The Girls' Club was formed the following year.

The tendency of the Jew to go to extremes is particularly marked in the dress of the Jewish girl. Most of them are tailoresses and dressmakers or milliners, so that they learn the latest and most outrageous fashions before they come into vogue in the West End, and are able to make their own garments. Thus with their inartistic use of cosmetics, many quite innocent girls look like prostitutes. The warfare waged in the club against paint and powder has been a continuous one, and though on the whole it has been victorious, many girls have left on account of it. The warfare has been difficult in that the example set by so-called Society girls of the West could so often be quoted against us. Personally I have an abhorrence of cosmetics. I feel it to be contrary to Nature and I never believe that a girl who spends time in altering her features can be natural or sincere. I love to see a girl dressed smartly, but I detest to see them looking unnatural.

Figure 16   A concert at the Jewish Working Girls' Club, Soho, 1901   One of several wholesome clubs designed to keep juvenile Jewesses off the streets and preserve their character as 'nice Yiddishe girls'. Apart from concerts, dances and debates, members could choose to learn dressmaking, millinery, reading, writing, singing, cooking, chip-carving, basket-making and Hebrew (G.R. Sims (ed.), *Living London*, 3 vols (London: Cassell, 1901), I, p. 118).

e)   Samuel Rosen, 1919

Source: *The Toynbee Record*, XXX (1919), p. 51

The role of non-Jewish philanthropy in the socialisation process is well illustrated in the following obituary notice.

The death – after a prolonged illness – of Samuel Rosen has deprived Toynbee of a regular worker, although he was probably unknown to most of those who frequent "the house." He took a great interest in the housing question, when it was acute in Whitechapel some years ago, and was associated with Canon Barnett, the Rev. Harry S. Lewis, the first Lord Swaythling, and Mr. N.L. Cohen in their efforts to prevent the scandals which were frequent at that time. He became a member of the Committee that was formed under their auspices to provide legal assistance for oppressed tenants, and when that Committee amalgamated with the Poor Man's Lawyer he continued to attend every week, and to assist as interpreter to the Yiddish-speaking applicants. A man of singular modesty, he never pushed himself forward, but was content to go on with his self-imposed task without thanks or recognition.

He belonged to a type of unworldly idealists that is almost unknown in this country, and was proprietor of a small – and not too flourishing – grocer's shop in a back street in Whitechapel. He was a scholar of considerable erudition in Hebrew literature and rabbinical learning, and an enthusiastic worker on behalf of the Zionist cause. His one ambition was to see his children successful in life, and he sacrificed his own comfort to secure their education; it was a great satisfaction to him when his elder son became a teacher in a secondary school, and the younger was able to serve the country of his adoption during the War as a wireless operator for the Navy.

Samuel Rosen was one of those "alien-immigrants" whose presence here was of great advantage to us, and he will long be missed by the few whose privilege it was to know his sterling worth and his unassuming modesty.

E.M.

VIII
THE JEWISH QUESTION

The conflict between native and immigrant Jew was cultural, religious and, above all, political in character. It was the political implications of mass immigration which agitated Anglo-Jewry and conditioned its responses to the newcomers. The rapid increase in the foreign Jewish population, its ghetto-like concentration in East London, Leeds and Manchester and the hostile response it engendered, alarmed British Jews. Overcrowded insanitary slums let at exorbitant rents were, it was claimed, the result of unrestricted alien immigration. Not only had the Briton been ousted from his home, his job too had been seized by aliens who were willing to work without regard to hours, conditions or rates of pay. Public health and private employment were not the sole considerations; public morals were threatened by the alleged licentiousness of the immigrant and public order by his criminal and political subversion. The coincidence of mass immigration with economic depression and increased foreign competition gave rise to fears of national degeneration and demands for a revision of the traditional policy of free trade in goods and the free movement in persons. These fears were central to the definition of a 'Jewish Question' and the growing clamour for the abolition of unrestricted immigration. Political anti-Semitism, hitherto absent from these islands, now found institutionalized expression in the British Brothers League, which stomped the streets of East London at the turn of the century.

Anti-Semitism, if less marginal to British culture than is sometimes supposed, was by no means the only response to the minority community. Jews occupied a unique place in English Protestant thought. The study of Scripture in general and the Prophets in particular focused attention upon the futurity of the Chosen People, arousing millenial expectations and a conversionist philosemitism which found forceful expression in seventeenth-century Puritanism and remained an important influence upon Victorian Evangelicalism. Interest in Jewish habits, customs and practices was more widespread than is usually allowed, and not uniformly hostile (**doc. 1** and see **doc. III.2**).

The popular case against the immigrants was developed in the journalism and political agitation of Arnold White, a Social Darwinist, imperialist, social reformer and avowed anti-Semite. The ways in which these often incoherent and irrational fragments inform a wider political ideology should not be lost sight of (**doc. 3**). Organized labour, though wary of the protectionists who were drawn to the opponents of unrestricted immigration, in general found the allegations respecting labour displacement and the degradation of work and wages convincing (**doc. 4**). Clergy, concerned about the effects of Jewish settlement upon parish life and the Christian character of the country, also found the case for tighter immigration controls appealing (**doc. 5**). The intellectual case against Jewish immigration, however, was put most cogently by Goldwin Smith, one of the 'lights of Liberalism', and a former Regius Professor of Modern History at Oxford. Goldwin Smith, who had been slighted by Disraeli in an earlier encounter and never got over it, found in the Eastern Crisis of 1875 the opportunity to revenge himself, got carried away and proceeded to move from a personal attack on an individual Jew to a racist attack on Jews and Judaism in general. The arguments that British foreign policy was being manipulated in the interests of sinister Jewish influences, that Jews could not be good patriots, and that further immigration was not in the national interest, helped create a framework of debate that was to culminate in a significant shift within British liberalism (**doc. 2**).

Anglo-Jewry itself responded, first, by doing its utmost to dissuade the victims of Tsarist persecution from seeking permanent residence in this country. The immigrants from the East were perceived as a de-stabilising element whose settlement imperilled both themselves and their hosts. Apart from the threat to its position in the polity, Anglo-Jewry, like their acculturated and assimilated co-religionists in Germany and France, saw in the 'ghetto Jew' a challenge to its self-image. But, for all its ambivalence, it could not support the abandonment of traditional British freedoms. Anglo-Jewry argued that in general terms the immigrants were assets who had developed new industries and contributed to national economic growth, that the charges against them were unfounded or not proved and that therefore it was right to err on the side of liberty (**docs. 5–6**).

The anti-alien, anti-Semitic, campaign forced the government to appoint a Royal Commission on Alien Immigration which reported in 1903 in favour of legislation to prevent unauthorized entry into the country with extensive powers of deportation for undesirables. These recommendations were embodied in the Aliens Act, 1905 (**doc. 7**).

Popular anti-Semitism was little affected. It was deeply embedded in the culture of Christianity and easily triggered by local economic difficulties as the disturbances in Limerick in 1904 were to show (**doc. 8(a)**). The anti-Jewish riots in South Wales in August 1911 also owed something to Christianity (in this case Baptist hostility) and were bound up with social and economic tensions associated with the industrial conflicts in the region (**doc. 8(b)**). The victims in both cases were comparative newcomers, immigrant Jews to whom the locals were indebted. The anti-Jewish disturbances in Leeds and London in the summer of 1917 were of a rather different character. Even before 1914 relations between the immigrant and indigenous populations were tense: as we have seen native and foreigner struggled over jobs, houses, neighbourhood and community. With the outbreak of hostilities things went from bad to worse; wartime pressures made peacetime antagonisms sharper and more explosive. The manpower crisis constituted the heart of the matter. There were approximately 25,000 to 30,000 male Russian subjects of military age, mostly of the Jewish faith, domiciled in Leeds and London. Large numbers were either unwilling or unfit to serve in allied armies. The introduction of compulsory military service at the beginning of 1916 made their position untenable. Increasingly the 'foreign Jew' was presented as a parasite and predator, snatching the jobs and comforts of the indigenous population while Britannia's sons sacrificed all for freedom, democracy and decency. The government, fearing public disorder, took powers to deport or conscript the resistant Russians. It made no difference (**docs. 8(c)–8(f)**).

The alien population, perceived as a threat to national security and public order, became subject to registration, enumeration, classification and continuous observation by the police and intelligence services. Demands for further restrictions, as voiced in the press, were widely supported (**docs. 9–11**). The government succumbed (**doc. 13**). The Aliens Restriction Act of 1919, and the deportations that accompanied it, cast a long shadow over a Jewish community which included large numbers of long-settled immigrants whose status was no longer assured (**doc. 14**).

The war experience may well have served to confirm the view that the only lasting solution to the Jewish Question lay in the restoration of a Jewish national home. Zionism as a source of cultural resistance to the integrationist enthusiasms of the leaders of Anglo-Jewry was attractive and growing in popularity within the immigrant community (see **doc. VI.8**). The triumph of political Zionism in 1917, though prompted by the superior lobbying of Chaim Weizmann and associates, owed more to considerations of military strategy, American opinion and Britain's post-war ambitions in the Middle East (**docs. 12(a)–(b)**). For all that, it marked a critical stage within the Jewish community in the transfer of power from the scions of Anglo-Jewry to the representatives of the immigrants and their children.

1. Jewish separatism, 1867

Source: H.T. Armfield, 'Jewish Domestic Economy', *Good Words* VIII (1867), pp. 731–36

Interest in Jews and Judaism in Victorian Britain was by no means confined to the effects of immigration upon labour displacement, wages and housing. There was an older, Protestant form of philosemitism which was neither uncritical nor hostile.

By the furniture of a Jewish kitchen, of all places in the world, I was recently made to feel that one portion of the Bible, which to most of us is scarcely more than a record of the past, or, at the best, only a shadowy prefigurement of Christian truth, is very far from being the dead letter it is commonly supposed to be. On the contrary, for a considerable section of men living in the same cities as ourselves, it is, I saw, the regulator of the most trivial details of house-life just as much now as it was thousands of years ago, when it fell fresh from the lips of the lawgiver.

. . .

. . . One is more inclined to suppose that those modes of interpretation which Christianity has introduced must have had some influence, however small, upon the older systems with which they have come in contact; and that, whether rightly or wrongly, a modern residence among Christians must have gradually insinuated a new principle into the minds of a scattered people, even though, when they lived in the enjoyment of their isolated compactness as a nation, they had learned to hold themselves bound not so much by the spirit as by the exact letter of their Divine law. Hence arises a popular mistake that the regard paid by a modern Jew to his ceremonial law is limited to one or two representative acts, as they may be termed.

. . . Such, however, is very far from being the case. In our own streets the injunctions of the Law of Moses, with the commentaries of ancient and learned writers upon it, are still interwoven with every thread of the domestic life of the Jew, giving a colour of singularity to the whole, and originating numberless odd ways and customs of which the outer world has but little suspicion.

The kitchen which suggested these thoughts was one belonging to a large Jewish establishment, and was accordingly on a considerable scale. The feature of it which would at once arrest the attention of a Christian was the presence of an entire duplicate set of utensils for culinary purposes and for the table.

. . .

. . . In no case are animal food and milk food either cooked in the same vessels or eaten from the same plates and dishes; and a complete service is therefore set apart for each of these two kinds of nutriment, lest by any inadvertency the milk food should come in contact with the flesh. It is quite necessary that the service for the table should be duplicate as well as the utensils for cooking; because the guilt of cooking milk and flesh together appears to attach also to him who partakes of food so cooked. . . .

. . .

Another feature in this Jewish kitchen and its contents, strongly insisted on by their laws, deserves to be remarked. It was kept most scrupulously, if not almost ostentatiously, clean. It is the more important to remark this, because an idea prevails extensively in England that the Jew does not much concern himself about cleanliness either of his own person or anything belonging to him. But such an idea requires considerable qualification. The truth, perhaps, is, that the type of Jew known to the generality of English people is not the man of affluence, of cultivated intellect, moving gracefully in refined society, and whom everyone delights to honour; but rather a man taken from the humbler walks of life, a man doomed by exile, and persecution, and poverty, to occupy the meanest home in the narrowest street, – an Ishmael of society, baffled at every turn by a national suspicion, and succeeding, in so far as he does succeed, in scraping together his maintenance in spite of a hostile public opinion. Of course, if you compare a man like this with the average well-to-do Englishman of your acquaintance, the comparison will tend very much to the disparagement of the Jew. His social position and advantages are less august, and therefore his attributes, both of person and of household, may be expected on the whole to be inferior. But measure such a man by the side of those classes of our own people with whom he is compelled to live, and it becomes a question whether the parallel does not go rather to the credit of the Jew. But be this as it may, it is undeniable that, if the Jew be not a clean man both in his house and in his person, he is dirty, not in accordance with, but in the very teeth of, his religious profession. For his religion is to the very bottom essentially one of washings. To look at their laws, one would imagine that a pious Jew must be engaged in ablutions, either of himself or of his goods and chattels, all day long. . . .

But to return to the dietary system of the Jews. There is a command in the Book of Deuteronomy to this effect:– "Be sure that thou eat not the blood: for the blood is the life: and thou mayest not eat the life with the flesh." From this and the directions akin to it, there springs up a most elaborate code of rules, according to which animal food must be prepared for the consumption of a devout Jew. In the first place, he cannot range through the market at large and buy wherever it might suit his fancy to buy, because at the shops where everyone else gets supplied he could have no guarantee that the meat he would get is not unclean, from default of the necessary observances in the slaughter or preparation of it. . . .

. . .

Indicative of the same habit of mind which underlies these regulations about diet, is a small item of the appointments of the Jew's house. It takes its rise from the commandment of Moses in reference to the words of the law, "Thou shalt write them upon the doorposts of thy house, and upon thy gates." . . .

. . .

. . . The ceremonial of affixing the *Mezuza*, like everything else connected with the Jewish religion, is laid down with great exactness. . . . and on the occasion of fixing it another of the ubiquitous forms of benediction comes in for recital, . . . But although the words of Moses about writing the law upon the posts are thus interpreted by the Jew strictly in the letter, it must not be supposed that the spirit of them is forgotten. Whether they be taken literally, as the Jew takes them, or figuratively, as most Christians would take them, all would agree in declaring that his ultimate object was to assert in the strongest possible language the claims of the law upon the respect of his people. And accordingly, to complete the usages of the *Mezuza*, this respect, which presumably exists in the heart of a true Israelite, has its outward expression in attitudes of the body. He passes it with an obeisance, or he reverently kisses the hand with which he has first touched the sacred memorial of his faith.

But it is not only in matters of food, dress, or furniture that the faith of the Jew interweaves itself with the customs and arrangements in his house. As might be anticipated, the domestic power of his religion is seen most clearly in religious services performed at home. Not, however, that regular family worship appears to be made so much of amongst the Jews as it ordinarily is amongst Christians in this country. On the contrary, the strict letter of the law would seem to require that even a man's ordinary daily prayers should be said in the synagogue with his brethren; the right to say them in private being accorded by authority, as a sort of gracious dispensation only, in consequence of the pressure of a man's avocations, a deficiency in the number of resident Jews legally requisite to form a congregation, or other insurmountable obstacle. Yet there are in the course of the year many religious services and ceremonials which it is obligatory to perform at home, and for which the ordinary business of the household has to be for the time completely suspended. . . .

. . .

The domestic rite of "saying grace" at meals, usually so brief in Christendom, is elongated into quite a formidable service at Jewish tables.
. . .

. . .

But what is the meaning of all this? Is it to be set down as mere antiquarianism? or as an obstinate commemoration of an extinct nationality? or – what purpose is it supposed to serve? It would be almost unfair to draw attention to all these minute observances of Jewish household religion without a word in answer to this question, to prevent the import of the system being misunderstood. The more so because it is undeniable that the current idea of the religion of the Israelites is a very one-sided, and, therefore, a very erroneous one. It is commonly represented as nothing better than a system of heartless formalities; but candour demands that we should ask ourselves occasionally, Is this true? After recounting these singularities of religious usage, I say, without hesitation, that it is not true that the religion of the Jews is a heartless formalism. At the close of an account like this it would be absurd to deny that it *is* formal in the very highest degree; but it is very much more than this. Their books and teachers, indeed, perhaps from only too sad an experience of the evil, seem to be incessant in their protests against the substitution of the letter for the spirit. Christianity herself cannot be more resolute in declaring the worthlessness of outward conformity with a religious ordinance, while its inner significance and purpose are lost sight of. Viewed in its relation to man, perfect self-control is the apex of the whole system, precisely as it is the highest ideal of regenerated manhood in our own faith; and in this branch of the subject the parallel holds throughout. Those virtues and characters which hold the highest rank in Christian ethics are exactly those which are the most sedulously cultivated by the religion of the Jew. Here he is entirely one with us. He labours for the well-being of man upon the same principles, with the same instrumentality, under the same influences, with the same ideal before his eyes, that we adopt ourselves; and so far he commands, not only our toleration, but our willing sympathy and respect. In his conceptions of man, that is, he is at one with us, but in his conceptions of God he is at issue with us; in his religious creed he must continue to be our antagonist, but in his views of life he is our fellow-labourer and ally.

2. The Jewish Question, 1881

Source: Goldwin Smith, 'The Jewish Question', The Nineteenth Century, X (1881), pp. 494–515

Goldwin Smith (1823–1910), the son of a Reading physician, was educated at Eton and Magdalen College, Oxford. 'He wrote many books', said the New York Times obituary, 'though none of the first grade of importance'. As a publicist he was more successful. His article on the Eastern Crisis in the Contemporary Review of 1877–78 raised disturbing questions about the status of Jews in British society. It brought a rejoinder from Hermann Adler and a counter response from the author. The text printed below is a trenchant re-statement of Smith's original position.

On opening the *Nineteenth Century* the other day in Canada, I was surprised to find that Mr. Lucien Wolf, of the *Jewish World*, in his paper on the Anti-Jewish agitation had set me down as having commenced the agitation in England. . . .

It had happened that when I was last in England we were on the brink of a war with Russia, . . . The Jewish interest throughout Europe, with the Jewish Press of Vienna as its chief organ, was doing its utmost to push us in. . . . At such a crisis it was necessary and right to remind the English people that Israel was a separate race, with tribal objects, and that its enmities could not be safely allowed to sway the councils of England. . . .

I heartily supported, and, were it needful, would heartily support again, the political enfranchisement of the Jews, though I do not pretend to believe that people who intrench themselves in tribal exclusiveness, refuse intermarriage, and treat the rest of the community as Gentiles, are the very best of candidates for citizenship. But the franchise is a trust, in the exercise of which every one must expect to be watched, especially those who are liable to any peculiar bias, above all when their allegiance is divided between the nation and some other power or interest. . . .

If patriotism means merely a willingness to perform all social duties and to do good to the community, nobody can deny that it may be possessed in the largest measure by the kinsmen of Sir Moses Montefiore. But if it means undivided devotion to the national interest, there is difficulty in seeing how it can be possessed without abatement by the members of a cosmopolitan and wandering race, with a tribal bond, tribal aspirations, and tribal feelings of its own. Far be it from Liberals to set up a narrow patriotism as the highest of virtues, or to make an idol of the nation. There is something higher than nationality, something which nationality at present ought to serve, and in which it will ultimately be merged. Mazzini taught us how to think upon that subject. But tribalism is not higher nor more liberal than nationality; it is lower and less liberal; it is the primeval germ of which nationality is the more civilised development. Nor does the narrowest patriot make such a religious idol of his nation as the Jew makes of his tribe. All the other races profess at least allegiance to humanity: they all look forward, however vaguely, to a day of universal brotherhood; they cannot help doing this if they are Christian, and have accepted the ideal of the Christian Church. The Jew alone regards his race as superior to humanity, and looks forward not to its ultimate union with other races, but to its triumph over them all, and to its final ascendancy under the leadership of a tribal Messiah. I mean of course the genuine, or, as the Americans would say with rough picturesqueness, the 'hard-shell' Jews. About the position of these alone can there be any question. As to the men of Jewish descent who have put off tribalism altogether, we have only to welcome them as citizens in the fullest sense of the term and to rejoice in any good gifts, peculiar to their stock, which they may bring to the common store. . . .

Of the existence of Israel as a power and an interest apart from the nations, though domiciled among them, there can scarcely be a doubt. One who has deeply studied the question, Mr. Oliphant, in his recent and very interesting work *The Land of Gilead*, dwells more than once on the great advantages which any European Government might gain over its rivals by an alliance with the Jews. 'It is evident,' he says, 'that the policy which I have proposed to the Turkish Government (*i.e.* the restoration of Palestine) might be adopted with equal advantage by England or any other European Power. The nation that espoused the cause of the Jews and their restoration to Palestine would be able to rely on their support in financial operations on the largest scale, upon the powerful influence which they wield in the Press of many countries, and on their political co-operation in those countries, which would of necessity tend to paralyse the diplomatic and even hostile action of Powers antagonistic to the one with which they were allied. Owing to the financial, political, and commercial importance to which the Jews have now attained, there is probably no one power in Europe that would prove so valuable an ally to a nation likely to be engaged in a European war as this wealthy, powerful, and cosmopolitan race.' Perhaps the writer of these words hardly realises the state of things which they present to our minds. We see the Governments of Europe bidding against each other for the favour and support of an anti-national money power, which would itself be morally unfettered by any allegiance, would be ever ready to betray and secretly paralyse for its own objects the Governments under the protection of which its members were living, and of course would be always gaining strength and predominance at the expense of a divided and subservient world. The least part of the evil would be the wound inflicted on our pride. It is the highest treason against civilisation that Mr. Oliphant unwittingly suggests. . . .

The allusion to the influence wielded by the Jews in the European Press has a particularly sinister sound. This, as has already been said, is a danger the growth of which specially justifies our vigilance. In the social as in the physical sphere new diseases are continually making their appearance. One of the new social diseases of the present day, and certainly not the least deadly, is the perversion of public opinion in the interest of private or sectional objects, by the clandestine manipulation of the Press.

. . .

In such German pamphlets as I have seen upon this question I have not noticed strong traces of theological antagonism. Herr Stöcker seems fully imbued with the old-fashioned reverence for the faith of Israel: his complaint is rather that there is too little of it among the modern Israelites than that there is too much. The Jewish antipathy to labour offends him as a Christian Socialist, with whom the duty and the dignity of labour are primary articles of faith: this is the nearest approach to religious antagonism that I have observed. Herr Stöcker complains, it is true, of the attacks made by the Jewish Press on Christianity; but this he might do without exposing himself to the charge of intolerance, though perhaps there is some exaggeration in his complaints.

The belief that these troubles are wholly or mainly religious flows naturally from the notion almost universally entertained, that Israel is merely a dissenting sect. Talleyrand, . . . fancied that a Jew was just like other citizens, saving his theological opinions, and that when toleration was extended to those opinions he would become like other citizens in every respect. The advocacy of Jewish emancipation in England proceeded on the same assumption, while the opposition was founded on that of a religious crime and a divine sentence. The result has proved that though emancipation was wise and right, the impression under which debate was conducted was mistaken. We now see that Israel is not a sect, but a vast relic of primæval tribalism, with its tribal mark, its tribal separatism, and its tribal God. The affinity of Judaism is not to nonconformity but to caste. If Judaism were a religion as Christianity or Buddhism is, it would, like Christianity and Buddhism, proselytise: . . .

It is partly under the influence of the same erroneous impression, as I venture to think, that Mr. Wolf ascribes whatever is not lofty in the commercial character and habits of the Jews to the 'demoniac attitude' of Christianity, . . .

There are features common to the characters of Orientals generally, and visible in that of the Jew, for which Christendom plainly is not responsible. Nor is Christendom responsible for anything that originally marked, for good or for evil, either the Semitic stock generally of the Hebrew branch of it. . . . It was not the attitude of Christianity that caused the Jews to adopt as a typical hero the man who takes advantage of his brother's hunger to buy him out of his birthright with a mess of pottage, . . . It was not Christianity that penned passages in Hebrew books instinct with sanguinary tribalism and vindictive malediction. But a more unhappy element probably in the special character of the modern Jew than any Oriental or Semitic defect is the accumulated effect of the wandering life, with its homelessness, its combination of degrading vagrancy with unpopular exclusiveness, its almost inevitable tendency to mean and hateful trades. And to the wandering life the Jews were led partly by untoward circumstances, partly by their own choice, certainly not by the attitude or the conduct of Christendom. They seem to have been not less unpopular with the nations of the pagan world, . . . and their unpopularity seems to have arisen always from much the same causes. Either the whole human race except the Jews is demoniac, or there is something naturally unpopular in the habits and bearing of the Jew.

. . .

'The Jew,' says Renan, 'from that time [that of the final dispersion] to this has insinuated himself everywhere, claiming the benefit of common rights. But in reality he has not been within the pale of common rights; he has kept his status apart; he has wanted to have the same securities as the rest, with his exceptional privileges and special laws into the bargain. He has wished to enjoy the advantages of nationality without being a member of the nation, or bearing his share of national burdens. And this no people has ever been able to endure.' There is no reason why any people should endure it, at all events if the number and influence of the intruders are such as to constitute a serious danger to the nation, and the parasite seems likely to injure the growth of the tree. In England the Jews are few; and though some of them have made colossal fortunes by stock-broking, the aggregate amount of their wealth is not great compared with that of the whole country. English writers are therefore able, much at their ease, to preach the lessons of a serene philosophy to the Germans, who have as many Jews in a single city as there are in the whole of England or France, and are moreover threatened with fresh irruptions from Poland, that grand reservoir, as even Jewish writers admit, of all that is least admirable in Israel. Seeing the growth of the Jewish power in Germany, the immense wealth which it has amassed by stock-broking, and which, refusing intermarriage, it holds with a grasp almost as tight as mortmain, its influence over the Press, the lines of sumptuous mansions which bespeak its riches and its pride, the rapid multiplication of its people and the reinforcements which it receives from abroad, its tribal exclusiveness and compactness, its disdain of manual labour and increasing appropriation of the higher and more influential places in the community, a German may be excused for feeling apprehensions which in an Englishman would be absurd. No wonder if he fancies, as he walks along the principal street of his chief city, that he is in some danger of being reduced to the condition of a hewer of wood and a drawer of water for an intrusive race in his own land. Not the German only, but any one who feels an interest in the fortunes of Germany, may well regard the growth of Jewish influence there with some anxiety, at least if he deems it best for the world that the great Teutonic nation, at last united and liberated by efforts so heroic and at so great a cost, should be allowed to develop its character, and work out its destiny in its own way. . . .

The situation is a most unhappy one. Such consequences as have flowed from the dispersion of the Jews are enough to prove to the optimist that there are real and lasting calamities in history. Repression, though duty imposes it on a government, does not seem hopeful; soldiers may be sent, and some of the Anti-Semitic rioters may be shot down, but this will not make the rest of the people love the Jew. That the people should ever love the Jew while he adheres to his tribalism, his circumcision, and his favourite trades, seems to be morally impossible. . . . No real solution seems to present itself except the abandonment by the Hebrew of his tribalism, with its strange and savage rite, and of all that separates him socially from the people among who he dwells. . . .

What can, what ought, the Germans to do? It behoves them calmly to consider this question. Violence clearly in any form is neither right nor expedient. The Government is bound to put it down, and excesses which provoke a deserved reaction will only leave Semitism morally stronger and more formidable than ever. The withdrawal of political rights, once conceded, is also practically out of the question, more especially as the Jew has not only been permitted to vote but compelled to serve in the army. This last fact is decisive. On the other hand, no principle political or moral forbids a German to use his own vote for the purpose of keeping the government and guidance of the nation in German hands. Of course he is equally at liberty to encourage, or refuse to encourage, such journals as he thinks fit. Associations against anybody have a very ugly look, yet they may be justified by great compactness of tribal organisation and corporate activity on the side of the Hebrews. Restraints upon immigration are harsh and inhospitable, except in a case of absolute necessity. But a case of absolute necessity may be conceived, and the land of every nation is its own. The right of self-defence is not confined to those who are called upon to resist an armed invader. It might be exercised with equal propriety, though in a different way, by a nation the character and commercial life of which were threatened by a great irruption of Polish Jews. . . .

It has been said, and I believe truly, that religion is the least part of the matter. Yet there is between the modern Jew and the compatriot of Luther a certain divergence of general character and aim in life connected with religion which makes itself felt beside the antagonism of race, and the traces of which appear in the literature of this controversy. Judaism is material optimism with a preference to a chosen race, while Christianity, whether Catholic or Protestant, is neither material nor in a temporal sense optimist. Judaism is Legalism, of which the Talmud is the most signal embodiment, and here again it is contrasted with Christianity and the Christian Ideal; which is something widely different from the mere observance, however punctual, of the law. In the competition for this world's goods it is pretty clear that the legalist will be apt to have the advantage, and at the same time that his conduct will often appear not right to those whose highest monitor is not the law. The Agnostic, seeing what he deems the revelries of Christianity rejected by the Jew, and imaging this to be the cause of quarrel, is ready to take the Jew to his heart. But it may be questioned whether he will find the affinity so close as at first sight it appears. The Agnostic after all is the child of Christendom. He is still practically the liegeman of the Christian conscience, whatever account of its genesis he may have given to himself. He has a social ideal, not that of the Church, but that of humanity, which has come to him through the Church, and which is utterly at variance with the pretension of a chosen race. Mr. Wolf's text, 'Ye shall eat the riches of the Gentiles, and in their glory shall ye boast yourselves,' would not express the aspirations of a Positivist any more than those of a Christian.

Apart from these local collisions, there is a general curiosity, not unmingled with anxiety, to know what course in politics the enfranchised Jew will take. He is everywhere making his way into the political arena, which indeed, under the system of party government, suits his traditional habits almost as well as the stock exchange. A money power is sure in the main to be conservative, and the inclination of Jewish wealth to the side of reaction in England and other countries is already becoming apparent. Poor Jews will be found in the revolutionary, and even in the socialist, camp. But in whatever camp the Jew is found he will be apt for some time, unless the doctrine of heredity is utterly false, to retain the habits formed during eighteen centuries of itinerant existence, without a country, and under circumstances which rendered cunning, suppleness, and intrigue almost as necessary weapons of self-defence in his case as the sword and the lance were in the case of the feudal soldier. He will be often disposed to study 'the spirit of the age' much as he studies the stock list and to turn the knowledge to his own profit in the same way. It is very likely that he may sometimes outrun and overact national sentiment or even national passion, which he does not himself share. This is one of the dangerous liabilities of his character as a statesman. It might have been supposed that the Jews, having been for so many centuries shut out from military life, would be free from militarism; indeed, a high rank in civilisation has been plausibly claimed for them on that ground. Yet a Jewish statesman got up Jingoism much as he would have got up a speculative mania for a commercial purpose, and his consuming patriotism threw quite into the shade that of men who, though opposed to Jingoism, would have given their lives for the country. Among the ablest and most active organisers of that rebellion in the United States which cost a thousand millions sterling and half a million of lives, was a Jewish senator from Louisiana, who when the crash came, unlike the other leaders, went off to push his fortune elsewhere. There was no particular reason why he should not do so, being, as he was, a member of a cosmopolitan race; but there was a particular reason why the people who had no other country should receive his counsels with caution in a question of national life or death. A political adventurer will not be sparing of that which in the pride of Jewish superiority he regards as 'gutter blood.' Joseph, being the Prime Minister of Pharaoh, displays his statecraft for the benefit of his employer by teaching him to take advantage of the necessities of the people in a time of famine for the purpose of getting them to surrender their freeholds into the royal hands. He would no doubt have played the game of an aristocracy or even of a democracy in the same spirit, though his natural taste, as an Oriental, would lead him if possible to be the vizier of an absolute monarch. There are some who think that the Hebrew adventurer, with a cool head and a cool heart, may be specially useful as a mediator between heated political parties, and a reconciler of the interests which they represent. But this is surely a condemnation of party rather than a recommendation of the Hebrew.

Mr. Oliphant, in the work to which reference has already been made, proposes that Palestine should be restored to the Jew, with some of the vacant country adjoining; and it appears that this plan is not unlikely to be carried into effect. The restoration of their own land may have the same good influence upon the Jews which it has had upon the Greeks. It is not likely that of those now settled in the West any considerable number would ever turn their steps eastward. We know the anecdote of the Parisian Jew who said that if the Kingdom of Jerusalem was restored he should ask for the ambassadorship at Paris; but the westward flow of migration might be checked, and from the eastern parts of Europe, where the relations of the Jews to the native population are very bad, some of them might return to their own land. Mr. Oliphant seems to have little hope of seeing the Jews, even in Palestine, take to husbandry, and proposes that they should be the landowners, and that the land should be tilled for them by 'fellahs.' We must assume that fellahs convinced of the validity of the Jews' claim to exemption from the indignity of manual labour will be found. But necessity would in time compel the Jew once more to handle the plough. The situation at all events would be cleared, and the statesmen who are now inditing despatches about religious toleration would see that Israel is not a sect but a tribe, and that the difficulty with which they have to deal arises not merely from difference of opinion, or any animosities produced by it, but from consecrated exclusiveness of race.

In one respect the Jew certainly has a right to complain, even in a country where his emancipation has been most complete, not of persecution, but of what may be called a want of religious delicacy and courtesy on the part of Christians. He is singled out as the object of a special propagandism carried on by such societies as that for the conversion of the Jews. The conduct of those who are trying to impart to him the truth which they believe necessary to salvation is not 'demoniac,' but the reverse; yet it is easy to understand his annoyance and indignation. The barrenness of this propagandism in proportion to the money and effort spent on it is notorious; the object against which it is directed is not mere intellectual conviction, but something as ingrained and tenacious as caste. Simple respect for the Jew's opinion and perfect religious courtesy are more likely to reach his mind than any special propaganda.

Of the lack of theological interest in him the Jew can scarcely complain. If there has been error here, it has certainly been on the side of exaggeration. The formal relation of Christianity in its origin to Judaism perhaps we know; its essential relation, hardly. What was a peasant of Galilee? Under what influence, theological or social, did he live? Who can tell exactly? We have a series of Lives of Christ, from which eager readers fancy that they derive some new information about the Master, but which, in fact, are nothing but the gospel narrative shredded and mingled with highly-seasoned descriptions of Jewish customs and of the scenery of the lake of Gennesaret, while the personal idiosyncrasy of the biographer strongly flavours the whole. If there are any things of which we are sure, they are that Galilee was a place out of which orthodox Judaism thought that no good could come; that the teaching of the Galileans was essentially opposed to that of the Jewish doctor, and that Judaism strove to crush Christianity by all the means in its power. Thus if Israel was the parent of Christendom, it was as much in the way of antagonism as in that of generation. There is an incomparably greater affinity between Christianity and Platonism or Stoicism, than between Christianity and the Talmud. The exaggerated notion of Christians about the importance of the Jews has been curiously reproduced of late in an unexpected quarter, and under a most fantastic form. Even when theological belief has departed, religious sentiment is not easily expelled, nor does the love of the mysterious die out at once, especially in a woman's breast. Miss Martineau, after renouncing Theism, indemnified herself with mesmeric fancies. The authoress of 'Daniel Deronda' in like manner indemnified herself with the Jewish mystery. No Jewish mystery, except a financial one, exists. Daniel Deronda is a showman who, if, after taking our money, he were desired to raise the curtain, would be obliged to confess that he had nothing to show. A relic of Tribalism, however vast and interesting, is no more hallowed then any other boulder of a primæval world. Every tribe was the chosen people of its own God; and if it were necessary to institute a comparison between the different races in respect of their 'sacredness,' which it happily is not, the least sacred of all would be that which had most persistently refused to come into the allegiance of humanity.

One more remark is suggested by the discussion of the Jewish question, and perhaps it is the most important of all. It is surely time for the rulers of Christian Churches in general, and for those of the Established Church in particular, to consider whether the sacred books of the Hebrews ought any longer to be presented as they are now to Christian people as pictures of the Divine character and of the Divine dealings with mankind. Historical philosophy reads them with a discriminating eye. It severs the tribal and the primæval from the universal, that which is perennially moral, such as most of the commandments in the Decalogue, from that which by the progress of humanity has ceased to be so. It marks, in the midst of that which is utterly unspiritual and belongs merely to primitive society or to the Semite of Palestine, the faint dawn of the spiritual, and traces its growing brightness through the writings of prophets and psalmists till it becomes day. But the people are not historical philosophers. Either they will be misled by the uncritical reading of the Old Testament or they will be repelled. Hitherto they have been misled, and some of the darkest pages of Christian history, including those which record the maltreatment of Jews in so far as it was religious, have been the result of their aberrations. Now they are being repelled, and the repulsion is growing stronger and more visible every day. It is not necessary, and it might be irritating, to rehearse the long series of equivocal passages which shocked the moral sense of Bishop Colenso, and of which Mr. Ingersoll, the great apostle of Agnosticism in America, makes use in his popular lectures with terrible effect. The question is one of the most practical kind, and it will not well brook delay. It is incomparably more urgent than that of Biblical revision.

I cannot conclude without repeating that if this was a case of opposition to religious liberty, I should thoroughly share the emotions and heartily echo the words of Mr. Lucien Wolf. But I have convinced myself – and I think Mr. Wolf's own paper when carefully examined affords proof – that it is a case of a different kind.

3. Arnold White speaks, 1899

Source: Arnold White, *The Modern Jew* (1899), pp. xi–xv, 14–15, 52–64, 118, 139–61, 188.

Arnold White (1848–1925), social reformer, eugenist and imperialist, was, with the Earl of Dunraven, the leading anti-alienist of the 1880s and 1890s. A person of some substance, he was instrumental in bringing the issue before Parliament and in assisting the various official investigations that followed. He differed from most anti-alienists in not bothering to conceal his pronounced anti-Semitism.

To make the people of England think is the object of this book. If they refuse to think betimes, they will wake up one morning only to discover that they have parted with the realities of national life, and are dominated by cosmopolitan and materialist influences fatal to the existence of the English nation.

Dangers may be predicted from facts which may be unwelcome but cannot be denied. Each immigrant foreign Jew settling in this country joins, not the English community as the Huguenots and Hollander refugees from the Roman Catholic prosecutions of the seventeenth century joined us, but a community proudly separate, racially distinct, and existing preferentially aloof. Members of this community for successive generations, except in rare instances, decline to intermarry with non-Jews, maintain a different Sabbath, consume a different food, and are tied to alien communities of their own race and faith in other lands by closer bonds than any that unite them to the country of their adoption. This Jewish island in the sea of English life is small to-day. Few trades, interests, or classes are so directly affected by it as to create misgiving in the public mind that a danger menacing to national life has begun in our midst, is growing, and must be abated if sinister consequences are to be avoided. There are two methods, and only two, in which the evil results of a Jewish imperium inside the English Empire can be obviated. It can be destroyed and its members expelled as was done in the thirteenth century in most countries in Europe, including England, and is likely to be done over again in France before many years have passed, or the Jewish community, frankly recognising the peril that besets them, must review their conduct and heartily work for instead of against the process of absorption which in two generations made French Protestants of the day of Louis XIV an integral part of the English people. So far the enormous majority of them have resolutely declined even to consider methods which they allege would obliterate their racial entity as Jews. Except among the Jewish aristocracy, they refuse to intermarry, and while seeking no proselytes to their own faith, their proudest consciousness lies in the conviction that Jehovah has set them apart among the nations and destines them to a future more glorious and responsible than any that awaits the less gifted and favoured followers of the Nazarene. They have, they say, a mission and a message to the Gentiles.

England, therefore, is in this dilemma: She is either compelled to abandon her secular practice of complacent acceptance of every human being choosing to settle on these shores, or to face the certainty of the Jews becoming stronger, richer, and vastly more numerous; with the corresponding certainty of the press being captured as it has been captured on the Continent, and the national life stifled by the substitution of material aims for those which, however faulting, have formed the unselfish and imperial objects of the Englishmen who have made the Empire. . . . Humanity does not change its spirit in a day, a week, or a century, and we English have no right . . . to anticipate that when the Jews arrive at the position in Great Britain which they occupy in France to-day, the conduct of the bulk of them will be more humane, enlightened, or unselfish towards us than it has been towards the French or still more towards their six million co-religionists in the Russian Ghetto.

Those who are only acquainted with the faultless civic and social life of Anglicised Jewish subjects of the Queen are scarcely in a position to judge of the dangers which menace us as a nation, and which menace the English Jews along with the rest of their fellow subjects. In all countries and throughout the centuries, recurrent phenomena attending the protection, equality, popularity, strength, vices, and final ejection of the Jewish community are constant; and seem to form a code of inexorable law which, to be understood, must be examined. The mild spirit of Christian forbearance has promoted the undue economic predominance of a more powerful and intolerant race. When the spirit of Christianity began to wane in France, the religious indifference which followed the Revolution removed the checks to Jewish prosperity, and there, whether by Christian forbearance or religious indifference, no impediment to the aloofness of Israel exists. The intolerance of Christendom towards the Jews is reflected by an intolerance even deeper and more lasting of Judaism towards non-Jews. They resemble the Roman Catholic Church in this, that until they have obtained freedom and equality they are humbler, more suppliant, and meeker than other men; but when once equality is accorded, the spiritual despotism of Rome herself is not more absolute than the iron intolerance of the prosperous but non-spiritual Jew.

. . .

. . . Is it true that international finance has fallen captive to Jewish energy and skill? In London, Paris, Vienna, and Berlin the Jew banker is easily first among the merchants in money. In England the fall of the Barings has given a lonely supremacy to a Jewish banking-house with princely traditions. But money trading is not the only walk of life in which the Jew has been found to take the highest place. Wherever material comfort and personal safety are obtainable, there are nimble brain, deft finger, and sensitive organisation found on the topmost rung of the ladder. Medicine, music, law, surgery, politics, journalism, and art are being progressively officered by men of the Jewish race. The intellectual pre-eminence of the Jew is not to be regretted by the Anglo-Saxon race, itself built up from materials thrown out by other nations. Stupid and self-indulgent people who are passed in the race of life by earnest and clever men, whether Jew or Gentile, naturally join the ranks of the anti-Semites; but there is another class of Jew-hater, who is not so much concerned with the alleged parasitism of the Jew as with the mental and spiritual effects of the worship of the modern equivalent of the Golden Calf. It can scarcely be denied by the warmest advocates of equality and freedom for all, even among the more enlightened Jews themselves, that from modern Israel a river of materialism emerges. Russian statesmen perceive that the decay of faith in England, France, and Central Europe leaves the ground open for the operation of a new social morality. They dread the modern democracy, acknowledging neither God nor master, that has ceased to hold in reverence the ideals its fathers worshipped; and they attribute to Jewish materialism a large responsibility for the evil. . . .

. . .

. . . Six centuries back Jews were, as now, the backbone of the trade in money. Financial operations were entirely in their hands, and so completely had they monopolised the manufactures, that the sacred vessels used in the service of the church were supplied by Jewish goldsmiths. The English armies in Normandy and Gascony contained no Jewish archers or javelin men; no Jew was found in the train of knight or baron; they grew rich and prospered at home while the blood of Norman nobles and English men-at-arms was fertilising the plains of France. Such being the case, their unpopularity among men of action is not surprising. They were tolerated simply as the mechanical sources of money. Nor was the fault of this state of things simply on the side of the English. The Jew, in his capacity of money-lender, cannot reasonably have been expected to forego his pound of flesh with unvarying persistency. Money-lenders are always few and debtors invariably in the majority. Lenders, as a class, have never succeeded in acquiring popularity among borrowers. Lord James of Hereford's Bill against money-lenders enshrines a view of the favourite trade of the Hebrew race which has prevailed in England since Jews settled here. When they are of different religion and race, creditors are still further separated from their debtors. A memorable example of this hatred and desire for the plunder of opulent Hebrews is found at the coronation of Richard Cœur de Lion. Jews were excluded from this pageant at Westminster Abbey. Some few of them, impelled by Oriental curiosity, still characteristic of their race, slipped in with the crowd. They were discovered. A hue and cry was raised and the Jews were chased out of the Abbey by the followers of Jesus of Nazareth. Not content with mere expulsion, religious fervour was quickly reinforced by a desire for loot. The London citizens hunted their prey into the Jewry and revelled in the sack of Hebrew merchandise precisely as the Russian or Galician populace hunts and robs them today. Frightful atrocities were committed on the inmates of Jewry. The roar of flames mingled with the screams of tortured Israelites until the murderers drew off, sated with blood and plunder. This is but a single instance of the Jewish massacres which occurred periodically throughout England, and exemplifies the pushful inquisitiveness of a race which to this day is, for the most part, honestly oblivious to the chief causes of its unpopularity.

. . .

Besides the social and racial aloofness of the foreign immigrants there is a further element which differentiates the most Anglicised Jew who remains loyal to his faith from all other foreigners. This element in the problem is the fact of his close connection both by blood and religion with a kindred community in every foreign country. This is seen whenever the question of the good or evil conduct of a Jew is discussed in the public press. At the outset of the recent Dreyfus case Jews believed Dreyfus to be innocent for the same reason that the crazy anti-Semites believed him to be guilty, the judgment in both cases being arrived at without one tittle of evidence on either side, although the illegality of the trial was not in question. There is not a synagogue or a Jewish congregation in Poland, Lithuania, or Galicia which does not in case of need justly exercise over humane Jews in Western Christendom a stronger influence than any of the social or religious forces of the country in which they are domiciled. Under the stress of persecution, or even of criticism, the solidarity of the modern Jews is complete, and it is completer between Jews of different nationalities than between the Jewish community of a given country and the native inhabitants when persecution and criticism are absent. Jews quarrel among themselves as ferociously as the most exemplary Christians. Whatever an Englishman may or may not be, it is clear that the members of no race or fragment of a race can be deemed English when their diet is foreign, their origin Oriental, when their ties with alien co-religionists in other lands are closer than with Britons, and when, for successive generations, they have proudly declined to intermarry with the people of their adopted country. It is no answer to say that some of the richest, the most enlightened and Anglicised of the Jews have married Christians, and will do so again. The fact is indisputable, and is greatly to the advantage both of Christendom and of Jewry. The proportion of mixed marriages, however, between Jews and non-Jews is so small as to constitute an immaterial factor in the problem, while Jewesses who marry Christians are looked on by the bulk of their own people, even in the middle classes, as the victims of *mésalliance.*

A brilliant but sinister novel, "Dr. Phillips," written by a Jewess, throws light on this point. A number of Jewish middle class matrons are discussing the prospect of a daughter of one of them marrying a Christian:

> Mrs. Collings said she would rather see one of her children dead than married to a Christian. Mrs. Detmar would not go quite as far as that; only she would, certainly, rather see hers married to the poorest Jew that ever walked, even to an absolute pauper. Mrs. Jeddington said she did not think things were as bad as that; she would rather see Soph married to "one of their own people," of course, but she did not think her father would mind either way.
>
> Mrs. Montague Levy said: "Mixed marriages never came to any good," and instances were cited (p. 165).

Speaking of the quality of aloofness in the middle class Jews, the talented authoress of "Dr. Phillips" continues:

> Theirs is a society worth describing before, as must be in the natural order of things, it decays or amalgamates. It is a fact little understood that here, in the heart of a great and cosmopolitan city, sharing in, and appropriating its riches, there is a whole nation dwelling apart in an inviolable seclusion, which they at once

cultivate, boast of, and are ashamed at. There are houses upon houses in the West Central districts, in Maida-Vale, in the City, which are barred to Christians, to which the very name of Jew is an open sesame.

All the burning questions of the hour are to them a dead letter; art, literature, and politics exist not for them. They have but one aim, the acquisition of wealth. Playing cards at each other's houses is their sole experience of the charms of social intercourse; their interests are bounded by their homes and those of their neighbouring brethren (p. 168).

In a sort of jealous exclusiveness these Jews lived by and among themselves. They fancies they did so from choice. It was not so; it was a remnant of the time when the yellow cap and curiously shaped gaberdine marked them out as lepers in the crowd. The garb had been discarded, but the shrinking feeling of generations was still lingering. There is a certain pride in these people; they are at once the creatures and the outcasts of civilisation. The difference between Jew and Gentile was once one of religion. Now it is a difference that it will take as many centuries of intermarriage to bring about. The Jews feel this acutely. They remember the leper mark that has been taken from them, and they shrink from accentuating the remembrance by association with the people whose ancestors affixed it.

Put two strange Jews, one from London and one from the Antipodes, amid a hundred people of other nationalities, and in a quarter of an hour they will have recognised their kinship, and have gravitated towards each other in unconscious Ishmaelitism against the rest of the company.

Sections of them are trying very hard to struggle against this race barrier, and with a modicum of success. But they have much to contend against (p. 60).

. . .

Another matter that leads to the aloofness of Israel is the fondness of poor Jewish parents for the Chedorim, or elementary school, in which children are taught the elements of Hebrew and religion. The pedagogic principles employed are very primitive, instruction being merely an exercise in memory. The sanitary conditions also often leave much to be desired. In civilised communities, the tendency has been to replace these Chedorim by schools on more modern principles, which include secular subjects in their curriculum ("Jewish Year Book." 1898–1899.)

Lord Rothschild has sent the following circular letter (in English and Yiddish) to the parents of every male pupil in the Jews' Free School:

Jews' Free School
Bell Lane, Spitalfields, E.
December 1898

Dear friend, I desire to address you on a subject of very great importance concerning the health and well-being of your sons, and affecting their future development, physical and intellectual.

Figure 17   Alien types, 1901   Immigrant Jews, with their beards and distinctive clothing, were as readily identifiable by appearance as by language (G.R. Sims (ed.), *Living London*, 3 vols (London: Cassell, 1901), I, p. 54).

I know what love and devotion Jewish parents feel for their children, how hard they work for them and what sacrifices they submit to in order to promote their welfare. I know also how ardently they desire to see their children brought up in the doctrines of our holy religion, and that they should be properly instructed in Hebrew and in the tenets of our sacred faith.

But it has long seemed to me that you may be doing your children harm by the over-zeal which prompts you to send them to the Chedorim for so many hours a day. Visitors have noticed how pale and tired the boys attending the free school look, and how their weariness increases with each hour of the day. This was particularly noticed by H.M. Inspector during a recent visit. He was impressed by the appearance of fatigue so noticeable among the boys. At first he thought they might be underfed, or that they suffered from some form of home neglect. But being assured that the children were well looked after by their parents, he questioned them and then discovered the true cause of their tired looks. He found that many boys attend the

Chedorim as early as 7 o'clock in the morning and remain there till it is time to go to school. Immediately school is over, they return to the Chedorim and stay there until 8 or 9 o'clock at night. They thus spend twelve or thirteen hours a day in their studies, a large proportion of this time being passed among insanitary surroundings.

In consequence of this over-pressure, H.M. Inspector has strongly urged the committee of the free school to shorten the school hours. The committee have this matter now under their serious consideration. There is little doubt they will carry out the suggestion of H.M. Inspector. The inevitable result of such a change will be that you will have to keep your children longer at school than you do at present, and you will thus be deprived of their services at a time when you can ill afford to spare them.

I ask you, are you not expecting too much of children of tender age? Do not these long hours seriously injure their health? Some time ago, Dr. Schorstein stated publicly that his experience at the London Hospital showed him that the Chedorim were ruining the health of the children attending them, that the bodies and minds of your little ones became enfeebled, and that in consequence they were less able to withstand the various illnesses to which children are subject.

While appreciating your motives, I would beg to point out to you how unwise is your action. Far be it from me to under-value the religious instruction your children should receive, but I venture to think, that sufficient teaching in this most important subject is given at the free school, where the Hebrew and religious syllabus, issued and sanctioned by the Chief Rabbi, is thoroughly well taught. A great many hours a week are given to Hebrew reading, translation, Bible history, Hebrew grammar, the observances of the Calendar, and last but not least, to Ethics and the Moral Law. Surely, this instruction should prove sufficient.

By the course you are pursuing you are positively injuring the future prospects of your children, for, if they come to school tired and unrefreshed, how can they do themselves justice in their secular studies? Their progress is hindered, and either you must keep them at school more years than would otherwise be necessary, or, if you take them away at the legal age, they are not sufficiently educated to acquit themselves well in the battle of life. Instead of rising in the industrial world, they sink into the ruck of ill-paid and over-crowded occupations and remain the mere drudges of society.

I earnestly beg of you, therefore, to take my words to heart and withdraw your children from the Chedorim altogether, or at least reduce the hours during which they attend. They will then grow up healthy and strong, fitted in every way to pursue an honourable career, and with a reasonable prospect of becoming good and worthy English citizens.

I am,
Very truly yours,
Rothschild.

Another instance of the separation of the Jews from their Gentile fellow subjects is to be discovered in the recent claims of the Cohanim, or priestly class, for exemption from service at inquests. In consequence of their priestly descent the Cohens claim certain privileges, and among others, under the command of Leviticus xxi. I, 3, refuse to contaminate themselves by being in the same place as the dead.

A further symptom of the gradual growth of Jewish power in England, and the success with which privileges denied to other races and to every other form of religion except the Anglican, Roman Catholic, Presbyterian, and Wesleyan bodies, which number millions, not thousands, among their followers, are granted to the Jews, is the expenditure of State funds in the erection of synagogues at Wormwood Scrubs, Parkhurst, and Pentonville Prisons. Government have apparently admitted the right of Jewish prisoners to separate worship at the public expense.

The refusal to intermarry, the maintenance of separation as a Chosen People, the different diet, the non-observance of Sunday, the claims of the Cohanim to evade civic duties, the Talmudic education given in the Chedorim or elementary schools, the religious claims of prisoners for synagogues at the public expense, are examples of the separate tendencies of the Jewish people domiciled in England.

What is true of the middle-class Jew in England is even more pronounced in the destitute and recent immigrants from Russia or Poland, who form, with their descendants, the bulk of the Jewish colonists in Great Britain and Ireland. Assiduous, supple, temperate, many of them succeed in shaking off the chains of their poverty. In the second or third generation individuals among their descendants may become successful in letters or in art. But the language employed by the authoress of "Dr. Phillips" is applicable to the poorer classes of the Jews to an even greater extent than to those above them in social rank.

In the words of a German writer (Robert Hessen, *Preussische Jarbucher*, November 1889): "As long as the Jews do not find it to their advantage to become national in their feelings, so long every exhortation and every measure will be in vain."

One of the chief difficulties in the way of nationalising and absorbing the Jewish element is the persistence with which they adhere to the dietary system laid down by Moses. It is true that the conditions that existed in the days of the great Hebrew legislator were totally different from those prevailing to-day. Still, the general immunity of the Jewish race from zymotic disease is probably due, to a large extent, to the purity of the materials composing their repasts, and the special care taken in the examination and preparation of the flesh of animals. Since hygiene has become in all civilised countries the object of a national and municipal care, the necessity for separate diet, demanded and insisted on by the stricter class of Jews – which practically includes the best members of the community – has completely passed away. There is no religious significance in separate food; its provision is neither a Mosaic nor a Talmudic command, the breach of which constitutes a breach of the law. Still, the aloofness of the Jews is largely due to the unwillingness of the vast majority of them to eat with Christians. In some cases this tendency is carried to an absurd point. One of the most eminent Rabbis in Russia, the late Isaac of Mohilieff, recently visited this country. Looking upon the preparation of food even in the kitchens of his co-religionists as not complying with the canon prevalent among the strict Jews in Russia, he ate and drank nothing during the whole of his sojourn in this country except bread and wine.

A recent instance of Jewish aloofness in the matter of diet is afforded in the applications made to the authorities of one of our public schools to arrange for special cooking for the Jewish boys attending that school. This request was refused, and I understand with the full assent of the more liberal, progressive, and Anglicised members of the community in this country.

Since the Jewish Question is by no means a question merely of race rivalry or of "bread envy," there are no greater enemies of Judaism than the idealists among the Jews themselves, who encourage aloofness and separation in matters of no importance. Prejudice and envy alone could never have produced the anti-Semitic feeling now universal throughout the world. Money is no longer merely earned. It is won as the result of a struggle which stands in closer relation to war itself than to the exchange or sale of commodities. It is no longer necessary that fortunes should be gained by industry, although it is true that this quality is important. There is another element which seems to be almost universal in the Semitic race – viz., the inborn proclivity to perceive with lightning glance the right moment to "corner" the market. During the present century, therefore, the evolution of a new influence may be detected – that of the self-made millionaire.

Under existing conditions it is impossible that any man, however clever or able, can honestly make a million sterling within the space of a year or two, and if he succeed in doing so, his triumph is attained at the expense of others; not by making two blades of grass grow where one grew before, nor by fulfilling the useful function of intermediary between individuals and communities. As a promoter or as an expert in the flotation of companies, in deluding the public by inflating worthless securities with an artificial and effervescent value, and in the art of hypnotising large communities of shareholders into the belief that something is to be made out of nothing, or that vast risks and the hundred to one chances may be taken with impunity, there is no equal to the Jew. His success is almost imperial, and has introduced, as I have said, a completely new and dangerous element into modern society. . . .

. . .

. . . This is a phenomenon that adds to the aloofness of Israel, and causes masses of the community to regard the whole race with silent aversion. . . .

. . .

Suppressions of fact are even less serious than statements that are not true. The Board of Trade raises public sympathy with the undesirable mendicants and middlemen who come here, by expressly stating . . . that the "certain residuum, principally of Jewish refugees," remains here. All Englishmen wish to maintain England as the asylum of the *bonâ fide* refugee. But the idea that the dregs of Russian cities who remain here are mainly refugees is a fiction concocted in the Labour Department of the Board of Trade. A Royal Commission, or other impartial inquiry, would at once ascertain that not one immigrant in ten even claims to be a refugee. The bulk of immigrants come here, not because Russians persecute them, but because they are hungry and the English are charitable. Russian Jews quickly learn that £120,000 is left in one legacy to a Jewish body in London. . . . I contend that England is unwise to extend national hospitality to persons belonging to the submerged tenth of other countries, who refuse absorption into our community; and the device of the Board of Trade in calling them "refugees" is an unusual departure from the best traditions of English public offices.

4. The voice of Labour, 1892

Source: Minutes of Evidence taken before the Royal Commission on Labour Group 'C', Parliamentary Papers, [C.6795—vi] XXXVI Part II (1892), qq. 15,096—15,205

George Edwin Green was the Secretary of the National Union of Boot Clickers, a London-based union, whose 1,650 members cut the uppers of boots by hand. His opinions and attitudes with respect to Jewish immigration are particularly noteworthy.

15,096. Do you think that the proper course would be to prohibit all foreigners from landing here unless they had something in their pockets which would indicate a visible means of subsistence? – As regards their having something in their pockets, we tried to pass a resolution at the Trades Council some time back that a foreigner when he lands must be worth 3*l.* in English money, and 1*l.* for every child, or a man and wife 5*l.* But that seems to me absurd, and I will tell you why. If the employers of labour want these men they will very soon send over to Poland and Germany this amount, and then, as soon as ever these people land, they will take it back again. That is easily got over. It would not meet the case at all. I would suggest although I have not worked out any scheme, that no one should be allowed to land unless he knew a trade. We do not object to men who know a trade and who will stick up for their wages. We would welcome them. But as soon as they do get into the country they cut our people down something frightful. They can live on about 2*d.* a day, whereas an Englishman would not, or could not if he would. It is a fact that seven of these Jewish or Polish workmen will work in one room from 7 o'clock in the morning to about 10 o'clock at night with half-a-quartern loaf. You will admit that an Englishman cannot compete with that.

15,097.   But they do not work for the half-quartern loaf, they are paid wages, are they not? – Yes, they are paid wages, but very much under price, about half the price of English. What they do earn they save until they are able to start themselves. They must do that with it, because they do not spend it in living.

15,098.   You say they start in business themselves? – Yes. . . .

15,101.   Then they are not an improvident class? – No, they are not improvident, not by any means. As I said before, they debar themselves from the common and absolute necessaries of life. They spend nothing in soap, for instance, or anything of that kind. As for clothing, what they wear is filthy.

. . .

15,203.   You say no man should be allowed to come to this country who had not a trade at his fingers' ends? – Not unless he knows a trade of some description.

15,204.   You have heard of such men as Hungarian refugees, and Italian refugees, and others; you would not allow those to land in England, would you? – Refugees and political people are, of course, different; but I do not believe in making England a refuse heap, as it is at the present time.

15,205.   Are not these Russian Jews political refugees to a large extent? – I do not think they have any political opinions at all. I do not think they have got the pluck to have an opinion – the majority of them. If you saw them walking about you would think they were animals rather than men. They do not even know what morality means. They do not even know what cleanliness means, or anything of that kind. I could startle you with some things I have seen in what they call the "dens" they live in in the East end. . . .

5.   Sunday Bloody Sunday! 1905

Source: Minutes of Evidence taken before the Select Committee of the House of Lords on the Sunday Closing (Shops) Bill, Parliamentary Papers [344] VIII, 1905, qq. 1643–737

The Revd Alfred James Poynder, rector of Whitechapel, presented the problem of Jewish immigration as one of anti-alienism rather than anti-Semitism. The issue of

Sunday trading, he seemed to suggest, showed all too clearly that the immigrant minority were too far at variance with Christian culture and Christian values to be successfully integrated into English society.

1643. ... by the stress at which we are all living down there, by our alien population not observing the Lords Day, it has become practically like any other day. The only day observed in our parish is Good Friday, when the alien population chiefly shut and we shut. The police estimate that between 30,000 and 50,000 on a Sunday morning, who are not of the alien population, do their shopping in our streets and crowd our neighbourhood right up till noon, practically converting the whole of the morning into an enormous fair. This is the more detrimental, because the police are there in numbers to keep the peace, but in effect to permit the vendors to break the law. ... The British population say that they would lose their custom in a great measure if they in self-defence, did not open on the Sunday. ... One is deeply interested in the religious difficulty of the Jews. We have some 14,000, roughly, of Jews in our own parish, in the mother parish, and, of course, one greatly respects their religious convictions and does not want to feel that they are in any way worsted by any laws we make, but, on the other hand, we must always remember, I suppose, that if they get the benefit of our excellent police force our sanitary laws, and all our other laws, they must also conform to the laws of the country which, we feel, are for the good of the people ...

1645. ... I should wish to guard my remarks very closely against the feeling that I was in any way trying to deal harshly with the *bona fide* religious Jews. Of course, we greatly respect their convictions, and deeply appreciate all their religious fervour and earnestness. It seems to me that this question is not one between Gentile and Jew, but rather between British and alien, the former having made their Sunday laws, for the good of their own land, and guarded them very safely and carefully all through the centuries; and because aliens settle with us are we therefore to break down the laws which past experience through the centuries has taught us are good for the brain and body of our people as well as for their spiritual life. That is the line I have always sought to take in this question. . .

1711. *Duke of Northumberland*. I should like to press you a little more about this question of the Jews. You said just now, as I understood, that a Jew had come to this country and received the benefits which our good form of Government gives him, and, therefore, it was fair that he should obey our rules, but there is a large number of Jews who are born in this country and whose ancestors were born in this country, are there not? – Yes.

1712. Therefore they are in all respects the subjects of the country as much as the Christian population? – Yes.

1713.   They get no benefits which the Christian population does not get, do they? – No they get all the benefits, which the Christian population has arranged for them through the centuries.

1714.   You think for that reason it is fair to handicap them by taking away two days or nearly two days out of the week on which they cannot trade? – But do we do that?

1715.   I suppose if they, by their own law, cannot trade on Saturday and we, by our law will not allow them to trade on the Sunday, that makes two days? Not two working days . . . after sundown they may all of them work according to their own law.

1718.   We will confine ourselves to the Jew who is a really earnest Jew. I wish to know exactly what is the extent of his disability? – I would like you first to realise that a great many people are working seven days a week whether they call themselves Jews or do not. You must start with that proviso. You cannot beg that fact. Not only are they working, but they are causing the old fashioned British population, who are also earnest Christians in self-defence because they really cannot live, they say, to work on Sunday. You have to see the thing from both aspects.

1719.   I am only asking you it is a fact that you do heavily handicap the faithful Jews? – You heavily handicap the faithful Christian if you enable the Jew to open by his side. I want you to face that fact too . . .

6. Immigration, 1905

Source: Herbert Samuel 'Immigration', *Economic Journal*, XV (1905), pp. 318–39

Herbert Samuel (1870–1963), politician and intellectual, was born into a prominent Jewish banking family and educated at Balliol College, Oxford. He entered the Cabinet as Chancellor of the Duchy of Lancaster in 1909, was President of the Local Government Board in 1914–15 and Home Secretary in the last Liberal administration. Here the theorist of the New Liberalism explores the duties of the state in relation to freedom of movement.

. . . Problems of immigration have been given remarkably little attention by English economists and publicists. The so-called classical economists offer no guidance. . . . But since the writers of this school, in their lists of admissible forms of State action, never include the regulation of immigration, there can be little doubt that they considered it to be covered by the general rule of *laissez faire*. . . . To meddle with the freedom of movement from country to country was looked upon as obviously illegitimate. . . . The change of view was inevitable. The theory that under no circumstances should a State restrict the right of entry into its dominions is clearly unsound. . . .

No political scientist nowadays believes in the doctrine of natural rights. The well-being of the society concerned is the only test that can be applied, qualified, though it must be, by duty to the world at large. If one nation can help the members of other nations by admitting them into its territories, it should be chary of refusing the boon. But if the admission results in appreciably lowering its own civilisation, in degrading the standard of comfort of its people, in lessening, therefore, its influence for good on the other nations, then surely its duty to the world, as well as its duty to itself, would justify exclusion.

. . .

Nor can we accept . . . that every form of immigration is to be viewed with suspicion, and that most forms should be forbidden by the State. The alien is almost always unpopular. Nations, like individuals, are very conscious of their own virtues and of other peoples' faults. . . . There is no need to argue here against this kind of insular stupidity. And indeed anti-foreign prejudice nowadays more usually springs from industrial than from racial motives. There are numbers of workmen unemployed. This proves, it is said, that the country is over-populated. To encourage fresh additions to the population is like pouring water into a vessel already full above the brim. The new arrivals will either find no lodgment or will displace others; they must themselves starve or make others starve. Therefore, it is the obvious duty of Government to admit the fewest possible number of immigrants. This fallacy is, of course, a variant of the old Wage-Fund Theory, now as universally rejected by economists as it was once universally accepted – the doctrine that there is a certain amount of capital available to provide employment and wages for the working classes, and that the more numerous those classes become the smaller will be each individual's share. But the believer in the Wage-Fund Theory forgot that the more workmen there are, the more profit; the more profit, the more accumulation of capital; the more capital, the more opportunities for employment. He fell into the error, as Arnold Toynbee put it, "of looking upon the working man as a divisor and not as a multiplier."

The crude doctrine, now very commonly held in England, that to add to the population, by immigration or otherwise, is to add by so much to the difficulty of finding employment, is contradicted, not only by economic theory, but by the most notorious facts. Forty years ago the United Kingdom had a population of thirty millions; now it has a population of over forty-two millions. At that time there was a certain percentage of the working classes unemployed; according to the interesting figures lately published by the Board of Trade, in recent years the percentage has been almost precisely the same. But the doctrine we are considering would require us to believe that, since there were men unemployed forty years ago, the whole addition of twelve millions must have gone to swell their ranks, and that more than a quarter of the population are now permanently without work – a *reductio ad absurdum* which leaves nothing more to be said. If our industrial system has been able to absorb those twelve millions in the last forty years, the general standard of comfort rising at the same time and the ratio of out-of-works not increasing, it must be an error to say that the addition in the future of some thousands by immigration must necessarily make more acute the difficulty of unemployment. The contrary is often the case. In most countries to which they have come, aliens have fostered trade through the industries they have transplanted.

. . .

. . . And our most recent immigrants have brought with them new methods of division of labour which have given a powerful stimulus to the trades of tailoring, cabinet-making, slipper- and cap-making, and they have introduced in London the new industry of cigar-making. . . .

. . . It is plain that there is no single principle, ready to the hand of the politician, applicable universally. Each case, or group of cases, must be judged on its individual merits.

Let us consider some of these cases. And let us take first the classes of immigrants whom all would admit to be undesirable, choosing our illustrations from the present situation in our own country. Aliens may be classed as obviously undesirable for physical, for moral, or for economic reasons. In the first category are those who are suffering from infectious or loathsome diseases, and the insane and imbecile; in the second are criminals and prostitutes; in the third are persons who cannot maintain themselves, and who must necessarily become charges upon public funds. . . . In principle, then, the exclusion of persons falling within these categories will be held to be both desirable and just. But before we consent to apply the principle, we have to ask whether, if these classes are alone to be excluded, it is in practice possible to construct a sieve which can separate them from other immigrants. Of these groups of undesirables, the diseased, with a few exceptions, and the imbecile can alone be detected with certainty by examination at the ports. The criminal, the vicious, the intermittently insane, the vagrant, can obviously not be identified at sight, and carry no label to tell their character. . . .

Consider, again, the category of paupers. What human power will be able to detect which among a thousand immigrants is to become a public charge? The Röntgen ray has yet to be discovered which will reveal a man's character and future capacity as now his bones can be revealed. Certainly a money test is valueless. Among the aliens who have come to settle in England in recent years, the proportion who bring little or no money is large, but the proportion who seek Poor Law relief is remarkably small, They have, as is well known, a marked capacity for improving their position, and no assumption could be more false than to suppose that their initial poverty means ultimate pauperism. Any such

attempts to divide the sheep who will prosper from the goats who will
become a public charge must necessarily fail. . . .
. . . There remains the broader question whether, . . . the immigration of
foreigners is in general to be deprecated or tolerated or encouraged; how
far, and under what circumstances, the State should regulate it. The
subject divides for convenient treatment into two parts – the effect of
immigration economically on the industrial conditions of the population
into which it comes, and its effect socially on their national
characteristics. In countries in an early stage of development, and where
capital is available, . . . immigration, viewed from an economic
standpoint, must be beneficial, since the demand for labour will much
exceed the supply, and the chief need for the conquest of nature and the
general increase of wealth is population. . . . But in old countries, where
the industries are not capable of expanding more rapidly than the native
population increases, immigration might be economically injurious. . . . It
is in the last case only . . . that the State would be justified, if no other
means existed by which the evil could be met, in forbidding immigration.
That it would be justified in such a case, few would dispute. For we are
assuming, first, that the existing population suffices, in numbers and in
character, for all present industrial needs, and that its increase will suffice
for future needs; we are assuming also that the new arrivals, being ready
to accept the conditions of employment belonging to a lower civilisation,
find situations for themselves only by undercutting and ousting those who
are employed already; and we are assuming, thirdly, that by no
distribution of the aliens over various industries, and by no trade-union
action, can these results be avoided. Unless we are to believe that it is of
no social importance to maintain a proper standard of living among the
masses of the population, we are forced to the conclusion that in such a
case the State would be justified, would indeed be imperatively required,
to intervene. (This conclusion need not, of course, involve us in a
Protectionist position with regard to the importation of foreign goods
which displace native workers from their employment, for there the
counterbalancing export provides, in the long run, equal employment – a
fact which prevents the two instances from being treated as parallel.) In
such a case, then, State action would be legitimate. Whether such a case
has ever occurred is more doubtful. It is asserted, indeed, with much
emphasis, that all these conditions are present before our eyes, now and
in England. But with equal vigour this assertion is denied. . . .

. . .

Leaving the economic side, we come now to the last division of the
subject, the social effect of immigration . . . We may conclude that the
immigration is as yet far too small in volume to work any appreciable
change in the customs, the character, or the institutions of the British
people. . . .

. . .

Finally, . . . every system of regulation is in its nature an invasion of freedom. To watch at the ports all the ships that arrive, to investigate the antecedents and try to gauge the capacities of the people who come, to prevent individuals from going where they will and settling amongst you if they wish, to stigmatise, perhaps, all the members of a specified race as unfit to land on your shores and to live in your midst – all this derogates from liberty, and must be distasteful to any nation which holds liberty to be precious. It is a consideration which . . . should make us ask for clear proof of the necessity for restrictions before we consent to impose them.

To sum up what has been said: The political student has no universal rule to offer to the legislator. He cannot urge that, without exception, every country should be open to all who come; nor can he urge that, whenever circumstances permit, the foreigner, if he be poor, should be shut out. Each case, or group of cases, must be judged on its merits. It would be right to exclude the criminal, the diseased, the insane, and the pauper, were it possible to detect them, but in practice it would usually be found preferable to repatriate them after they had disclosed their character than to attempt to exclude them before. For the rest, it is necessary to weigh a number of elements, some of which may have to be put into one scale, some into the other: whether, in point of fact, the immigration does lead to unemployment and distress among the native workers, or whether, through the introduction of new trades or the expansion of old ones, the labour force of the nation is strengthened without, in the long run, anyone being the worse; whether or not the immigrants are so few in number and so near akin in race that they can be absorbed into the population and leave no mark upon it; if not, the legislator must judge as best he may from the character of the aliens in what respects their intermixture will strengthen and in what respects it will injure his people, whether the net result of their presence is likely to better or worsen the race. And if, when all these elements have been weighed, it seems still uncertain which way the balance inclines, then he will decide the issue by placing in the scale against restriction an unwillingness to interfere with individual freedom. For in political affairs it is at least a safe rule, if there be a doubt, rather to err on the side of liberty.

7.   Aliens Act, 1905

Source: An Act to amend the Law with regard to Aliens, 11 August 1905 (5 Edw. 7. c.13)

The Aliens Act of 1905 marked a significant break in the liberal tradition with respect to the movement of peoples into Britain. The right of asylum was preserved but unrestricted entry was abrogated and controls introduced for certain categories of person.

Regulation of Alien Immigration

1. – (1) An immigrant shall not be landed in the United Kingdom from an immigrant ship except at a port at which there is an immigration officer appointed under this Act, and shall not be landed at any such port without the leave of that officer given after an inspection of the immigrants made by him on the ship, or elsewhere if the immigrants are conditionally disembarked for the purpose, in company with a medical inspector, such inspection to be made as soon as practicable, and the immigration officer shall withhold leave in the case of any immigrant who appears to him to be an undesirable immigrant within the meaning of this section.

. . .

(3) For the purposes of this section an immigrant shall be considered an undesirable immigrant –
  (a) if he cannot show that he has in his possession or is in a position to obtain the means of decently supporting himself and his dependents (if any); or
  (b) if he is a lunatic or an idiot, or owing to any disease or infirmity appears likely to become a charge upon the rates or otherwise a detriment to the public; or
  (c) if he has been sentenced in a foreign country with which there is an extradition treaty for a crime, not being an offence of a political character, which is, as respects that country, an extradition crime within the meaning of the Extradition Act, 1870; or
  (d) if an expulsion order under this Act has been made in his case;
but, in the case of an immigrant who proves that he is seeking admission to this country solely to avoid prosecution or punishment on religious or political grounds or for an offence of a political character, or persecution, involving danger of imprisonment or danger to life or limb, on account of religious belief, leave to land shall not be refused on the ground merely of want of means, or the probability of his becoming a charge on the rates, nor shall leave to land be withheld in the case of an immigrant who shows to the satisfaction of the immigration officer or board concerned with the case that, having taken his ticket in the United Kingdom and embarked direct therefrom for some other country immediately after a period of residence in the United Kingdom of not less than six months, he has been refused admission in that country and returned direct therefrom to a port in the United Kingdom, and leave to land shall not be refused merely on the ground of want of means to any immigrant who satisfies the immigration officer or board concerned with the case that he was born in the United Kingdom, his father being a British subject.

. . .

Expulsion of Undesirable Aliens

3. – (1) The Secretary of State may, if he thinks fit, make an order (in this Act referred to as an expulsion order) requiring an alien to leave the

United Kingdom within a time fixed by the order, and thereafter to remain out of the United Kingdom –

(a) if it is certified to him by any court (including a court of summary jurisdiction) that the alien has been convicted by that court of any felony, or misdemeanour, or other offence for which the court has power to impose imprisonment without the option of a fine, or of an offence under . . . the Burgh Police (Scotland) Act, 1892, . . . , or paragraph eleven of section fifty-four of the Metropolitan Police Act, 1839, and that the court recommend that an expulsion order should be made in his case, either in addition to or in lieu of his sentence; and

(b) if it is certified to him by a court of summary jurisdiction after proceedings taken for the purpose within twelve months after the alien has last entered the United Kingdom, in accordance with rules of court made under section twenty-nine of the Summary Jurisdiction Act, 1879, that the alien –

(i) has, within three months from the time at which proceedings for the certificate are commenced, been in receipt of any such parochial relief as disqualifies a person for the parliamentary franchise, or been found wandering without ostensible means of subsistence, or been living under insanitary conditions due to overcrowding; or

(ii) has entered the United Kingdom after the passing of this Act, and has been sentenced in a foreign country with which there is an extradition treaty for a crime not being an offence of a political character which is, as respects that country, an extradition crime within the meaning of the Extradition Act, 1870.

(2) If any alien in whose case an expulsion order has been made is at any time found within the United Kingdom in contravention of the order, he shall be guilty of an offence under this Act.

. . .

7. – (1) Any person guilty of an offence under this Act shall, if the offence is committed by him as the master of a ship, be liable, on summary conviction, to a fine not exceeding one hundred pounds, and, if the offence is committed by him as an immigrant or alien, be deemed a rogue and vagabond within the meaning of the Vagrancy Act, 1824, and be liable to be dealt with accordingly as if the offence were an offence under section four of that Act.

. . .

(4) If any immigrant, master of a ship, or other person, for the purposes of this Act, makes any false statement or false representation to an immigration officer, medical inspector, immigration board, or to the Secretary of State, he shall be liable on summary conviction to imprisonment for a term not exceeding three months with hard labour.

Figure 18 Reading room (Free Library), Mile End Road, 1901 Apart from the loan of books, the public library provided readers with Yiddish newspapers for information and instruction and a place to study in (G.R. Sims (ed.), *Living London*, 3 vols (London: Cassell, 1901), III, p. 97).

(5) If any question arises on any proceedings under this Act, or with reference to anything done or proposed to be done under this Act, whether any person is an alien or not, the onus of proving that that person is not an alien shall lie on that person.

(6) In carrying out the provisions of this Act, due regard shall be had to any treaty, convention, arrangement, or engagement with any foreign country. . . .

8.   Anti-Jewish disturbances

a)   Limerick, 1904

Source: The Times, 1, 4 and 5 April 1904

On 12 January 1904 Father Creagh, a monk of the Redemptionist order, preached a blatantly anti-Semitic sermon to the indebted peasants of Limerick which provoked physical violence against the tiny Jewish community and the inauguration of a ruinous boycott. It was an extraordinary outburst that made national headlines. *The Times* included letters from apologists and critics with a leading article which are printed below.

Boycott of Jews in Limerick

To the editor of *The Times*

Sir, – I beg a little space in your valuable journal to bring before the public the serious condition of the Hebrew community in Limerick. I notice by a letter from the Lord Lieutenant of Ireland to the Jewish Board of Deputies that he assures the said board that things have quieted down and show an "un-interrupted improvement," and that so far as his Majesty's Government is concerned it does not intend to take any measures in the matter. Sir, I have spent a whole week visiting daily the Hebrew community in Limerick, from where I have just returned, and all I can say is that their condition at present is simply appalling. The boycott is in full force: and not only do the people decline to deal with the Jews, but they even refuse to pay what is due to them for goods purchased in the past. No Jew or Jewess can walk along the streets of Limerick without being insulted or assaulted. The police give them, so far as I was able to see, passive protection. Only last Friday a man was charged with seriously assaulting a Jew in the public street of Limerick. It was proved by the Crown and admitted by the prisoner that the Jew did not offer the slightest provocation; and although the police in their evidence stated that the Jew had to be taken to a doctor to have his injuries attended to, yet the magistrates thought it sufficient merely to fine the "catholic" prisoner 20s. Justice, however, has long since departed from lawless Limerick, and this fact was confirmed only two weeks ago by the Lord Chief Baron, who told the jury and the public that "there is no justice in Limerick."

The boycott, unfortunately, does not apply to the city of Limerick alone; for those responsible for the present trouble are not satisfied with having incited the mob in the city, but they have been sending out circulars all over the country with the most inflammatory extracts from Father Creagh's sermon telling the peasantry and others that they are not to deal with the Jews. A case of high-handed conduct on the part of an Irish priest occurred last week 20 miles distant from Limerick. A Jew peddler called in a certain village to sell his goods. A woman had just purchased from the man a pair of blankets, and arranged to pay for them at the rate of 1s. per week, the man not receiving at the time any money. He was just about to leave the house when a car drove up and the parish priest, entering the house, met the Jew and demanded from him what he was doing there. The Jew said that he was about his ordinary business. The priest then asked the woman what she had bought, and when she pointed to the blankets which were lying on the table he took them up, threw them out of the doorway, and told the man to leave the village and never enter his parish again, at the same time remarking to the woman "Do you not know that you must not deal with the Jews?"

Such, Sir, is the state of affairs existing at present in Limerick and that part of the country. The number of Jews in Limerick consists of 35 families. With the exception of two or three the majority of them are ruined and on the verge of starvation. Two or three Protestant gentlemen have been obliged already to give immediate relief to at least 15 families. The Jewish Rabbi told me, and I know from personal knowledge, that up to this no relief was ever required by any of the Jewish residents in Limerick. I know of the members of one family who have resided there for nearly 20 years, and the man was able to support himself and family on the 25s. per week which he earned. His children are now grown up. A son of his graduated last year in the Royal University. Yet the same man has, within the last two months, had to sell all his furniture and other personal belongings for the purpose of buying food, as since the boycott came into force he has been ruined and prevented from earning anything. The same thing applies to the majority of the other Jewish families in Limerick.

The few Protestants in Limerick can only sympathise deeply with the Jews, whom they always found to be a sober, quiet, and law-abiding community. The Protestants dare not help them openly, as they do not know when their own turn may come or when they too may find themselves at the mercy of Redemptorist priests (which, like justice in Limerick, is conspicuous by its absence).

May I, therefore, in all sincerity and earnestness, ask the Anglo-Jewish Association or other responsible members of Anglo-Jewry, and all who pity the down-trodden and persecuted Jew, to come to the assistance of the perishing and boycotted Israelites in Limerick? The matter admits of no delay; starvation and homelessness stare them in the face.

I may mention that while in Limerick I had a long interview with Father Creagh, the Roman Catholic priest, whom the Jews and others charge with being the cause of all their present misery; and after 55 minutes' talk, during which we discussed fully and freely the Jewish question in Limerick, I am convinced that while Father Creagh remains in that city directing its Roman Catholicism the Jews will have to leave, and many of them have not as many shillings in the world as would pay their fares even as far as Dublin.

Yours
I. Julian Grande, Director of the Irish Mission to the Jews

The Jewish question in Limerick

To the editor of *The Times*

Sir, – The suggestion of your correspondent on this subject in your issue of to-day that it is religious in-tolerance that prompts the feeling against the Jews in Limerick is not warranted by the facts, and tends to obscure the true cause of a growing evil, which it is to be hoped the legislation just introduced by the Government may prove instrumental in checking.

Notwithstanding some isolated cases, in which the conduct of individuals who had gone out of their way to insult the religious feeling of the South may have provoked ill-will amongst the lower order, there is no part of Europe more free from religious intolerance per se, and there is no people who have less cause to dread the display of such feeling than the Jews, whose religion has never been identified with any great changes in the possession of the land. Jews have resided in Ireland for centuries, but the majority of them have been people of respectable origin, as well as of refinement and education. Notwithstanding that they have usually engaged in pursuits which did not tend to endear them to society at large, their dealings have been, for the most part, with the better classes of Irish society, and never brought them into conflict with the people.

It is different with the present invasion of low-class Polish and Russian Jews. At first these people were rather welcomed than otherwise, but as they gradually developed this system of peddling goods to the peasantry, and began to foreshadow the evils that have caused them to be so ill-treated by the corresponding class in Russia, the feeling of people in Ireland has gradually undergone a change. The very instance quoted by your correspondent convicts the priest of nothing more than an intemperate zeal to protect his flock against one of the worst forms of usury. Some idea of the extent to which an evil which, with the carelessness of the Irish people regarding debt, is becoming a very serious one may be judged from the fact that three-fourths and more of the civil bill processes at quarter sessions in Ireland are those of Jews against the peasantry and labouring classes for arrears of payment for goods supplied on a system which is not at all as easy as *The Times's* method of selling an encyclopaedia. A legal official of the Limerick district informed me the other day that of some 200 civil bills over 170 were of this character, and he seemed to think that the evil was a growing one and would have to be met by legislation against, a class of people who are renewing in Ireland the class of dealings for which other countries have been made too hot for them. There is no doubt there is a very strong feeling against these people, but it is chiefly against their luxury and extortion. However, it must be admitted that when people owe money which they cannot pay, especially to Jews, it does not take very long to pass over the border which separates the man from his religion. In such cases "any stick is good enough to beat the dog with". At the same time the sympathy of the better class of people is with their own countrymen, and I heard a Protestant gentleman, who certainly could not be accused of religious intolerance to any one, asking the other day should what survived of Ireland from the Norman and Cromwellian invasions have its bones picked by the Russian Jews, and going on to quote Byron:-

"So whom the lion quite his fell repast
Next prowls the wolf, the filthy jackal last."

Your correspondent is altogether wrong; the question is merely a
financial, not a religious, one, and it is to be hoped that the
Government, which showed such scant mercy to the Irish proprietors,
will not unduly favour a much less desirable class of invaders of
Ireland.

Your obedient servant
Milesian

Leading article
A comfortable belief has of late become widely defused among the
people of Great Britain crediting the Irish masses with an abatement of
intolerance and a desire to live and work in harmony with unpopular
minorities. We published on Good Friday a letter describing the
position of the Jews in Limerick, which warns us that the optimistic
views we refer to cannot be accepted without serious qualification.
Limerick, though its population is dwindling and its commercial
importance is slight, is still one of the chief cities of Ireland. It has an
historic past, and is better known to British tourists than any town in
the South except Cork and Killarney. In such a community we should
not expect to find ominous signs of a persecuting spirit too closely akin
to that which has broken out so cruelly against the Jewish denizens in
some of the less advanced countries of the Continent. In Limerick,
indeed, and generally throughout Ireland, the Jews are still few in
numbers and, for the most part, in a humble and inconspicuous
condition. Not many years ago they were practically non-existent in
any part of the sister island, with the exception of Dublin and Belfast.
The census of 1871, which for the first time marked a very slight
advance in the number of Jews in Ireland, showed that there were then
only six in Cork, two in Limerick (where there are now thirty-five
families), and one in Waterford. But more recently the increase, though
still relatively insignificant, has been sufficiently marked to arouse the
suspicion and the jealousy both of the artisans and small traders in the
towns and of the peasantry in the country districts. They have drawn
upon themselves the unfavourable notice of the Roman Catholic clergy
and the denunciations of some firebrands of the pulpit. The growth of
a Jewish quarter in Dublin, and on a smaller scale in Cork, and other
towns, has been watched with feelings of rancour which have at length
found vent at Limerick in a series of discreditable outrages. There
seems to be no question that something like a state of terrorism is
being organized, which may assume very serious proportions unless it
is taken promptly in hand. Yet it would appear, from a communication
addressed the other day by the LORD LIEUTENANT to the Jewish
"Board of Deputies" that the Irish Executive are satisfied with the signs

of "improvement" which are visible, to the official eye, and are not disposed to take any further steps in the matter. The authorities of the Roman Catholic Church seem inclined to maintain an equally dignified Olympian attitude. The priest, whose sermons inciting the Roman Catholic masses to have nothing to do with the Jews, were the proximate cause of the present excitement, and whose vicious inflammatory language has been widely circulated among an ignorant peasantry, has neither been silenced nor removed.

The facts stated in the letter we have referred to by the "Director of the Irish Mission to the Jews" ought not to be ignored, especially at this season, when in Roman Catholic countries anti-Jewish passion is liable to rise to fever-heat. If these statements are exaggerated or perverted the Irish Executive is, no doubt, in a position to disclose the real state of things. At present, such apologies for intolerance as that put forward yesterday in our own columns by a correspondent signing himself "Milesian" appear to give up the whole case, and to start with the dangerous assumption that, because the ways of the Jews are unpopular, they have no right to expect protection under the law. It is, at any rate, beyond dispute that, only a few days ago, a man employed in a large bacon factory was brought up before the magistrates at the Limerick Petty Sessions for an unprovoked and brutal assault on a Jewish milk-dealer, and was discharged with a fine and a warning. The victim, according to the evidence of the police, had to be taken away, bruised and bleeding, to have his injuries attended to by a medical man, and his assailant thought it sufficient to plead in his defence that the whole thing was merely a joke. It is a joke which the unhappy people who are marked out by ecclesiastical incendiaries for popular contempt and hatred can hardly be expected to appreciate. We are assured that "no" Jew or Jewess can walk along the streets of "Limerick without being insulted or assaulted," and the significance of the fact is increased by its origin. It is directly connected with an organized scheme of boycotting the Jews and of starving them out of the town and of the surrounding districts. It is known from the history of the Land League and its operations that boycotting almost invariably leads to acts of lawless violence, which, indeed, form its sanction, and particularly the proscribed minority have the courage or the obstinacy to persevere in their daily business in spite of threatening language. Unfortunately, the pretensions of terrorism are supported in Limerick by some well-remembered precedents. The corporation, some years ago, successfully defied the Government by refusing to pay an extra police tax levied at a time of disorder and danger. More recently some Protestant "vangelists" have been treated as the Jews are being treated to-day, and met with little sympathy either from the magistrates or from the Executive. It may have been alleged that the Protestant Evangelists were provocative in their methods of preaching the Gospel, though this is not an excuse which the British people are very willing to admit when Christian missionaries are attacked by Chinese mobs. At any rate, in the case of the Limerick Jews there is not the slightest ground for pretending that there has been anything which can, by the most reckless abuse of language, be described as provocation.

The thirty-five families of Jews in Limerick are, we are told, "sober, quiet, and law-abiding," and this may well be believed. "Milesian" has told us, indeed, that the Jews in Limerick, since they have developed a system of peddling goods among the peasantry, and especially since they have claimed payment through the Courts for what is owing to them, have incurred popular displeasure. But they are not, we understand, to any large extent engaged in money-lending, and have not come into conflict with the agricultural population, as is so often the case in Continental countries, over mortgage debts. They are generally engaged in the smaller branches of retail trading, such as milk-selling, and as hucksters and hawkers in the rural districts. But they have fallen under the boycotting ban, since some of the clerical firebrands have begun to denounce them from the pulpit and to carry out the persecution by those arts of personal and violent authority to which the Irish priest, dealing with an ignorant and timorous body of peasants, is unfortunately too prone. The result is, our Correspondent declares, that the majority of the Limerick Jews are ruined and on the verge of starvation. The populace are told by their clerical guides that they must not deal with the Jews, and they extend the doctrine to include the prohibition of payment for goods they have already received and consumed. A self-supporting and, in a small say, an independent and prosperous little community, which has never before required relief, is thus thrown upon the assistance of a few of the Protestants of the city, themselves regarded with an evil eye by the organizers of the clerical boycott. We cannot accept the view of "Milesian" that the Jew-baiters in Limerick are justified by Continental precedents, which the people of this country has always condemned. It is certainly not the case that the Anti-Semite persecutions in Russia, renewed incitements to which at Odessa were recorded yesterday by our Vienna Correspondent, have been due to peddling goods and asking to be paid for them. But it is really too much to ask us to believe that the presence in Limerick of a little body of Jews – hardly 200 individuals, all told, of every sex and age – constitutes a grave social problem that excuses street violence and pulpit excerations. The appeal of the Director of the Irish Mission to the Jews to the Anglo-Jewish Association and its leading men is not likely to be disregarded. But the question has another and a graver aspect. Local self-government in Ireland is in the experimental stage, and there is a good deal of controversy as to the manner in which it has been worked. But nothing could so deeply discredit it as the belief that among the results of administration dominated by intolerant clerics and animated by the exclusive spirit of the Catholic Association, which **Archbishop Walsh** has recently deemed it prudent to disavow, would have to be reckoned a "squalid version" of Kishineff. The reality of the social peace in Ireland will be open to more than doubt if the persecution of a handful of Jews in Limerick is deemed a subject too small and unimportant for the attention of the Executive, for the efforts of the police, and for the energetic and courageous enforcement of the law by the magistracy. The elements of lawlessness have not ceased to exist and to operate in Ireland because, in anticipation of the King's visit, some ecclesiastics are for the moment endeavouring to keep things quiet. The most outspoken of the Nationalist newspapers are boasting of the policy of cutting down the numbers of the constabulary as a triumph for their party objects, and on the remission of the extra police charges as a proof that measures for repressing and penalizing disorder are not seriously meant.

b) South Wales, 1911

Source: PRO HO 144/1160/212967/5a, Statement of Mr Joseph Cohen regarding the Tredegar Riot, 23 August 1911

Serious disturbances directed at Jews and their property began in the industrial districts of South Wales on Saturday 19 August 1911. In the course of the following week the riots spread and were only suppressed with the assistance of the military. A graphic eye–witness account, preserved in the minute of a conversation which took place in the Home Office between A.L. Dixon (1881–1969), Private Secretary to the Under Secretary, and Joseph Cohen, is given below together with Dixon's further observations.

Statement of Mr Joseph Cohen regarding the Tredegar Riots
23rd August 1911

One of the Jewish refugees from Tredegar, Mr Joseph Cohen (103 High Street, Tredegar) called here to-day and gave me an account (which impressed me very much) of the terrible nature of the riots which have occurred. Mr Cohen himself is a mineral water manufacturer employing several hands. He has a brother, also living in Tredegar, Mr Michael Cohen of 15 Commercial Road, who keeps (or, rather, kept) a drapery shop. Mr Cohen told me that the Jews of Tredegar had had some inkling that trouble was coming from the roughs; he himself had mentioned their fears to the Police who made light of them. On Saturday the attack on the shops of the Jews commenced in a small way by one or two boys throwing stones at windows. The bystanders began laughing and jeering, and gradually as the crowd collected the spirit of disorder grew until what at first seemed a small matter developed into a serious riot and attack on the shops and houses of Jewish residents. Mr Michael Cohen's shop was looted so thoroughly that he could not find a change of garments for his children when he had to flee. Mr Joseph Cohen's English neighbours banded together and protected his house on Saturday; but on Sunday the crowd became so menacing that he fled to the house of a friendly neighbour, taking his wife (who had recently been confined) and child and invalid mother with him. His sisters found refuge in another house and were so terrified that they spent Sunday in the cellar. Yesterday Mr Cohen brought his family to London but was so much in fear that he had not ventured to go to his house to change from his working clothes before he came. His house, he understands, has been ransacked from top to bottom; he does not know what has come to his factory but he presumes that has suffered too. The loss which Mr Cohen has suffered, including the damage to his house and property and to his factory, which he had recently rebuilt and installed with fresh machinery, and also the interruption of his business, will, he says, have quite ruined him, and there are many other Jews – for instance, those who have larger families – who are in worse plight even than he. All the Jews, he says, have fled from the neighbourhood and a good many English residents are fleeing too.

A.L.D.

The above was Mr Cohen's story

The Supt. of Police, to whom I have since spoken, adds that this Mr Cohen is the man who, in his opinion, is, more than any other Jew, the cause of the anti Jewish feeling. He has been buying up old house property and raising the rent etc. He does not appear to have exaggerated the violence of the rioters: the Police offered to afford him protection, with military aid, to go to his house and bring away any valuables, but he did not accept the offer. His house has not, however, been ransacked. It is very likely that he will put in a substantial claim against the Police Authority. The Board of Jewish Deputies are arranging, through the Jewish Guardians for Mr Cohen's pauper accommodation for the time being.

A.L.D.

c) Leeds, June 1917

Source: PRO HO 45/10810/311932/40a, Telegram of Abraham Bezalel to National Council of Civil Liberties, 5 June 1917

Abraham Bezalel, also known as Solly Abrahams, was an East End Jewish radical, opposed to military service in defence of Tsardom, whose activities were closely monitored by the police and intelligence services. He was deported to Russia shortly after the following telegram was sent.

Most serious antisemitic outbreaks rioting looting attacks on helpless woman and children have started here Sunday 4 pm and continued until late Monday night all jewish shops and houses in bridge street regent street york road neighbourhood and other streets smashed and contents scattered in the streets many jews wounded private Max Rose Rosenbloom 7 byron St who joined voluntarily July 1916 is under treatment of Doctor Richardson public dispensary his aggressor released by the police who seemed to enjoy this affair and offered no protection untill last night I approached the deputy chief constable Handley and warned him of the anticipated danger to life because of inadequate protection and at last when it assumed alarming proportion protection was given and resulted in 19 arrests all charged to-day with disorderly conduct and sentenced 40/21 days those charged with assaulting police-men two months a jewish young man Myer Berson 5 Rugby Terrace who expressed his surprise on Doctor Pickles Camp Road Surgery hurting a jewish woman and calling her sheeny dog sentenced 40/ because of attempting to defend the woman danger not over yet please take immediate steps put question parliament ask public inquiry and assurances for protection jews are terrified and helpless I count upon you to act swiftly.

d) What the papers said, 1917

Source: *The Leeds Mercury*, 4 June 1917; *Yorkshire Evening Post*, 4 June 1917; *Yorkshire Evening News*, 4–5 June 1917

The invasion of the Jewish quarter in Leeds began on Sunday 3 June at 7.30 p.m. and was resumed the following evening. No lives were lost but an enormous amount of damage was done. Local newspapers covered the story in depth. Below is a selection from their reports.

The Leeds Mercury 4 June 1917
Anti-Jewish Disturbance in York Road Vicinity

The bitterness against the Jewish section of the community in Leeds, which has been existing in certain quarters for a considerable time, found expression last night in a serious outbreak in the neighbourhood of Bridge-street and Regent-street.

Gangs of youths, whose ages ranged from fourteen to seventeen, smashed almost all the windows of the Jewish traders in the vicinity, dragged out the contents of the windows, and scattered them about the streets.

The residents in the neighbourhood were in a terrified condition, and up to the early hours of this morning they were huddled together in doorways afraid to go to bed.

One woman, in talking to our representative, said she could not understand why she had been molested. If it was because of the desire of young Jews to avoid military service, it could not apply in her case, because she had two brothers and a husband in the Army.

On the other hand, it is alleged by the English people that the Jewish youths are provocative in their conduct, and there have been several cases in which they have molested peaceable citizens as they have been passing through the district.

But there cannot be much doubt of the intensity of the feeling. The damage done is of a serious character, and it is fortunate there were not a good many people hurt when the youths, backed by a number of women, were hurling bricks and stones through the shop windows, and in some instances through the bedroom windows in the houses.

At midnight there was another disturbance in York-road, near Burmantofts-street. A draper named Samuels had two huge glass windows smashed to atoms. At one o'clock this morning crowds of people were standing about in the streets eagerly discussing the situation.

The immediate cause of the outbreak appears to be unknown, but it is rumoured that a young woman was molested during the course of the evening, and there were those who suggested that the riots bore some relation to the fact. The whole affair, however, is a matter of conjecture up to the present, but the police are pursuing the case with vigilance, and in all probability will be able to unearth the trouble.

Yorkshire Evening Post, 4 June 1917
Riotous Street Scenes in Leeds

Riotous scenes arising out of the racial animosity between the young hooligans of the Gentile and Jewish communities in Leeds were witnessed last night, and to-day there is distress and anxiety in the Ghetto. From early morning, small crowds of people gathered in Bridge Street, York Road and that part of Quarry Hill where Jews and Gentiles live in close contact.

Latterly they have scarcely been neighbourly. One heard many expressions of bitterness on both hands to-day and after a particularly violent wordy collision between two voluble sets of womenfolk in Bridge Street at ten o'clock this morning there was imminent danger of a recrudescence of last night's window-smashing riot. Stones were thrown, an ugly scene was nipped in the bud. Still, considerable feeling was displayed throughout the day, and one gathered that many among the Jewish people in the districts affected are very revengeful for the happenings of Sunday night.

For two or three hours last night there was serious rioting and unmistakable evidence of Jew-baiting. Windows of Jewish shop-keepers were broken by the score, and until dawn broke this morning there were many Hebrew families in Bridge Street, Quarry Hill and York Road remaining in the streets, fearing to go to bed, and wondering if they were safe. They were the victims of an attack which was as indiscriminate as it was violent, for amongst the shop-keepers whose windows were smashed was one whose husband and two brothers are in the army.

Many explanations are given to account for the rising. The story of an attack by young Jewish hooligans upon a wounded soldier whose crutches they broke has been bandied about a good deal, and whether it be true or not, it has apparently aggravated the feeling of bitterness against the young Jews. In certain districts, too, resentment has been shown that so many young Jews have avoided military service. A further reason given for the outbreak is that the hooligan element in the Jewish community has been particularly aggressive of late. One who is in a position to know declared to-day that there is no class in Leeds so provocative as the young Jewish hooligan class which has been very much in evidence of late.

Whilst granting that there may have been a growing feeling of bitterness against that class it seems probable that last night's anti-Jewish disturbance was due more to accident than design. At all events it had its origins in a very small affair of stone-throwing between English and Jewish children, who opposed each other on that disused piece of land known as Mabgate Green, which was the site of some of the slum property cleared away a short time ago by the Corporation. Unfortunately the clearing-away process was not completed. Heaps of brick-bats and stones were left, and these as it turned out – though an attempt was made to get them away this morning – supplied the ammunition with which all the subsequent destruction was brought about.

It was the stone-throwing episode at the back of the Yorkshire Penny Bank Buildings at the bottom of New York Road which began the trouble. The Jewish lads were outnumbered, and when a lot more lads from the York Road district came to oppose them, the former were driven into the almost wholly Jewish locality of Regent Street. Still, there was probably more mischief than malice in the affair – some of the lads were heard to say "Let's 'kid' we're Germans" – until a stone accidentally broke a window of the corner shop occupied by Lewis Cohen, licensed broker, who had a varied assortment of goods in his window. Cohen went out to remonstrate with the stone-throwers, and, as he explained to a "Yorkshire Evening Post" representative, "that seemed to make them worse".

The young mob had by this time been reinforced by older children of both sexes, and by a distinct gang of youths whose ages probably ranged from 14 to 17. These proceeded to make short work of Cohen's shop. Every window was smashed; two suits, a dozen vests, and three pairs of boots were taken from one window; and the nine children of the family had to be crowded into a back scullery to escape injury. This occurred at about six o'clock, and, having whetted their appetite, the mob pursued a career of destruction which took them all round the district. Whether organised or not, the occasion was seized to make an attack upon the Jewish community, as is evident from the fact that the only windows broken were those of shops bearing Jewish names.

Altogether some hundreds of windows were smashed. The principal damage was done to shops in the lower part of Bridge Street. Here the shop windows of practically all the Jewish traders were smashed, though most of the tradesmen apparently conducted their business as usual this morning. A short distance up York Road two plate-glass windows were broken, and stock carried away from a shop which it is estimated it will cost £100 to replace. Other windows were broken, principally in Macaulay Street, Argyll Road, and Green Road. The glass lay in the gutters until the early hours of this morning, when it was removed.

Two dozen police of the special and regular constabulary were rushed to the scene as soon as the seriousness of the affair was realised, but they had to deal with a mob of about 1,500 young people. It was not until after ten o'clock that this mob was dispersed, and there were still straggling parties who caused alarms at various points until after midnight.

It is significant that Briggate and Boar Lane were unusually free from the hooligan element last night. Some personal violence is reported, the most serious case being that of a Jewish soldier named Mark Rosenbloom, who was home on leave, and who, in taking the part of his co-religionists, was struck on the head with a stone. He had his injuries attended to at the Dispensary.

Yorkshire Evening News, 4 June 1917
Sunday Night Disorder in Jewish Quarter of Leeds

The lawlessness which raged last night in that section of the Leeds Jewish quarter known as the Leylands has resulted in considerable damage to property and the alarm of peaceful persons. In that part of Bridge-street where the tenants are almost exclusively Jewish shopkeepers nearly every pane of glass was smashed by the insensate mob, and in several instances provisions and articles of clothing were looted from the wrecked premises.

A peculiar feature of last night's discreditable episode is the fact that while the centre of the disturbance was that part of the Leylands which is bounded on the north by the York-road viaduct, riotous conduct occurred almost at the same time – 9.30 pm – at places distant a quarter of a mile from Bridge-street, Argyle-road and Green-road were visited by the lawless crowd, windows were smashed, and goods carried off by that section of the gang which was out for loot.

The gathering of a large number of men and lads – and a score or so of undisciplined women – on the open space near the viaduct, about nine o'clock last night, did not cause any alarm in the minds of the inhabitants. Suddenly, however, a rush was made through the archway, and in less than two minutes – according to an eye-witness of the shameful scene – every window on both sides of the streets was smashed, and some of the shops plundered, amidst the shrieks of terrified women and children.

The appearance of the police in force caused the mob to scatter in haste and abandon the evident intention of wrecking the Jewish factories and workrooms in Templar-street. The windows of one factory in that thoroughfare were smashed, an enormous sheet of plate-glass being shivered into a thousand fragments.

This morning the despoiled tenants had boarded up their damaged premises, and were eagerly taking counsel together about the amount of compensation to which they may be entitled through the violence of the mob.

The affair is said to have had its origin in a plan to make reprisals for the alleged offensive conduct of a gang of Jewish lads in Briggate on a number of recent occasions.

Superintendent Blakey said the trouble arose out of a serious melee which took place last night and which seemed to have been organised by a gang of youths. A racial feud had for some reason obtained in Leeds for some time past between the Jewish boys and the English boys, and the youths had been going about in gangs armed with sticks. A number of cases of disorder had been already dealt with by the magistrates, but the scenes of last night were infinitely worse than anything that had occurred previously.

Last night's trouble appeared to have originated about seven o'clock when a number of youths assembled in the Leylands, which is recognised as Jewish district. When admonished by a Jewish family to behave themselves they began to smash windows and a crowd of from 1,500 to 2,000 people assembled. The police on duty in the district were reinforced and the youths then scattered in all directions, breaking the windows of premises which showed any signs of Jewish occupation.

Yorkshire Evening News, 5 June 1917
Another Raid on the Leeds Jewish Quarters

The renewal of the anti-Jewish riots in Leeds last evening was, fortunately, restricted to window-breaking and looting on a much smaller scale than prevailed on Sunday. There seems to be quite a large number of youthful persons living in York-road, on the fringe of the Leylands, who, having no useful work to do, are naturally inclined to mischief.

One by one the various pretexts by which the malicious mob sought to justify its evil-doing have been examined and refuted. At a meeting of the leaders of the Jewish community, held yesterday – and at which the Rev. Mr Abraham, B.A., Mr Victor Lightman, and Mr Isaacson were present – the existing disturbing situation was carefully considered, and it was decided that the matter was perfectly safe in the competent hands of the Chief Constable.

Mr Victor Lightman, J.P., an influential captain of industry in Leeds Jewry, strongly repudiated this afternoon to a representative of the "Yorkshire Evening News" the baseless charges of molesting wounded soldiers which have been made against Jewish lads in Leeds.

Lieutenant-Colonel Littlewood, Administrator of the 2nd Northern Military Hospital Area, has already contradicted the unkind story which centred around the imaginery assaults upon wounded soldiers.

An example of how the wicked fairy tales do grow is given by an incident in yesterday's turbulence and turmoil.

Just as the mischievous gang ran howling southwards along Bridge-street, towards Lady-lane, a wounded soldier was struck by a missile – either stone or half-brick – and was assisted into an adjacent house by a gentleman in naval uniform and another wounded soldier.

Mr L. Rosenberg, of New York-road, who has done priceless work in military recruiting in Leeds Jewry, rendered prompt aid. It has been said, in this instance, that a threatening crowd assembled when the soldier was hurt by a missile from the ranks of the gang which invaded the Leylands.

An "Evening News" representative witnessed the occurrence from the viaduct which spans Bridge-street, and he has no doubt whatever that the unthinking crowd were simply swarming around the soldier with the same unthinking spirit of morbid curiosity which causes the crush around a man who has fallen by the way and is panting for breath.

The marauders who went out last night on mischief bent did not succeed in greatly extending the area of their nefarious operations. They managed to get into a previously undamaged part of the Leylands – that division to the south of Templar-street and nearest to Lady Lane – and several smashed windows and boarded shop-fronts testified to their dangerous activities in the evening.

At the line of demarcation, somewhere near Argyle-road the over-swelling eastward tide of Jewish occupation has so corresponded with the receding waves of the Gentile tenantry that the two races are found in the same melancholy one-sided thoroughfare to which some long bygone local house-builder with unconscious humour, has labelled Mean-street, and libelled the might Macaulay.

Here the two races (Gentile and Jew) have dwelt cheek by jowl in peace and unity until this wave of passion swept over the least desirable of the much-mixed population in those parts.

"I have lived many, many years amongst Christians", said an aged Israelite this afternoon, "and although they do not buy in our shops, I have never, in all the years, had a word of trouble with them."

At the angle of Gower-street and Regent-street, as the noontime crowds were hurrying along, a Jewish matron was calling heaven and earth to witness the havoc which has been wrought in her home. She was hunted like a wild beast from Odessa, in the days of the "pogrom" and the horrors of the "Black Hundred", and sought sanctuary in hospitable, generous England.

Last night she heard once more the hurrying feet of the mob of the senseless crowd.

It is a hard case! . . .

In opening the proceedings the Chief Constable (Mr. W. Burne Lindley) said that there had been disturbances in the past few days between youths of the English and Jewish communities. There were riotous scenes last night, and 20 persons, including four females and five boys, were arrested.

Considerable damage was done, chiefly to plate-glass windows in shops and work-shops, and in the melee Detective-inspector Dalton sustained an injury to his eye, which would prevent him from coming to the court for at least a week. A special constable and a civilian were also assaulted.

The disorders were not spontaneous, but appeared to be little ones in various parts of the city. He spoke of the difficulties of the police in consequence of war depletion, and said that from 200 to 400 "specials" were called out last night.

e)   Bethnal Green, September 1917

Source: PRO HO 45/10822/318095/478, 'Anti-Jewish Demonstration', Report of Superintendent J. Best, Hackney Police Station, J Division, 24 September 1917

On 23 September 1917, immediately before Yom Kippur, street fighting broke out on the fringe of the Jewish East End. The following day there was a recurrence of disorder; Jews were stoned and windows broken.

I beg to report that at 4 p.m., on Sunday, 23rd September 1917, a dispute, during which blows were exchanged, took place at Blythe Street, Bethnal Green, between several Englishmen and Russian Jews.

A crowd, numbering some 5,000 persons – a large proportion being women and children – quickly assembled, and took sides with the disputants. The Jewish element were outnumbered, and retired indoors to their residences in Blythe and Teesdale Streets, which are parallel, at right angles with Bethnal Green Road, and almost exclusively occupied by Russian Jews engaged in the tailoring trades.

Many Jews appeared at their windows, and in some way angered the crowd, as stones were thrown and several panes of glass were broken.

Police were promptly on the spot, and the disturbance was confined to Blythe and Teesdale Streets. At 4.45 p.m. the crowd was well under control, and further police assistance having arrived, the assembly was dispersed at 5.30 p.m., although a considerable number of persons, mainly curious people and women and children, continued to perambulate the streets. These were kept moving, and by 7 p.m., the neighbourhood was in a comparatively normal condition.

The trouble originated in a dispute between an Englishman and a Russian Jew (both unknown) which occurred at Bethnal Green Road, on the evening of Saturday, 22nd September 1917. The parties met again on the afternoon of the next day, when the dispute was renewed, leading to the disturbance described.

One case of assault was reported to police – Abraham Cohen, age 22 years, British Subject, tailor, of 32, Kerbella Street, Bethnal Green, who sustained two cuts on his head (not serious) caused by some unknown person with a blunt instrument at Teesdale Street. The injury was treated at the London Hospital, and Cohen was allowed to go home.

One arrest was made – Benjamin Parker, age 16 years, British Subject, carman, of 1, Manchester Buildings, Monmouth Street, Bethnal Green, was arrested for using insulting words at Bethnal Green Road at 5.45

p.m. This youth, seeing several men of Jewish appearance passing, said to some companions "There's another gang of f——g Jews" and ran towards them, when he was at once taken into custody.

. . .

Police present:– 1 Superintendent, 1 Chief Inspector, 3 Inspectors, 6 P.Ss. 61 P.Cs. (foot), 7 P.Cs. (mounted), with 2 Sub Inspectors, 4 Sergeants, and 28 Constables of the Special Constabulary.

The whole were dismissed at 10 p.m.

f) A Comment from the Commissioner, 1917

Source: PRO HO 45/10810/311932/56, Anti-Semitic Riots in London and Leeds, 24 October 1917

The German Press, having got hold of the story, presented the anti-Jewish disturbances as a pogrom damaging to British interests. The Commissioner of Police was pressed by the Department of Information for a refutation and replied as follows.

The story is grossly exaggerated; in fact there is only the slightest foundation for it.

Two men, an Englishman and a Russian Jew, quarrelled in a public house in the East End, on the evening of the 23rd September. They went into the street where an excited crowd quickly gathered and took sides, with the result that missiles were thrown and several panes of glass were broken. No further mischief was done, and here the matter ended.

On the following afternoon, Sunday, 24th September, the two men met again at the same spot, and not unnaturally resumed their quarrel. Again a crowd collected, stones were thrown, a few panes of glass were broken and one man was hurt, sustaining nothing worse however, than two slight cuts on the head. Beyond charging a lad of 16 with insulting behaviour, and dispersing the crowd there was nothing for the Police to do. The whole incident was no more than a street brawl. There was nothing in any way approaching a riot or pogrom, anti-Semitic or other; one man slightly injured and 30 panes of glass broken in 8 houses on the two days (19 panes in one house, 11 in the other seven houses) representing the total damage done. There was no shooting, no plundering and no maltreating; in fact nothing more troublesome to the Police than the curbing of an excitable crowd. There has been no trouble since in that district or elsewhere in the Metropolis – in fact nothing in the nature of rioting since the disturbances that followed the wrecking of the "Lusitania".

9.   The New Book of Exodus, 1918

Source: The Evening News, 22 March 1918

Migration from London to avoid air raids, prudent when undertaken by the indigenous middle classes, was presented as dysfunctional and disruptive when undertaken by East End Russian Jews.

The selfishness and cowardice displayed by certain of our alien "guests" is rapidly becoming a matter of concern to Englishmen and Englishwomen, who are suffering discomfort and even grave hardship as a consequence.

It is, no doubt, a good thing for London that people who fly into a panic at the first hint of an air raid should be as far away as possible from the place where they can make mischief, but the migration of East End Russians to Brighton, Maidenhead, and other places has exceedingly unpleasant effects for those who live in the invaded areas.

The present state of things is simply intolerable. We find people who sought this country as a refuge largely in order to avoid the necessity of training to defend their own, not only helping us to consume the food which we now need for ourselves, not only snatching the jobs of the men who are fighting, but absolutely refusing, as far as the men of military age are concerned, to lift a finger in defence of the land in which they have chosen to reside.

We have not forgotten that when our relations with Russia allowed us to offer the Cuthbertskys the choice of fighting in the British or the Russian Army the friends of those unwilling conscripts created something like a riot in London, assaulting peaceable citizens and cheering for the Kaiser. These same people and their compatriots are now swarming into towns and villages relatively near to London, and forcibly ejecting English tenants in order that they may find a lodging.

We have no words to express our contempt for English landlords who are tempted by alien money to do such shameful wrong to their own countryfolk, but since these mean and sordid creatures do exist the law must be altered to deal with them. . . .

. . .

The whole question is one which merits the immediate attention of the Government, not only in regard to the protection of English homes and the decencies of life, but of the continued presence in our midst of the Cuthbertskys, who take all they can grab with both hands and offer nothing in return.

10. The Russian Jewish alien shirker, 1918

Source: The Morning Post, 9 March 1918

The resurgent anti–alien agitation after 1915 was centred upon the position of the Russian Jewish 'friendly alien' with a demand for further restrictive legislation underscored by threats of popular violence.

The East-End Russian Jew
An Enemy to Neutrality (By a Correspondent)
On Thursday, February 14, a number of young Russian Jews celebrated Germany's great peace-offensive victory at Brest Litovsk by noisy applause outside Caxton Hall. Every legal trick had been tried to leave them free to profiteer out of the calling-up of their British-born neighbours. The besting of the Tribunal by the news of Trotzky's cynical treachery produced this outburst. Not for the first time since the war has the Russian Jew made public display of his hostility to an Empire of whose generous hospitality he avails himself freely, and it will be a grave injustice to British East End populations, where in the days of voluntary enlistment recruiting percentages were higher than almost anywhere else in London, if these young Russian Jews are allowed to become neutral aliens through an act so unneutral as Trotzky's. Those who know him know that the Russian Jew will remain what he has ever been since hostilities began, an alien enemy at heart. The Caxton Hall decision has released 20,000 Russian Jews of military age from all obligation to this country save to profiteer out of her troubles. Other Russian Jews who refused to enlist, and left Euston Station cheering for Germany and groaning for the King, are returning from Russia, fresh from Bolshevik orgies. These are to be the "neutral aliens" who are to be turned loose like a hostile garrison among intensely patriotic British people, whose able-bodied men are all away fighting for their country. The bullying of loyal British populations in East London districts infested by Bolshevik peace revolutionaries ought to be better known. Complaint of the behaviour of Russian Jews is always stifled by the silly, ignorant cry of anti-Semitism. Among the poor of the East End, poor because of parasite aliens who boycott all dealers but themselves, anti-Semitism is never heard. But no local policeman, public servant, cleric, or school teacher is ignorant of the existence of that system of anti-Briticism which prevails throughout East London for sweating, profiteering, and politically oppressing the British working class for the benefit of the alien Jew. The British East Enders are soldiers and workers. The alien Jew East Enders are dealers and shirkers. Their presence here, never at any time very desirable, has grown into a national menace because of the pacifist terrorism which is being imported from Russia. In London as in Petrograd, they are revealing traits totally different from the law-abiding, ill-treated martyrs of liberty which fiction and film drama have hitherto

represented them to be. By alien organisation inside an unorganised community, by money made in dealing in necessaries at 300 per cent above their proper price, and by civilian violence – for though the young Russian Jew's cowardice is the laughing-stock of even the women and children he upsets in his blind rush for shelter from air raids, his gangs are the street bullies of Whitechapel, Stepney, Shoreditch, and Bethnal Green – East London is being filled with revolutionary peace terrorism against the will of its national population. The Workers' and Soldiers' Council, an offshoot of the Union of Democratic Control, was started last summer, directly it was seen that the demoralisation of the Russian Army had succeeded. At the first London meeting of the Workers' and Soldiers' Council, which was to have been held in the Memorial Hall last July, the principal speaker announced was a Russian Jew named J. Fineberg, who has since been elevated to the dignity of "first secretary" to the Bolshevik "ambassador" passing under the name of Litvinoff. This meeting was transferred later to the Brotherhood church, which is largely frequented by Russian Jews for the sake of their anti-national peace propaganda.

When conscription became law, hundreds of small streets in Shoreditch and Bethnal Green were found where nearly every available recruit had joined up. These are the people who have to listen to abuse of British patriotism, spouted at open-air peace meetings by British defeatists, backed up by alien bullies of military age. The Shoreditch and Bethnal Green tribunals have protested against sending back wounded soldiers, while the intolerable nuisance of the immunity of the young Russian Jews is unredressed. War Aims meetings have been broken up by singing the "Red Flag" in broken English. Street shrines are pilfered of their poor adornments, and mud bespattered. Children carrying Union Jacks in patriotic school festivals are molested by Jew boys called Red Scouts. Save in certain Sinn Fein-ridden parts of Ireland, nowhere else in the British Empire have British soldiers been insulted in the street, except in certain Russian Jew-ridden parts of East London. These young Russian Jews are no longer "friendly" aliens now, and they have no title to be allowed to become "neutral".

Best Jobs go to the Foreigner
The alien problem in the East End of London, as was indicated in an article by "A Correspondent" in the *Morning Post* last Saturday, has lately assumed a phase which will lead to a serious disturbance of the peace unless it is carefully and judiciously handled. Once again the antagonism, slumbering but ever-present, between the native English and the alien is approaching a point which is all the more dangerous because national prejudices have come into play. Put in a nutshell, the problem is this – that, while the British-born resident, both Jew and Gentile, of the East End has done and is doing his duty by England in her hour of peril, the alien-born, both Jew and Gentile, but particularly Jew, refuses to move a finger to aid the country which has given him protection, and stands calmly by, ready and eager to seize every commercial advantage

which the exigencies of the war may bring forth. For him it is "Bizness as usual", yesterday, today, and forever. From this selfish avarice on the one hand and the natural resentment provoked by it on the other you have the elements of a fierce and alarming quarrel.

East End Sinn Feiners

To get a proper perspective of the situation it is necessary to recall a few facts which are often forgotten in dealing with the alien problem in the East End; and here let it be remembered that the alien problem is not necessarily the Jewish problem, and does not imply that the English Jew has not done his duty in the national crisis. The problem is with the alien immigrant, Jew and Gentile, who has descended on the East End of London from nearly every part of Europe. This crowd of foreigners has come like a moving bog down a mountain side in overwhelming mass. Some of the inhabitants have escaped submergence, others have gone under, and it is possible to point to parishes of ten thousand inhabitants where only one thousand were aliens a few years ago, but today the position is quite reversed, having no country, these aliens have no conscience either. In some respects they are more Sinn Fein than the extremists in Ireland, inasmuch as they are for "ourselves alone" and have not the instinct of an insular patriotism even in the slightest degree. To commercial morality they are utter strangers, and competition to them is a game of "all in". It is to this unfair competition that Bethnal Green owes its Sunday market, the despair of the Church and the source of infinite annoyance to the better section of the trading community who would be satisfied with six days' work a week, and who know that their rivals' plea of "We never trade on our Sabbath" is more or less of a religious pretence, under which a further cut can be made into the market.

Cuckoo Practices by the Alien

The evils thus briefly sketched became far more acute on the outbreak of the war, for the acumen previously displayed in commercial pursuits was sharpened so that the double purpose of "business as usual" and of avoiding military service might be accomplished. Registration became a dead letter to a considerable extent, owing to the facility with which an alien could change his name and disappear, and to other means of evading the law. It is well known that under the shelter of this Act many Austrian and German Jews blossomed out as subjects of the Tsar; they had no mind to fight for the Kaiser or the Emperor Charles, still less to be interned as alien enemies, and they had cunningly calculated on the fact that even if everything went well in Russia some considerable time must elapse before arrangements could be made whereby they must have to take service in either the British or the Russian Armies. As events turned out, they managed to escape either obligation. So long as the Russian Tribunal was sitting there was some prospect of leaving these defaulters by the heels, but now that the Russian Tribunal is a thing of the past that hope is gone. It is no pleasure or consolation to the mother

who has given five sons to the Army, one of whom is lying beneath a
wooden cross in Flanders, to see the fifth and youngest go forth, and to
know that across the street, maybe, are a dozen able-bodied young aliens
who are cynically watching the exodus of Englishmen to possible death,
and waiting to seize their jobs as the cuckoo seizes a ready-made nest.
Occasionally you will see a notice in a shop window that "This business is
closed, as the owner has joined his Majesty's Forces"; but too often the
business is open, for the simple fact that an alien has stepped into the
English owner's place.

Curious Form of "National Service"
This exploitation of commercial possibilities takes various and subtle
forms. In normal times, it is necessary to explain, there is a certain
freemasonry among the alien population of the East End which ensures
that its members shall get the best of whatever is going in the way of
trade. In Bethnal Green, a vast centre of cabinet-making and allied trades,
for instance, while the British-born worker may be held up for want of
stuff. When the British-born worker is called to the Army the alien has
visions of an industrial paradise. Sometimes he does not wait for the gates
to open; he is equal to giving them a push on his own account. Such a
course was pursued in the tailoring trade, which, it may be remarked, is
to some extent a house trade carried on in defiance of any factory laws
which may be made by people who are content to work the round of the
clock, so that their British rivals may be ousted. The raising of the citizen
army gave an immense impetus to this trade by creating a demand for
uniforms, and where these were made by the thousand in East End
factories a subtle device was entered into by which the work was secured
to the Jewish workers. In some cases the Christians were discharged and
their places were filled by Jews. As the demand for recruits became more
and more urgent the workless Christian was drafted into the Army; while
the Jew who had stepped into his place was secure in the plea that he was
doing "work of national service". He had a double-edged security which
was more of a tribute to his cunning than his patriotism. Incidentally it
may be mentioned that even the refugee question was exploited. A large
proportion of the so-called "Belgian refugees" who appeared in the East
End were nothing more nor less than Russian Jews from Antwerp. They
were awaiting shipment to America, and the journey to London was
welcomed as a step on the way, but America being now impossible they
have been content to settle in the East End and be absorbed in its ever-
growing population of aliens.

Continuity of Employment Secured
The employment of these men has a certain attraction for the less
scrupulous and more selfish class of employer, especially in trades which
are worked on the "team" system, where the absence of one man may
mean the idleness of many. The calling-up for military service of a single
man from the team throws the others out; they cannot continue their
work until the place of the absentee is filled. And what more natural than

in choosing a new employee the manufacturer gives preference to one who is under no obligation to military service or any other kind of influence which is likely to disturb the continuity of his work? In this manner patriotism becomes the "refuge of a scoundrel" though not in the meaning of that sturdy old Englishman, Dr Johnson.

A Vast Army of Ishmaelites
This, then, is the problem in the East End. A vast population of alien Ishmaelites. A remedy must be found, but is hard to discover. The wholesale deportation of these people back to their own country is suggested, but so long as the war continues that scheme is impracticable; even if the native country of each could be determined. Again, it is suggested that the alien districts in the East End should be made into a sort of compound, where the inhabitants should do work only and essentially for national service. It is a popular idea in many quarters, and possibly along its lines a remedy may be found for a situation which is becoming more and more exasperating every day. At present the anger is confined to the women who have seen their husbands, brothers, sons, and sweethearts go forth to war, maybe never to return, and if they have the will they have not the power to make a change. Bethnal Green, which has the highest record for voluntary enlistment in London and the highest but two in the country, is now manless and voiceless. But what will be said – and done – "when the boys come home" and find the alien usurper in snug, comfortable, and profitable billets from which he has to be dislodged? The boys may well ask themselves then if that is what they fought for.

11. Protest of the Jewish National Labour Council, 1918

Source: PRO HO/45/10822/318095/619, Statement passed by the Executive Committee of the Jewish National Labour Council of Great Britain at a meeting held on Sunday 9 June 1918, at 131 Whitechapel Road, London E1

The text that follows was a response to the alarming growth of anti-alien sentiment in the community at large. The role of representative public bodies in fomenting unrest was particularly disturbing.

It is with the deepest regret that we have to record the fact, that many of the East London Borough Councils have developed the custom of indulging, from time to time, in the passing of Anti-Alien resolutions.
    As it is well known, these resolutions are mostly directed against the Jewish population, who are law abiding and who have contributed thousands of men to his Majesty's forces, or to the National Service of this country. These resolutions attain nothing but the creation of bad

feeling between one part of the population and another a state of affairs which the Borough Councils ought to avoid and combat.

The last contribution to the Anti-Alien, better said, to the anti-Jewish agitation, is a resolution passed by the Hackney Borough Council. At the meeting when this resolution was passed, most disgraceful words, referring to Aliens, were used in many of the speeches held. . . . The resolution states that the Government ought to prevent "aliens" from opening new businesses in the place of those closed by British called to the colours. The fact is that a regulation under the Defence of Realm Act, forbids the opening of new retail businesses without special permits, and aliens do not apply for such permits. The said resolution also demands that aliens should be prevented from buying businesses of the British called to the colours. This demand of the Hackney Borough Council means that the British are to be prevented from selling their businesses and compelled to close them, and so be totally ruined. The fact is that there are no buyers amongst the "aliens" to buy the businesses of those aliens (Russian subjects) who have been called to the colours or to National service. Surely the Borough Councils should show more sense and fair play than to pass such resolutions. . . .

We also call the attention of the Government, . . . that resolutions of the kind . . . can inflame the minds of low elements who are always on the look out for trouble.

You . . . have taken thousands of alien youths for the Army or National Service; . . . it is, therefore, you who should protect the Jewish population from calumnies and from dangerous results which may follow.

M. Green, Chairman
Morris Myer, Honorary Gen: Secretary

12.   The Balfour Declaration, 1917

a)   Dear Lord Rothschild . . . 1917

Source: Leonard Stein, The Balfour Declaration (1961), p. 664

The most famous document in modern Jewish history is reproduced in its various drafts below. The final text differed significantly from the proposal submitted to the government by Chaim Weizmann and Nahum Sokolow.

(a) Zionist drafts, July 1917
1. His Majesty's Government accepts the principle that Palestine should be reconstituted as the national home of the Jewish people.
2. His Majesty's Government will use its best endeavours to secure the achievement of this object and will discuss the necessary methods and means with the Zionist Organisation.

(b) Balfour draft, August 1917
His Majesty's Government accept the principle that Palestine should be reconstituted as the national home of the Jewish people and will use their best endeavours to secure the achievement of this object and will be ready to consider any suggestions on the subject which the Zionist Organisation may desire to lay before them.

(c) Milner draft, August 1917
His Majesty's Government accepts the principle that every opportunity should be afforded for the establishment of a home for the Jewish people in Palestine and will use its best endeavours to facilitate the achievement of this object and will be ready to consider any suggestions on the subject which the Zionist organisation may desire to lay before them.

(d) Milner–Amery draft, 4 October 1917
His Majesty's Government views with favour the establishment in Palestine of a national home for the Jewish race and will use its best endeavours to facilitate the achievement of this object, it being clearly understood that nothing shall be done which may prejudice the civil and religious rights of existing non-Jewish communities in Palestine or the rights and political status enjoyed in any other country by such Jews who are fully contented with their existing nationality [and citizenship].

[Note: Words in brackets added subsequently.]

(e) Final text, 31 October 1917
His Majesty's Government view with favour the establishment in Palestine of a national home for the Jewish people and will use their best endeavours to facilitate the achievement of this object, it being clearly understood that nothing shall be done which may prejudice the civil and religious rights of existing non-Jewish communities in Palestine or the rights and political status enjoyed by Jews in any other country.

b) A new epoch for our race, 1917

Source: Jewish Chronicle, 9 November 1917

To the leaders of Anglo-Jewry the Zionist project appeared dangerous and divisive and at odds with their view of themselves as Englishmen of the Jewish persuasion. To those of Russo-Polish parentage, by contrast, Zionism seemed like the saviour of the Jewish people and their faith. These differences in due course made a change of leaders inevitable. The feelings stirred by Zionism, as the next document suggests, were simply too deep.

With one step the Jewish cause has made a great bound forward. The declaration of His Majesty's Government as to the future of Palestine in relation to the Jewish people marks a new epoch for our race. For the British Government, in accord – it is without doubt to be assumed – with the rest of the Allies, has declared itself in favour of the setting-up in Palestine of a National Home for the Jewish people, and has undertaken to use its best endeavours to facilitate the achievement of that object. Amidst all that is so dark and dismal and tragic throughout the world, there has thus arisen for the Jews a great light. It is the perceptible lifting of the cloud of centuries, the palpable sign that the Jew – condemned for two thousand years to unparalleled wrong – is at last coming to his right. The prospect has at last definitely opened of a rectification of the Jew's anomalous position among the nations of the earth. He is to be given the opportunity and the means whereby, in place of being a hyphenation, he can become a nation. Instead of, as Jew, filling a place at best equivocal and doubtful, even to himself, and always with an apologetic cringing inseparable from his position, he can – as Jew – stand proud and erect, endowed with national being. In place of being a wanderer on every clime, there is to be a Home for him in his ancient land. The day of his exile is to be ended.

The declaration of the Government, which concedes the Zionist position on principle, must have effects, far-reaching and vital, upon the future of Jews and Judaism. A National Home for the Jewish people established in Palestine – whatever the exact form it may take in the circumstances in which it may be initiated – is certain to develop and in good time fulfil the fondest traditional aspirations of the Jewish people. They will become an entity of which the world will have no doubt. Questions of religion, of race and all others which to-day are set up and tend to confuse Jewish issues, will have no significance in face of the fact that the world will have recognised Jews as a nation.

It would be niggardly indeed if the fullest acknowledgement were not accorded to the Zionist movement for the success to which it has now attained. Through years of agitation and propaganda, and let it be acknowledged, of opposition that not occasionally was venomous and bitter, Zionists have carried on their work for the Jewish cause as they saw it. With splendid energy and matchless devotion, in face of many a setback and many a disappointment, they have never turned from the work that was to them a sacred mission. And now they have obtained not merely an historic acknowledgement that their view of the Jewish position was the right and the practical one, but that their activity – so often misrepresented, so often condemned, so often baulked by the most powerful sections of Jewry – was politically sound and ethically just. It is a great victory, which must encourage the movement from end to end of the world and give to it an enormous impetus for the labours, the heavy labours, that are now before it. Where all, from the most prominent leader to the humblest follower, have wrought so valorously, it may possibly seem invidious to mention specially any names in connection with the Government declaration. But it would be churlish to withhold from Dr. Weizmann the fullest measure of praise and congratulation, of honour and of respect; for it is his diplomatic achievement of which the declaration is the result. In his work in this connection he has been magnificently seconded by M. Sokolow, who was specially delegated as a member of the executive body of the organisation for Zionist work in this country.

We have called the Government declaration "a Jewish triumph." It is in truth much more. It is a triumph for civilisation and for humanity. For it points the way to not alone an ending of the brutal suppression of our people from which directly they have suffered the last two thousand years, but from which civilisation, albeit indirectly, has suffered no less certainly. It will mean releasing for mankind, as a great spiritual force, the soul of our people, cramped and bound as it has hitherto been because of the world-position till now assigned to the Jew. The time can at least be described when the Jew will be able, without let or hindrance, to perform for the world his mission of Judaism, that mission which alone is the justification for his existence as a Jew, and the sense of his responsibility for which has alone enabled him to endure the untellable suffering to which our people have been subjected.

Let us, however, not be mistaken. The Jewish fight is, we are fully conscious, not finished; complete victory is not won. Indeed, we are not sure that just now is not beginning the real testing-time for Jews and for the Jewish National spirit; that just now is being proved for the first time the real measure of Zionism. We are not in the least unmindful of the great and sacred work which the Government declaration has opened out for Jewry. None the less, a position, a great, a vital, a decisive position, has been won for the Jew and won for humanity. The Government declaration marks the definite opening of a new chapter, we believe a great and glorious chapter, in the history of our people. It is a memorable day for Israel: "This is the day the Lord hath made; we will rejoice and be glad therein."

13. The Aliens Restrictions Act, 1919

Source: An Act to continue and extend the provisions of the Aliens Restriction Act, 1914, 23 December 1919 (9 & 10 Geo. 5. c.92)

The growth of anti-alien opinion reached a triumphant conclusion with the legislation printed below. The Jewish community, with its large numbers of immigrants of uncertain status, had good cause to study the provisions closely.

CONTINUANCE AND EXTENSION OF EMERGENCY POWERS
1. (1) The powers which under subsection (1) of section one of the Aliens Restriction Act, 1914 (which Act, as amended by this Act, is hereinafter

in this Act referred to as the principal Act), are exerciseable with respect to aliens at any time when a state of war exists between His Majesty and any foreign power, or when it appears that an occasion of imminent national danger or great emergency has arisen, shall, for a period of one year after the passing of this Act, be exerciseable, not only in those circumstances, but at any time; . . .

(2) Any order made under the principal Act during the currency of this section shall be laid before each House of Parliament forthwith, and, if an address is presented to His Majesty by either House of Parliament within the next subsequent twenty-one days on which that House has sat after any such order is laid before it praying that the order may be annulled, His Majesty in Council may annul the order, and it shall thenceforth be void, but without prejudice to the validity of anything previously done thereunder . . .

2. (2) For the purpose of enforcing the provisions of any Treaty of Peace concluded or to be concluded between His Majesty and any Power with which His Majesty was at war in the year nineteen hundred and eighteen, His Majesty may by Order in Council under the principal Act make regulations requiring information to be given as to the property, liabilities, and interests of former enemy aliens, and for preventing (without notice or authority) the transfer of or other dealings with the property of such aliens.

FURTHER RESTRICTIONS OF ALIENS

3. (1) If any alien attempts or does any act calculated or likely to cause sedition or disaffection amongst any of His Majesty's Forces or the forces of His Majesty's allies, or amongst the civilian population, he shall be liable on conviction on indictment to penal servitude for a term not exceeding ten years, or on summary conviction to imprisonment for a term not exceeding three months.

(2) If any alien promotes or attempts to promote industrial unrest in any industry in which he has not been bonâ fide engaged for at least two years immediately preceding in the United Kingdom, he shall be liable on summary conviction to imprisonment for a term not exceeding three months.

. . .

6. After the passing of this Act no alien shall be appointed to any office or place in the Civil Service of the State.

7. (1) An alien shall not for any purpose assume or use or purport to assume or use or continue after the commencement of this Act the assumption or use of any name other than that by which he was ordinarily known on the fourth day of August nineteen hundred and fourteen.

(2) Where any alien carries on or purports or continues to carry on, or is a member of a partnership or firm which carries on, or which purports or continues to carry on any trade or business in any name

other than that under which the trade or business was carried on on the fourth of August nineteen hundred and fourteen, he shall, for the purpose of this section, be deemed to be using or purporting or continuing to use a name other than that by which he was ordinarily known on the said date.

(3) A Secretary of State may, if it appears desirable on special grounds in any particular case, grant an exemption from the provisions of this section, but shall not do so unless he is satisfied that the name proposed to be assumed, used, or continued is in the circumstances of the case a suitable name. . . .

(5) A fee of ten guineas shall be paid by any alien on obtaining an exemption under this section; but the Secretary of State may remit the whole or any part of such fee in special cases. . . .

(7) Any person to whom any such exemption is granted shall, unless the Secretary of State shall expressly dispense with such publication, within one calendar month thereafter publish at his own expense, in some paper circulating in the district in which he resides, an advertisement stating the fact that the exemption has been granted.
8. No alien shall sit upon a jury in any judicial or other proceedings if challenged by any party to such proceedings.

SPECIAL PROVISIONS AS TO FORMER ENEMY ALIENS
9. (1) Every former enemy alien who is now in the United Kingdom and to whom this section applies shall be deported forthwith unless the Secretary of State on the recommendation of the advisory committee, to be constituted under this section, shall grant him a licence to remain.

(2) The Secretary of State may, if he is satisfied on the recommendation of the said advisory committee that there is no reason to the contrary, grant such licence, subject to such terms and conditions (if any) as he shall think fit.

(3) This section shall apply to any former enemy alien now in the United Kingdom (not being a former enemy alien exempted from internment or repatriation on the recommendation of any advisory committee appointed after the 1st day of January nineteen hundred and eighteen and before the passing of this Act) as to whom there shall be delivered to the Secretary of State, within two months after the passing of this Act, a statement in writing signed by any credible person to the effect that the continued residence in the United Kingdom of that alien is, for reasons relating to the alien, undesirable in the public interest, and giving particulars of the allegations upon which such reasons are based.

. . .

GENERAL
13. (2) If any person aids or abets any person in any contravention of this Act or knowingly harbours any person whom he knows or has reasonable

ground for believing to have acted in contravention of this Act, he shall be guilty of an offence against this Act.

(3) Where a person lands in the United Kingdom in contravention of this Act, the master of the ship or the pilot or commander of the aircraft from which he lands shall, unless he proves to the contrary, be deemed to have aided and abetted the offence.

(4) A person who is guilty of an offence against this Act shall be liable on summary conviction to a fine not exceeding one hundred pounds or to imprisonment, with or without hard labour, for a term not exceeding six months, or, on a second or subsequent conviction, twelve months, or, in either case to both such fine and imprisonment. . . .

15. The expression "former enemy alien" means an alien who is a subject or citizen of the German Empire or any component state thereof, or of Austria, Hungary, Bulgaria, or Turkey, or who, having at any time been such subject or citizen, has not changed his allegiance as a result of the recognition of new states or territorial re-arrangements, or been naturalised in any other foreign state or in any British Possession in accordance with the laws thereof and when actually resident therein, and does not retain according to the law of his state of origin the nationality of that state.

Provided that the special provisions of this Act as to former enemy aliens, except the provisions of subsection (2) of section two of this Act, shall not apply to any woman who was at the time of her marriage a British subject.

16. (1) This Act may be cited as the Aliens Restriction (Amendment) Act, 1919, and the principal Act and this Act may be cited together as the Aliens Restriction Acts, 1914 and 1919.

14.   Deportations and the Deputies, 1923

Source: PRO HO 45/24765/432156/3, Charles H.L. Emanuel, Solicitor and Secretary, Board of Deputies of British Jews, to Rt. Hon. W.C. Bridgeman, MP 14 February 1923

The Board of Deputies, alarmed by the enlargement and extension of alien restrictions in peacetime, pressed the Home Office for modifications of a less oppressive nature.

. . . The Aliens Act of 1905 contained powers of Deportation of Aliens, strictly limited, however, to cases in which a Court of Competent Jurisdiction had convicted and recommended that a Deportation Order should be made, and to the cases of Aliens who had been certified by such a Court, on grounds set out in the Act, to be undesirable persons. These limited powers were greatly extended by the Aliens Restriction Act

1914 passed on the outbreak of the Great War to meet the national emergency which then confronted this country. They were further extended by the Aliens Restriction Amendment Act 1919 after hostilities had ceased.

These enlarged powers were continued in force for a further year from December last by the Expiring Laws Act of 1922.

The existence of these exceptional powers places a considerable section of the population, consisting largely of old settlers, outside the ordinary law of the country so far as the protection of their persons is concerned, and the Board begs to be permitted to submit to you its urgent representations that these powers are no longer necessary and that their existence in times of Peace is inconsistent with the general principles of Justice which form the basis of the Law as applied to British Subjects, and which were in force as regards Aliens until the passing of the Act of 1914.

In the case of Deportations under the powers accorded by the 1905 Act, the Alien had the protection of trial before a Court of Competent Jurisdiction, and the usual rights of Appeal lay open to him. If he was ordered to be deported, it was on a recommendation or certificate of a Court after due consideration of the circumstances. This protection is no longer open to him. He may now be deported even when, after trial, no recommendation for Deportation has been made, or when the Court, having been asked to make such a recommendation, has definitely refused to do so. Deportations have been made in a series of cases where no recommendation was made, many months after the Alien had paid his fine or served his sentence and had reason to believe that he had thus expiated his offence. In some of these cases he had in the interim, married, and his innocent Wife also became a sufferer. Another case is that of the Alien tried, sentenced, and recommended for deportation, but whose sentence had been subsequently quashed on appeal. Nevertheless he is liable to deportation without further trial. But perhaps the type of case which most clearly illustrates the hardship occasioned by these special powers, is that of the person who, without trial, is suddenly ordered to be deported. He has had no notification of the nature of the charge against him or even of the name of his accuser. He is deprived of that right of trial which is extended even to the criminal who is caught red-handed. He is not able to obtain any Hearing at which he can personally answer the unknown charge, and bring witnesses to clear his character.

It is not suggested that these powers vested in you are exercised without mature consideration, but it is respectfully urged that the strongest circumstantial evidence is sometimes misleadiing, and that, however convincing the suspicion may be, no harm could ensue from permitting the suspected person to know the nature of the charge and the name of the person who makes it, and to avail himself of the protection of a trial before a Competent Court. The number of convictions which, even after hearing by such Courts, are quashed on appeal, is itself eloquent proof that miscarriages of Justice are not unusual even in Courts of Law. The risk must be infinitely greater where the accused is not permitted to have a trial.

I am instructed to ask that you should be so good as to receive a small Deputation which could lay before you, in detail, its grounds for urging that Section 1 of the Aliens Restriction Amendment Act of 1919 should not be continued after the termination of the current year.

IX

JEWS AT WAR 1914–18

'England has been all she could to the Jews. The Jews will be all they can to England', so wrote the *Jewish Chronicle* in August 1914. Its confidence was not misplaced. More than 50,000 Jews served during the four bloody years that lay ahead, and more than 10,000 were killed or wounded. There was, however, a sizeable number who resisted the call to arms. Non-naturalized Russian Jews who refused to serve with the Tsarist army were not, as foreign nationals, liable for service with the British military. Their position became the subject of deepest controversy following the introduction of conscription at the beginning of 1916. Opinion among native Jews and the general population was that those who enjoyed the privileges of life in Britain should also share the burden of its defence (**doc. 1(a)**).

The government with the support of the Anglo-Jewish community first tried persuasion. Naturalization was offered free to those who enlisted voluntarily. Service with their co-religionists in a specially-created Jewish unit, a scheme advanced by Vladimir Jabotinsky with the support of the Liberal press, was also rejected (**docs. 1(c)–1(d)**). The government and the East End were at daggers drawn. Resistance to military service was in some cases a matter of conscience based on religious considerations (**see above docs. II.6(a)–II.6(c)**), but there was also a strong political and ideological element involved. Opposition was organised and sustained by the socialist internationalists and anarchists who, as noted in a previous chapter, were the moving force in Jewish labour politics. The Foreign Jews Protection Committee against Conscription, Deportation to Russia and Compulsory Military Service (FJPC) involved Abraham Bezalel, a former French army corporal, whom the police considered a dangerous subversive, Y.M. Zalkind, editor of the sinister Yiddish newspaper *The Jewish Voice*, and representatives from revolutionary bodies like the International Workers of the World and other firebrands (**doc. 1(b)**). Their activities kept Special Branch under its anti-Semitic commander, Basil Thomson, fully occupied (**doc. 4**). The police, fearful of public disorder, pressed for tougher action (**doc. 1(g)**).

The War Cabinet considered the options. Persuasion, though not abandoned, was tempered by a more coercive approach. The War Office, warming to the idea of a Jewish Legion, announced at the end of July 1917 that such a unit was to be formed. Shortly afterwards a Convention on Anglo-Russian military service was implemented by Order in Council. Russian alien men of military age would be conscripted for service in the British army or repatriated for service to their country of origin (**docs. 2–2(a)**). About a third of the 6,000 Russian Jews who opted for service in Russia under the terms of the Convention actually sailed. The want of transport, however, compelled the families of these Conventionists to remain behind. The plight of divided families intensified the growing antagonism between the government and the East End. Wives and dependents languished on relief in Whitechapel; children were embarrassed by the absence of their fathers; mothers were apprehensive and uncertain (**doc. 7 and see IV.5(b)**)

The Russian Revolution held forth the promise of a better future. Immigrant Jews of the East End were overjoyed as news filtered through of the destruction of Tsarism. The February Revolution was perceived as marking the end of oppression and the beginnings of a new era of peace and reconstruction to which returning socialists might make a useful contribution (**doc. 3**). But it also re-opened the question of Jewish military participation. The revolutionary defeatists who seized power in October had no interest in the forced repatriation of Russian Jewish soldiers from England and proceeded to issue wholesale exemptions through consular officials before repudiating the military service agreement and withdrawing from the war (**docs. 5 and 6**). In these circumstances it was decided to retain those who had already enlisted but to suspend recruitment other than for service with the labour battalions. About 5,000 Russian Jews served in non-combatant roles with the latter; approximately 1,500 served with the Jewish units of the Royal Fusiliers – the 38th, 39th and 40th battalions of the Royal Fusiliers, subsequently designated the Judean Regiment in recognition of its distinguished service in the Palestine campaign.

The Jewish military effort in the war of 1914–18 was, indeed, impressive. No doubt the over-representation of Jews in the British armed forces reflected the demographic and occupational peculiarities of the minority and the fact that Jewish men were more available for service than the comparable indigenous population. But it also reflects the creeping process of acculturation. Although there was a generalised prejudice against Jews as soldiers, the Boer War experience had shown that the immigrant community was not totally impervious to popular imperialism and that the blast of war might sound as loudly in Jewish ears as in any other (**docs. 8(a)–8(c)**).

The tendency to view the minority war experience in 1914–18 in relation to the development of Jewish self-defence and the origins of the armed forces of the state of Israel too often obscures further consideration of the religious, cultural and political effects of military participation upon the Jewish community in Britain. Contemporary accounts of Jewish war service are as varied as those of non-Jews: those written for publication contain a fair proportion of eye-wash; private correspondence is often more revealing (**docs. 9(a)–9(c)**). The possible effects of war service upon the secularisation and acculturation of the immigrant minority is suggested. Young men removed from an observant community into a disciplined Gentile environment, with little provision for Jewish requirements, sometimes found it prudent and pleasurable to conform more closely to the ways of the majority. Anti-Semitism was not diminished thereby, but Jewish self-confidence may well have grown significantly. In the post-war years Jewish self-defence may have been practised as widely in the Leylands as in the Land of the Bible. War-related changes in relation to religious observances may well have proved enduring. But like the influence of war service upon occupation and authority relations in the family, the precise effects remain to be established.

1. The East End and the Government

a) *Government policy explained, 1916*

Source: PRO HO 45/10819/318095/95, Herbert Samuel to Rev. John Clifford D.D., 20 September 1916

Herbert Samuel, Home Secretary in the Asquith Coalition Government, here explains public policy respecting the position of Russian subjects and military service to a leading Nonconformist Liberal.

Dear Dr. Clifford,

I am glad to have this opportunity of explaining to you the position about Russian political or religious refugees. For a long time past, Frenchmen, Belgians and Italians of military age, living in the United Kingdom have been sent back at the call of their respective Governments. The Russian Government has made no such call, and has expressed its willingness that its subjects should serve in the Armies of its Allies. Russian subjects in the United Kingdom have consequently been in an exceptional and privileged position. There are some 25/30,000 Russian subjects of military age in this country, and I came to the conclusion that it was not right that men of an allied nationality, resident in this country, should avoid taking their part in the present struggle. I trust that you will agree that this view is sound, both for the reason that here are a large number of men of military age doing nothing to help the allied cause in the war, and on account of the resentment of our own people, who are called on to make heavy sacrifices whilst these men of allied nationality remain in their midst as though there were no war at all.

Mainly on my suggestion, the War Office arranged to admit Russian subjects into the British Army, but as the opportunity for voluntary enlistment was not very widely accepted, I came to the conclusion that some measure of compulsion must be applied. Russian subjects are not liable to the provisions of our Military Service Acts, and therefore the only practicable means of pressure was ... to say that a Russian subject, who failed to get an exemption from military service on any ground on which a British subject may get exemption, should no longer be permitted to remain in this country, but should return to his country of origin, as other aliens of allied nationality are required to do.

I have no desire, and never have had, to send any Russian back to Russia, but the possibility of repatriation has been fastened on and it has been represented that the Government's main object is to send people back to Russia. This is an entire misconception, and I am afraid that in some quarters the misconception has been deliberately fostered.

As soon as the possibility of repatriation was mentioned, the position of the political or religious refugee was at once raised. I explained in the House of Commons more than once that because a man was a refugee from Russia was no good reason for his refusing to serve in the British Army and to help to defend the country he had made his home, and that no question of repatriation could arise unless a man deliberately refused, without good reason, to join the British Army. I made it clear also that if any such case did occur and the man claimed that he was a political or religious refugee from Russia, his case would be specially considered by a Tribunal to be established for the purpose before the question whether he should be required to return to Russia was decided.

I attach on a separate sheet copies of statements which I have made in the House on this point from time to time.

On the 22nd August I stated in the House of Commons that I had decided in response to a request from a responsible Russo-Jewish Committee to leave the question of repatriation in abeyance for the present and to give an opportunity for a voluntary recruiting campaign amongst Russians in this country. The question of the further measures, which it may be necessary to take, will be considered at the close of that campaign when we are in a position to ascertain its results. . . .

b)   Russian socialist groups in London, 1916

Source: PRO HO 45/10819/318095/110, Brief Summary of the activities of the Committee of Delegates of the Russian Socialist Groups in London (1916)

The following document, published by the Committee of Delegates of the Russian Jewish Groups in London on 16 September 1916, summarises the work of the Committee in defence of the right of asylum.

After half-a-year of intense activity, the Committee of Delegates of the Russian Socialist Groups in London finds it necessary to summarise its work and to make it known to broad circles of the Russian Emigrants in England, without whose confidence and co-operation this work cannot be effective.

. . .

The Committee was formed on March 13th, 1916, and consisted of the Delegates of the:

London Section of the Social Democratic L.P. of Russia.
London Group "   "   "   "   "
London Group of the Social Revolutionary Party.
London Group of the Boond.
London Group of the Social Democracy of Lettland.
London Group of the Lithuanian Socialist Federation in Great Britain.

Later the Delegate of the Polish Social Democratic Club also joined the Committee. From the middle of May the Jewish Social Democratic Organisation in Great Britain has constantly and closely participated in the activity of the Committee.

At that time rumours were only beginning to circulate about the impending plan of compulsion of Russian Subjects to enlist in the British Army, under the threat of deportation to Russia. The Committee utilized the connections that had been created by the previous activity of the Russian Socialist Groups in London, in order to prepare the ground for the struggle against the danger that threatened the Right of Asylum. Realising the necessity of making the question widely known through Parliamentary discussion, the Committee entered into communication with Members of Parliament, . . . The work and aims of the Committee have been made widely known in Socialist, Trade Union and Radical circles by Comrade Mrs. Bridges Adams, who has worked with the Committee throughout.

In March and April many Russian Subjects were forcibly taken into the Army in Scotland; in consequence of the action of Messrs. King and Snowden in Parliament, to whom the Committee addressed itself, the Military Authorities withdrew these measures.

. . .

In the end of June . . . the Committee prepared for circulation at the Conference of the British Trade Unions (June 30th) an English leaflet entitled "Right of Asylum," in which the question was thoroughly examined and for the first time a definite declaration made, that the more consequent among the emigrants will not submit to the brutal act and will fight against it to the bitter end. . . . Comrade Mrs. Bridges Adams who distributed the leaflet was arrested and kept over 24 hours in custody; 4,000 copies were confiscated.

The following two months were a time of the most feverish activity of the Committee. First it issued a strongly worded protest against the new crime that was being prepared by reaction. . . . Only the *New Age* published this protest. . . .

Soon afterwards the Committee issued a pamphlet under the title: "An appeal to public opinion: Should the Russian Refugees be deported?" . . .

. . .

. . . In general, the Committee and the English comrades who are in touch with it are carrying on an extensive correspondence with British Socialist and Trade Union Organisations, and are contributing to the development amongst the advanced elements of the working class of a strong current against the policy of Mr. Samuel. . . .

. . .

In the middle of August the general meeting of the Russian Socialist Groups that was convened by the Committee, fixed the line of action to be taken at all the likely stages of the coming crisis. Amongst other things it examined the question of the proposed special Tribunal, . . . the Groups declared themselves emphatically against the gratuitous distinction which the Government proposes to make between "genuine" politicals and non-politicals, and they decided that no member of the Groups shall make use of any privileges which may be granted and which will not be within the reach of all emigrants who are unwilling to enlist or to go to Russia. They further enjoined upon all their members, and called upon all others in the event of the said special Tribunals for politicals being set up, to go to such Tribunals and to declare themselves political refugees, protesting against deportation, but producing no proof or evidence of political refugeeism, because in so doing they would acknowledge that the Right of Asylum extends only to one category of emigrants, and because such proofs are not within the reach of all those who refuse to enlist, and would be equivalent to participating in the policy of Mr. Samuel, who in sparing *some* would have a cover for deporting *others*.

The Committee took part also in the work of the emigrants outside the Groups. . . .

The Committee also took steps to be in touch with other organisations struggling against the violation of the Right of Asylum, and for that purpose it sent Delegates with watching briefs to a series of East End Conferences.

Its members are closely participating in the very useful work of the

Russian League against Compulsion, an organisation of Russian Subjects liable to Military Service, who have decided to struggle against the violation of the Right of Asylum, proceeding from the principles of international proletarian solidarity.

On August 22nd, Mr. Samuel made in the House of Commons a declaration about the postponement of the application of his plan and about the organization up to September 30th of a recruiting campaign for Russian Subjects. . . .

. . .

Looking back upon the work done until now, the Committee of Delegates of the Russian Socialist Groups in London has the right to state that it has done a very great work in rousing advanced British public opinion in the struggle for the Right of Asylum. Numerous resolutions adopted by Socialist and Labour organisations, many utterances of the adversaries of Mr. Samuel's policy in Parliament, in the Press, at meetings – have been in a large measure influenced by the activity of the Committee. Being the unifying organ and the expression of the will of the London Organisations of the Russian Socialist Parties, the Committee has introduced into the action of the emigration from Russia at this critical time a consequent line of principle, based upon the system of views of the international socialist working class faithful to its banner. In the sense of these views the Committee illuminates the problems facing now in England the emigrants from Russia. It has decisively and categorically made clear to the Government and to the whole British society that the idea of compelling by threats the whole Russian emigration to submission to the intended act of brutality is a baseless illusion. The Committee has not asked for the reception of deputations from it by a Cabinet Minister and would have refused to take part in such deputations, but it has opposed to the Government the only force that cannot be crushed, the force of the consequent action based upon principle of the conscious working class, indissolubly connecting the struggle carried on here with the international struggle of the proletariat of all Countries against world wide reaction, and seeing in the problems that face the Russian emigration in England only a partial expression of the general, fundamental problems of the present historical moment.

THE RIGHT OF ASYLUM

In all countries with free political institutions, the Right of Asylum for all those who have escaped from political, national or religious persecutions in their native countries, is considered a fundamental principle of democracy. In Great Britain this principle remained unassailable for centuries, and many prominent fighters for political or religious freedom or for the cause of Labour – in old times the Huguenots and other Protestants, in the nineteenth century Mazzini, Kossuth, Marx, Engels, Bakounine, Alexander Herzen, Kropotkine, numerous French Communards – have found in this country a safe refuge.

The maintenance of the Right of Asylum is of vital importance, especially for the future development of the Labour movement. In view of the antagonism between Labour and Capital now developing with unprecedented violence, there is no doubt that in all countries the number of victims in the fight for the cause of Labour will grow in ever-increasing proportion. Once the Right of Asylum is done away with in one country, it will vanish everywhere, not only in war, but also in peace, and the foremost fighters in every country will be at the mercy of their oppressors if there is no place abroad where they can find shelter under the protection of the Right of Asylum.

Mr. Herbert Samuel, the Home Secretary, has struck the axe at this Right. He proposes to deport to Russia all Russian subjects of military age who will not "voluntarily" enlist here – although he himself acknowledges that the Government has no right to press foreigners forcibly into the Army. We have not enjoyed here the citizen-rights, we are subjected to constant restrictions, and being in the country, we are not of the country, therefore it would be monstrous to apply to us compulsion either directly or indirectly. As for Russia, we have escaped from political persecutions there and from the horrors attending the Russian despotic regime. Not only those who have taken an active part in the movement for freedom and for the elementary rights of the working-class in Russia, but also the members of the subject nationalities and in general all those who have fled from the terrible oppression there, would have before them in case of their enforced return the certain prospect of persecution and heavy punishment. Mr. Herbert Samuel's "compulsory repatriation," for the victims of Russian despotism who are now here, means, as the "Nation" puts it: "sending them to gaol, exile or death."

In the announcement made by Mr. Samuel in the House of Commons on August 22, the decision as to deportation is delayed, but the threat is not abandoned. The British workers must not be lulled by this apparent concession into false security about the fate of the Right of Asylum. If the Right of Asylum is to be saved, keen watchfulness is necessary. "Eternal vigilance is the price of liberty."

We appeal once more to British Labour not to relax their efforts in the fight against the abolition of the Right of Asylum and to prevent the forces of reaction from perpetrating this crime against democracy, against the interests of Labour.

THE COMMITTEE OF DELEGATES OF THE RUSSIAN
SOCIALIST GROUPS IN LONDON

September 4 1916

c)   A Jewish legion, 1916

Source: Manchester Guardian, 23 August 1916

Opponents of the conscription or coercion of Russian Jews pressed upon the government a compromise arrangement to allow for the military participation of the East End. Their case is argued below.

Mr. Samuel made important concessions last night on the question of conscription for Russian Jews. The outrageous proposal to force these unhappy people to enlist in the British army, under threat of being sent back to Russia, where they would be liable to heavy penalties as defaulters from the Russian army, has not, indeed, been formally abandoned, but it has been suspended, and it is incredible that it should be revived. A vastly more defensible course has now been adopted. Reason and persuasion are to be substituted for threatenings and force. "A responsible committee of leading Russian Jews" has, Mr. Samuel tells us, been formed which will conduct "an active recruiting campaign in London and in other centres" among the foreign Jewish population, and definite inducements will be held out to them voluntarily to enlist. Almost all of them are aliens, and the high naturalisation fee of £5, plus law fees, is, as a rule, quite beyond their resources. Mr. Samuel offers that any of them who enlist before September 30 shall, if after three months' service they desire to be naturalised, have this fee remitted. Thus, if they are called upon to fight for this country, they may at least be able to feel that they can become its citizens.

Still more important is the proposal to form a special Jewish corps. Mr. Samuel did not give a positive undertaking on this head, but he said that "so far as practicable arrangements would be made for men wishing to serve together to do so." The foreign Jew would undoubtedly feel very differently about enlisting in a Jewish legion, officered by Jews, and where his special interests and needs, whether spiritual or dietetic, could be considered. This has, we understand, been done in France with the best results. There the foreign Jew, when dispersed among the ordinary soldiery, was found to be brilliant indeed in attack, but undisciplined and difficult to manage in the routine of the camp. When assembled in a single corps this difficulty largely disappeared. It is partly one of language. Many of these immigrants know no English, and the difficulty of language can only be adequately met where they can be dealt with together. These people have strong feelings, perhaps prejudices. Their love of England has hardly had time to grow, and Russia they regard as a cruel stepmother. They deserve and they must receive consideration. If they are wisely handled and addressed by men not only of their own faith but of their own nation – the wealthy English Jew is perhaps the last person to appeal to them, – most of them, we do not doubt, will willingly respond. . . .

d)   Enter Mr Jabotinsky, 1916

Source: PRO HO 45/10819/318095/94, Vladimir Jabotinsky to Rt. Hon. Herbert Samuel MP, 16 September 1916

Vladimir [Ze'ev] Jabotinsky (1880–1940) was a Russian-born writer, soldier and orator who became a Zionist after witnessing the pogroms. His interest in Jewish self-defence prompted the formation of the Jewish Legion and Jewish battalions to assist the British war effort. His plans are outlined below.

Dear Sir,

I apologise for not having answered your letter of 5 inst. before; but I was very busy with preparations for our propaganda campaign, and things were not sufficiently clear to myself, so I thought it better to postpone my reply. I regret very much that your messenger did not find me at home and thus I lost the chance of an indispensable interview. If I had seen you that day my task would have become much easier; as it is, I feel still doubtful about many essential points, and forced either to give up or to start the work without exactly seeing my way. I chose the latter course, because the situation is very serious. I formed a committee of young men from Whitechapel; we opened an office at 150, Minories, Aldgate, E.; to-day we posted in the East End a 1000 placards and will distribute handbills with the same text (I enclose a translation); the first number of the paper "Unser Tribune" will appear on Tuesday, and it will soon be published daily. The first public meeting will take place, I hope, before the week end.

Now it is my duty to put on record frankly and clearly what is my purpose in undertaking this campaign. I believe that it is absolutely impossible to enlist our men otherwise than for a limited service-area. Even compulsion will not help, but will only result in an ugly campaign for wholesale exemptions, more disgraceful than anything else. I see from the "Daily Chronicle" that Mr Lucien Wolf, too, is of opinion that immigrants ought to be reserved for home defense; I know from himself that he had mentioned Egypt also, but that part of his article was censored. I am glad to see that a man whose British patriotism is above all doubt confirms the necessity of a limited service scheme – it shows that this concession is suggested by life itself. And it is much more honourable than the other suggestion – "labour battalions", which has a strong flavour of degradation if applied to a whole racial group. Home defense with Egypt is not a sham but real fighting service. At the same time the big majority of the immigrants would accept it.

There is also the question of separate units. I would be insincere if I told you that batches of 100 satisfy me or any of my friends. But I will accept in this matter the interpretation of Mr Lucien Wolf who wrote me that the size of the units is an open question.

According to all these considerations, I propose to lead the campaign on the following lines:

(1) Immigrants must enlist.
(2) They must be posted in distinct groups, sufficiently large to be welded afterwards into a legion, should the necessity arise.
(3) They must be reserved for home-defense, including dominions, i.e. Egypt.
(4) They will be considered as fighting units, not labour or transport companies, and will undergo the regular military training.
(5) If Palestine should come within the scope of British operations, they will form a sort of Legion and will be employed there.

Provided my campaign is not hampered by unforeseen interferences, I hope to be able within a reasonable time to present the Authorities convincing evidence, in form of signed petitions, meeting resolutions and other manifestations, of a considerable number of young men willing to enlist on these or similar conditions.

At the same time I think – although this is not my aim – that the fact of a strong pro-service propaganda will favourably influence the ordinary unconditional recruiting, which is slowly going on even now.

Of course, the whole campaign will have a nationalistic and "legionistic" character, with the hope of participation in the conquest of Palestine as one of the principal motives. Apart from my own opinions, this is the only way to raise any enthusiasm at this hour of general and Jewish disappointment; and I do not believe in the success of a propaganda where the only argument for voluntary enlistment is the frightfulness of the alternatives.

In conclusion I beg you to consider that this matter can only be settled by a compromise. I guess you have already come to this conviction yourself. But the compromise must be honourable, not one bound to throw a slur of cowardice on the Jewish name; therefore it must not be limited to "labour", or to insular defense only. The scheme which I am going to promote is, so far as I know, the only plan of mutual concessions which excludes this reproach.

If after these explanations you think my work useless or harmful I should be obliged for a frank disapproval; otherwise I shall hope that my two years' endeavours will not have been in vain.

e)   *Exit Mr Jabotinsky, 1916*

Source: PRO HO 4510819/318095/112a, Special Branch Report No. 6758/ 15 of Sergeant A. Albers, 18 October 1916

Although keen to support the British war effort, Jabotinsky was kept under close surveillance by Sergeant Albers of Special Branch, one of the few Yiddish-speaking policemen in the land. Jabotinsky's initial efforts did not seem promising.

I beg to report having attended meetings in connection with the Jewish Legion Committee of the English Zionist Federation, one of which was held at St. Mark's Hall, Chapel Road, Notting Hill, Monday 16th inst., and the other at Ganymede Hall, Berwick Street, W., Tuesday 17th. The audience at both these places consisted of the Jewish element, chiefly Russians of military age. From the commencement of the proceedings in each case, they were antagonistic towards the speakers and a considerable amount of booing and hissing greeted them, the noise being so great as to drown anything being uttered. At the Berwick Street meeting the people present several times rushed the platform and among the conflagration cries of "Traitors" could be heard. At both the meetings it was found necessary to have the hall cleared by Police.

In my opinion it appears useless to hold these gatherings as the Jewish folk seem to greatly resent the arguments put forward, and in view of the hostile attitude of the crowd, no good purpose could be served by continuing to advocate Mr. Jabotinsky's propaganda. . . .

f) English and Russian Jews, 1916

Source: PRO HO 45/10518/318095/14, Committee of Delegates of the Russian Socialist Groups in London, An Appeal to Public Opinion: Should the Russian Refugees be Deported? (1916)

The differences between native and immigrant Jews were thrown into sharp relief by their divergent attitudes towards the war in general and military service in particular. The bitterness engendered is conveyed in the sixpenny pamphlet from which the following is extracted.

. . . In conclusion, it is necessary to say a few words about the leaders of English Jewry and their Press (the *Jewish World* and *Jewish Chronicle*) who have joined in the clamour for conscription for the Russian Jews. Those leaders represent nobody except the well-to-do British-born Jews, mostly of the financial world, who have nothing in common, either in ideas, feeling, or language, with the foreign Jewish population, who belong almost entirely to the working classes and earn their bread in the sweat of their brow. To the rich English Jew the suffering of his brethren in Russia is at best an abstract problem, otherwise valuable in so much as it affords him the opportunity of displaying his charity.

The bulk of the Jewish emigrants here come from Russia, and almost everyone has some relation in the "old" home. To the emigrants here, the tragedy of the Jews in the Empire of the Czar was their own tragedy. It was as if they themselves had undergone all the horrors and terrors suffered by their brethren in the old country. The picture of these horrors was continually before their eyes: they could not rest. This revival of barbarism, this nightmare of the dark ages had to be stopped, . . .

To their horror and consternation the Jewish masses discovered that England was deaf to the agonised cry of the Jews in Russia. . . .

g) Lock 'em up, 1916

Source: PRO HO 45/10819/318095/91, Basil Thomson to J.F. Henderson (with enclosure), 14 September 1916

The head of Special Branch had no doubt that Russian Jews were dangerous subversives who ought to be locked up. In the following letter to J.F. Henderson, the Under Secretary at the Home Office, he supports his recommendation with a damaging report from PC 100 Greenberg of Leman Street, possibly the only Jewish policeman in the Metropolitan Force at that time.

I am sending you a copy of the police report. From what I know of these people, I think it is a case for an immediate action against Bezalel, Bernard, Mindlen, Prager and Salkind, but particularly Bernard. It may be difficult on the evidence of a single witness to obtain a conviction, but it will be possible for the Military Authorities to remove them from London. The effect of tackling the leaders would be, in my opinion, to stop the whole of this kind of agitation, but it will be useless unless action is taken at once.

Leman Street   'H'
                                                                13th September

I beg to report that a meeting was held at the New King's Hall, Commercial Road, E., on Tuesday 12th inst, by the Russian Jewish (French Refugees) Protection Committee, which I attended.

The above meeting was called (1) to consider what, if any, compromise should be made in the matter of Military Service, (2) the establishing of an organization of French Refugees. There were about 200 persons present.

This Committee is affiliated with the Foreign Jews Protection Committee against Deportation to Russia and Compulsory Military Service, of which Dr. I. Kruk, A. Bezalel and Dr. I.M. Salkind are Chairman, Hon. Sec. and Hon. Treasurer respectively.

Dr. I.M. Salkind occupied the Chair and was supported by Abraham Bezalel, G. Bernard, Prager, Mindlen and several others.

Dr. Salkind, in opening the meeting, said . . . I think . . . you will all be in favour of forming an organization, as the more organization and bodies we have the better for our cause. As to compromise, . . . I wish to say the slightest departure on your part from a firm principle will give the English Government a hold they are looking for. . . .

Mr. G. Bernard, Hon. Sec., Russian-Jewish (French Refugees) Protection Committee, then addressed the meeting, saying:– . . . "As

Translation from Yiddish

ON MILITARY SERVICE

Jewish Youth!

The situation is very serious. Words and "memoranda" will not do. The only way that remains is to search for an honourable compromise with fair concessions on the two sides.

We must not forget that this is not a question of our personal interest only. It is a question of the Jewish future in England, and not only in England.

The form in which the appeal to the foreign Jews was made can be severely criticised. But the world will forget the forms and will only remember the essence. And the essence of the present situation is this:

England, in an hour of need and danger, came to the Jewish immigrant with the call: "Come and help me to defend my life!"

Be careful in your answer to such a call. You do not answer for yourself only – you answer for the Jewish nation.

This reply will never be forgotten.

If we answer England: "No, we do not want to defend you" – that will be a deadly blow to our struggle for the Jewish rights in all the Eastern countries, and a deadly blow to the Jewish immigration to all the Western countries. Because even America will not care for such immigrants upon whom she cannot rely in a time of danger. Be careful. Do not forfeit the Jewish position in the few lands where it is good.

"No" cannot be our answer to England's call. If we feel that our position in the war is different, we must look for a compromise; but the compromise must be an honourable one, fair and worthy of the Jewish name.

However deep the difference between citizen and immigrant may be, one duty is clear: to defend the country itself. We must not degrade ourselves by begging that we may be employed for works which old men, women and children can do. A healthy youth who lives in a country must be ready to defend it like a man, with a gun in his hand. This is the sacred duty of "home-defence".

The development of the war, especially in the East, may put before us in the nearest future another obligation which no Jew will have the right to repudiate. For this second duty – the defence of our right on a Jewish "heim" – we must declare ourselves, too, ready and willing.

These two obligations – "home" and "heim" – are expressed for us in the words: JEWISH LEGION.

Young Jew! Think it over before it is too late. Give England a friendly, fair and worthy reply to her call. In your hands is the Jewish honour and the Jewish future.

On behalf of the Committee
"For Jewish Future"
W. Jabotinsky, Press.

Those who agree with the spirit of our appeal are invited to come to the Committee's office at 150, Minories, Aldgate, EC.

Figure 19 On military service (Yiddish poster), 1916 Appeals issued in Yiddish failed to persuade those with bitter memories of pogroms and persecution to sacrifice their lives for England's ally, Russia (Public Record Office HO 45/10819/318095/94).

to compromise, have nothing to do with it. To do work of national importance is a trick by the Government. Up to now the Government has not found it in their power to compel you to join the Army, and they are trying to extract from you some form of compromise by which you will become in their power, as all work at the present time of national importance is under military law, and once you submit to that you are yourself no more. You must get out of your minds the question of strikes on Government work, as to my mind it would be an absolute failure. The Government would not tolerate such an action, and the next day you would receive a card to report yourself to the recruiting authorities and sent off to France, where you would be shot for your cause as Englishmen have been. So leave strikes alone and undertake no work of national importance. They have even sent engineers out to the trenches, some of whom have been recalled, so what chance have we, who are tailors and cap-makers? . . . With regard to naturalization after three months. That is another trick. No one will be naturalized unless he has resided in this country 5 years, and to be able to read and write. . . .

. . .

Mr. Bezalel then addressed the meeting and said:– "Friends, you have heard the result of the conference of last Sunday. You must follow the same. Don't be afraid, Don't be afraid of the Police. Be firm and resolute, take on nothing offered by the Government. Don't let them trap you into work of national importance, and fool you by naturalization. What friend Bernard said is right. Five years, not three months. Don't give way, stand fast and hold together and defy the Government with your solidarity, then we shall win." . . .

The whole of the speeches made were delivered in Yiddish, and the entire meeting was orderly with the exception of the incident reported. The meeting, which commenced at 9.5 p.m. terminated at 12.20 a.m., 13th inst.

I beg to state that all the foregoing speeches are dictated from memory, as any attempt to take shorthand or other notes at the time, would have brought my immediate ejectment from the Hall. . . .

(Signed) P.C. Greenberg

2. Military Service (Conventions with Allied States) Act, 1917

Source: An Act to enable His Majesty in Council to carry into effect conventions which may be made with Allied and other States as to the mutual leadership of His Majesty's subjects and subjects of the Allied and other States to military service, 10 July 1917. [7 & 8 Geo. 5.] C.26

The Russian Revolution had, it seemed removed any objection to military service in the East End. The British government certainly thought so and hastened to conclude an agreement with the Kerensky government that might do little for the war effort but much for the peace of East London. The enabling legislation and the agreement to which it refers are printed below.

1. His Majesty may by Order in Council, signifying that a convention has been made with a foreign country allied or otherwise acting in naval or military co-operation with His Majesty in the present war (in this Act referred to as the contracting country) which imposes a mutual liability to military service on British subjects in that country and on subjects of that country in the United Kingdom, direct that this Act shall have effect with respect to the contracting country and the subjects of that country, and on any such Order in Council being made, this Act shall have effect accordingly: Provided that –

(a) No such Order in Council shall be made unless the convention secures to His Majesty's Ambassador or other public Minister in the contracting country power to grant to British subjects in that country exemption from military service, and such Ambassador or Minister shall grant such exemption in any case where a British subject proves that he is not domiciled in the contracting country, and that before proceeding to the contracting country he was ordinarily resident in some part of His Majesty's dominions other than Great Britain:

(b) No such Order in Council shall be made unless the convention contains provisions to the effect that British subjects in the contracting country and subjects of the contracting country in the United Kingdom shall, before becoming liable to military service, have an opportunity, if they make application for the purpose, of returning to the United Kingdom or the contracting country, as the case may be:

(c) An Order in Council shall not be made until the expiration of thirty days from the date when the convention has been laid before Parliament.

2. (1) Where this Act is so applied with respect to any country, subjects of that country shall, if they have not, within twenty-one days after the convention has been laid before Parliament, made an application in such manner as may be prescribed by a Secretary of State to return to the contracting country, or if, having made such an application, they have failed to avail themselves of an opportunity to do so, be liable to military service under the Military Service Acts, 1916, in the same manner as British subjects; and those Acts shall apply accordingly, subject to the following modifications:–

(a) The appointed date shall, as respects subjects of the contracting country who come within the operation of the Military Service Acts, 1916 and 1917, on the application of this Act in respect of that country, be the thirtieth day after the date of the Order in Council applying the Act, and as respects subjects of the contracting country who come within the operation of the Military Service Acts, 1916 and 1917, after that date, be the thirtieth day after the date on which they so come within the operation of those Acts, except that when such subjects come within the operations of those Acts by reason of their failing to avail themselves of an opportunity of returning to the contracting country, the appointed date shall be the date of such failure:

(b) A subject of the contracting country who has not made such an application as aforesaid to return to that country shall have the same rights with regard to exemption and exceptions conferred by the Military Service Acts, 1916 and 1917, other than the exceptions mentioned in paragraph (1) of the First Schedule to the first-mentioned Act, as he would have if he were a British Subject, and, whether he has made such an application or not, shall be deemed to be within the exceptions under the Military Service Acts, 1916 and 1917, if he is the holder of a certificate of exemption for the time being in force granted by the Ambassador or a duly authorised public Minister of that country in the United Kingdom.

(c) Regulations issued under the Military Service Acts, 1916 and 1917, may provide for the establishment of special tribunals for dealing with applications or appeals for exemption in respect of men who are rendered liable to military service by virtue of this Act and for the appointment of additional members to tribunals when dealing with such applications or appeals:

(d) Any British subjects arriving in Great Britain from the contracting country after the date of an Order in Council applying this Act to the subjects of that contracting country shall, if not ordinarily resident in Great Britain, be deemed for the purposes of the Military Service Acts, 1916 and 1917, to be ordinarily resident in Great Britain as from the date of his arrival, unless he shows that the part of His Majesty's dominions in which he last resided was some part other than Great Britain.

(2) For the purposes of the limitation on the number of aliens who may serve together at any one time in any corps of the regular forces imposed by section ninety-five of the Army Act, subjects of a contracting country who become liable to military service by virtue of the application of this Act in respect of their country shall not be reckoned in that number.

(3) For the purposes of this Act the expression "convention" includes an agreement.

3. This Act may be cited as the Military Service (Conventions with Allied States) Act, 1917, and shall be included amongst the Acts which may be cited as the Military Service Acts, 1916 and 1917.

a)   Anglo-Russian Military Service Agreement, 1917

Source: An agreement concluded between His Majesty's Government and the Provisional Government of Russia relative to the Reciprocal Liability to Military Service of British subjects resident in Russia and Russian subjects resident in Great Britain, 16 July 1917, Parliamentary Papers [Cd. 8588], XXXVIII (1917–18), pp. 735–737

His Brittanic Majesty's Government and the Provisional Government of Russia, being convinced that it is in the interests of their countries for the better prosecution of the present war that British subjects resident in Russia, and Russian subjects resident in Great Britain, should return to their respective countries there to fulfil their military duty in the ranks of the army of their country, or that they should enrol themselves in the army of the country of their residence, have concluded the following agreement:

1. His Brittanic Majesty's Government and the Provisional Government of Russia will reciprocally bid their subjects inhabiting respectively Russia and Great Britain, and belonging to the categories called to the colours in their own country, to proceed to their respective countries.

2. His Britannic Majesty's Government undertake as far as possible to effect during the course of the summer of 1917 the transport by sea of the above-mentioned persons.

3. Such of these persons as refuse, after due notice given, to return to their own country, either at their own expense or by profiting by the means set forth in article 2 of the present agreement, will be compelled to undertake military service in the country of their residence.

The call of these persons to arms will be effected by the competent authorities if the country of their residence, who will for this purpose apply the dispositions in force in their respective countries as regards absentees.

4. Will be exempt from the obligation to the call to arms set forth in the preceding article persons who furnish documents delivered by their diplomatic or consular authorities certifying their exemption from military service.

5. This agreement shall cease to have force from the date of the conclusion of the present war.

In faith whereof the undersigned, His Britannic Majesty's Ambassador and the Russian Minister for Foreign Affairs, duly authorised to this effect, have concluded the present agreement and have attached thereto their seals.

Done at Petrograd, in duplicate, the 3rd 16th July, 1917

(Signed) George W. Buchanan
        Michel Terestchenko

July 16, 1917

3.   The Russian Revolution and the Jews, 1917

Source: The Herald, 31 March 1917

News of the collapse of the Tsarist autocracy was received with extraordinary enthusiasm in the Jewish East End. The Russian Revolution brought together libertarians concerned to uphold the right of asylum, socialist revolutionaries, pacifists and progressive dissidents in a series of public celebrations to welcome the opening of a new era for humanity in general and the Russian Jew in particular.

GREAT RUSSIAN RALLY IN LONDON

On Saturday, March 24, a great mass meeting was held, under the auspices of the Committee of Delegates of the Russian Socialist Groups in London, in the Great Assembly Hall (Mile End Road), to celebrate the Russian revolution. Over 7,000 persons were present, and many thousands were unable to get in and had to go away.

Telegrams with congratulations, expressions of joy, greetings to the revolutionary proletariat in Russia, and best wishes for its future fight were received from the London Jewish Trades Council, the United Furnishing Trades Union (Cohen, Secretary), the East London Branch of the Amalgamated Society of Tailors and Tailoresses (Leipovitch, Secretary), the National Hat- and Cap-makers Union of Great Britain, the Workers' Circle (N. Weiver, General Secretary), Mr. Morris Myer, Editor of the *Jewish Times,* the London Jewish Cleaners and Repairers Union (Leipovitch, Secretary), The Jewish Socialist-Labour Party Poaley Sion in London, The Amalgamated Society of Tailors (Manchester).

Earnest speeches were made by Robert Williams (Transport Workers' Federation), E.C. Fairchild (B.S.P.), V. MacEntee (B.S.P.), J. Fineberg (B.S.P.), Mrs Bridges Adams and delegates of the Committee of the Russian Socialist Groups, of the London Groups of the various Socialist Parties of Russia, and of the Jewish Social Democracy (B.S.P.). The highest enthusiasm was reached when Russian sailors appeared on the platform, fraternising with the Socialists, and one of them spoke of their solidarity with the revolution; the same solidarity was also expressed by a soldier, who had been a prisoner and had escaped, and expressed the wish of fighting for other aims.

The following resolution was unanimously adopted by the meeting:

This meeting, at one with the broad masses of Russia, rejoices at the overthrow of Tsarist despotism – the monstrous system of oppression, which hampered in every possible way the development of the material and spiritual forces of the country, was the source of innumerable sufferings, especially for the workers, the oppressed nationalities, and the fighters for freedom, and was the stronghold and the chief supporter of reaction and tyranny throughout the world.

The meeting further considered that the task of the true democratic forces in Russia, headed by the class-conscious proletariat struggling for its revolutionary class-aims, is to carry through the complete democratisation of the country.

The meeting demanded from the British Government the immediate release of Petroff, Mrs. Petroff, Sairo, Hazle, and of the other Russian citizens who are deprived of their liberty in contravention of the elementary principles of the freedom of the subject.

Another meeting was held on Sunday last at Camperdown House, East London, presided over by Lord Sheffield. This was under the auspices of the Foreign Jews' Protection Committee, and was also filled to overflowing. On Monday, March 26, a further meeting to congratulate the Russian people on the overthrow of Tsardom was held at the Memorial Hall, under the auspices of the British Socialist Party. These enthusiastic meetings go to show that democracy is now awakening to its great responsibilities in Great Britain; and London, which is always looked upon as the centre of reaction as far as Great Britain is concerned, will rouse itself and show its appreciation of the magnificent turn of events in Russia. In the words of Edward Carpenter, we may now sing sincerely and truthfully, "Faint in the East behold the dawn appear."

4.   Russian Jewish matters, 1917

Source: PRO HO 45/10819/318095/525, Police Report on Russian Jewish Matters, 22 December 1917

The complexities of Russian Jewish politics, the fragments that composed and recomposed the radical movement, and the Yiddish in which its proceedings were conducted, made it exceptionally difficult for outsiders to make sense of it all. The British police did surprisingly well.

With reference to Russian Jewish matters in London: I beg to report that a Conference was held by the United Russian Committee on Wednesday the 12th December at the Old King's Hall, Commercial Road, E.

Dr. Jochelman, the Chairman of the Committee who presided, declared that arrangements have been made between the Russian authorities and the Local Government Board that the Russian families who have hitherto been receiving their weekly allowance through the United Russian Committee will henceforth receive the same allowance through the Local Guardians of the respective districts where the families reside. An official letter from the Local Government Board to the Russian Consulate was read by Dr. Jochelman to convince the delegates that the families will not be looked upon as paupers receiving charity, but that the allowance will be made by the British Treasury and charged to the Russian Government.

A resolution was put before the Conference to appreciate the action of the Local Government Board towards the Russian families, but an opposition was formed by the following:– Morris Myer, editor of the "Jewish Times", representing the Jewish Workers Relief Emergency Fund; Jack Bernstein and H. Trabitchoff, representing the Jewish Anarchist Federation; A. Fisher and P. Segal, representing the "Bund"; S. Drin and S. Leemel (anarchists), representing the United Ladies Tailors Trade Union (the former being the Chairman of the Union, the latter the Chairman of the West End Branch of the same Body; J. Weiner, Secretary of and representing the "Free Workers Circle"; Mr. Gradel, Secretary of and representing the Cigarette Makers Trade Union; Mrs King and Mrs Soloveitchik, and Weinberg of the Gibraltar Press, representing the West End Branch of the Jewish Protection Committee.

The reason the aforementioned opposed the resolution was because they considered it will be a degradation for the families to go to the Guardians, and secondly because the Local Government Board are aiming to place a trap for the Russians, to utilise them later on for their vile purposes. . . .

. . . Some members of the opposition (Bernstein, Weinberg, Trobatchoff, Fisher, Mrs King, Mrs Soloveitchik and L. Katzel) have formed a Committee, called the "Ladies Committee for protecting the interests of the dependent families of Russian Citizens". Mrs Soloveitchik is acting as Chairman. They are going to agitate among the women to press the Russian and British authorities to be sent back to their husbands in Russia.

A temporary Committee in opposition to the Anglo-Zionist Federation and the Government's declaration regarding Palestine for the Jews, has been formed, comprising S. Joseph, Jack Bernstein, J. Lush, P. Himmelfarb, J. Habergritz, A. Alexander, S. Hertzberg, Morris Levy, J. Yampolsky, Sabotinsky and J. Weiner. The first meeting was held at the New Home Restaurant on the 14th December when it was resolved that every member of the Committee should make an effort to enlighten the Jewish Working men that the declaration of Britain to Lord Rothschild re Palestine for the Jews is merely a political trick, and that it will be detrimental to the proletariat as a whole to make Palestine as a Jewish National home in the form of a Colony or State, predominated by the British Government and Anglo-Jewish Capitalists. The actions of that Committee so far consists of verbal propaganda in private circles, as well as in their respective organisations.

The group of the Russian Political Emigrants called a special committee meeting on Sunday the 16th December at 107 Charlotte Street, W. Dr. Margolin presided and a Mr. D. Chuchim, acting secretary. It was decided to advise those Russians receiving calling-up letters for the British Army that they should return same to the Recruiting Office with a remark that as Russia has now declared an Armistice, those Russians in this country are not liable to serve. . . .

A Mrs Goldberg, whose husband is in Wormwood Scrubbs prison as a Conscientious Objector, appears to be a prominent figure in the Jewish

Anarchists Federation and the No-Conscription Fellowship.

The Jews Protection Committee have removed their offices from 10 Great Garden Street, E. to the New Home Restaurant.

The enclosed is a copy of the Russian Newspaper "Golos-Truda" (Voice of Labour). It has been read by an Informant but does not contain anything of special importance. There is an article by the pen of the anarchist Schapiro, editor of the paper, entitled "The Totals of Party Work". A watch is being kept for other copies of this paper in case anything worthy of attention should appear therein.

5.   Minutes of the War Cabinet, 1918

Source: PRO Cab. 23/5 WC 329 (12), Minutes of a Meeting of the War Cabinet, 23 January 1918

The collapse of the Kerensky government and the hostile attitude of its successor re-opened the barely closed question of the Russian Jews and military service. The War Cabinet's conclusions are printed below.

12. The War Cabinet had before them a Paper by Mr. Balfour on the subject of the conscription of Russian subjects in this country (Paper G.T.3411).

Mr. Balfour explained the difficulty which had arisen in the working of the convention agreed between His Majesty's Government and the last Russian Government. Under the Act of Parliament upon which the convention was founded, power was given, without appeal, to the Ambassadors in both countries to grant exemptions from military service. M. Litvinoff, the representative of the Bolshevik Government, would undoubtedly exempt all the East End Jews from military service, if he could. This would create an intolerable position in the East End, where these Russian Jews were making large sums of money by supplanting British shopkeepers who had been called up for military service.

General Macdonogh stated that there were about 25,000 of these Russians of military age in this country, of whom only about 4,000 had so far been called up. From the counter-espionage point of view, it was most desirable that these aliens should be either got into the Army, interned, or deported to Russia. The majority of them were Jews. He had accordingly seen Dr. Weizmann, the President of the English Zionist Federation, who had expressed the opinion that it was important that the Jewish regiment, to which these Russian Jews were usually sent, should be despatched to Palestine at the earliest possible date. Orders had accordingly been given to the regiment, which was now stationed at Plymouth, to prepare for service overseas, and transport was being awaited. He feared that a majority of the remaining East End Jews cared very little for Zionism, and were only anxious to make profits. Under the convention an option was given to these aliens either to serve in the British Army or else to return to Russia. The tonnage difficulty prevented the latter alternative being made use of in practice, and this fact was known to a good many of the aliens.

Lord Derby stated that there had been some trouble in the Jewish regiment at Plymouth, but on being addressed by their Commanding Officer, Colonel Paterson, who had a great hold over them, they were unanimous to proceed to Palestine to fight. He hopes that the Government would remain firm, and continue to enforce the Military Service Acts in regard to these Russians. Rather than allow them to remain in the East End, he thought that, failing their being got into the army, the most practical suggestion would be to send them to a concentration camp at Aberdeen or Hull, to await transport to Russia, and that they should be made to understand distinctly that they would not be allowed to return to this country.

The War Cabinet decided that –

The Military Service Acts should continue to be applied to Russian subjects in this country, and that, in the event of it being impossible to get all of them into the army, they should be sent to camps, as suggested by Lord Derby, and be made to understand that their return would not be permitted.

The working out of this decision was to be left to an Inter-Departmental Committee, to be arranged by Lord Derby, consisting of representatives of –

The War Office,
The Foreign Office,
The Home Office,
The Ministry of National Service.

6.   Mr Trotsky's instructions awaited, 1918

Source: PRO HO 45/10819/318095/558, Maxim Litvinoff, Provisional Plenipotentiary for Great Britain of the Russian Peoples' Commissary for Foreign Affairs, to Arthur Balfour, Secretary of State for Foreign Affairs, 31 January 1918

Ironically, the essentially domestic issues for which the Anglo-Russian Military Service Convention had been negotiated were fast becoming a source of international conflict and embarrassment.

Sir
I have been inundated with letters from Russian citizens of military age, living in this country, complaining of what they regard as a great injustice done to them by the enforcement of the Military Service Act

(Convention with Allied States) 1917. They resent very strongly the position in which they are placed by being called upon to enter the Army and take active part in a War in which their country no longer participates, having entered into negotiations for peace. They also point to the vigorous haste with which the Military Authorities of this country have begun of late to enforce the above Act, the impression being created in their minds that, anticipating the approaching annulment of the Convention, the Authorities are trying to exploit to the full the opportunities they at present have to force into the Army as many Russian recruits as possible and to keep them there, afterwards, whether the Convention is annulled or not.

As the representative here of the Russian Republic, I cannot but sympathise with my fellow citizens in their present situation, and hope, by taking up the matter now, to be able to prevent it from becoming a new source of friction and misunderstanding between our respective countries.

I would say, first of all, that the Convention has never met with the approval of Russian Democracy and that the Provisional Government of Russia in concluding it were acting not from motives of expediency and right, but in response to pressure from the Allies. Thus the very origin of the Convention makes it unacceptable to the great majority of the Russian people, who regard with the same feeling of mistrust and discontent all the agreements, secret or public, entered into by the previous Government.

The British Government is undoubtedly aware that the demobilisation of the Russian Army has already begun, that all men above 35 years have been sent home, an Army of Volunteers being in course of creation instead of a conscript army. As there is, accordingly, no conscription for Russian citizens in Russia, and more especially as the Convention is no longer being applied in respect of British subjects in Russia, the forcible enlistment of Russians in this country can have no justification. Moreover, I would point out that the French Government is no longer applying the terms of the Convention to Russian Citizens living in France.

I expect very shortly to receive definite instructions on this matter from Mr. Trotsky. In the meantime I venture to suggest to you, Sir, that it would be only just, as well as highly expedient, to discontinue applying the Convention to Russian citizens in this country, and to release from barracks and prison all those Russians who have already been enlisted.

I desire to intimate to you that I reserve to myself the right to publish the correspondence between us on this matter, a course to which I am sure you will have no objection.

7.   By the waters of Whitechapel! 1919–20

Source: PRO MH/57/204, Leonard L. Cohen Chairman of Russian Dependents Committee, to Minister of Health, 24 June 1921

Those who had opted for repatriation and war service under the terms of the Anglo–Russian Military Agreement were unable to take their families with them. The plight of the dependents of these 'Conventionists' may be glimpsed at from the administrative and financial arrangements made for their maintenance.

Sir,

I am desired by my Committee to inform you that they have taken a careful review of the present position of the work entrusted to them by the Ministry, and to put before you an outline of the conclusions at which the Committee have arrived. . . .

The Russian Dependants Committee, a Committee of voluntary workers, was constituted at the request of the Ministry of Health in March 1920 under a Minute of the Ministry dated 16th March 1920, and its functions were stated in the Minute to be the following:–

"To co-ordinate the relief given from Government and charitable sources to the dependants of Russians who returned to Russia in compliance with the terms of the Anglo-Russian Military Service Convention".

Before the Committee came into existence relief to Russian Dependants had been administered through various bodies of Local Guardians who received the necessary funds from the Ministry of Health, and attended to the distribution.

The reasons which led to the transfer of the work from the Local Guardians to the present Committee were inter alia, as far as is known to us, that it was considered that a Committee of voluntary workers was likely to be able to take a closer and more individual interest in the work than Local Guardians were able to do, and that thereby a gradual reduction in the number of those in receipt of relief would be effected, either by showing the dependants the way to become self-supporting or through effecting repatriation of dependants or bringing back the bread winners of the families. It was also thought that the centralisation of the relief work in one body would result in more effective supervision, avoidance of overlapping of relief, and a more equitable distribution of the available funds according to the needs of the individual cases.

In organising and carrying out their work the Committee were greatly assisted by the fact that they were able to take over the existing organisation of the Jewish War Refugees Committee, whose headquarters are at 82 Leman Street, E, and whose work was just coming to an end. The Russian Dependants Committee established its headquarters at 82 Leman Street, E., (premises placed at their disposal free of charge by the Jews Temporary Shelter) and appointed sub-committees at Manchester and Leeds. All other provincial cases, distinct from those living in the Manchester and Leeds areas, are being administered from 82 Leman Street, E. The work of the Committee embraces all cases of Russian Dependants (under the Military Convention) irrespective of race or religion; amongst the dependants taken over by the Committee were 96 Adults and 187 Children non-Jews, the remaining cases being Jews.

When the Committee began its work the Ministry of Health authorised the payment to the Committee of a Capitation Fee, based on the total number of Dependants under the Committee's charge, at the rate of 12/6d per Adult (practically all women) and 3/- per Child. It became soon apparent that this Capitation Fee was insufficient, and as from the 1st July 1920 the fee was raised by the Ministry of Health to 15/6d per Adult and 5/- per Child. The allocation of these funds amongst the Dependants was left in the discretion of the Committee.

In addition to the funds supplied by the Ministry of Health the Committee was able, at the beginning of the work, to rely on some limited contributions from private persons, or other bodies, collections, proceeds of cinema performances etc., but these contributions, owing to bad times intervening, and general unemployment, have for some time past practically ceased.

With every desire to keep financial requirements to the lowest possible point, the Committee have been faced with the greatest difficulties to make both ends meet. Having regard to the cost of living the Capitation Fees hardly allow a bare existence; moreover the Committee was at a disadvantage as compared with the Local Guardians, in as much as the latter have been allowed considerable latitude in granting supplementary relief in case of illness or when the necessity was shown by medical certificate.

The relief work of the Committee commenced on the 5th April 1920. At the end of the first week there were in receipt of relief:–

414 Adults and 852 Children

The transfer of the cases from the different bodies of Local Guardians distributed over the country took a number of weeks, and the maximum figures were reached during the first and second weeks of July 1920. The total of cases registered with the Committee have been as follows:–

London Administration	639 Adults	1145 Children	
Manchester	27 "	63 "	
Leeds	12 "	14 "	
Total	678 Adults	1222 Children	

From that time onwards, largely through the efforts of the Committee, the number of Dependants has gradually become reduced for the following reasons:–

1) Dependants becoming self-supporting,
2) Repatriation,
3) Dependants being taken over by husband re-admitted into England,
4) Death,
5) Emigration on their own accord,
6) Remarriage,
7) Relief stopped for other reasons.

The following table shows the reduction in numbers under the aforesaid headings, up to the 31st May 1921:–

1) Dependants becoming self-supporting
       Adults 15   Children 22
2) Repatriated
       Adults 58   Children 103
3) Dependants taken over by husbands re-admitted into England
       Adults 134 Children 278
4) Death
       Adults 2   Children 1
5) Emigrated on own accord
       Adults 7   Children 3
6) Re-marriage
       Adults 2   Children 1
7) Relief stopped for other reasons
       Adults 20   Children 17

At the 31st May 1921 the total numbers in receipt of relief were as follows (including Manchester and Leeds):

      440 Adults 797 Children

The attempt to make the women and children under the care of the Committee self-supporting has at all times been a difficult one. The task has become almost impossible owing to the setback in Trade and Industry, which set in soon after the Committee commenced work. It may safely be stated that unless conditions of employment change entirely no work can be found for the women at present under the care of the Committee, and no reduction in numbers can be expected in this way.

With regard to securing permission for the husbands to return to this country, and to resume responsibility for their families, the Committee wish again to place on record the great assistance which they have received from the Home Office Authorities, as shown by the fact that 134 husbands have so far been allowed to come back to this country, and it is expected that a further gradual reduction of numbers will take place as and when further applications are granted.

The question of repatriation remains very much in the same position as previously reported. For all practical purposes Russia still is a closed country, nor would it be feasible to send women and children to

Russia unless previous arrangements for their reception could be made with either the Russian Government or the individual husbands of the respective families.

The Committee has recently caused enquiries to be made into every case for the purpose of ascertaining how many of the women at present under the care of the Committee (440) have had news from their husbands during the last five months i.e. since the 1st January last. The result of this enquiry has been as follows:-

News received and whereabouts of husband known
107 Adults with 212 Children
No news received
333 Adults with 585 Children

It is expected that as and when communication with Russia gets more normal a greater number of women will receive news from their husbands or sons in Russia.

It will be seen from the figures given above that an appreciable reduction in numbers has taken place since the Committee took over the care of the dependants from the Local Guardians. At the same time the number of women and children dependent upon public relief still remains considerable.

My Committee would be glad to have an opportunity of discussing with the Ministry of Health the various questions bearing upon the care of these dependants. A small delegation of the Committee will be pleased to hold themselves at the disposal of the Minister of Health for a verbal discussion at any time that may be convenient to him.

8.   The Jewish soldier

a)   Heart and hand, 1900

Source: G.W.E. Russell, 'The Jewish Regiment', Daily News, 17 September 1917

These exhilarating verses were written by a Jewish lady at the time of the Boer War

Long ago and far away, O Mother England,
We were warriors brave and bold,
But a hundred nations rose in arms against us,
And the shades of exile closed o'er those heroic
    Days of old.

Thou has given us home and freedom,
Mother England,
Thou hast let us live again

Free and fearless 'midst thy free and fearless children,
Sharing with them, as one people, grief and gladness,
   Joy and pain.

Now we Jews, we English Jews, O Mother England,
Ask another boon of thee!
Let us share with them the danger and the glory,
Where thy best bravest lead, there let us follow,
   O'er the sea!

For the Jew has a heart and hand, our Mother England,
And they both are thine to-day –
Thine for life, and thine for death, yea, thine for ever!
Wilt thou take them as we give them, freely, gladly?
   England, say!

b)   Mafeking Day in Brick Lane, 1900

Source: Jewish Chronicle, 25 May 1900

The making of immigrants into Britons found its most dramatic expression in the over-representation of Jews in the British armed forces during the First World War. The Boer War in which Jews also served with distinction was a sign of things to come.

Although the news of the Relief of Mafeking was already known on Friday evening, East End Jewry did not celebrate the happy event until the conclusion of Sabbath, extending the *simcha* till late on Sunday. . . . East End Jewry has a method of its own in commemorating any auspicious occasion. First comes the religious ceremony and then the civil celebration. In every Chevra Synagogue, wherever a Maggid discoursed on Saturday afternoon, the preacher referred to the none too timely relief of the gallant little garrison. The men bowed their heads with acquiescence in their favourite Maggid's remarks. The Sabbath clothes were not doffed, for was it not a *Yomtov*? Never did Brick Lane and Hanbury Street present such a sight. Not only the young were decorated with red, white and blue, and Baden-Powell medallions, but the old as well adopted the colours of the favourite. The poor old Jewish traveller selling rosettes and medallions at the corner of Osborn Street, Whitechapel, will have no cause to regret the relief of Mafeking; over £4 were his takings from the moment Sabbath was at an end till midnight, and he still could have sold more. Every draper's shop was soon out of bunting and flags, and on Sunday morning the whole of the Ghetto was beflagged. From the Bethnal Green end of Brick Lane to St. George's-in-the-East, from High Street, Whitechapel, to Stepney, every shop and every house had some sort of decoration. The streets were crowded with cheering men and women, girls and boys, and the hard-worked machinist refused to go back to his machine, the laster to his last and the joiner to his bench. . . .

The greatest display of flags was however in the "Lane." Every stall, every barrow had its flag. One could get "Mafeking fish," "Mafeking oranges" and "Mafeking lemons," cakes *l'kovod* Mafeking and what not. Everything was being sold in honour of Mafeking and, every minute or so, one could hear patriotic airs sung and played; the Yiddish bands – there are several, one consisting of four girls and two men – being greatly in demand, and reaping a "coppery" harvest for their selection of patriotic music. All were happy. The sentence, "Mafeking is relieved," was like an abracadabra, opening the way to joy, levelling the rich and poor, ending the terrible anxiety. "Mafeking relieved. Mazzeltov, Mazzeltov."

c) Jews as soldiers, 1903

Source: 'Jews as Soldiers', *The Spectator*, 3 January 1903

Jewish military participation in the Boer War came as something of a revelation to those whose thinking rarely progressed beyond stereotype images. The following is interesting because it does seek to penetrate beyond convention and prejudice.

Lord Roberts attended on Sunday last the special military service held at the Central Synagogue in Great Portland Street for Jewish members of the Regular and Auxiliary Forces. The gathering took place, not inappropriately, in connection with the yearly religious ceremony commemorating the warlike exploits of the Maccabees and the struggle which terminated in the overthrow of the Syrian dominance in Palestine by the Asmoneans and their followers. It is the first time in the annals of this country that the acting Commander-in-Chief of the British Army has been present in his official capacity at a military function of this kind limited exclusively to soldiers and Volunteers who are members of the Judaic community. On the Continent, where the number of Jews serving with the colours or passed into the Reserves runs into thousands, such parades honoured by the attendance of the higher officers have been far from uncommon. On more than one occasion – as with the German forces investing Paris, and the Russians around Plevna – the Sons of the Synagogue have met to observe their solemn anniversaries amid the tumult and stress of actual warfare. Here, in England, the soldier element has not, until within the past few years, been strong enough to admit of such a parade as that of Sunday. The last two decades have, however, seen a change in the temperament of the younger generation of Jews in the United Kingdom. The rise of a wider, broader Imperialism which has

marked this period, and the spread of a martial spirit among the people
which has accompanied it, have quickened the dormant fighting instincts
of the race. The result is seen in the larger number of Jews now found in
the Army and Reserve Forces. In the operations recently terminated in
South Africa it is estimated that over twelve hundred officers and men
belonging to the Hebrew community took active part. This would be a
very goodly proportion having regard to their total in the three kingdoms.
The deaths among the Jewish soldiers have been, it is said, in excess of
their due quota. In any event, the bulk of the native-born Jews here have
come well to the fore in the recent struggle, and it is understood that the
presence of Lord Roberts at Sunday's Synagogue parade is intended to
mark in some measure the Commander-in-Chief's satisfaction with the
conduct of the Jewish troops during the South African War.

The Jew ought to make a good soldier. After all, he comes of a fighting
stock, and the fighting instinct must be latent in him. . . . The anomalous
position of the Jew during the Middle Ages, the absence of all incentive
or motive for any form of active patriotic life, was fatal to those
sympathies and aspirations in which military ardour has its spring and
origin. The mass of the Jewish people were cowed into a timidity fatal to
all true manliness, and altogether incompatible with anything like a
soldierly spirit. But the instinct was only repressed, for where the Jew was
permitted to take part in the stirring events of the time, he played a bold
and courageous part. In the turbulent movements characterising Italy
from the twelfth to the sixteenth century more than one Jew came into
prominence as a valiant and skilful soldier. In our East Indian possessions
Jews have from time to time shown conspicuous gallantry as combatants
and rendered important services in the field. It is not generally known,
but the Indian native army regiments have always had a proportionately
larger number of recruits from the Jews than from any other of the tribal
units of Hindostan which contribute to the Indian Army. These Jews
belong to the so-called "Beni Yisrael" of Bombay, natives who have been
settled there from time immemorial. They are, singularly enough, the only
people in the country whose occupation is put down in the official returns
as "soldiering." . . . That the Jew is not deficient in mere animal courage
and pluck the prize ring here sufficiently showed in the last century, when
"The Star of the East," Barney Aarons, with his coreligionists, Dutch
Sam and David Belasco and Daniel Mendoza, stood in the very front
rank of noted pugilists. . . .

. . .

In this country no followers of the Synagogue have ever attained high
rank in the Army. . . . At the present time there are not, probably, more
than three Jewish officers of field rank on the lists of the British Army, –
Colonel Montefiore, a nephew of the late Sir Moses Montefiore, who
served in the Artillery; Colonel Leverson; and Colonel Goldsmid. . . . On
the whole, the number of officers is small considering the large number of
young men in the Hebraic community who have ample means, plenty of

brain, and no serious calling or occupation to which to devote themselves.

If military service is not popular among the great bulk of the poorer class of Jews in Russia and Eastern Europe, it is easily accounted for without going into any question of racial inclination or predisposition. The *Kolonist* system, as it was termed, formerly in vogue, is sufficient to explain the Russian Jew's hatred of the Army and all connected with it. Under this abominable system, Jewish children destined for the Army were taken, often from the mother's arms, when three or even two years old, placed in special barracks, and brought up there as *Kolonists* for the Army. There they served twenty-six years. It can hardly be deemed matter of surprise that human nature rebelled at such treatment, and that the Jew looked upon military service as something akin to a life-long punishment. Even now the lot of the Hebrew in the Russian Army is exceptionally hard. His life is made bitter to him by every species of insult, often by ill-treatment of the grossest kind. And when he shows anything like bravery or courage, how is it rewarded? Here is an instance from the *War Gazette* which transpired within the past six weeks. A Jewish drummer of the Fanagorski Grenadier Regiment named Teitelbaum was going home during the time of the recent riots in and about Moscow. He saw a policeman suddenly attacked by a mob, and severely hurt. Without staying a moment to consider, he rushed into the fray to rescue the constable, and was at once set upon by a score of the peasants, receiving a severe wound in the head. In spite of this, he drew his weapon, and beat about right and left, until he drove the mob of rowdies off and rescued the policeman from certain death. So pleased was the Colonel of the regiment with the man's bravery that he specially reported it to the Czar. The Czar endorsed the report "a stout and brave man," and ordered him to receive as a reward – five roubles! Five roubles would be about 11s.6d., and this magnificent sum was duly handed to the Jewish soldier by the commander of the regiment. There are fifty thousand Jews in the Russian Army, that is, two full army corps of twenty-five thousand each. Teitelbaum's reward for bravery is not exactly calculated to stimulate others to the like course in similar emergencies.

In Galicia the ancient prejudice against military service is rapidly disappearing even among the more orthodox followers of the Synagogue. Formerly the Service was so dreaded that when a boy was born he was compelled to wear a pair of narrow stays, which were laced in tighter and tighter as the child grew older so as gradually to narrow his chest, and thus bring the measurement and girth below what were required for the Army recruits. The abominable practice brought with it its own punishment in the shape of chest diseases and consumption, which are still the scourges of the Austro-Polish Jewries. The reduction of the term of training with the colours and the spread of schools have done much to reconcile Jewish parents to the conditions of service in the Dual Empire. The effect, too, of military training upon the younger generation has been beneficial to an incredible extent. Galicia furnishes the larger proportion of infantry required for the Austro-Hungarian Army, while the Jews form nearly one-half of the Galician contingent. And a smarter, neater-looking set of men than the Jewish foot-soldiers, in their shapely dark uniform, as they may be seen by hundreds any day in the streets of Lemberg or Cracow, it would be hard to find. They have lost in Jewishness – if the phrase be allowable – but gained in manliness. And they, as well as the State, are the better for this. The same may be said of the martial spirit which, from the nation at large here, has spread in recent years to the members of the Synagogue in this country, and is leading them in increasing numbers to take their stand in the defensive ranks of the Empire. It cannot but broaden their mental ideals, stimulate their patriotism, raise their standard of manliness and manly duty, and bring them in closer touch with the general population of which they form an increasingly important element.

9.   King and country, 1914–18

a)   A Jewish Chaplain on the Western Front, 1915–18

Source: M. Adler, A Jewish Chaplain on the Western Front (1920), pp. 16–19

Michael Adler (1868–1944), Senior Jewish Chaplain with the British armed forces, here shows that his Christian counterparts had no monopoly of eye-wash.

I have frequently been asked whether there were any signs of anti-Semitism in the life of the great British Army, and I say, without the slightest hesitation, that whatever indication of ill-feeling there was towards the Jew was so small as to be entirely negligible. The Christian soldier was warmly attached to his Jewish "pal," and the relations between the soldiers of all denominations were remarkably cordial. I received frequent letters from Christian soldiers telling me about their Jewish friends in most affectionate terms, and, almost without exception, Jewish men spoke very highly of their treatment by their brothers-in-arms. . . .

. . .

The general conduct of the Jewish soldier won for him an excellent record throughout the Army, and tended in every way to reflect credit upon the Jewish name. The number of court-martials which were brought to my notice throughout the war in which Jewish soldiers were involved was agreeably small. . . . I only heard of one case throughout the whole war of a Jewish soldier being shot for cowardice, and he was entered in his battalion as a member of the Church of England. All other offences with which Jews were charged belonged to the ordinary category of military misdemeanours.

Figure 20 Jewish soldiers in uniform, 1918 A company of the Jewish Regiment: 12 officers and 426 men marched through the City and the East End. Everywhere the force, which presented a very smart appearance, was greeted with enthusiasm and ringing cheers (*Daily Graphic*, 5 February 1918).

In the early days of the war certain of our men attempted to conceal their identity by not reporting themselves as Jews. Some, whilst remaining Jews, changed their names, as in the classic example of Gunner Leib Kalmanovitch adopting the name of Louis Bonaparte, whilst the name of Smith became a favourite. I was once asked by a Colonel to discover if a certain soldier who had applied for Passover leave was a Jew, as his name was Private McKennell. The man seemed to know very little of Judaism, and I was rather puzzled at his ignorance, when I chanced to ask him where his father lived. "Oh," he replied, "my father, *Olov Ha-sholom*, is dead." This decided me. One day I met an Australian soldier with the un-Jewish name of McPaul. He was entered as a Jew, and I asked him if he was born in the faith. He was not, he stated, but as he was out of sympathy with Christianity, he had resolved not to attend religious worship. When attesting in Sydney, he had been asked, "What religion do you profess?" He answered, "What religions have you got?" and upon learning that Judaism was officially recognised, he answered, "Then put me down as a Jew!" At a certain service I held, the only man present who wore an "Arba Kanfoth" was entered as a Roman Catholic in his unit. On the whole, however, the number of Jewish soldiers who did not confess their faith publicly was small, so that our records are reliable as to the number of men on active service. The total for all the war areas, including the Labour Companies, is about 50,000.

b)   Letters from the Front, 1919

Source: J.H. Patterson, *With the Judaeans in the Palestine Campaign* (1922), pp. 230–36

The following letters from Jewish soldiers serving in the Palestine theatre are not necessarily representative of the experience of all units but they do point to the persistence of prejudice in the armed forces.

Ludd,
4–7–19
A7/48

Sir,
I beg to report that the men are discontented, not only in our battalion, but also in the other Jewish units, which cannot fail to influence our men still more.

The causes of their discontent are much deeper than delay of Demobilization. Over 3/7ths of the Judæans in this country are men who volunteered to serve in Palestine in the name of their Zionist ideals, and in reply to the pledge embodied in the declaration which Mr. Balfour, on behalf of H.M. Government, issued on the 2nd November, 1917.

It is now a general impression among our soldiers, an impression shared by the public opinion of Palestine, that this pledge has been broken, so far as local authorities are concerned.

Palestine has become the theatre of an undisguised anti-Semitic policy. Elementary equality of rights is denied the Jewish inhabitants; the Holy City, where the Jews are by far the largest community, has been handed over to a militantly anti-Semitic municipality; violence against Jews is tolerated, and whole districts are closed to them by threats of such violence under the very eyes of the authorities; high officials, guilty of acts which any Court would qualify as instigation to anti-Jewish pogroms, not only go unpunished, but retain their official positions. The Hebrew language is officially disregarded and humiliated; anti-Semitism and anti-Zionism is the fashionable attitude among officials who take their cue from superior authority; and honest attempts to come to an agreement with Arabs are being frustrated by such means as penalising those Arab notables who betray pro-Jewish feeling.

The Jewish soldier is treated as an outcast. The hard and honest work of our battalions is recompensed by scorn and slander, which, starting from centres of high authority, have now reached the rank and file, and envenomed the relations between Jewish and English soldiers. When there is a danger of anti-Jewish excesses, Jewish soldiers are removed from the threatened areas and employed on fatigues, and not even granted the right to defend their own flesh and blood.

Passover was selected to insult their deepest religious feelings, by barring them access to the Wailing Wall during that week. No Jewish detachment is allowed to be stationed in Jerusalem or any of the other Holy Cities of Jewry.

When a Jewish sentry is attacked and beaten by a dozen drunken soldiers, and a drunken officer disarms with ignominy a Jewish guard, nobody is punished. Leave to certain towns has become a torture because the Military Police have been specially instructed to hunt the Jew, and the weaker ones among our men escape this humiliation by concealing their regimental badge, and substituting the badge of some other unit.

In addition, army pledges given to them are also disregarded; men who were recruited for service in Palestine are sent against their will to Messina or Egypt or Cyprus; men who enlisted under the understanding that their pay would be equal to that of any British soldier suddenly discover that no allowances will be paid to their wives and children.

Under these conditions, even some of the best among them give way to despair; they see no purpose in carrying on, conscious that the great pledge has been broken, that instead of a National Home for the Jewish people, Palestine has become the field of operations of official anti-Semitism; they abhor the idea of covering with their tacit connivance what they – and not they alone – consider a fraud.

They cannot formulate these grievances in full, nor gather the documents necessary to prove them, but under their desire to "get out of the show" there is bitter disappointment, one of the most cruel even in Jewish history.

You, Sir, have always been in favour of speeding up their demobilization; I, as you know, was of the opinion that it is the duty of every volunteer to stick to the Jewish Regiment as long as circumstances might demand, and I still hope that many will stick to it in spite of all. But even I myself am compelled to admit that things have reached a stage when no further moral sacrifice can fairly be demanded of men whose faith has been shattered.

I only hope that those who give up the struggle will not follow the example of a few misguided irresponsibles who chose the wrong way to support a right claim. I hope that they will await their release in a calm and dignified manner, discharging their duties to the last moment, and thus giving those who misrule this country a lesson in fair play – a lesson badly needed.

I remain, Sir,
Your obedient Servant,
XX

To Lieutenant-Colonel J.H. Patterson,
 D.S.O., Commanding 38th Battalion
 Royal Fusiliers

————

Bir Salem
17–7–1919

To Officer Commanding 38th Royal Fusiliers
Sir,
I have the honour to request that this application praying that I may be permitted to resign my Commission in His Majesty's Forces be forwarded through the usual channels, together with the under-mentioned reasons for my taking this step after having originally volunteered for the Army of Occupation.

My resignation, Sir, is my only method of protest against the grossly unfair and all too prevalent discrimination against the battalion to which I have the honour to belong. I desire to point out to you, Sir, the fact that this unfair and un-British attitude affects not only my honour as a Jew, but my prestige as a British officer, and this latter point must inevitably handicap me in the efficient discharge of my military duties.

The disgraceful exhibition of yesterday morning is but a fitting climax to the endless series of insults and annoyances to which this battalion – because it is a *Jewish Battalion* – has been subjected, almost since our first arrival in the E.E.F. Insults to a battalion as a whole, Sir, are insults directed to every individual member of that battalion, and as long as I remain a member of His Majesty's Forces, I regret to say I find myself unable to fittingly resent in a manner compatible with my own honour, and the honour of my race, the insulting attitude towards my race, and through my race, towards me, of my military superiors.

In passing, may I point out that my being a Jew did not prevent me doing my duty in France, in Flanders, and in Palestine, and in the name of the countless dead of my race who fell doing their duty in every theatre of war, I resent, and resent very strongly indeed, the abusive attitude at present prevalent towards Jewish troops.

I have innumerable instances of petty spite, and not a few cases of a very serious character indeed, all of which I can readily produce should the occasion ever arise.

I have the honour to be, Sir,
Your obedient Servant,
Y.Y.

c)   *The bacon tasted good, 1919*

Source: Jewish Chronicl, 28 February 1919

The unsettling effects of war service upon religious beliefs and behaviour are vividly illustrated by the letter of the Rev. Arthur Barnett, a Jewish chaplain in France, who hoped that the changes might not prove permanent but feared that they would.

Sir, – I have read with deep interest the recent contributions by Rabbi Dr Gollancz and the Revs. A.A. Green and J.F. Stern on the subject of Religious Reconstruction. These ministers speak from a wealth of experience and a depth of knowledge of our communal and religious life.

Let me deal with but one large and important class in the Community for whom the need for religious construction is vitally urgent. Much has been written about, but, as far as I am aware, nothing has been prepared for the religious needs of the soldier now returning to civil life. Is the Community going to allow many thousands of young men who have upheld Jewish honour during these long and terrible years to slip through its hands and pass out into civil life uncared and uncatered for?

There has been much speculation during the War on the question of "the Soldiers' Religion." Personally I have never been able to persuade myself that the experiences of War have brought any permanent religion to those who previously lived without it. There have been spasmodic appearances of what looked remarkably like a deeper spirituality in the fighting man, but on examination, I think it has proved to be founded rather on the fear of Death than on the love of God. It seemed to vanish in direct proportion to the distance from the front line. The religion of the Base was quite different to that of the Trench.

There is, to my mind, but one great gain that this War experience has brought to all, and that is a sense of values, of *religious values*, as of other values in life. This psychological fact will have to be borne in mind in any attempt to deal with the religious needs of the returning soldier.

Generally speaking, I believe the effect of war on the Jewish soldier will have been to make him less Jewish in life and outlook. Men who before had lived a fairly Jewish life, will now, after those years of de-Judaising tendencies and influences, find it difficult to recover their faded Jewish consciousness. Army life has produced a sort of Jewish anaesthesia. It has been impossible for the Jew in the Army, cut off, as he has been from practically all Jewish influence – living, working, playing, eating and sleeping, in intimate association at every hour of the day with his non-Jewish comrades – it has been impossible for him to preserve his Jewish consciousness against the forces of his environment. The only corrective afforded him have been the efforts of the Chaplains and the distribution of suitable Jewish literature.

Let me give an illustration of what has happened to one type of Jew in the Army. I have had a good deal to do recently with certain Labour Units consisting for the most part of Jews, the majority of whom come from the East End of London, and all of whom came originally from a country that is, or was, regarded as the home of Jewish orthodoxy. In one of these companies, where the Jews are about 500 strong, they were getting an issue of bacon and pork in their daily rations. I therefore applied to the Army Headquarters for some substitute to be provided, and the request was immediately granted. Imagine my surprise and disgust upon my next visit to their camp at hearing from their Commanding Officer that the men had protested in large bodies and practically threatened to refuse work unless the bacon ration was restored for their breakfast. Now I have no doubt that these men had never tasted bacon before entering the Army; yet, in spite of a comparatively favourable Jewish environment, a short period of Army life had so reduced their Jewish consciousness as to make them actually prefer and demand swine flesh when other food was offered them in its stead. The only reply I received upon remonstrating with them was: "It's not so bad when you get used to it!"

In another similar company I applied for the same change in rations. The Army authorities again were perfectly willing to accede to my request, but informed me that the C.O. of the unit stated that the majority of the men did not desire any change. Only 15 out of more than 400 Jewish men were found to be "objectors".

Further, I have obtained Saturday as the day of rest for these Companies. Yet a large number prefer to lounge and smoke and play cards on the Sabbath rather than attend a voluntary service in the morning.

Surely all this is but symptomatic of the apathy and indifference to Judaism of the East End Jew, as described in the Rev. J.F. Stern's report. Had the Judaism of these men any deep-rooted foundations, they surely would not have presented such a miserable and pathetic exhibition, and dragged themselves and their religion into such contempt in the eyes of their Christian Officers as they certainly did.

Happily, such conduct is by no means characteristic of all Jewish soldiers. The men who have fought, suffered, and endured bravely, though they have perforce forsaken a good deal in essential Jewish life and practice, will be found to have preserved and even strengthened their sense of *honour* and *responsibility* towards their People and Faith. It is through this attitude that they will be most accessible on their return to normal life. . . .

And I ask myself whether men who have for so long faced life at close grips, who have so long stood at the brink of Eternity, who, if they have gained nothing else, have at all events learned something about the real and false values in Life – I ask whether such men are going placidly back to their pre-war synagogues, with all the shams, unrealities, and vulgarities still to be found there. Three years among them out here make me answer emphatically, "No". We shall have to simplify, purify, and elevate the synagogue if it is to have any attraction for, or influence upon, these men. By this, I do not mean "Christianizing" the service. There is enough and to spare in our traditional Sabbath Liturgy, which if properly selected, and honestly and intelligently presented, will satisfy the needs of the most sincere and devout worshipper.

If, however, the synagogue cannot, or will not, reach out its hand to the returning soldier, then, unless we are willing to stand by and see him engulfed in the assimilative tendencies that the army has taught him, some other institution must arise to do the work. Here I offer as a suggestion that an extensive Y.M.C.A. movement on Jewish lines be inaugurated throughout the country. Nothing has done more for the social, moral, and religious welfare of the soldier during the War than has the Y.M.C.A. What it has done for the Christian a similar Jewish movement can do for us. Why not extend such a Jewish movement to civil life and open Jewish Huts in the various metropolitan districts and the larger provincial centres, which should serve exactly the same social and religious purposes as the Y.M.C.A. Huts have done. Here men could meet for healthy recreation, find old comrades, renew old friendships, seek the guidance of past Jewish officers who would be willing to lend a hand at management, and of the local Jewish minister who would be responsible for the religious side of the work and for its Jewish influence. Regular services could be arranged suitable to the acquirements and requirements of the men using the huts.

Such a movement would reach large numbers of young Jews who would otherwise be lost sight of. These Jewish lectures, debates, and religious services would help to restore to Jewish consciousness men who, through superior forces, have abandoned much that is essential in Jewish life and thought.

Some scheme of Religious and Social Reconstruction on an extensive basis is necessary if we are to fulfil our duty to those returning warriors. They have earned the right to be cared for, whatever be the demand made upon the Community. No sacrifices you make will ever equal those they endured for you. The voices of the dead men from some two thousand Jewish graves scattered amid the lonely ruins of the desolate places of war should cry out to you across the sea to stretch out both your hands to receive those living comrades who were spared their fate. Let British Jewry now pay its debt of honour!

CHRONOLOGICAL SUMMARY

1290:   Expulsion of Jews from England

1656:   Readmission of Jews to England

1701:   Sephardi synagogue established at Bevis Marks on east side of City of London

1722:   Ashkenazi Great Synagogue, Duke's Place, founded

1726:   Hambro Synagogue, Fenchurch Street, founded

1761:   New Synagogue, Leadenhall Street, founded

1826:   Anglican sacrament as a condition of naturalisation abolished

1832:   Jews allowed to become freemen of City of London

1833:   Jews admitted to the Bar

1835:   Jews allowed to vote at parliamentary elections without oath of abjuration; David Salomans elected Sheriff of City of London

1836:   Moses Montefiore elected President of Board of Deputies and first Constitution adopted

1837:   Board of Deputies made certifying authority for marriage secretaries of synagogues

1841:   *Jewish Chronicle* founded

1841-2: Formation of West London Synagogue of British Jews from secessionist grandees provokes temporary disruption of community; Jewish schools opened in Birmingham, Liverpool and Manchester to improve manners and morals

1845:   N.M. Adler elected Chief Rabbi

1847:   *Laws and Regulations of all the Synagogues of the British Empire* assert supremacy of Chief Rabbi; David Salomans admitted as alderman of City of London; Lionel de Rothschild elected MP for City of London but unable to take his seat

1851:   David Salomans elected MP for Greenwich

1855:   Jews' College, London, founded to supply new-style Jewish ministry; Alderman Salomans chosen as Lord Mayor of London

1856:   Dissenters' Marriage Act includes provision for Reform synagogues to appoint their own marriage secretary

1858:   Baron Lionel de Rothschild becomes first Jewish MP having been returned on five previous occasions without taking his seat. Jewish Emancipation complete. First known strike by Jewish cigar makers in East London indicates nascent industrial proletariat within the minority

1859:   Creation of Jewish Board of Guardians in London to make Jewish poor self-supporting

1860:   Jewish Association for the Diffusion of Religious Knowledge founded (later renamed Jewish Religious Education Board)

1867:   Manchester Jewish Board of Guardians established

1870:   United Synagogue created by private act of parliament; Education Act shifts burden of provision from community to taxpayer; Sandys Row Synagogue formed from *chevra* organised by 50 Dutch cigar makers twelve years earlier; Anglo-Jewish Association founded

1871:   Promissory Oaths Act removes last significant disability enabling Jews to become Lord Chancellor

1872:   Jewish Working Men's Club in East London founded by Samuel Montagu

1872-3:   Bradford Reform congregation established

1873:   *Jewish World* published

1874:   Short-lived Lithuanian Jewish tailors union formed in East London

1876:   Hebrew Socialist Union, the first such body in East London, represents a harbinger of immigrant radicalism

1878:   Conjoint Foreign Committee of Anglo-Jewish Association (est. 1871) and Board of Deputies, a kind of Anglo-Jewish Foreign Office, created

1881:   Assassination of Tsar Alexander II on 13 March provokes series of pogroms; Great Garden Street Talmud Torah opened in East London, the first of a new kind to provide a traditional education in English

1882:   Temporary Orders Concerning the Jews, the 'May Laws', passed restricting the Tsar's Jewish subjects to the Pale of Settlement; Mansion House Fund inaugurated by Lord Mayor to assist Jewish victims of Russian persecution

1883: Hovevei Zion groups formed in South Wales, Leeds and Manchester

1884: Publication of *The Lancet* report on conditions among Polish Jews provokes controversy; *Polish Yidel*, first Yiddish socialist newspaper, published by Morris Winchevsky in Spitalfields, East London

1885: Poor Jews' Temporary Shelter opened; *Arbeiter Fraint*, a revolutionary socialist monthly, published; strike of Leeds tailors marks a first for Jewish industrial unions

1886: Poles expelled from Prussia; formation of London Tailors and Machinists Union to press for 12-hour day; Jewish Girls' Club opened in London; ultra-Orthodox German immigrants establish a Beth Hamedrash in North London, the forerunner of the Adath Yisroel (est. 1911); Manchester Jewish Working Men's Club patronised by immigrant workers

1887: Jewish movement further restricted within the Pale of Settlement; 16 *chevroth* organised into the Federation of Minor Synagogues on initiative of Samuel Montague; Hebrew Cabinet Makers' Alliance founded; West Central Jewish Girls' Club opened

1888: Appointment of House of Lords Committee on the Sweating System chaired by Lord Dunraven and of House of Commons Select Committee on Emigration and Immigration (Foreigners)

1889: Socialist 'synagogue parade' at Great Synagogue outrages Anglo-Jewry; strike wave affects Jewish workers in London and Manchester culminating in great tailors' strike of 27 August–20 October

1890: Publication of Revd Simeon Singer's authorised Ashkenazi prayer book standardises ritual of United Synagogue

1890: Rigorous enforcement of 'May Laws'; Jews expelled from Moscow and Kiev

1891: 7,000 Russian Jewish immigrants settle in Britain; Hermann Adler, who had acted delegate for his father since 1879, succeeded him as Chief Rabbi; national federation of Hovevei Zion societies formed

1892: 3,000 Russian Jewish immigrants settle in Britain; Claude G. Montefiore restates case for Judaism in light of modern biblical criticism in Hibbert Lectures; *Machzike Hadath* secede alleging deficient *kashruth* supervision of Chief Rabbinate

1894: TUC reaffirms anti-immigration resolutions first passed two years earlier; Maggid of Kamenitz, Chaim Zundel Maccoby (1859-1916) appointed Preacher to Federation of Synagogues

1895: Jewish Lads' Brigade founded; Machzike Hadath join with Shomrei Shabbat *chevra* in Booth Street to form independent Jewish community

1896:   Brady Street Boys Club founded; messianic reception given to Theodore Herzl in Whitechapel; varieties of Zionism beginning to emerge

1897:   English Zionist Federation founded to mobilise communal support for Jewish national home

1898:   *Machzike Hadath* acquire the former Huguenot Church in Spitalfields for refurbishment as synagogue and talmud torah; West Central Lads Club founded

1899:   Jewish Athletic Association established; outbreak of South African War

1900:   Russian Jews seek home in Britain from persecution; Stepney Jewish Lads Club founded

1901:   British Brothers League founded to mobilise East London against alien immigration; Factory Act tightened regulations in sweated trades

1902:   Education Act provides for cost of all but religious instruction and physical maintenance to be defrayed by the state; Jewish Religious Union founded to promote Liberal Judaism; Peace of Verining brings South African War to close

1903:   Royal Commission on Alien Immigration, appointed on 21 March 1902, reported on 10 August 1903; Jewish labour demonstration in Hyde Park on 21 June 1903 to protest at Kishinev pogrom, attended by 25,000

1904:   Outbreak of Russo-Japanese War

1905:   Compromise settlement brings *Machzike Hadath* within authority of Chief Rabbi in face of growing public concern over alleged inhumanity of *kashruth* procedures; end of Russo-Japanese War; outbreak of Russian Revolution; 300 Jews killed in Odessa pogrom; demonstration in Jewish East London in support of Russian Revolution

1906:   700 pogroms in Ukraine and Bessarabia

1907:   Union of Hebrew and Religious Classes formed to co-ordinate provision of synagogal religious instruction

1909:   Trade Boards Act stimulates growth of trade unionism among Jewish garment workers

1910:   10 December 3 policemen shot and killed by alien desperados in Houndsditch

1911:   Samuel Montague ennobled as Lord Swaythling; Siege of Sidney Street served to identify Jews with political terrorism

1912:   Feinman Yiddish People's Theatre opened in East London; Joseph

Herman Hertz (1879-1946) becomes Chief Rabbi; Workers' Circle hold first annual conference in May with 814 members; Jewish tailors strike brings East London clothing industry to standstill

1912-13: Marconi and Indian Silver scandals become focus for expression of anti-Semitism; Beilis ritual murder trial in Kiev

1914: Outbreak of First World War and passage of Aliens Restriction Act in August

1915: Zion Mule Corps formed in March; sinking of *Lusitania* in April provokes anti-German riots

1916: Conscription introduced in January and becomes law in May; statement of Home Secretary on 29 June that Russian Jews who refused to serve in British Army would be repatriated; resistance organised by Foreign Jews' Protection Committee

1917: March (February) Revolution in Russia; anti-Jewish riots in Leeds and London in summer; proposed formation of Jewish unit to serve in British Army announced by War Office in July; Anglo-Russian Military Service Convention passed by Order in Council in August; November (October) Revolution in Russia; Balfour Declaration announced on 2 November; Russo-German armistice concluded on 4 December

1918: British Cabinet decides on recruitment of resistant Russians for labour service only

1919: *Protocols of the Elders of Zion* published promoting idea of international Jewish-Bolshevik conspiracy; Aliens Restrictions (Amendment) Act

GLOSSARY

Arba Kanfoth fringed woolen undergarment; also called *tsitsith*

Ashkenazi (*plural* Ashkenazim), Jews of Central and Eastern European origin; their ritual and Hebrew pronunciation is distinct from the Sephardim

Ba'al K'riah "Master of the Reading", the office, paid or voluntary of one who reads a portion of the Law from the *Torah* on Sabbaths, festivals and other occasions

Bar Mitzvah the ceremony in the synagogue that marks the attainment of his religious majority by a boy at the age of thirteen

bemah elevated platform with reading desk in synagogue

Beth Hamadrush literally House of Study

Beth Din ecclesiastical court of Chief Rabbi with jurisdiction over marriage and divorce, in civil disputes and *shechita*

bube grandmother

Chaham head of Spanish and Portuguese congregation in London

chalitza ritual ceremony releasing widow from obligation of a levirate marriage

Chatan Torah and *Chatan Bereshit* bridegroom of the Law and bridegroom of Genesis; principal honours on the Festival of the Rejoicing of the Law (*Simchat Torah*)

chazan cantor

cheder (*plural* chedarim) schoolroom in which Hebrew language and Bible taught

cherem ban or excommunication

chillul hashem blasphemy; an act on the part of a Jew likely to bring disgrace on the individual and on the Jewish people *daven* act of prayer sometimes accompanied by a swaying movement

dayan (*plural* dayanim) judge of *Beth Din*

ethrog (*plural* ethrogim) citron, one of four species, for ceremonial use in Festival of Tabernacles

Galizianers Jews from Galicia reputed to be exceedingly sharp

Gemora commentary on the *Mishnah*; a constitutive element of the *Talmud*

get bill of divorcement

goy (*plural* goyim) gentiles

gregger rattle sounded in the synagogue on Purim at each mention of the name of Haman in the course of reading the *Megilla*

Haftorah Sabbath reading from Prophetic book

judenhetze hatred of Jews or popular form of judeophobia

kashrut Jewish dietary laws. See also *kosher*

Kedusha proclamation of the holiness of God, inserted in public services prior to third benediction of the *Amidah*

Kehilla (*plural* Kehillot) self-governing Jewish community

ketubah marriage contract

kosher term commonly applied to those categories of food that Jews are permitted to eat, and also to the preparation of such food in accordance with the dietary laws

landsleit compatriots from same area, town or *shtetl*

landsmann person from same town or region as oneself

landsmannschaft a form of association based upon common origin from a particular town or district

Litvak Jew originating from Lithuania

lulav (*plural* lulavin) palm branch for ceremonial use in Festival of Tabernacles

Ma'ariv evening service

Machzike Hadath "Upholder of Religion", a secessionist ultra-orthodox congregation located in the Jewish East End

machzor festival prayer book

maggid popular Yiddish-speaking preacher

masseltov good luck; a congratulatory term

Midrash rabbinical, teachings and commentaries

mikva ritual bath for purification of observant women

Mincha afternoon service

minhag religious rite or custom

Mishnah basic text of *Talmud*

mitzvah (*plural* mitzvot) religious commandment or obligation

Megilla Book of Esther read on Feast of *Purim*

melammed teacher in a *cheder*

meshumet convert to Christianity

mezuzah small tube containing religious texts affixed to a doorpost

Mizrah ornamentation being on east wall of synagogue to indicate direction of Jerusalem and prayer

Musat additional Sabbath service

olav hasholem may his soul rest in peace

pinkes minute book

pogrom anti-Jewish outbreaks in last decades of Tsarist Russia; nowadays a generic term for any organised massacre or expulsion of Jews

Polak Jews originating from Poland

Purim feast of lots derived from Book of Esther

rav rabbi

Rosh Hashana Jewish New Year

Rosh Hashochtim chief supervisor of ritual slaughterers of animals for food

schnorrer a beggar

Sephardi (*plural* Sephardim) Jews originating from Spain and Portugal at close of the fifteenth century having a distinctive rite and pronunciation of Hebrew

Sepher Torah Scroll of the Law

Sepharim Scrolls of the Law

shammash beadle of synagogue

Shechita slaughter of animals for food in accordance with Jewish law

sheitel wig worn by observant married Jewesses

shlep to haul or drag

shochet person who slaughters animals for food in accordance with Jewish rites

shofar ram's horn used as trumpet in Jewish ceremonies and rites

Shomer (*plural* shomerim) supervisor of slaughter of animals for food to ensure compliance with Jewish Law

Shomerei Shabbat "Guardians of the Sabbath"; ultra orthodox congregations in Jewish East London

Shul (*shool*) synagogue

Shulchan Aruch sixteenth-century code of Jewish Law prepared by Joseph Caro

Sidra portion of *Torah* read during Sabbath service

stetl East European village

stiebl (*plural* stieblech) small conventicle for worship

stille chuppah marriage, valid in Jewish ecclesiastical law, usually conducted in private

streimel furry hat worn by Hasidic Jews

Succah tabernacle or booth erected to celebrate Festival of Tabernacles

Succoth Festival of Tabernacles

Tallith fringed prayer shawl worn by observant Jews

Talmud fundamental texts and commentaries on rabbinic law embodying legal decisions and discussions from c.200 BCE to 450 CE

Talmud Torah (*plural* talmudei torah) school for study of the Talmud and the Bible

Torah five scrolls of Moses; also used as a shorthand for whole corpus of Jewish law

tryfer food forbidden by Jewish Law

tsitsith fringed undergarment worn by observant Jewish males

yehidim Board of Elders of Spanish and Portuguese congregation in London

yeshivah (*plural* yeshivoth) school for advanced religious study

Yiddishkeit Jewish way of life

Yom Kippur Day of Atonement

Yomtov religious festival

FURTHER READING

The following is neither a comprehensive nor a select bibliography of works consulted, but a guide for those who wish to read further into the recent secondary literature. Items with valuable bibliographies are starred with an asterisk. The place of publication is London unless stated otherwise.

Useful general studies include V.D. Lipman, *A History of the Jews in Britain Since 1858** (Leicester University Press, Leicester, 1991) and G. Alderman, *Modern British Jewry* (Clarendon Press, Oxford, 1992). The latter is stimulating and strong on politics; the former, though for the most part sound, tails off after World War I. A valuable comparative framework is supplied by S. Sharot, *Judaism: A Sociology* (David and Charles, Newton Abbot, 1976).

The starting point of all serious analysis is L.P. Gartner's path-breaking study *The Jewish Immigrant in England 1870–1914* (Allen and Unwin, 1960). Since its appearance more than thirty years ago, the Anglo-Jewish experience has moved from the margins into the mainstream of modern social history. On both sides of the Atlantic there has been a substantial growth of interest in the assimilation and acculturation of the Jewish minority in Britain. The old insularity and metropolitain-mindedness have gone. British Jews are no longer presented as an undifferentiated mass. Provincial Jewry has come into its own and there is a new awareness of class and gender, number and variation. The work of the Research Unit of the Board of Deputies has brought striking advances in our understanding of the demography of the immigrant minority. Marriage and mortality statistics have been employed to indicate population trends by S.J. Prais and M. Schmool, 'Statistics of Jewish Marriages in Great Britain, 1901–1965', *The Jewish Journal of Sociology*, IX (1967), pp. 149–74 and 'Statistics of Milah and the Jewish birth-rate in Britain', *The Jewish Journal of Sociology*, XII (1970), pp. 187–93. War losses to illuminate the shape and structure of the minority population have been used to considerable effect by B.A. Kosmin, S. Waterman and N. Grizzard, 'The Jewish Dead in the Great War as an indication for the location, size and social structure of Anglo-Jewry in 1914', *Immigrants and Minorities*, V (1986), pp. 181–92. Nuptiality and fertility are well covered in B. Kosmin, 'Nuptiality and fertility patterns of British Jewry,

1850–1980: An Immigrant Transition?', *Papers in Jewish Demography in 1981* (1983), pp. 199–214. Particularly important for its findings on infant and maternal mortality is the imaginative study by Lara Marks, 'Irish and Jewish Women's Experience of Childbirth and Infant Care in East London, 1870–1939; The Responses of Host Society and Immigrant Communities to Medical Welfare Needs'* (Unpublished D.Phil thesis, University of Oxford, 1990) and the same author's 'The Luckless Waifs and Strays of Humanity: The Irish and Jewish Immigrant Unwed Mothers in London 1870–1939', *20th Century British History*, III (1992), pp. 113–37. Noteworthy, too, is G.D. Black, 'Health and Medical Care of the Jewish Poor in the East End of London 1880–1939'* (Unpublished PhD thesis, University of Leicester, 1987).

Progress has been rapid but uneven. The institutional life of the community is reasonably well covered. Synagogal organization is dealt with in standard studies from A. Newman, *The United Synagogue, 1870–1970* (Routledge and Kegan Paul, 1976) and G. Alderman, *The Federation of Synagogues 1887–1987* (Federation of Synagogues, 1987). The history of Reform and Liberal Judaism is currently being written by A.J. Kershen and J. Romain. An outline account is available in A.J. Kershen (ed.), *1840–1990: 150 years of Progressive Judaism in Britain* (London Museum of Jewish Life, 1990). Charitable provision is better served. V.D. Lipman's *A Century of Social Service, 1859–1959: The Jewish Board of Guardians* (Routledge and Kegan Paul, 1959) still stands up but should be supplemented with E.C. Black's *The Social Politics of Anglo-Jewry, 1880–1920** (Basil Blackwell, Oxford, 1988), which is very good on the effects of mass immigration upon communal institutions. There are no satisfactory studies of the Office of Chief Rabbi or of the Board of Deputies. Provisional accounts are available in G. Alderman, 'The British Chief Rabbinate: a most peculiar practice', *European Judaism* (Autumn, 1990), pp. 45–59 and A. Newman, *The Board of Deputies of British Jews 1760–1985: A Brief Survey* (Valentine Mitchell, 1987).

Studies which try to relate the immigrant minority in a specific local and regional context to mainstream social developments include E. Krausz, *Leeds Jewry: Its History and Social Structure* (William Heffer for Jewish Historical Society of England, Cambridge, 1964); N. Kokosalakis, *Ethnic Identity and Religion: Tradition and Change in Liverpool Jewry* (University Press of America, Washington, DC 1982); K.E. Collins, *Second City Jewry: The Jews of Glasgow in the Age of Expansion, 1790–1919* (Scottish Jewish Archives, Glasgow, 1990); U. Henriques, ed., *The Jews of South Wales* (University of Wales Press, Cardiff, 1993). A model local study is B. Williams, *The Making of Manchester Jewry, 1740–1875* (Manchester University Press, Manchester, 1976). Commendable, too, is the same author's *Manchester Jewry: A Pictorial History 1799–1988* (Manchester Archives Publications, Manchester, 1988).

Some of the gaps in our knowledge, though, are startling. The Jewish family, of all things, remains largely under-researched. The disruptive effects of immigration upon family life are examined in E.J. Bristow, *Prostitution and Prejudice: The Jewish Fight against White Slavery 1870–1939* (Clarendon

Press, Oxford, 1983); Lara Marks, 'The Experience of Jewish Prostitutes and Jewish Women in the East End of London at the Turn of the Century', *The Jewish Quarterly*, XXXIV (1987) pp. 6–10 and in David Englander, 'Stille Huppah (Quiet Marriage) Among Jewish Immigrants in Britain', *The Jewish Journal of Sociology* XXXIV (1992), pp. 85–109. Gender roles are explored by Rickie Burman in 'The Jewish Woman as the Breadwinner', *Oral History Journal*, X (1982), pp. 27–39; 'Growing up in Manchester Jewry – the Story of Clara Weingard', *Oral History Journal*, XII (1984), pp. 56–63 and 'Jewish Women and the Household Economy in Manchester', in D. Cesarani ed., *The Making of Modern Anglo-Jewry* (Basil Blackwell, Oxford, 1990), pp. 55–78. The internal life of selected families is explored with sensitivity and imagination, again by means of oral sources, by Rosalind O'Brien, 'The Establishment of the Jewish Minority in Leeds' (Unpublished PhD thesis, University of Bristol, 1975). Jerry White's *Rothschild Buildings, Life in an East End Tenement Block 1887–1920* (Routledge and Kegan Paul, 1980) is an outstanding example of interview-based research and an engaging study of family and locality.

The immigrant quarter is finely evoked in W.J. Fishman, *East End 1888: A Year in a London Borough among the Labouring Poor** (Duckworth, 1988). J. Green, *A Social History of the Jewish East End of London 1914–1939* (Edward Mellen Press, Lampeter, 1991) is lively and imaginative. The role of the East End as a reception centre is developed by the equally readable C. Bermant, *Point of Arrival: A Study of London's East End* (Methuen, 1975). A rather different perspective is supplied by J. Connell, 'The Jewish Ghetto in Nineteenth Century Leeds: A Case of Urban Involution', *Urban Anthropology*, X (1981), pp. 1–26. The popular culture of the settlement locality would repay systematic study. One aspect is usefully described by D. Mazower, *Yiddish Theatre in London* (London Museum of Jewish Life, 1987). Problems of settlement are explored in David Englander, 'Booth's Jews: The Presentation of Jews and Judaism' in *Life and Labour of the People in London, Victorian Studies*, XXXII (1989), pp. 551–71. Questions of group and personal relations are reviewed by the same author in 'Community and territoriality: Jewish East London 1850–1950' in W.T.R. Pryce ed., *From Family History to Community History* (Cambridge University Press, forthcoming), and explored in the perceptive contribution of T. Kushner, 'Jew and Non-Jew in the East End of London: Towards an Anthropology of "everyday" Relations' in G. Alderman and C. Holmes, eds, *Outsiders and Outcasts: Essays in Honour of William J. Fishman* (Duckworth, London, 1993), pp. 32—52.

The material circumstances of the Jewish community are conveniently summarised in Harold Pollins, *Economic History of the Jews in England* (Associated University Presses, London, 1982). Work and its organisation are dealt with in J. Buckman, *Immigrants and the Class Struggle: The Jewish Immigrant in Leeds, 1880–1914* (Manchester University Press, Manchester, 1983); James A. Schmiechen, *Sweated Industries and Sweated Labour: The London Clothing Trades 1860–1914* (Croom Helm, Beckenham, 1984) and in D. Feldman, 'Immigrants and Workers, Englishmen and Jews: Jewish Immigration to the East End of London 1880–1906' (Unpublished PhD thesis, University of Cambridge, 1986). On work and home see also the suggestive observations in R. O'Day 'Before the Webbs: Beatrice Potter's Early Investigations for Charles Booth's Inquiry', *History*, LXXVIII (1993), pp. 218–420.

The problems of the Jewish labour movement are examined in W.J. Fishman, *East End Jewish Radicals 1875–1914* (Duckworth, 1975). Developments outside of London are examined in Bill Williams, 'The beginnings of Jewish Trade Unionism in Manchester 1889–1891', in K. Lunn ed., *Hosts, Immigrant and Minorities, Historical Responses to Newcomers in British Society 1870–1914* (Dawson, Folkstone, 1980), pp. 263–307; and H. Maitles, 'Jewish Trade Unionists in Glasgow', *Immigrants and Minorities*, X (1993), pp. 46–69. A comparative perspective is supplied by Anne J. Kershen 'Trade Unionism amongst the Jewish Tailoring Workers of London and Leeds, 1872–1915', in D. Cesarani, ed., *The Making of Modern Anglo-Jewry* (Basil Blackwell, Oxford, 1990), pp. 34–54 and A.S. Reutlinger, 'Reflections on the Anglo-American Jewish Experience: Workers and Entrepreneurs in New York and London', *American Jewish Historical Quarterly*, 66, (1977), pp. 473–484. Electoral politics are the subject of specialised studies by G. Alderman, *The Jewish Community in British Politics* (Clarendon Press, Oxford, 1984), and *London Jewry and London Politics 1889–1986* (Routledge, 1989). Women's participation is explored in L.G. Kuzmack, *Women's Cause: The Jewish Woman's Movement In England and the United States 1881–1933* (Ohio State University Press, Columbus, Ohio, 1990). The wider framework is the subject of Jonathan Frankel's difficult but rewarding monograph, *Prophecy and Politics: Socialism, Nationalism and the Russian Jews, 1862–1917** (Cambridge University Press, Cambridge, 1981).

Recent research on the religion of the immigrant has tended to emphasise the institutional at the expense of the spiritual. A notable attempt to locate Judaism within a wider sociological setting is made by S. Sharot, 'Religious change in native orthodoxy in London 1870–1914: the Synagogue Service' *The Jewish Journal of Sociology*, XV (1973), pp. 57–77; 'Religious change in native orthodoxy in London 1870–1914: Rabbinate and Clergy', *The Jewish Journal of Sociology* XV (1973), pp. 167–87. A suggestive contribution is from J. Carlebach, 'The Impact of German Jews on Anglo-Jewry-Orthodoxy, 1850–1950', in W.E. Mosse et al. eds, *Second Chance: Two Centuries of German Speaking Jews in the United Kingdom* (J.C.B. Mohr, Tubingen, 1990), pp. 405–24. The peculiarities of Reform Judaism are explored in R. Liberles, 'The origins of the Jewish Reform Movement in England', *Association for Jewish Studies Review*, I (1976), pp. 121–50. Its arrested development is dealt with, brilliantly in my view, by S. Singer, 'Orthodox Judaism in Early Victorian London 1840–1858' (Unpublished PhD thesis, Yeshiva University, New York 1981). The gendered nature of much of the writing in this sphere has been challenged by Rickie Burman, 'She looketh Well to the Ways of Her Household; the Changing Role of Jewish Women in Religious Life c. 1800–1930', in G. Malmgreen, ed., *Religion in the Lives of English Women 1760–1930* (Croom Helm, 1986), pp. 234–59 and the same author's 'Women in Jewish Religious Life, Manchester 1880–1930' in J. Obelkevich, L. Roper and R. Samuel, eds, *Disciplines of*

Faith: Studies in Religion, Politics and Patriarchy (Routledge and Kegan Paul, 1987), pp. 37–54. Important, too, is E.M. Umansky, *Lily Montagu and the Advancement of Liberal Judaism: From Vision to Vocation* (Edward Mellen Press, New York, 1983). A historian who uses her eyes as well as her head is J. Glasman, 'London Synagogues in the late Nineteenth Century: Design in Context', *London Journal*, XIII (1987–88), pp. 143–55. The loss of identity, then as now a central Jewish concern, is examined in the suggestive volume of essays edited by Todd M. Endelman, *Jewish Apostasy in the Modern World* (Holmes and Meir, New York, 1987) and, more controversially, in the same author's *Radical Assimilation in English Jewish History 1656–1945* (University of Indiana Press, Bloomington, Ind., 1990). The meaning of Zionism in this context is well brought out in S. Cohen, *Zionists and British Jews. The Communal Politics of Anglo-Jewry, 1895–1920* (Princeton University Press, Princeton, New Jersey, 1982).

Jewish education, rather surprisingly, remains a subject in search of a historian. For the moment we must make do with sundry theses and articles in lieu of the required comprehensive study. Those such as P.S.L. Quinn, 'The Jewish Schooling Systems of London 1656–1956' 2 vols, (Unpublished PhD thesis, University of London, 1958) or C. Hershon, 'The Evolution of Jewish Elementary Education in England with special reference to Liverpool' (Unpublished PhD theses, University of Sheffield, 1973) are worth consulting for details. More promising is S. Singer, 'Jewish Education in the Mid Nineteenth Century: A Study of the Early Victorian London Community', *Jewish Quarterly Review*, LXXVII (1986–87), pp. 163–78 and S.K. Greenberg, 'Anglicanisation and the Education of Jewish Immigrant Children in the East End of London', in A. Rapoport-Albert and S.J. Zipperstein, eds, *Jewish History: Essays in Honour of Chimen Abramsky* (Peter Halban, 1988), pp. 111–26. The *chedarim*, which will also stand further scrutiny, need to be examined in relation to the development of other forms of social provision for Jewish youth. S. Bunt's *Jewish Youth Work in Britain* (Bedford Square Press, 1975) is helpful, but, as with education, we are waiting upon a systematic study that is long overdue.

Education generally received primacy in the acculturation process. That process, though, has been treated in rather general terms. Gartner's work, for all its merits, gave insufficient space to the acculturation of immigrant women and children. That gap is now beginning to be filled. Works by Rosalind Livschin, 'The Acculturation of Children of Immigrant Jews in Manchester, 1890–1930' in D. Cesarani, ed., *The Making of Modern Anglo-Jewry* (Basil Blackwell, Oxford, 1990), pp. 79–96 and Susan L. Tananbaum, 'Generations of Change: The Anglicisation of Russian Jewish Immigrant Women London 1880–1939' (Unpublished PhD thesis, Brandeis University, 1991) point the way forward to a more subtly differentiated account.

The character of Britain as a receiving society, and its tolerance of ethnic, cultural and religious diversity, is questioned in a short study by Colin Holmes, *A Tolerant Country* (Faber, 1991), and in the disturbing collection edited by T. Kushner and K. Lunn, *Traditions of Intolerance: Historical Perspectives on Fascism and Race Discourse in Britain* (Manchester University Press, Manchester, 1989). Antagonism to immigrant Jews is well-documented in Colin Holmes, *Anti-Semitism in British Society, 1870–1939* (Edward Arnold, 1979). Anti-Jewish disturbances before the First World War are examined in L. Hyman, *The Jews of Ireland* (Jewish Historical Society of England, 1972); G. Alderman 'The Jew as Scapegoat: The Settlement and Reception of Jews in South Wales before 1914', *Transactions of the Jewish Historical Society of England* XXVI (1974–78), pp. 62–70 and C. Holmes, 'The Tredegar Riots of 1911: Anti-Jewish Disturbances in South Wales', *Welsh History Review* XI (1982), pp. 214–25. Wartime influences are examined by David Cesarani, 'An Embattled Minority: The Jews in Britain during the First World War', *Immigrants and Minorities* VIII (1989), pp. 61–81 and touched upon by D. Englander, 'Police and Public Order in Britain 1914–1918' in C. Emsley and B. Weinberger eds, *Policing Western Europe: Politics, Professionalism and Public Order 1850–1940* (Greenwood, West Port, Connecticut, 1991), pp. 90–138. Important, too, is S. Almog 'Anti-semitism as a Dynamic Phenomenon: The "Jewish Question" in England at the End of the First World War', *Patterns of Prejudice*, XXI (1987), pp. 3–18. The single most important work on Zionism in this context is David Cesarani, 'Zionism in England 1917–1939' (Unpublished D.Phil. thesis, University of Oxford, 1986).

The Jewish experience of the war at home has made some headway in recent years. A good workmanlike monograph, based primarily upon newspaper sources, is provided by J. Bush, *Behind the Lines; East London Labour 1914–1919* (Merlin, 1984) which relates the Jewish labour movement to larger war-induced changes in what was still the key area of settlement. Narrower in focus but greater in depth is S. Kadish *Bolsheviks and British Jews: The Anglo-Jewish Community, Britain and the Russian Revolution* (Frank Cass, 1992), which makes good use of the Home Office files to examine the radical opposition to Jewish military participation and the impact of the Russian Revolution. New light on official responses is supplied in B. Wasserstein's study of the then Home Secretary *Herbert Samuel, A Biography* (Clarendon Press, Oxford, 1992). Informative, too, are E.C. Sterne, *Leeds Jewry and the Great War 1914–1918: The Home Front* (Jewish Historical Society of England: Leeds Branch, Leeds, 1982) and N. Grizzard, *Leeds Jewry and the Great War 1914–1918* (Jewish Historical Society of England: Leeds Branch, Leeds, 1982). The effects of the war on immigrant Jews are examined in D. Cesarani, 'Anti Alienism in England after the First World War', *Immigrants and Minorities* VI (1987), pp. 5–29. Alas, there has been no comparable progress in the analysis of Jewish war service. Pity. The debate on war and social reform might look different from the perspective of an immigrant minority.

Index